The Fateful Alliance

The Fateful Alliance

GERMAN CONSERVATIVES AND NAZIS IN 1933:
THE *MACHTERGREIFUNG* IN A NEW LIGHT

HERMANN BECK

Berghahn Books
New York • Oxford

Published in 2008 by

Berghahn Books
www.berghahnbooks.com

©2008 Hermann Beck

Library of Congress Cataloging-in-Publication Data
Beck, Hermann, 1955–
    The fateful alliance : German conservatives and Nazis in 1933 : the Machtergreifung
in a new light / Hermann Beck.
        p. cm.
    Includes bibliographical references.
    ISBN 978-1-84545-496-8 (hardback : alk. paper)   1. Germany—Politics
and government—1918–1933.   2. Deutschnationale Volkspartei—History.
3. Nationalsozialistische Deutsche Arbeiter-Partei—History.   4. Conservatism—
Germany—History.   5. National socialism.   I. Title.

DD240.B3389 2008
943.086'2--dc22   2008007615

British Library Cataloguing in Publication Data
A catalogue record for this book is available from the British Library

A version of Chapter IV was originally published in 2005 as Hermann Beck,
"The Nazis and their Conservative Alliance Partner in 1933: The Seizure of Power
in a New Light," Totalitarian Movements and Political Religions 6:2 (2005),
215–243, Taylor & Francis, journal website: http://www.informaworld.com.

A version of Chapter V was published in 2006 as Hermann Beck, "Between
the Dictates of Conscience and Political Expediency: Hitler's Conservative
Alliance Partner and Anti-Semitism during the Nazi Seizure of Power," The
Journal of Contemporary History 41:4 (October 2006), 611–640, Copyright
@ SAGE Publications, 2006, by permission of Sage Publications Ltd.

Printed in the United States on acid-free paper

ISBN-13: 978-1-84545-496-8   hardback

CONTENTS

Contents

PREFACE

This study has a long history. In 1996, when I shifted the focus of my research from nineteenth-century conservatives and bureaucrats to the late Weimar Republic and the early Nazi period, I was interested initially in the political behavior of German professional classes and higher officials, commonly summarized under the term *Bildungsbürgertum*, or "cultivated" bourgeoisie. Germany owed its reputation in scholarship, administration, and technical expertise to this numerically small, but socially influential, university-trained elite. The *Bildungsbürgertum* was a uniquely German phenomenon that originated as a distinct social class in the second half of the eighteenth and early nineteenth centuries. From the first, it was characterized by its close relationship to the state, since its strongest component came from the upper echelons of state bureaucracies in the various German states. In addition to high officials, this class included the academically trained professions, notably university professors, members of the legal profession, the Protestant clergy, and medical doctors, most of whom were state officials as well. Until 1879 lawyers, for example, had to be licensed by the state, and medical doctors had barely managed to extricate themselves from the fetters of state governments by the revolutions of 1848. University education and examinations in Germany continue to be state-regulated to this day.

The constituent element of the *Bildungsbürgertum* was the common *Bildung* of its members.[1] *Bildung* was shaped by a belief in human perfectibility, specifically that an individual's potential could be realized through a classical education. This was the central notion of German Idealism and a cornerstone of Wilhelm von Humboldt's reform of the Prussian university system, from where the concept spread throughout Germany. Between the Reform Era and the Revolutions of 1848, the power wielded by high officials in the larger states of the German Confederation added to the prestige of the group and served as justification for its corporate pride and feeling of self–importance. Germany's late industrialization, as well as the initial weakness of a bourgeoisie often hampered by state regulations, further advanced the ascendancy of the educated elite and the social prestige bestowed on those with academic achievements and titles. In the hierarchically structured world of Central Europe before 1933, established members of the *Bildungsbürgertum* were thus bound to become role models, whose behavior set social and occasionally even political standards that were eagerly emulated by their social inferiors.[2]

Politically, the *Bildungsbürgertum* initially tended toward liberal ideas, though there were great differences within the group as a whole: lawyers and members of the emerging free professions were more liberal than civil servants. In the revolutionary Frankfurt parliament *Bildungsbürger* represented all political orientations, though liberals clearly outnumbered conservatives. The liberalism of the majority of the *Bildungsbürgertum* was determined by its opposition to the aristocracy, its struggle for constitutional reform, and the quest for a sovereign nation–state. Before 1866, nationalism was a liberal

1. The concept cannot be exactly translated. A recent rendering of *Bildung* as "the experience of personal growth through an individualized appropriation of classical high culture" is unwieldy, but approximates the German meaning. See Jonathan Sperber, "Bürger, Bürgerlichkeit, bürgerliche Gesellschaft: Studies of the German (Upper) Middle Class and Its Sociocultural World," *Journal of Modern History* 69 (1997), 276 (note 9). The term *Bildungsbürgertum* has been in use only since about 1920; it evolved from "gebildete Stände," and "Gebildete," to "gebildete bürgerliche Gesellschaftskreise" and "gebildetes Bürgertum." See Ulrich Engelhardt, *"Bildungsbürgertum." Begriffs- und Dogmengeschichte eines Etiketts* (Stuttgart, 1986).

2. William S. Allen, in *The Nazi Seizure of Power*, makes the point that it became socially acceptable (in the small town studied in his book) to join the Nazi party once a prominent *Bildungsbürger* had spoken out publicly in support of Hitler.

ideal; the aristocracy and other conservatives all across the German
states were opposed to a national unification that would entail partial forfeiture of their privileges. But as opposition to Bismarck's
policies evolved into support, "progressive" liberalism turned into
"national" liberalism and, gradually, by the end of the 1870s, the
bulk of the *Bildungsbürgertum* had lost its forward-driving liberal orientation. By the 1890s, many had turned into advocates of impe-
rialist policies and defenders of an aggressive nationalism. In this
shift to conservatism, as later to National Socialism at the end of the
Weimar Republic, the future members of the *Bildungsbürgertum*—
university students—were in the vanguard of political change: students preceded the established *Bildungsbürgertum* in appropriating a
new conservatism. Before the German defeat in the First World War
and the subsequent economic turmoil and inflation, this cultivated
bourgeoisie had enjoyed significant material security and comfort,
as well as greater social prestige than its counterparts in other European countries. To them, defeat in the war was more than a military disaster: it signified a personal humiliation and the loss of a
distinct cultural identity. As a result, large sections of the educated
elite moved further to the political right. From the beginning, they
vehemently rejected the new Republic that bore the birthmark
of a humiliating defeat. The educated elite's fate had been closely
aligned with that of the Empire; with the Empire's demise, it suffered a decline in reputation that increased its alienation from Weimar, to which inflation added the grievance of material destitution.
The inflation broke the economic spine of the *Bildungsbürgertum*,
whose lifestyle had been supported largely by their savings, as regular salaries rarely sufficed to maintain the material accoutrements
that went with their exalted social position, such as domestic servants, *Bildungsreisen*, and a costly education for their offspring. Probably no part of the German population felt the humiliating changes
in everyday life more deeply than the educated elite; none felt more
distant from a republican regime with which reconciliation seemed
impossible. Dispossession destroyed its political instinct, making it
susceptible to political choices that formerly pride alone might well
have precluded.

Pervaded by the certainty of their social and cultural superiority,
the majority of the conservative and national-minded *Bildungsbürgertum* initially showed little interest in the Nazi movement, despite the
economic decline of a majority of its members. Until about a year
before Hitler came to power, it was thus mostly the academic proletariat, the déplacé among the cultivated bourgeoisie, those filled

xii   *Preface*

with festering resentment toward their more successful colleagues, who expressed their spite by voting for the NSDAP. Even though extreme nationalism, the hatred of Versailles and the "November criminals" and, in some instances, anti-Semitism provided common ground with National Socialism, the message put forth by National Socialists was too simplistic for the average member of the *Bildungsbürgertum*. Its claim to epitomize a culturally superior segment of the population ran counter to the anti-intellectualism of the Nazis.

But why then did a vast segment of the *Bildungsbürgertum* go over to the Nazis, and how could the gradually evolving affinities between the Nazi movement and the cultivated bourgeoisie be explained? That many did defect to Nazism has been documented beyond doubt. Already in 1982 Richard Hamilton showed that, beginning with the spring of 1932, large segments of the haute bourgeoisie, including the *Bildungsbürgertum*, voted for the Nazi party. In his electoral analysis of Germany's larger cities Hamilton impressively demonstrated that inhabitants of the *Villenvororte*, the more affluent suburbs of large German cities from Berlin to Hamburg and Munich to Mannheim, voted in disproportionate numbers for Hitler and the NSDAP. Apart from factory owners and businessmen, the population of these *Villenvororte* was made up largely of members of the educated middle classes, professionals, and various categories of higher civil servants employed by the Reich, the respective federal states, or municipalities.[3] As Michael Kater has shown, in relationship to the rest of the population, the educated upper middle class increased both its proportionate representation in the Nazi party and its membership in affiliated organizations, such as the National Socialist Physicians' or Jurists' Leagues, in the wake of the transfer of power to Hitler.[4] Already in 1932, university graduates entered the Nazi party at twice the rate of their percentage in the overall population. And after Hitler became Chancellor on 30 January 1933, the academically trained flocked into the NSDAP to

---

3. Richard Hamilton, *Who Voted for Hitler* (Princeton, 1982). Hamilton also established the fact that those who could still afford a summer holiday in 1932 and thus voted by *Stimmschein* in the elections of 31 July 1932 also favored the NSDAP in disproportionate numbers. Here, too, one may surmise that members of the *Bildungsbürgertum* made up a substantial percentage of those still able to afford a summer holiday at the high point of the depression.

4. Michael Kater, "Sozialer Wandel der NSDAP im Zuge der nationalsozialistischen Machtergreifung," in Wolfgang Schieder, ed., *Faschismus als soziale Bewegung*, 2nd ed. (Göttingen, 1983), 25–69.

the point that there was a marked shift in the party's sociological profile, since the membership quota of the educated elite was four times as high as their share in the population. According to Kater, members of the legal profession, as well as doctors and dentists, were overrepresented in the SS by a factor of seven, tenured university lecturers and professors by a factor of four. It is beyond doubt that the cultivated bourgeoisie's initial enthusiasm for the regime helped to consolidate Hitler's dictatorship and contributed to making the new regime socially acceptable.

The motivation for this fundamental shift in political orientation seemed well worth investigating. Were *Bildungsbürger* turncoats out of conviction? Opportunism alone did not seem to explain the wholehearted (and often unsolicited) enthusiasm with which the "National Revolution" was welcomed. In the fever accompanying the Nazi successes after 30 January, the conversion of many *Bildungsbürger* appeared to be genuine. To what exactly could National Socialism appeal in this segment of the population which, by dint of education, breeding, and social background, seemed unlikely prey for the "temptations" of Nazism, the early public image of which was dominated by vulgarity, social animosity, and street violence? Could nationalism and the promise to restore domestic unity and order, combined with a concerted effort to rebuild German might, alone account for the enthusiastic conversion? Was an anti-Semitism that subtly insisted on cultural incompatibility a major factor? The actual search for specific reasons proved difficult. A careful perusal of the files of civil service organizations and the correspondence among, for example, *Philologenvereine*, yielded few concrete results, while sources of a more personal nature, such as collections of letters, literary bequests, and autobiographies, were often so general that they might be applied to everyone or so dependent on the individual lives of the respective writers that generalizations were impossible. Here I could not quite ward off the suspicion that authors of some prominence, whose letters were important enough to be published, or who later left their papers to an archive, might have taken care to leave out any letter or other document that might be too "incriminating" with respect to their relationship with National Socialism. Admissions of early euphoria for Nazism could well harm their posthumous reputations with the postwar German audience. Because of this attempt to protect one's personal reputation, the kinds of documents I was looking for would thus be difficult to unearth. My subsequent search in local archives for the reaction of the conservative bourgeoisie to the Nazi takeover in

1933 was hardly more fruitful. I contacted more than forty local and regional archives whose personnel were all kind enough to respond in detail to my inquiries. With a number of significant exceptions, either few relevant materials existed or the bulk of the holdings on 1933 were destroyed by air raids in the second half of the war.[5] It was startling to see that the protocols of city council meetings for 1933, or at least for the decisive first half of 1933, when the Nazis arrogated plenipotentiary powers to themselves on the national, regional, and local level, were consistently missing. This was the case even in cities such as Mannheim, where protocols of city council meetings had been completely preserved since the mid-eighteenth century. Here, too, it was difficult, for obvious reasons, to believe in mere coincidence, and more feasible to presume that, in the last days of the war, local politicians who helped seize power in the winter and spring of 1933 (or acquiesced in it) did their best to suppress the all-too-obvious confirmation of their involvement with the regime. But it is, of course, also true that in times of revolution (contemporaries of all political persuasions referred to the winter and spring 1933 as such), few or no meetings took place and, when they did, insignificant and nonpolitical issues topped the agenda. The *Quellenlage* changed when I turned to the party that until about 1932 was the most likely political home of the *Bildungsbürgertum*, the Deutschnationale Volkspartei (German National People's Party or DNVP). This party, as is well known, entered the governmental coalition with the NSDAP that brought Hitler into power in 1933. Substantial sections of its party files survived the war and were kept in the former East German Zentrales Staatsarchiv I at Potsdam and then, in the wake of German reunification, relocated to the newly opened Bundesarchiv at Berlin-Lichterfelde. Under the impact of these new and unexpected findings, I modified my initial topic so that the relationship between conservatives and Nazis during the period of the seizure of power became the focal point of analysis and the conservative *Bildungsbürgertum* receded—for the time being—into the background. In a later study, I hope to be able to deal with this compelling topic.

One is often most impressed by the unexpected and, in my case, this was the open conflict between German Nationals and Nazis in March, April, and May 1933, especially the Nazis' almost frenetic

---

5. This severely affected the holdings at Essen, Köln, Hamburg, Heilbronn, Hildesheim, and Kassel.

hatred for their conservative allies. This extreme loathing was occasionally even expressed in physical terms, with the result that members of German National organizations had to be hospitalized. From mid-March onwards, everything that smacked of "conservatism" or "bourgeois" (*bürgerlich*) was denounced as reactionary. Once the original enemies of Nazism—such as Communists and Socialists—had been repressed and others (like the Center Party) neutralized, the Nazis could afford to vent their fury on their conservative brother-in-arms and coalition partner. As the following chapters will show, during the winter and spring of 1933, no "alliance of elites" existed. Traditional conservative political and social bastions were willfully destroyed and then—under different auspices—reconstructed, but only after they had fully acknowledged Nazi leadership. The following chapters will also show that the complete and ignominious collapse of conservatism was not only brought about by judicious and shrewd Nazi maneuvering, but also accelerated by sheer violence and intimidation and fostered by the *Zeitgeist*, the unique climate of opinion that pervaded Germany between February and July 1933. Already by the end of 1933, disillusionment and disappointment dashed the high hopes with which the new government had been greeted, and many felt that they had misjudged the nature of the Nazi regime.[6] But political reality, once created, could no longer be undone under the conditions of a repressive dictatorship that was already firmly ensconced in power by July 1933. When German conservatives, the conservative bourgeoisie, and parts of the *Bildungsbürgertum* realized their gross miscalculation, it was too late.

In the course of this study, several organizations have supported my research, and a number of colleagues have generously lent me their time and expertise. I should especially like to thank the School of Historical Studies at the Institute for Advanced Study at Princeton, where I spent a year during the early stages of this project, as well as the University of Miami, which has consistently supported my research with a series of Orovitz Summer Research Awards and travel grants. Among the libraries whose debt I have incurred, special thanks are due to the staffs at Princeton University Library, the Württembergische Landesbibliothek in Stuttgart, and the University Library in Heidelberg. I am obliged to the staffs of the following archives,

---

6. This point is convincingly made by Norbert Frei, *Der Führerstaat. Nationalsozialistische Herrschaft 1933 bis 1945*, 6th ed. (Munich, 2001).

who diligently responded to my various inquiries: the Stadtarchive at Augsburg, Baden-Baden, Bonn, Bremen, Dortmund, Düsseldorf, Duisburg, Essen, Freiburg, Göttingen, Hannover, Heidelberg, Heilbronn, Hildesheim, Kaiserslautern, Karlsruhe, Kassel, Köln, Leipzig, Magdeburg, Mannheim, München, Münster, Saarbrücken, Stuttgart, Ulm, and Wiesbaden; the Landesarchive in Berlin and Magdeburg; the Hessisches Staatsarchiv Darmstadt, Staatsarchive in Bremen, Hamburg, and München; the Generallandesarchiv Karlsruhe, the Bayerisches Hauptstaatsarchiv München, Hessisches Hauptstaatsarchiv Wiesbaden, Niedersächsisches Hauptstaatsarchiv Hannover, Landesarchiv Koblenz, Nordrhein-Westfälisches Hauptstaatsarchiv Düsseldorf, Hauptstaatsarchiv Stuttgart, and Sächsisches Hauptstaatsarchiv Dresden, as well as the Westpreussisches Landesmuseum in Münster. I am especially indebted to the accommodating and cooperative archivists at the Bundesarchiv Berlin-Lichterfelde, who unfailingly answered all my questions and furnished me with the necessary materials, notably to Herr Lange, Herr Klein, Frau Müller, and Frau Hessel. For their generous support in helping me locate archival materials, I am also grateful to Herr Fehlauer at the Berlin Document Center, Frau Klauß at the Geheimes Staatsarchiv Preußischer Kulturbesitz at Berlin-Dahlem, Frau Annegret Neupert and Herr Alois Fischer at the Bundesarchiv Koblenz, Eva Rimmele at the Institut für Zeitgeschichte in Munich, Agnes Petersen and Helen Solanum at the West European Collections of the Hoover Institution at Stanford University, Susanne Knoblich at the Landesarchiv Berlin, Dr. Böhme at the Stadtarchiv Göttingen, Dr. Blum at the Stadtarchiv Heidelberg, Michael Caroli and Dr. Rings at the Stadtarchiv Mannheim, Dr. Becker at the Stadtarchiv Saarbrücken, Dr. Margareta Bull-Reichenmüller at the Hauptstaatsarchiv Stuttgart, and Dr. Roland Müller at the Stadtarchiv Stuttgart. Of the numerous colleagues who read selected chapters of the manuscript, I wish to thank in particular my colleagues at the University of Miami, Edward L. Dreyer and Michael Miller. A great debt remains to Henry Turner, who read the manuscript for the press and made valuable suggestions for improvement; James Retallack, who provided important insight and constructive criticism that led to a number of necessary changes; as well as to David Barclay, Larry E. Jones, Stanley Payne, and James Tent, who read the entire manuscript and generously offered suggestions, criticisms, and incisive comments. It goes without saying that any shortcomings remain the responsibility of the author. No words can sufficiently express the debt of gratitude I owe to Marcia, who indefatigably read several versions of this book and spent countless hours with me discussing its arguments, fine-tuning its style, meticulously critiquing every paragraph, and forcing me to be more precise in expression and economical in wording. Her unfailing attention to detail, not least when dealing with problems of intricate document translations from the German, have made this a more coherent and readable book.

Introduction

Perspectives on the Nazi Seizure of Power,
30 January to 14 July 1933

During the past fifty years much detailed historical research has been devoted to explaining the prehistory of Hitler's rise to power: why Hitler became Chancellor less than three months after the NSDAP suffered a major defeat in the 6 November 1932 elections; how the transfer of power was affected after much confusion, prevarication, and behind-the-scenes intrigue, all of which resulted in Hitler becoming head of government on 30 January 1933; and why, after the democratic press in their 1933 New Year's editions had predicted the premature death of his movement and its certain decline into oblivion, National Socialism could emerge triumphant.[1] Much less is known, however, about the development of the relationship between the German National People's Party (DNVP or German Nationals), Germany's main conservative party during the Weimar Republic, and the NSDAP—the political coalition that helped bring Hitler into power. Little scholarly attention has been paid to the tension-ridden relations between the NSDAP and its conservative ally, whose leaders thought Hitler boxed in by their superior

---

1. Henry A. Turner, *Hitler's Thirty Days to Power. January 1933* (Harlow, 1996) offers the most detailed account; see also Martin Broszat, *Die Machtergreifung. Der Aufstieg der NSDAP und die Zerstörung der Weimarer Republik*, 5th ed. (Munich, 1994).

numbers in the Cabinet, or to the astonishing speed with which the Nazi movement succeeded in turning the Weimar Republic into a dictatorship. A number of detailed studies focus on the main historical figures, such as Alfred Hugenberg, chairman of the DNVP from October 1928 to June 1933.[2] There is also a series of well-researched books, dissertations, and articles on various aspects of the DNVP during the Weimar Republic.[3] But there is no comprehensive overview of the history of the DNVP, and no study that addresses the dynamic between the DNVP and the NSDAP during the period of the seizure of power or, more broadly, between German Nationals and their supporters, on the one hand, and National Socialism, on

2. See John A. Leopold, *Alfred Hugenberg. The Radical Nationalist Campaign against the Weimar Republic* (New Haven and London, 1977); Denis P. Walker, *Alfred Hugenberg and the Deutschnationale Volkspartei 1918 to 1930* (D.Phil., Cambridge, 1976); Heidrun Holzbach, *Das "System Hugenberg"* (Stuttgart, 1981); Klaus Wernecke and Peter Heller, *Der vergessene Führer Alfred Hugenberg. Pressemacht und Nationalsozialismus* (Hamburg, 1982); Rüdiger Stutz, *Die politische Entwicklung Eduard Stadtlers von 1918 bis 1933* (Jena, 1985).

3. Werner Liebe, *Die Deutschnationale Volkspartei, 1918–1924* (Düsseldorf, 1956); Elisabeth Friedenthal, *Volksbegehren und Volksentscheid über den Youngplan und die deutschnationale Sezession* (Diss. Tübingen, 1957); Jan Striesow, *Die Deutschnationale Volkspartei und die Völkisch-Radikalen 1918–1922*, 2 vols. (Frankfurt, 1981); Lewis Hertzman, *DNVP. Right-wing Opposition in the Weimar Republic, 1918–1924* (Lincoln, 1963); Manfred Dörr, *Die Deutschnationale Volkspartei 1925–1928* (Diss. Phil., Marburg, 1964); Gisbert J. Gemein, *The DNVP in Düsseldorf* (Diss., Cologne, 1968); Anneliese Thimme, *Flucht in den Mythos. Die Deutschnationale Volkspartei und die Niederlage von 1918* (Göttingen, 1969); Herbert Blechschmidt, *Die Deutschnationale Volkspartei 1918–1920* (Diss., Berlin/East, 1970); Erika Schwarz, *Rivalität und Bündnis in den Beziehungen der DNVP zur NSDAP: Sommer 1929 bis 1933* (Diss., Berlin/East, 1977); Reinhard Behrens, *Die Deutschnationalen in Hamburg 1918–1933* (Diss., Hamburg, 1973); Dankwart Guratzsch, *Macht durch Organisation. Die Grundlegung des Hugenbergschen Presseimperiums* (Düsseldorf, 1973); Amrei Stupperich, *Volksgemeinschaft oder Arbeitersolidarität. Studien zur Arbeitnehmerpolitik der DNVP, 1918–1933* (Göttingen, 1982); Wolfgang Ruge, "Deutschnationale Volkspartei 1918–1933," in Dieter Fricke et al., eds., *Lexikon zur Parteiengeschichte*, vol. II (Köln, 1983–1986), 476–528; Hermann Weiß und Paul Hoser, eds., *Die Deutschnationalen und die Zerstörung der Weimarer Republik. Aus dem Tagebuch von Reinhold Quaatz 1928–1933* (Munich, 1989); Larry E. Jones, "'The Greatest Stupidity of My Life:' Alfred Hugenberg and the Formation of the Hitler Cabinet, January 1933," *Journal of Contemporary History*, 27 (1992), 63–87; Thomas Mergel, "Das Scheitern des deutschen Tory-Konservatismus. Die Umformung der DNVP zu einer rechtsradikalen Partei 1928–1932," *Historische Zeitschrift*, 276 (2003), 323–368.

the other.[4] Why did the DNVP and its supporters acquiesce in Nazi transgressions and violent attacks, and why did they not stop the "implementation of Nazism's racial idiocies,"[5] as expected by some prominent German Jews, such as Georg Bernhard, even after they had fled the country? And exactly how did the relationship between the Nazis and the DNVP (and their conservative supporters) evolve and change between 30 January and 14 July 1933, when Hitler outlawed all parties, save his own, and thus formally sealed the establishment of the one-party state?

This book addresses these questions. It examines the relationship between German conservatism and National Socialism, as reflected in the coalition between the DNVP and the NSDAP. It analyzes the prehistory of the alliance, as well as the often-violent conflicts that characterized it between 30 January and the demise of the DNVP in late June 1933. The period of the Nazi seizure of power from 30 January to 14 July 1933 (also referred to as the *Machtergreifung*) is characterized here as an era of all-pervasive violence and lawlessness marked by incessant conflicts between Nazis and their alliance partner, a far cry from its traditional depiction in much of the previous literature as a relatively bloodless, virtually sterile assumption of power by one vast impersonal apparatus wresting control from another. The present study reinterprets the process of the Nazi seizure of power as more "revolutionary," violent, and far less orderly than previously assumed. It allocates greater importance to the role of violence and rabble-rousing grassroots initiatives by local Nazi organizations as the essential lubricants of the Nazi takeover. Contrary to common assumptions, as early as March and April 1933, Nazi violence spared no one who dared oppose the victorious movement; neither social status nor political prominence offered protection. The analysis then turns to the question of the DNVP's role as the NSDAP's governing alliance

---

4. The long article by Friedrich Freiherr Hiller von Gaertingen, closest to the present work with respect to topic and time frame, concentrates exclusively on the internal history and development of the DNVP between 1928 and the dissolution of the party in June 1933, omitting the relationship between German Nationals and Nazis, as well as the surrounding historical context. Friedrich Freiherr Hiller von Gaertingen, "Die Deutschnationale Volkspartei" (hereafter "DNVP"), in Erich Matthias und Rudolf Morsey, eds., *Das Ende der Parteien 1933* (Düsseldorf, 1960), 543–652.

5. Georg Bernhard, *Die deutsche Tragödie. Selbstmord einer Republik* (Prague, 1933), 25.

partner in the early months of 1933: Could the party have acted as a brake on Nazi excesses, or was it a pawn caught up in the spirit of the times? The examination of the DNVP's vacillating approach toward Nazi anti-Semitic attacks, and the party's own inconsistent actions concerning "the Jewish question," highlights the different nature of conservative anti-Semitism and shows that, partly out of concern for its own position, the party did nothing to alter the fate of German Jews. By investigating the fundamental changes in Germany's political climate and the astonishing, often genuine, increase in Nazi support during this period, the book seeks to provide answers to the question of how, within a span of six months, a democratic, if crisis-ridden state such as the Weimar Republic could be turned into a tightly controlled dictatorship that enjoyed significant popular acclaim. The book scrutinizes the revolutionary character of the Nazi seizure of power, the Nazis' attack on bourgeois values, and their co-optation of conservative symbols of state power to serve radically new goals, while addressing the issue of why the DNVP was complicit in these actions and paradoxically participated in eroding the foundations of its very own principles and bases of support.

The present study thus focuses less on people and events than on changes in political climate, the behavior of groups, and differences in political interests and mentality between Nazis and supporters of the DNVP. It examines the policies of the DNVP and, even more importantly, explores the party's relationship to National Socialism, which is integrated into the larger historical context and Zeitgeist of the age, and takes into account the different mindsets and identities of the two "national" parties. The numerous incidences of unbridled violence directed against conservative *Honoratioren* and DNVP members highlighted here show that the "Bündnis der Eliten" (pact of elites) was suspended during the *Machtergreifung*, as many local Nazi and SA leaders violently turned against local conservative elites. This took place within the mental climate prevalent during the winter and spring of 1933: the all-pervasive fear of communism after the Reichstag fire and the enormous *Aufbruchsstimmung*— the atmosphere of awakening—generated by the Nazis in March and April 1933. By this point, Nazism had succeeded in putting itself forward as a protest movement against bourgeois lifestyles and claimed to offer a better alternative for the future, just as potential political opponents to Nazism faltered and caved in without resistance or defected to the enemy out of genuine conviction, opportunism, or outright fear.

New Aspects of the Nazi Seizure of Power

Over time, our understanding of the nature of the Nazi seizure of power has changed, with significant consequences for the interpretation of the character of Nazism as a whole. Until the 1980s, historians generally underestimated the wanton violence that accompanied the Nazi seizure of power, not only in the takeover of the different German states (Länder) after 5 March 1933, but at all levels. This violence manifested itself not only in anti-Semitic attacks throughout Germany, but also in countless acts of revenge and intimidation against political opponents, neighbors, business rivals, or anyone who had ever fallen foul of prominent Nazis or Nazi organizations. Ubiquitous terror was the lubricating oil in the process of eliminating opponents, in rendering innocuous potential enemies, and in "persuading" organizations like the Catholic Church that accommodation with the new masters was the better part of valor. The threat of violence that was present in all spheres of life in the wake of the Reichstag Fire Decree of 28 February 1933 accelerated the process of *Gleichschaltung,* the "bringing into line" of the manifold associations and interest groups of German society. This book highlights one aspect of violence that historians have tended to overlook: Nazi attacks against their coalition partner, the DNVP, including its members and supporters. The tendency to disregard Nazi attacks on German Nationals and their supporters in the conservative *Bürgertum* is connected with a failure—or possibly an unwillingness—to recognize the social revolutionary overtones of the Nazi movement, in particular the Nazis' loathing of the *Bürgertum,* its values, and its entire bourgeois way of life, which many Nazis saw reflected in the DNVP. When analyzing the relationship between the DNVP and the Nazi movement, historians have emphasized their commonalities, shared beliefs, congruence of interests, and practical collaboration, without taking into account Nazi attacks on German National organizations, interest groups, and values.[6] To overlook strife and discord in the relationship between Nazis and the DNVP means to ignore, or at least minimize, the social revolutionary thrust of the Nazi movement during the winter and spring of 1933 and thus, to

---

6. It goes without saying that leftist forces in Germany were subjected to incomparably more severe forms of persecution; the difference in the level and severity of the violence, however, does not negate the significance of Nazi attacks against their conservative coalition partner.

a certain extent, misrepresent the complex and often contradictory reality of the period between 30 January and 14 July 1933.

Two main reasons may explain the tendency to disregard the open conflict between the Nazis and their conservative alliance partner. First, the overt cooperation between Mussolini and conservative elites in Italy, and the fact that the Italian variant of fascism rarely came into conflict with traditional forces in society, might have affected interpretations of the German case. Secondly, the Marxist interpretation of fascism, which played an important role in discussions of the 1960s and 1970s, emphasized the connection between fascism and the capitalist bourgeoisie. Those who subscribed to Marxist interpretations tended to reject "the significance of any distinction between the core fascist groups and forces of right authoritarianism," as Stanley Payne put it.[7] Proponents of Marxist theories, from the orthodox Soviet historians to August Thalheimer, Otto Bauer, and Max Horkheimer, all argued that fascist movements were at bottom manifestations of bourgeois interests and agents of the traditional upper classes.[8] But even those Western historians who rejected Marxist interpretations tended to downplay clashes and conflicts of interest between conservative elites and Nazis. Were they reluctant to counter Marxist positions by appearing to depict German conservatives as victims and thus be accused of vindicating or even exonerating them from the burden of their responsibility? Or, given that conservatives around Papen and Hindenburg had transferred power (albeit reluctantly) to Hitler on 30 January, did it seem justifiable to dismiss the issue of conflict between the traditional forces in German society and the Nazis altogether?

The argument here is that neither the transfer of power to Hitler nor the tactical alliance between the DNVP and NSDAP should obscure the confrontation between Nazis and the conservative forces in German society during the Nazi seizure of power. The "revolutionary fervor" of the Nazi Party and its organizations, notably the SA, was at its height during the months of the takeover when, with great speed and brutality, the Nazis wrested power from a largely conservative state apparatus. In the winter and spring of 1933, all leading Nazis behaved in a "revolutionary" fashion, blurring

7. Stanley Payne, *Fascism: Comparison and Definition* (Madison, 1980), 180.

8. Wolfgang Wippermann, *Europäischer Faschismus im Vergleich, 1922–1982* (Frankfurt, 1983); Wolfgang Wippermann, *Faschismustheorien. Zum Stand der gegenwärtigen Forschung*, 5th ed. (Darmstadt, 1989); Stanley Payne, *A History of Fascism, 1914–1945* (Madison, 1995), 441–496.

differences within the Nazi leadership between a more "conservative" Hermann Göring and a more "radical" Joseph Goebbels. Once their more obvious political adversaries, such as Communists, Social Democrats, and the Catholic Center had been broken or browbeaten into submission, the Nazis trained their aggression on their ally, the DNVP. The social revolutionary overtones of Nazi attacks against conservatives were complemented by their political instrumentality. Nazis needed to break the strongholds of conservative power in local politics and gain control of the state apparatus to facilitate the *Gleichschaltung*. Once the position of German Nationals and their supporters in the conservative *Bürgertum* had been successfully undermined, their organizations broken, and—what Nazis perceived as—their outmoded values scorned and ridiculed, the new masters could turn once again to establishing closer cooperation with a now-chastened establishment. After declaring the revolution ended in July 1933, Hitler needed their experience and expertise to help run the complex machinery of state. Thus, later cooperation between the German conservative establishment and the Nazi party should not be interpreted as cooperation between equal partners. By the summer of 1933, the conservative establishment had been shown who was really in charge, and its members fell into line more compliantly. The following section concentrates on the historiography of the Nazi seizure of power and highlights the more important interpretations of the period since the early 1960s.

Previous Assessments of the Nazi Seizure of Power

The most detailed study of the Nazi seizure of power, the monumental *Die nationalsozialistische Machtergreifung*, first published in 1960 by Karl-Dietrich Bracher and his collaborators Wolfgang Sauer and Gerhard Schultz, examines every aspect of state, society, bureaucracy, economy, military, ideology, education, and foreign policy in the first year and a half of Hitler's rule.[9] This magisterial analysis, which offers not only detailed chronological discussions of events and developments but also structural sociological analysis, omits the element of political mobilization from below—of chaos, disorder, and turmoil—almost completely. Instead, the reader is left with the impression that the gigantic apparatus of state is taken over by an

---

9. Karl-Dietrich Bracher, Wolfgang Sauer, Gerhard Schulz, *Die nationalsozialistische Machtergreifung*, 2nd ed. (Köln and Opladen, 1962).

impersonal, tenaciously moving machine that gradually permeates bureaucracy and society. The work stresses the "pseudo-legal" character of the Nazi takeover, but there is little sense of the dynamism of the seizure of power, of the ubiquitous random violence, of acts of revenge, SA units out of control, and innumerable instances of anti-Semitic bestiality. Even though Wolfgang Sauer deals with the terror of the SA in the last third of the book (pp. 855–880), the central aspect of violence remains curiously peripheral and never fully integrated into the overall explanation of the Nazi seizure of power.

In the same vein, Bracher's next classic, comprehensive work, *Die deutsche Diktatur*, which also devotes a good deal of attention to the Nazi takeover, stresses the "semblance of legality" that characterized the process, but again neglects to emphasize more emphatically the mobilization of grassroots violence.[10] Bracher correctly stresses the fact that "none of the institutions responsible for the maintenance of the Rechtsstaat" opposed Nazi actions,[11] but he fails to impress upon the reader that a central reason for their failure to act was raw fear of Nazi reprisals. When referring to acts of violence, Bracher employs concepts such as "terrorist seizure-of-power acts" (p. 290) that defy description and lack plasticity. Since he offers no concrete examples that would fill these concepts with life, his account of the period invariably leaves the reader with the wrong mental image of a more-or-less orderly process, without taking into account the turmoil and upheavals that contemporaries felt when, supporters and opponents alike, they employed the term "revolution" in referring to the months of March through June 1933. Bracher uses terms such as the "at any rate unstoppable revolution" and speaks of a "regime with a tempestuous and violent bearing" (p. 291), but since his analysis focuses largely on the sphere of state, bureaucracy, and the content of emergency ordinances without giving due weight to the pressure of the street, his precise examination of events remains strangely colorless and at variance with the perception of contemporaries.[12]

10. Karl-Dietrich Bracher, *Die deutsche Diktatur. Entstehung, Struktur, Folgen des Nationalsozialismus*, 7th ed. (Berlin, 1997), 282–335 (first ed. 1969; English translation 1970).

11. Ibid., 289.

12. The importance of disorder and "revolutionary violence" is consistently stressed in autobiographies dealing with the period. Two recent examples are Theodor Eschenburg, *Letzten Endes meine ich doch. Erinnerungen 1933–1999* (Berlin, 2000) and Sebastian Haffner, *Geschichte eines Deutschen. Die Erinnerungen 1914–1933*, 2nd ed. (Munich, 2002).

Undoubtedly, Bracher's analytical approach and the almost complete absence of narrative are partially to blame for the curiously neutral feeling with which the reader is left after reading his account. By not giving sufficient weight to details and telling episodes that were part of the changes and upheavals of the age, Bracher fails to capture the mood of intimidation and powerlessness on the part of potential and actual victims, on the one hand, and the exhilaration and exultation—a mood which had taken hold of Germany in those months—of Nazis and Nazi supporters, on the other.[13] Bracher aptly depicts Nazi control of society by arguing that "the characteristic, exceedingly successful method consisted in the mixture of pseudo-legal governmental decrees with revolutionary threats and terrorist pressure" (p. 299). This was very true, but since little is said about the nature of revolutionary threats and forms of terrorist pressure, these concepts serve only to stifle historical reality and fail to render a realistic depiction of the past.

Martin Broszat's *Der Staat Hitlers*, the classic work on the Nazi state that analyzes in detail the seizure of power, again evinces the tendency to convey the image of an impersonal takeover of a gigantic machinery with a focus on legal and bureaucratic aspects.[14] This despite the fact that Broszat is far more concrete in his approach than Bracher. When exploring purges of the Prussian bureaucracy, for example, he lists the names of suspended *Oberpräsidenten* (provincial governors) and points to regional differences in the Nazi takeover. Broszat uses concepts such as "party revolution" and "revolution from below" (pp. 258–267) without, however, capturing the atmosphere of threat, panic, and disquietude. The reader gets little sense of the breakdown of civil society and law and order, or of the widespread brutality, mayhem, and confusion. The Nazi state appears to have superseded Weimar without the countless tremors, cracks, and fissures at the fault line that marked this all-encompassing earthquake.

Hans Mommsen, another key proponent of the structuralist approach to Nazism, also implicitly downplays the violent and revolutionary aspects of the Nazi takeover by postulating a *Verschränkung*

13. The political scientist in Bracher was interested in explaining how parliamentary democracy gave way to totalitarian dictatorship to the point that the underlying element of planning in Nazi actions appears to take precedence, which might explain Bracher's lack of interest in violence.

14. Martin Broszat, *Der Staat Hitlers*, 7th ed. (Munich, 1978), 82–173 (first published 1969; English translation, *The Hitler State*, 1981).

(crossing over) of traditional and Nazi elites, which he depicts as a relatively smooth, frictionless process.[15] Mommsen asserts that despite "the undeniable social and frequently also generational antagonism" (p. 158) between the traditional and National Socialist elite, a close cooperation between both groups came about in the course of the *Gleichschaltung*. The fact that cooperation could come to pass in spite of social and generational "antagonisms" was due largely to the "far-reaching congruence of interests that stood at the cradle of the alliance between conservative-authoritarian leadership groups and the National Socialist leadership."[16] My argument here is that this congruence of interests was less extensive than Mommsen has assumed. It was clearly not important enough to keep Nazi aggression and hatred for "conservative-authoritarian leadership groups" (as Mommsen put it) in check. In another article, Mommsen maintains that the relative stability of the National Socialist regime during the phase of the seizure of power stemmed from the fact that "Hitler had been obliged to make far-reaching concessions to the conservative elite controlling the army, economy, and administration, thereby frustrating those elements in the Nazi movement who pressed for total seizure of all social and political institutions."[17] The evidence presented here suggests that these concessions may not have been as far-reaching as Mommsen claims. In the same article, Mommsen affirms that Goebbels considered the process of *Gleichschaltung* a revolutionary act, insisting that "the German revolution had been carried out from below and not from above."[18] Elsewhere Mommsen conceded "that National Socialists succeeded in creating the impression that the Third Reich was an open society,"[19] which seems to indicate that Mommsen, too, is prepared to accept that National Socialism affected some kind of social revolution.

15. Hans Mommsen, "Zur Verschränkung traditioneller und faschistischer Führungsgruppen in Deutschland beim Übergang von der Bewegungs-zur Systemphase," in Wolfgang Schieder, ed., *Faschismus als soziale Bewegung*, 2nd ed. (Göttingen, 1983), 157–181 (first published in 1977).

16. Ibid., 158. Mommsen argues that this alliance led to "paralysis of action and passivity of the old leadership groups."

17. Hans Mommsen, "National Socialism: Continuity and Change," in Mommsen, *From Weimar to Auschwitz* (Princeton, 1991), 141–163, esp. 145.

18. Mommsen, ibid., 152. Alan Bullock, *Hitler, A Study in Tyranny*, rev. ed. (New York, 1964) and Joachim Fest, *Hitler. Eine Biographie* (Berlin and Frankfurt, 1973) stressed early on the revolutionary aspect of the Nazi seizure of power.

19. Hans Mommsen, "Nachwort," in David Schoenbaum, *Die braune Revolution* (Munich, 1980), 352–368, esp. 356.

Klaus Hildebrand, in his short survey of Nazi Germany that is coupled with an extensive discussion of the historiography, puts less weight on the aspect of *Scheinlegalität* (semblance of legality) in the Nazi takeover than Bracher twenty years earlier.[20] Hildebrand maintains that during the course of the "gradually accomplished conquest of power," legal and terrorist measures "dovetailed in such a way that it was difficult to keep them apart."[21] He claims that the Third Reich had been "nourished on a hitherto unknown combination of tradition and revolution." On the other hand, in concurring with the assessment of John Weiss, who considers German fascism to be "the last gasp of conservatism," Hildebrand de-emphasizes the anti-bourgeois element of National Socialism.[22] This runs counter to the findings of the present study. The Nazis' scorn and contempt for German conservatism and the classes that supported it—the infamous *"Reaktion"* of the Nazi marching song—burst forth violently during the *Machtergreifung*. Conservatives were considered unfit to have any share in the governance of Germany, blamed for the half-hearted conduct of the war, and accused of cowardice in 1918. As this book shows, there was a broad consensus among Nazis about not wanting to hear themselves mentioned in the same breath as conservatives.

During the 1980s, the emphasis of interpretation shifted. Accounts of the Nazi seizure of power in surveys of Nazi Germany that dealt with the events of 1933 in some detail, such as the works of Gotthard Jasper, Hans-Ulrich Thamer, and Norbert Frei, devote greater space to Nazi violence and accentuate less its "pseudo-legal" aspects.[23] These studies benefited from the results of detailed research on the SA that had brought out the importance of brute force

20. Klaus Hildebrand, *Das dritte Reich*, 3rd ed. (Munich, 1987), 2. First published in 1979; English translation, *The Third Reich*, 1984.

21. Ibid., 108–109.

22. Hildebrand, ibid., 165. Hildebrand approvingly quotes John Weiss, *The Fascist Tradition. Radical Right-wing Extremism in Modern Europe* (New York, 1967), 5: "Fascism was not the 'last gasp of monopoly capitalism.' If anything, it was the last gasp of conservatism." Hildebrand adds: "- of a conservatism of specifically Prussian-German vintage," that lacked the reformist capacity of English Toryism.

23. Gotthard Jasper, *Die gescheiterte Zähmung. Wege zur Machtergreifung Hitlers 1930–1934* (Frankfurt, 1986); Hans-Ulrich Thamer, *Verführung und Gewalt. Deutschland 1933–1945* (Berlin, 1986); Norbert Frei, *Der Führerstaat. Nationalsozialistische Herrrschaft 1933 bis 1945*, 6th ed. (Munich, 2001). The first German edition was published in 1987; the English translation in 1993.

and coercion during the Nazi takeover.[24] By the 1980s, it had become clear that lawlessness and violent transgressions had been the order of the day, so that the concept of *Scheinlegalität* was deprived of its heuristic value. Yet even in these more recent studies, the chaotic-arbitrary aspect of violence, its wanton willfulness, and lack of planning and coordination are mostly unappreciated. In his concise survey and interpretation of the years from 1930 to 1934, Jasper dismisses the term "legal revolution" as ultimately misrepresenting the character of the *Machtergreifung*, since considerations of legality would only obfuscate the lawlessness and illegal transgressions that actually took place.[25] Jasper contrasts the terror of the SA with the inactivity and collusion of the police that made a sham of the March elections while, in his analysis of the takeover of the Länder after 5 March, he stresses the importance of "spontaneous initiative from below" (p. 143). On the other hand, in castigating the gullibility of the Center Party and its halfhearted insistence on binding concessions to safeguard the rule of law in return for the Center's support for the Enabling Act (see the interpretation in chapter 3 below), Jasper slightly minimizes the weight of the Damocles sword that hung over Nazi opponents as they considered their options in light of the Nazis' capacity to browbeat them into submission. In his important account of the years between 1933 and 1945, Hans-Ulrich Thamer lays stress upon the revolutionary element of National Socialism, especially the component of protest against traditional authority that considerably added to the attractiveness and allure of Nazism.[26]

---

24. Among others: Richard Bessel, *Political Violence and the Rise of Nazism. The Storm Troopers in Eastern Germany, 1925–1934* (New Haven and London, 1984); Conan J. Fischer, *Stormtroopers. A Social, Economic and Ideological Analysis, 1929–1935* (London, 1983); Mathilde Jamin, *Zwischen den Klassen. Zur Sozialstruktur der SA-Führerschaft* (Wuppertal, 1984); and Peter Longerich, *Die braunen Bataillone. Geschichte der SA* (Munich, 1989).

25. Jasper, *Die gescheiterte Zähmung*, 138. See also Jasper's edited collection, *Von Weimar zu Hitler, 1930–1934* (Cologne and Berlin, 1968).

26. Thamer, *Verführung und Gewalt*, 186 and 232–310. The revolutionary element is also discussed in Ernst Nolte, "Europäische Revolutionen des 20. Jahrhunderts. Die nationalsozialistische Machtergreifung im historischen Zusammenhang," in Wolfgang Michalka, ed., *Die nationalsozialistische Machtergreifung* (Paderborn, 1984), 395–410; Martin Broszat et al., eds., *Deutschlands Weg in die Diktatur. Internationale Konferenz zur nationalsozialistischen Machtübernahme* (Berlin, 1983), 78–113. See particularly the contribution by Horst Möller, who argues that the term "revolution" characterizes the establishment of the Nazi dictatorship better than "*Machtergreifung*" (p. 78). See also Horst Möller, "Die

Thamer also presses home the often disregarded point that the speed of the Nazi takeover should not lead to the conclusion that a master plan had existed beforehand.[27] Here Thamer digresses significantly from Bracher's approach which, in its interpretation of different "stages of *Machtergreifung*," seems to imply a "rational progression to preconceived goals," as Ian Kershaw once put it.[28] Thamer best encapsulates the irrational component of the period by raising the question: "the 'national revolution'—a delirious whirl?"[29] Throughout his analysis, Thamer underlines "the revolutionary character" (p. 245) of the *Machtergreifung*, the lubricating function of terror that accelerated the pace of the takeover, and the importance of "pressure from below," without which political power could not have been usurped.[30] In the same vein, Norbert Frei's skillfully composed, compact survey, *Der Führerstaat*, gives prominence to the importance of the "party revolution from below," especially in the course of appropriating power in the Länder.[31] Frei is among the first to appreciate the fact that Nazi violence was not only anti-Semitic in nature, or directed solely against the "Marxist" milieu, but that it also targeted, if in a less comprehensive and systematic way, members of the *Bürgertum*. In an apposite summary, he concludes that the success of the Nazi Party and the SA "resulted from the chaos created and general intimidation, not from any systematic planning of how to proceed."[32]

The most recent German surveys of Nazism published in the 1990s lay increasing emphasis on the violent, terrorist aspects of

---

nationalsozialistische Machtergreifung: Konterrevolution oder Revolution?" *Vierteljahreshefte für Zeitgeschichte*, 31 (1983), 25–51.

27. Thamer, *Verführung und Gewalt*, 232. Thamer draws attention to the important function of the Communists, whose very existence and the perceived threat they represented frequently served as an excuse for Nazi violence against all political opponents. Ibid., 248–253.

28. Ian Kershaw, *The Nazi Dictatorship. Problems and Perspectives of Interpretation*, 4th ed. (London, 2000), 73. *Stufen der Machtergreifung* (Berlin, 1974) is also the title of the reprint of Bracher's contribution to Bracher, Sauer, Schulz, *Die nationalsozialistische Machtergreifung*.

29. Ibid., 238. Thamer uses the word "Taumel," though he unfortunately does not elaborate further.

30. Ibid., 245, 259. The function of the SA is aptly characterized as that of the "engine behind *Gleichschaltung*" (p. 264).

31. Frei, *Der Führerstaat*, 59.

32. Ibid., 59. Frei emphasizes that the traditional Right had always shown "fear of the social revolutionary potential" of the Nazis (p. 44).

the Third Reich, as reflected in their discussion of the *Machtergrei-fung.*[33] Jost Düffler underscores that "the use of intimidation, ter-ror, and deprivation of rights" was an essential element of the Nazi takeover, and mentions that "there was also persecution" directed against the German Nationals.[34] Still, he overstates the nature of the political alliance between conservatives and Nazis in asserting that: "*from the very beginning* an alliance developed between the new mass movement and important parts of the old German bureau-cratic, economic, and military elite."[35] While it is true that such an alliance eventually came about, it did not occur in as smooth a fashion as Düffler suggests.[36] In the same vein as Mommsen, Düff-ler argues that after the other parties had been abolished, "the alli-ance between National Socialists and the conservatives continued to develop, in public affairs and administration, a tendency toward a uniform elite loyal to the state" (p. 41). This, too, is questionable: it was hardly an alliance of equals; the traditional elites had to com-promise and adapt to the requirements of the new state. During the months of turmoil and upheaval following 30 January 1933, they were forced to learn the stark lesson of their powerlessness and must have realized that remaining in office meant seeking accommoda-tion with the new masters. This was a humbling experience but preferable, in their eyes, to losing power and influence altogether. Given the brevity of the space allocated, Düffler's synopsis is admi-rable in its comprehensiveness, though he, too, fails to account for the tumult and chaos of the winter and spring of 1933 that gave the Nazis greater ascendancy over German society than was believed possible and put the traditional elites, at least temporarily, in a posi-tion of dependency. In a competent and eminently readable survey, Ludolf Herbst impresses on the reader the importance of terror and propaganda in the course of the Nazi takeover.[37] In contrast to some of the other shorter surveys, Herbst's account gives prominence to

---

33. Jost Düffler, *Nazi Germany 1933–1945. Faith and Annihilation* (London and New York, 1996; German original published in 1992); Ludolf Herbst, *Das nationalsozialistische Deutschland, 1933–1945. Die Entfesselung der Gewalt: Rassismus und Krieg* (Frankfurt 1996).

34. Düffler, *Nazi Germany*, 28 and 35.

35. Ibid., 36–37, emphasis added.

36. For a similar line of reasoning, see Düffler, "Die Machtergreifung und die Rolle der alten Eliten im Dritten Reich," in Michalka, ed., *Die nationalso-zialistische Machtergreifung*, 182–194.

37. Herbst, *Das nationalsozialistische Deutschland*, 80–89.

the multitude of anti-Semitic attacks and the wanton brutality that characterized them (pp. 73–80). And he underlines the fact that initially even Hitler proved powerless to channel the chaotic terror of the party rank and file.

The most recent English-language studies that deal with the period of the Nazi *Machtergreifung* (albeit from very different vantage points), those of Saul Friedländer, Michael Burleigh, Ian Kershaw, and Richard Evans all give weight to the element of violence and terror.[38] Both Friedländer and Evans appreciate the mental climate of the months from March through June 1933 much better than most of the older, less empirical German studies. Yet, even these latest accounts do not always accord sufficient weight to the Nazis' hatred of their conservative alliance partner and the social revolutionary overtones of the *Machtergreifung*, though this may well be due to the specific focus of their analyses.

The DNVP: Mass Party or Party of Notables?

An overview of the roots, identity, and structure of the DNVP is needed to appreciate the full spectrum of conflicts, commonalities, and tactical collaboration between Nazis and German Nationals. The DNVP was founded in November 1918 as a confluence of all prewar conservative political parties. Never before in German history since the founding of the first conservative organizations in Prussia in the 1830s had conservatism, both as an ideology and a political organization, become more completely discredited than in the autumn of 1918, when the seemingly well-entrenched monarchical order that it represented collapsed without fanfare or resistance.[39]

38. Saul Friedländer, *Nazi Germany and the Jews. The Years of Persecution, 1933–1939* (New York, 1997), 9–73; Ian Kershaw, *Hitler. 1889–1936: Hubris* (New York, 1999), 429–483 offers a splendid narrative account; Michael Burleigh, *The Third Reich. A New History* (New York, 2000), 149–198 and 281–293, provides an extensive examination of anti-Semitic violence; and Richard J. Evans, *The Coming of the Third Reich* (New York, 2004), 309–390.

39. On the founding of the DNVP after the defeat of 1918, see Thimme, *Flucht in den Mythos*, 61–107; Liebe, *Volkspartei*, 7–42; Hertzman, *DNVP*; Peter-Christian Witt, "Eine Denkschrift Otto Hoetzschs vom 5. November 1918," in *Vierteljahreshefte für Zeitgeschichte* 21 (1973), 337–353; Peter Fritzsche, "Breakdown or Breakthrough? Conservatives and the November Revolution," in Larry E. Jones and James N. Retallack, eds., *Between Reform, Reaction and Resistance. Studies in the History of German Conservatism from 1789 to 1945* (Providence & Oxford, 1993), 299–329.

All the groups that gathered under the roof of the new party were keenly aware of the painful fact that they were in opposition to the prevailing postwar Zeitgeist. Given that they had supported the old order, they were considered at least partially responsible for the unexpected military and political catastrophe of November 1918. Graf Westarp expressed the prevailing sentiment in conservative circles in the fall of 1918: "No nation had ever collapsed more completely in the face of such a sudden turn of events as we have. We have been thrown down from a grand summit, the highest peak. At the beginning of the year, there we stood—crowned in a laurel wreath, proud, and powerful; now we lie in the dust. We have become poor and disgraced."[40]

Supporters of the German Conservative Party (DKP), the Free Conservative Party (FKP), the Christian Social Party, the Pan-German Association, anti-Semitic splinter parties, and a number of former National Liberals formed the DNVP in the late fall of 1918. The confluence of so many different groups, from conservative notables to petty bourgeois anti-Semites fearful of sliding into the proletariat, made the DNVP one of the most heterogeneous parties of the Weimar Republic. The numerically strongest and politically most significant element that flowed into the DNVP were members of the former German Conservative Party, the Empire's strongest conservative party, founded in 1876. Despite its name, which signified an orientation away from Prussia and toward the new Empire, the DKP had been primarily a Prussian party. Less than one-fifth of the 285 seats won by the DKP in Reichstag elections between 1890 and 1914 came from non-Prussian areas.[41] Within Prussia itself, the overwhelming majority of parliamentary deputies came from the Old Prussian provinces east of the Elbe, notably from Pomerania, East Prussia, and Brandenburg. Before 1918 the party vociferously safeguarded the interests of landowners, Prussian civil servants, and

---

40. Thimme, *Flucht in den Mythos*, 65.

41. Hans Booms, *Die Deutsch-Konservative Partei. Preußischer Charakter, Reichsauffassung, Nationalbegriff* (Düsseldorf, 1954), 7; Edgar Hartwig, "Konservative Partei," in Dieter Fricke et al., eds., *Lexikon zur Parteiengeschichte* (Köln, 1983–1986), vol. III, 283–309; James Retallack, *Notables of the Right. The Conservative Party and Political Mobilization in Germany, 1876–1918* (Boston, 1988); Hermann Beck, "The Changing Concerns of Prussian Conservatism," in Philip G. Dwyer, ed., *Modern Prussian History* (London, 2001), 86–106, and Ernst-Otto Schüddekopf, *Die deutsche Innenpolitik im letzten Jahrhundert und der konservative Gedanke* (Braunschweig, 1951). The DKP continued to exist as the *Konservativer Hauptverein* (Conservative Main Association) inside the DNVP after 1918.

the Protestant clergy and constituted an effective bloc that doggedly countered any tendencies toward further democratization. Since its power base lay in Prussia, the party strenuously resisted any weakening of Prussia's constitutional position within the Reich. Beginning in the late 1890s, the party fell increasingly under the influence of the Agrarian League (*Bund der Landwirte*), and thus gradually developed into a vehicle for agrarian interests.[42] During the First World War it supported the annexationist policies of the Pan-Germans, advocated unlimited submarine warfare, repudiated the Reichstag's Peace Resolution, and staunchly opposed the repeal of Prussia's three-class voting system.

The Free Conservative Party, by contrast, was a party of notables without an elaborate organization that recruited its more important representatives from the upper echelons of the bureaucracy and tended to favor heavy industry.[43] Despite its status as a numerically weak *Honoratiorenpartei*, the Free Conservative Party exercised considerable influence on national politics through its networks of personal contacts. It was considered to be the party of "Ministers and Diplomats"; a great many government ministers and undersecretaries of state came from its ranks. Like the DKP, Free Conservatives staunchly opposed efforts at democratization within the Reich. During the First World War, the party's policies resembled those of the DKP, even though, all told, Free Conservatives were less radical and more willing to compromise than the DKP. The third (numerically less significant) political force that flowed into the DNVP was the Christian Social Party, founded in 1878 as the Christian Social Workers Party led by Court Chaplain Adolf Stoecker. The party's main purpose was to shield the working class from Social Democratic influence by bringing workers closer to Christian beliefs and the idea of "King and Fatherland." In 1881, the Christian Socials, maintaining their status as an autonomous group, affiliated themselves with the German Conservative Party, whose members hoped,

42. Hans-Jürgen Puhle, *Agrarische Interessenpolitik und preußischer Konservatismus im wilhelminischen Reich, 1893–1914* (Hannover, 1966).

43. Frederick Aandahl, *The Rise of German Free Conservatism* (Ph.D. diss. Princeton, 1955); Thomas Nipperdey, *Die Organisation der deutschen Parteien vor 1918* (Düsseldorf, 1961), 241–265; Matthias Alexander, *Die Freikonservative Partei 1890–1914. Gemäßigter Konservatismus in der konstitutionellen Monarchie* (Düsseldorf, 2000). The Free Conservative Party, which, in contrast to "Old Prussian Conservatives" welcomed the creation of the new Reich, was also referred to as the *Reichspartei* outside Prussia.

in turn, that the anti-Semitic slogans of Christian Socialism might help them gain a mass following among the lower middle classes. This hope never materialized since anti-Semitic splinter groups other than the Christian Social Workers Party successfully appeared on the scene in the 1890s and won their own mandates.[44] Notwithstanding the fact that the German Conservative Party incorporated anti-Semitism into its "Tivoli Program" of 1892, Christian Socialism smacked too much of leftist politics to be fully palatable to most German Conservatives, while the Christian Socials, for their part, became increasingly alienated from the DKP.[45] After some initial successes in the 1890s, the anti-Semitic parties of the Empire disintegrated into mere splinter parties after the turn of the century; what remained of them also flowed into the DNVP after the war.[46] In contrast to the DKP, the geographical center of these anti-Semitic parties lay in the western part of the Reich, and their social basis of support was comprised mostly of small farmers and the lower middle classes.

The most immediate precursor of the DNVP was the "Fatherland Party," which had been founded in an atmosphere of anticipated victory and national exuberance on 2 September 1917 as a protest against the Reichstag's Peace Resolution. It included all shades of conservatives, nationalists, anti-Semites, and national liberals.[47] To some extent, the wartime Fatherland Party prepared the ground for a gathering of all conservative forces—a concept that was to be realized by the DNVP. But in November 1918, little more than a year later, at the height of the sudden and profound national humiliation, the political atmosphere had radically altered. Already the epithet "people's party" (*Volkspartei*), halfheartedly appended to the core

44. Peter Pulzer, *The Rise of Political Anti-Semitism in Germany and Austria*, rev. ed. (Cambridge, 1988); Werner E. Mosse, ed., *Juden im Wilhelminischen Deutschland* (Tübingen, 1974); Helmut Berding, *Moderner Antisemitismus in Deutschland* (Frankfurt, 1988). On the *Bildungsbürgertum*, see Uffa Jensen, *Gebildete Doppelgänger. Bürgerliche Juden und Protestanten im 19. Jahrhundert* (Göttingen, 2005).

45. See Helmut Gerlach, *Von Rechts nach Links* (Zürich, 1937); Walter Frank, *Hofprediger Adolf Stoecker und die christlichsoziale Bewegung.* 2nd ed. (Hamburg, 1935); Retallack, *Notables of the Right*, 91–100.

46. Richard S. Levy, *The Downfall of the Anti-Semitic Political Parties in Imperial Germany* (New Haven and London, 1975); Berding, *Moderner Antisemitismus*, 86–110.

47. Heinz Hagenlücke, *Deutsche Vaterlandspartei. Die nationale Rechte am Ende des Kaiserreiches* (Düsseldorf, 1997).

term "German National," was a reluctant concession to what DNVP leaders considered the odious democratic Zeitgeist. Yet, since the smaller conservative groups had brought the Christian trade unions into the party, the DNVP was a very heterogeneous party with a mass following.[48] Its social structure resembled the wartime Fatherland Party more than the DKP, and it no longer remained geographically confined to East Elbian Prussia, but extended its reach well into the middle classes of the large cities of western Germany.[49] The transition from the exclusive political style of cliquish notables to a people's party with a large apparatus and a mass organization had proceeded relatively smoothly, since the groundwork for the change had already been laid at the end of the nineteenth century with the political campaigning and propagandizing of the Agrarian League.[50] Before the war, the two main conservative parties had no very elaborate central party apparatus; this changed, to a certain extent, with the DNVP, even though the party's regional Land Associations remained of crucial importance, a fact that would later work to Hugenberg's advantage.[51]

The DNVP's indisputable influence on German society during the Weimar Republic transcended by far the party's share of the electorate. This was due to the fact that large parts of the upper and upper middle classes, the aristocracy, and the Protestant sections of the professional classes and educated bourgeoisie (*Bildungsbürgertum*), that is, the main share of the Protestant clergy and of university professors and grammar school (*Gymnasium*) teachers—all of whom had civil servant status—as well as substantial sections of the high bureaucracy in the Reich and Länder governments, supported the

---

48. Amrei Stupperich, *Volksgemeinschaft oder Arbeitersolidarität. Studien zur Arbeitnehmerpolitik in der Deutschnationalen Volkspartei, 1918–1933* (Göttingen, 1982). According to Stupperich, the DNVP received 2.2 million working-class votes in the December elections 1924 (ibid., 35).

49. Liebe, *Volkspartei*, 16–18. Almost half its seats in the National Assembly came from electoral constituencies in the west.

50. Puhle, *Agrarische Interessenpolitik und preußischer Konservatismus*; Geoff Eley, *Reshaping the German Right. Radical Nationalism and Political Change after Bismarck*, 2nd ed. (Ann Arbor, 1991).

51. In 1919, the DNVP had 35 Land Associations; between 1924 and 1928, the number rose to about 45. Between 1922 and 1928, the party had about 600–700 county associations (*Kreisvereine*). Party membership fluctuated between 300,000 and 400,000 in 1919, then rose to 700,000 in 1922 and 950,000 in 1923, before declining to 737,000 in 1924 and 696,000 in 1928. Ruge, "Deutschnationale Volkspartei," 477.

DNVP until 1930. The Reich Association of Higher Civil Servants was closer to the DNVP than to any other party.[52] Those political, social, and religious institutions that were of central importance in German life during the Weimar Republic, such as the Protestant churches, universities, the *Gymnasien*, and the upper echelons of the administrative and judicial bureaucracies, were thus influenced to a greater extent by the DNVP than by any other party. Parts of the lower middle classes, including craftsmen, white-collar employees (*Angestellte*), shopkeepers, and to some extent farmers, provided the mass basis of support for the DNVP before 1930.[53]

The diverse set of interests represented in the DNVP might well have stymied the modicum of party unity necessary for it to become a significant force in Weimar's political system. Ironically, the great common denominator of its diverse membership and source of party unity would be the irreconcilable hostility toward the very political system in which it had to function in order to pursue its members' interests. The conservative groups that comprised the DNVP shared a common animosity toward the very principles on which the Weimar Republic was based. From the beginning, the DNVP's main purpose was to organize counter-revolutionary forces: the party was vociferous in its opposition to democracy and the democratization of political life; it yearned for a return to the Empire, which had signified strength, material well-being, and relative unity under authoritarian leadership, while the Republic stood for defeat, revolution, and domestic strife. This opposition to Weimar lay at the root of the party's contradictory policies and inherent predicament: the DNVP had to operate productively in a system it was systematically trying to undermine. Absolute rejection of the Weimar Republic was thus bound to be counterproductive. Some measure of practical cooperation with other parties within the confines of the new

52. Rainer Fattmann, *Bildungsbürger in der Defensive. Die akademische Beamtenschaft und der "Reichsbund der höheren Beamten" in der Weimarer Republik* (Göttingen, 2001); Stephan Malinowski, *Vom König zum Führer. Deutscher Adel und Nationalsozialismus*, paperback ed. (Frankfurt, 2004); Daniel R. Borg, *The Old-Prussian Church and the Weimar Republic. A Study in Political Adjustment, 1917–1927* (Hanover and London, 1984), 79–80; Thimme, *Flucht in den Mythos*, 11–14; Heinrich-August Winkler, *Weimar, 1918–1933. Die Geschichte der ersten deutschen Demokratie* (München, 1993), 289–295. Winkler, in particular, stresses the alienation of the majority of the *Bildungsbürgertum* from the Republic.

53. Liebe, *Volkspartei*, 15–18; Christian F. Trippe, *Konservative Verfassungspolitik, 1918–1923 (Düsseldorf, 1995)*, 23–32; Stupperich, *Volksgemeinschaft oder Arbeitersolidarität*; Dörr, "Die Deutschnationale Volkspartei."

political rules was unavoidable and necessary, if only to safeguard the interests of the various groups that supported the party. The different economic interest groups close to the party each had their own agendas: the Rural League fought for protective tariffs (which the DNVP procured when it entered its first coalition government),[54] while the Association of German National Shop Assistants advocated the strengthening of social services for white-collar workers. None of these goals could be attained without close cooperation with other political forces within the framework of the State.

In addition to crafting optimal policies for their political clientele, it was incumbent upon the DNVP to preserve conservative cultural traditions so that those classes and occupational groups that were associated with the party, such as the upper echelons of the bureaucracy and East Elbian landowners, could maintain their influence. Most influential German Nationals had been reared in a tradition of political paternalism: they saw themselves as part of a public-spirited upper class working closely with the government to further the national interest. Despite the revolutionary upheavals of 1918–1919, the roots of the DNVP in the Empire thus, to a certain extent, had prepared the ground for a policy of constructive opposition. Leading DNVP politicians could not long remain unwilling to collaborate with other parties on particular practical matters in spite of their principled contempt for the populist, socialist-oriented, and divisive parliamentary Republic. This inner contradiction between fundamental opposition, on the one hand, and a willingness to cooperate actively within the framework of the Republic, on the other, gnawed away at the DNVP's identity during the first decade of its existence. The inherent dilemma of the DNVP was accentuated by the fact that the party's rigorously authoritarian political ideology stood in glaring contrast to the (new) democratic rules of politics. Weimar's political system demanded measures and modes of behavior that ran counter to the DNVP's *raison d'être*. Older DNVP deputies considered this new orientation especially reprehensible, for it seemed to call into question their conservative heritage and made the party appear as an offshoot of the revolution; whereas, for its younger members, many of whom yearned to participate in

54. On 1 January 1921, the Agrarian League fused with the *Deutscher Land-bund* (established in 1919) to form the *Reichslandbund* (Rural League), which had about five million members in 1928.

political life, the party's initial intransigent opposition to the Republic proved to be a strain.

The DNVP advocated a decentralized, federated Reich, opposed any further strengthening of central government, stood for the preservation of a strong Prussia and German customs and traditions, and promoted a national-minded, Christian system of education, the strengthening of matrimony and the family, and the sanctity of private property. In 1919, the first DNVP party conference prepared a program that remained in force until 1932, when it was superseded by Hugenberg's "Freedom Program," the elaboration of which had been entrusted to only two deputies, both closely associated with the Pan-German Association. The "Freedom Program" highlighted economic concerns and strongly emphasized the party's opposition to socialism, which was blamed for ruining the organically grown connections among state, economy, and society, and for undermining the institutions of the family and local government. Written at a time when the Nazis had become the DNVP's most dangerous rival and when German National voters were defecting in droves to the NSDAP, Hugenberg's program was positioned more against the Nazi party's putative socialism than that of the SPD. Consequently, the DNVP also contrasted its own "individualism" with the pernicious tenets of socialism: "soulless masses of men, standardized mass souls—that is its goal."[55]

Even after 1918, Germany's East Elbian regions, such as Pomerania, East Prussia, the eastern parts of Brandenburg, and lower Silesia, remained the electoral strongholds of conservatism. In the western parts, the DNVP did well in central Franconia and sections of Schleswig-Holstein.[56] In the elections of May 1924, for example, the DNVP emerged as the strongest political force in East Prussia; it received 49.5 percent of the vote in Pomerania, 40.5 in the electoral district Frankfurt an der Oder (which included mostly the Neumark east of the Oder), 38.9 in the Mark Brandenburg, 30.9 in Schleswig-Holstein, and 29.9 in the Liegnitz electoral district of Lower Silesia. The party was least successful in the electoral districts of Upper

---

55. Thimme, *Flucht in den Mythos*, 23–25; Ruge, "Deutschnationale Volkspartei," 476–528.

56. Of the 3,121,479 votes the DNVP received in the elections for the National Assembly, 1,251,108 came from provinces east of the Elbe; 982,997 from central and western Germany west of the Elbe; 153,863 from Hamburg, Lübeck, Bremen, Mecklenburg, Schleswig-Holstein, and the Regierungsbezirk Stade; and 733,511 from southern Germany. Liebe, *Volkspartei*, 17 and 78.

Bavaria–Swabia (7.5 percent), Koblenz–Trier (7.4), and lower Bavaria (2.9).[57] This picture remained largely unaltered in the elections of 20 May 1928. The regional strongholds of the DNVP tallied with those of the Nazi party. In areas where the DNVP was traditionally most successful, it lost large numbers of voters to the NSDAP. Martin Broszat has impressively documented this electoral change from conservatives to National Socialists.[58] In the confessionally mixed regions of southern and western Germany, where voting often correlated with the denominational character of political parties, the DNVP almost became the Protestant counterpart to the Center Party, though it never quite achieved similar stability in voting patterns.[59] In southern Germany, the party evinced a marked confessional character and in areas with pronounced Protestant diasporas, Protestant middle-class minorities usually voted for the DNVP. The DNVP's percentage of women voters and members was larger than that of most other parties, and the party also received a disproportionately large share of rural and small-town votes.[60] It was also successful in nonindustrialized cities with a high share of self-employed, salaried employees, pensioners, and service personnel, who voted for the DNVP under the influence of their employers.[61] While the total number of DNVP voters in the western parts of the Reich was lower, the stability of their voting behavior was greater. Here a high percentage of *bürgerliche* DNVP voters remained true to the party out of habit and tradition. In the party schisms of 1929 and 1930, the Rural League, the Christian Socials, and the Association of German National Shop Assistants had split from the party, and members and supporters of these groups no longer voted for the DNVP.[62] One may therefore assume that after 1930 it was primarily high officials, the portion of the *Bildungsbürgertum* that had escaped material destitution, and a part of the Protestant bourgeois middle classes that remained true to the DNVP.

In contrast to the DKP's parliamentary faction before 1914, the DNVP Reichstag faction saw a definite decline in the percentage

---

57. See Jürgen Falter, et al., *Wahlen und Abstimmungen in der Weimarer Republik. Materialien zum Wahlverhalten, 1919–1933* (Munich, 1986), 228–229.

58. See Table 1 in Appendix.

59. Karl-Dietrich Bracher, *Die Auflösung der Weimarer Republik*, 4th ed. (Villingen, 1964), 93.

60. Liebe, *Volkspartei*, 130–131.

61. Thimme, *Flucht in den Mythos*, 29–31.

62. Ibid., 31–32.

of nobility and large landowners, since members of *völkisch* splinter groups and Christian Socials, whose supporters came from the lower strata of society, streamed into the DNVP after the war.[63] After 1919, industrial and commercial interests, as well as members of occupational associations (*Verbände*), played a greater role in the DNVP parliamentary group. Declining numbers of deputies who represented agricultural interests were matched by an increase in the number of civil servants and representatives of industry and commerce. In the 1920s, about one-fifth of the DNVP Reichstag faction came from industry and commerce, while almost half were civil servants, including officers and members of the cloth (*Geistliche*); even in March 1933, civil servants still accounted for 43.8 percent, while the percentage of leaders of economic associations (*Verbandsvorsitzende*) fell from 13.6 (1919) to 5.7 by the end of the Republic. The decline was due largely to Alfred Hugenberg, who had an almost visceral aversion to any kind of interest-based politics.[64]

At the high point of German National electoral success in May 1924, the DNVP Reichstag faction was composed of thirty-four representatives of agriculture (mostly estate owners), twenty-one (mostly high-ranking) civil servants, thirteen salaried employees and workers, eight industrialists and representatives of big business, eight members of the professions, eight university professors and *Gymnasium* teachers with civil servant status, eight tradesmen and artisans, six former officers, and five clergymen.[65] The number of war veterans and reserve officers in the DNVP Reichstag faction increased during the course of the Republic. Whereas a full 80 percent of the members of the parliamentary faction had not actively served in the war in 1919 (mostly because of their age), tensions

63. The percentage of the nobility fell from 37.7 (1912) to 9.1 (1919); that of large landowners from 49.3 (1912) to 11.4 (1919). This was a reflection of the fact that the party's social basis was comprised of a wider spectrum of occupational groups than that of the prewar DKP. Thimme, *Flucht in den Mythos*, 26.

64. Thimme, *Flucht in den Mythos*, 26–29. There was little difference with the DKP faction with respect to deputies' educational level.

65. Liebe, *Volkspartei*, 78–79; deputies who were high administrative officials and at the same time large landowners are listed twice. Shortly before the elections, the National Liberal Union had switched from the DVP to the DNVP after disputes with Gustav Stresemann. Its members included the deputies Reinhold Quaatz, Moritz Klönne, Albert Vögler, Alfred Gildemeister, and Johann Becker. As a quid pro quo for their public appeal on behalf of the DNVP, Klönne and Quaatz were assured safe seats on the DNVP party list in Reichstag elections.

between the increasing number of ex-servicemen and members of
the prewar generation of representatives intensified in the 1920s.[66]
In fact, during Hugenberg's tenure as party leader, DNVP deputies
often complained that leading members of the party, such as Hugenberg himself, his confidante Paul Bang, and Axel von Freytagh-
Loringhoven, had seen no active service in the war.[67] The social
composition of the NSDAP parliamentary group was very different:
in October 1932, its 230 members consisted of fifty-five workers and
white-collar employees, fifty peasants, forty-three self-employed,
twenty-nine party functionaries, thirty-two civil servants, and nine
former officers.[68] In contrast to the DNVP, which—despite the social heterogeneity of its electorate before 1930—never quite succeeded in casting off its image as a *Klassenpartei*, the NSDAP was a
genuine *Integrationspartei*.[69]

From the beginning, clashes between the two parties were inevitable. While the DNVP was often torn in its attitude toward
the Republic, the NSDAP rejected Weimar with uncompromising
radicalism, as epitomized in Gregor Strasser's blunt dictum: "National Socialism is the very opposite of what we have today."[70] Ideological conflicts were rampant since the Nazi party was strongly
anti-bourgeois in orientation. Already in *Mein Kampf*, Hitler wrote
with derisive contempt about the "bourgeois *Wahlstimmvieh*" (electoral cattle), whose support would only water down his movement,
and criticized the bourgeoisie's cowardly behavior in 1918, as well as
its lack of national pride.[71] During the Republic's last years, opponents of Nazism gleefully highlighted the NSDAP's hatred for the
bourgeoisie and its lifestyle, thus underlining the incompatibility

66. Heinrich Brüning repeatedly stressed the camaraderie among deputies
who had participated in the war; see Heinrich Brüning, *Memoiren 1918–1934*
(Stuttgart, 1970).

67. Thimme, *Flucht in den Mythos*, 28–29.

68. Hans-Ulrich Wehler, *Deutsche Gesellschaftsgeschichte, 1914–1949*, vol. IV
(Munich, 2003), 779.

69. Eberhard Kolb, *Die Weimarer Republik*, 6th ed. (Munich, 2002), 124. Kolb
referred to it as a modern *Integrationspartei* and as a "schichtenübergreifende, ex-
trem nationalistische und antimarxistische Mobilisierungspartei" (ibid).

70. "Nationalsozialismus ist das Gegenteil von dem was heute ist." In a
speech on 20 October 1932; quoted in Bracher, *Auflösung*, 108.

71. Adolf Hitler, *Mein Kampf*, 210th ed. (Munich, 1936), 31, 367, 375, and
595.

of the two parties of the extreme right.[72] Finally, German Nationals and Nazis subscribed to very different political styles, though, beginning in 1931, DNVP leaders strenuously tried to imitate Nazi methods and techniques. Following the Stettin party congress in September 1931, the party decided to build up the hitherto neglected German National *Kampfstaffeln* (fighter squadrons), though their numbers never came close to rivaling those of the SA.[73] The *Kampfstaffeln* reached their greatest extension with about 100,000 members[74] shortly before they were banned in May and early June 1933 and never were a serious opponent of the much better organized SA with its more than half a million members in February 1933. Given all these differences and animosities, why then were DNVP leaders and parts of the party's rank and file still willing to consider an alliance with the Nazis? There were several reasons. The patronizing behavior of German Nationals indicated their view of Nazis as a less sophisticated national brother-in-arms who needed guidance, even after the strength of the NSDAP vastly exceeded their own. In the autumn of 1930, after the NSDAP's unexpected breakthrough at the polls, the German National press even spoke of the "votes of the national camp," as if Nazi votes rightly were also their own.[75] The fact that Nazi leaders made no bones about their ultimate goals was not recognized by the DNVP, but rather lightly dismissed as *Diktaturspielerei*[76] in the conservative press. German Nationals thus willfully underestimated and misjudged the nature of National Socialism. In the end, it was undoubtedly the opportunity to enter government and replace the hated Weimar Republic with a more authoritarian system that made Hugenberg and other DNVP leaders decide in favor of a coalition with the Nazi party. This was a fateful decision, even for the DNVP, for just how much the two camps were at loggerheads became evident only in the winter and

---

72. Bundesarchiv (BA) Koblenz, ZSg 103, Sammlung Lauterbach, no. 795: NSDAP und Bürgertum.

73. Ruge, "Deutschnationale Volkspartei," 476–528, esp. 527.

74. On the growing importance of the Kampfstaffeln in spring of 1933, see BA Koblenz, ZSg 1, no. 4412, *Der Nationale Wille*, 6 May 1933, 246, 250; 13 May 1933, 264; 20 May 1933, 278; 3 June 1933, 313; 10 June 1933, 327.

75. BA Koblenz, ZSg. 103, Sammlung Lauterbach, no. 828: NSDAP and DNVP. At the same time Goebbels wrote in his *Angriff* (no. 108) that he took exception to being mentioned in the same breath "with the stinking dung heap of rotting *Klassenparteien*," a clear allusion to the DNVP. Ibid.

76. "Die Bilanz von Boxheim," *Breisgauer Zeitung*, 1 December 1931; see also chapter 1 below.

spring of 1933, when conflicts that had long lain dormant burst out into the open.

Finally, an explanation of the use of "conservatives" and "conservative" is in order. Leaders, members, and supporters of the German National People's Party are denoted as conservative, though one might argue that Westarp was more of a traditional conservative, while Hugenberg was a radical nationalist who had little of the traditional conservative in him. In the Nazis's relationship with and struggles against German Nationals, such distinctions mattered little. In Nazi eyes all German Nationals were conservative reactionaries whom they despised, even the rabid anti–Semites among them. There were few German Nationals Hitler disliked more intensely than Paul Bang, Hugenberg's *Staatssekretär* in the Ministry of Economics, despite the fact that Bang was a dyed–in–the–wool, radical anti–Semite. The DNVP is referred to as a "conservative" party, even though it included remnants of anti–Semitic splinter parties, radical nationalists, and—as will be shown in Chapter Five below—uncompromising, racist anti–Semites. The term "conservatives" is thus used in a broad sense and includes all shades of traditional and radical conservatism, so that the subtitle of this book could also read: "conservative Germans and National Socialism." I felt that getting involved in a quagmire of definitions might result in making clear-cut statements impossible. In keeping with German custom, the DNVP is here referred to as a "*bürgerliche Partei*." Its aristocratic members and leaders were limited in number and significance.

Several of the chapters that follow offer a detailed documentation of Nazi attacks on German National organizations, meetings, and public office holders in the winter and spring of 1933. I would like to warn the reader against the temptation of interpreting this as sympathetic to the DNVP and German conservatism or as an attempt to characterize German Nationals as helpless victims of Nazi terror. Nothing could be further from the truth or from my intentions. Hugenberg and many of his supporters willingly entered into a governing coalition with Hitler and did so, one might say, with their eyes wide shut. If Nazi aggression against German Nationals is emphasized here, it is because it occupies a prominent place in DNVP party files, not because I intend to portray German Nationals as co-equal victims of Nazi terror. It is a truism that, as far as political conflict was concerned, the Left suffered incomparably more. Insofar as possible, it has been my intention to let the documents speak for themselves in order to enhance our understanding of the nuances of the Nazi seizure of power.

Overview of Contents

A brief synopsis of the contents of the present study reads as follows:
the first chapter outlines, in broad brushstrokes, the DNVP's development as it advanced through the thicket of Weimar party politics,
from its foundation in 1918 up to the transfer of power to Hitler on
30 January 1933. Though this chapter will not add substantially to
our factual knowledge, it offers the first continuous history of the
party from its inception to the eve of the *Machtergreifung*. The book's
six main chapters then focus on the troubled alliance between conservatives and Nazis between 30 January and 14 July 1933, when
the one-party state was legally sanctioned. Apart from examining
the internal development of the DNVP during this period, these
chapters analyze the rapidly changing Zeitgeist of winter and spring
1933 that greatly facilitated a swift Nazi takeover. Chapter Two
documents DNVP policy between 30 January and the elections of
5 March 1933, the struggle between the two national parties over
who would be the legitimate heir to the national heritage, as well as
the changing attitude of the *Bürgertum* which, for fear of Communism, became increasingly sympathetic to Nazi policies in the wake
of the Reichstag fire. Chapter Three focuses on the "revolution of
March" following that month's elections, the Nazi terror that acted
as the lubricant of this revolution, and the DNVP's reaction to both.
Chapter Four concentrates on ideological conflicts between Nazis
and the conservative establishment, especially the Nazi effort to undermine traditional hierarchies. It also analyzes the changing public
image of the Nazi movement, which increasingly portrayed itself as
a massive protest against bourgeois lifestyles. Chapter Five deals with
the DNVP's reaction to the proliferation of anti-Semitic attacks and
anti-Semitic measures in March and April, as well as with the party's own inherent anti-Semitism. Chapters Six and Seven cover the
period from early April to the party's dissolution in June. These two
chapters examine the political climate in the spring of 1933 and the
increasingly ferocious Nazi attacks on German Nationals, who desperately tried to keep the alliance intact, at a time when they were
losing their local strongholds of power to the Nazis. The last part
of Chapter Seven analyzes the dissolution of the DNVP, while the
Epilogue offers an examination of the relationship between German
conservatism and National Socialism in a larger historical context.

 As outlined above, this study presents the period of the seizure
of power in a new light. Here, for the first time, the complex and
contradictory relationship between National Socialism, on the one

hand, and the DNVP and the conservative *Bürgertum*, on the other, is examined within a larger political context, in all of its multifaceted nuances. The originality of the book's six main chapters lies in the following points: (I) the depiction of National Socialism's changing self-portrayal during the seizure of power as an anti-bourgeois, revolutionary movement, marked by the Nazis' attempt to discredit and undermine the *Bürgertum* and bourgeois forms of life; (II) the comprehensive documentation of the countless attacks on German National organizations, meetings, officeholders, and members of the bourgeoisie in general; (III) the analysis of the relationship between German Nationals and the Jewish community, highlighting the equivocation of the DNVP as its disparate membership groups reacted to the "Jewish question"; (IV) the examination of the Nazis' usurpation of the heritage of a conservative Prussian past and their intent to supplant conservatives as guardians of the national history, a phenomenon that goes over and beyond the Day of Potsdam; (V) the focus on the political climate of the age that clearly facilitated a speedy Nazi arrogation of power and exerted such powerful pressure that German Nationals succumbed to it, in part by imitating the style of their more powerful and successful ally.

If one agrees with the arguments presented here—the anti-bourgeois thrust of National Socialism, the continuous violence against all real and perceived obstacles that characterized the Nazi revolution, the emphasis on the Zeitgeist as a catalyst of revolutionary fervor and political change—our image of the *Machtergreifung* will require modification. For a proper understanding of the period between Hitler's accession to the Chancellorship at the end of January 1933 and the establishment of the one-party state in mid July, an appreciation not only of the "behavior of the elite," but also of the specific atmosphere and of people's "immense resentment, . . . feelings, traditions, hopes, desperation, and humiliations," as Fritz Stern once put it,[77] is imperative. The intention here is to capture this mood as viewed through the lens of the troubled alliance between conservatives and Nazis.

77. Fritz Stern as quoted in Broszat et al., eds., *Deutschlands Weg in die Diktatur*, 141–142.

Chapter I

PRAGMATISTS VERSUS FUNDAMENTALISTS

The DNVP in the Weimar Republic, 1918–1933

From its inception, the German National People's Party was divided between principled opposition to the Weimar Republic, on the one hand, and the desire for practical cooperation and participation in governmental coalitions, on the other—a conflict that was never overcome until Hugenberg became party chairman in 1928. Three phases in the relationship between the DNVP and the Weimar Republic can be distinguished: (I) uncompromising opposition and hope for the demise of the Republic before 1924, with tentative signs of a reluctant readiness for cooperation; (II) participation in coalition governments and political cooperation despite ongoing opposition to Gustav Stresemann's foreign policy during Weimar's "good years" between 1924 and 1928, the DNVP's politically most successful period; (III) increasing hostility toward the Republic with the accession of Alfred Hugenberg to the chairmanship of the party in October 1928. The rejection of all that Weimar represented became all-pervasive; this weakened the party and divided it further, while strengthening the radical forces within it.

In the first years after its formation in 1918, the DNVP was dominated by conservatives who had served in the ministerial bureaucracy of the Empire. Despite their principled opposition to the Weimar Republic, their experience in government administration had led them to pursue practical solutions to political problems. Given their personalities and life experiences, none of these men could remain intransigent in their opposition to the Republic; they thus proved willing to participate in the Weimar political system until a better solution could be found. The initial leadership group of the DNVP, despite harboring deep animosity toward the principles on which Weimar was based, was nonetheless moderate in orientation, though at times deceptively so. By contrast, the members of the former Deutsch-Konservative Partei (German Conservative Party or DKP) who had joined the DNVP, such as the party's former parliamentary faction leader Kuno Graf von Westarp, or those close to the Pan-German Association, such as Alfred Hugenberg, stubbornly emphasized their disdain for the Republic and were less willing to compromise their principles for the sake of practical politics. Initially, they remained in the background because they had become too discredited by their exaggerated annexationist demands during the war. During wartime their views had been considered to be a commendable reflection of national sentiment. Now, in the wake of defeat, they had become an embarrassing mortgage of a past best forgotten. In the shadow of wartime defeat and less burdened by the baggage of past annexationist claims, former Free Conservatives and Christian Socials thus initially exercised greater influence within the party than their relative strength warranted, especially in Weimar's constituent National Assembly and in the formulation of the DNVP's political program. The leadership team in this first phase, which determined the party's course in the immediate postwar period, consisted mainly of Imperial civil servants such as Oskar Hergt (1869–1967), former Prussian Finance Minister and, since December 1918, the first chairman of the DNVP; Clemens von Delbrück (1856–1921), former Free Conservative Lord Mayor of Danzig, Prussian Minister of Industry and Commerce, and later Undersecretary of State (*Staatssekretär*) of the Interior from 1909 to 1916, who became one of the major exponents of the DNVP in the National Assembly until his death in December 1921;[1] Arthur Graf von Posadowsky-Wehner (1845–1932), DNVP parliamentary faction leader in the National Assembly and one of Delbrück's predecessors as Undersecretary of State of the Interior from 1897 to 1907, who had made a name for himself as a social reformer during the

---

1. Delbrück, who had been mentioned as a candidate for party leadership even before Hergt, was opposed by the Pan-German Association due to his close relationship with Bethmann-Hollweg. See Christian F. Trippe, *Konservative Verfassungspolitik, 1918–1923. Die DNVP als Opposition in Reich und Ländern* (Düsseldorf, 1995).

Empire (he left the DNVP after the Kapp Putsch in 1920);[2] and Karl Helfferich (1872–1924), another high-ranking bureaucrat, financial expert and banker, Undersecretary of State in the Treasury Department and the Ministry of the Interior during the war, who had helped finance the war effort through loans instead of raising taxes, and who died an untimely death in a train accident in 1924.[3] Finally, there was Adalbert Dühringer (1855–1924), judicial reformer of the late nineteenth century, Councilor at the Supreme Court (*Reichsgerichtsrat*) in Leipzig (1902–1915), Baden's Minister of Justice in 1917–1918, and then cofounder of the DNVP in Baden in 1919. Dühringer left the DNVP in July 1922 in opposition to the growing anti-Semitism of the German Nationals during the so-called "Henning-Wulle" crisis and the overt approval of Foreign Minister Rathenau's murder by *völkisch* circles within the party.[4]

After the attrition through death or resignation of this group of moderate bureaucrats, representatives of various interest groups from industry, the Rural League (*Reichslandbund*), and the Association of German National Shop Assistants became increasingly influential within the DNVP. This second phase in the party's history was ushered in by the elections of 4 May and 7 December 1924 in which the party reached the zenith of its success by gaining approximately one-fifth of all votes cast. Subsequently, the DNVP participated twice in coalition governments, in which its deputies held a number of ministerial positions.[5] Upon assuming these governmental posts, the DNVP Ministers were obliged to take an oath to the Weimar Constitution, thereby tying the party more closely to the Republic. Despite its cooperation in economic and financial matters, the DNVP proved less amenable when it came to foreign policy and sabotaged Stresemann's conduct of foreign affairs

---

2. See Hans-Ulrich Wehler, *Deutsche Gesellschaftsgeschichte, 1849–1914,* vol. III (Munich, 1995), 1020–1022, 1088–1090.

3. John G. Williamson, *Karl Helfferich, 1872–1924. Economist, Financier, Politician* (Princeton, 1971).

4. This refers to deputies Wilhelm Henning and Reinhold Wulle, who pushed for a more anti-Semitic stance within the DNVP. See Jan Striesow, *Die Deutschnationale Volkspartei und die Völkisch-Radikalen, 1918–1922,* two vols. (Frankfurt, 1981); Trippe, *Konservative Verfassungspolitik,* 209.

5. In the First Luther Cabinet (January 1925 to January 1926) and the Fourth Marx Cabinet (January 1927 to June 1928). Ministerial posts held included Interior, Justice, Finance, Economics, Food and Nutrition, and Transportation.

whenever possible,[6] in particular since its members considered it a sellout of traditional German interests to effect a rapprochement with the West. Following the not–unexpected election defeat of 20 May 1928, in which the DNVP's share of the vote fell from 20.5 percent to 14.7 (from 6.206 to 4.381 million votes cast) and its Reichstag faction shrank from 103 to 73 seats, Kuno Graf von Westarp was forced to resign from the position of party chairman. He was replaced in October 1928 by Alfred Hugenberg, whose candidacy was championed by the Pan–German Association, and who was strongly supported by the DNVP Land Associations (*Landesverbände*), which had always been more fundamentalist in their outlook than the parliamentary faction in the Reichstag, and over which Hugenberg exerted some measure of control through his financial resources and growing ascendancy over the party apparatus.

With Hugenberg's accession to the leadership, the nationalist hotheads within the DNVP, who had always opposed the Republic with implacable hostility, gained the upper hand. Moderates within the DNVP, mindful of the need to come to terms with the Republic in order to wield at least a modicum of political influence, were increasingly pushed to the fringes. This growing influence of fundamentalists at the expense of pragmatists would soon lead to two major schisms in the DNVP Reichstag faction and further catastrophic election defeats. After 1929, the uncompromising anti-Republican course pursued by Hugenberg inexorably brought the DNVP into closer contact with its stronger and more vital rival, the Nazi party.

The DNVP during the Early Republic (1920–1924)

Already during the Kapp Putsch of March 1920, the DNVP was forced to show its true colors and indicate whether it was willing to follow up on its hostile attitude to the Republic with corresponding deeds. Wolfgang Kapp, the East Prussian *Generallandschaftsdirektor*,[7]

---

6. Robert Grathwol, *Stresemann and the DNVP. Reconciliation or Revenge in German Foreign Policy, 1924–1926* (Lawrence, Kansas, 1980); Peter Krüger, *Die Außenpolitik der Republik von Weimar*, 2nd ed. (Darmstadt, 1993); Klaus Hildebrand, *Das vergangene Reich* (Stuttgart, 1995), 383–560; Gottfried Niedhart, *Die Außenpolitik der Weimarer Republik* (Munich, 1999).

7. Director General of the East Prussian Agricultural Credit Bank (1906–1916). Kapp was born in 1858 in New York, where his father had been

son of a well-known revolutionary of 1848, who had made a name for himself as a founder of the Fatherland Party in 1917, tried to overthrow the Republic through a military coup in March 1920. The coup was sparked by Allied demands for a reduction of Reichswehr forces and the dissolution of the *Freikorps* (Free Corps), since many rightists feared that fulfillment of these demands might expose Germany's eastern provinces to Bolshevik invasion.[8] Support for Kapp was consequently strongest among the populations of Silesia and East Prussia, to the point that even the Social Democratic provincial governor (*Oberpräsident*) of East Prussia, August Winnig, recognized Kapp's new government.[9] Kuno Graf von Westarp and other members of the DNVP's right wing knew about the preparations and were ready to support the coup. Since General Walther von Lüttwitz, the military leader of the revolt, acted before Kapp had made the necessary political arrangements, many of those who might have participated under more advantageous circumstances now exercised restraint, so that the putsch was doomed to failure from the start. The DNVP leadership advised against participation in the putsch from the beginning, while the party manager, Hans Erdmann von Lindeiner-Wildau, went so far as to alert the Prussian official Herbert von Berger to the increasing unrest inside the Reichswehr on 8 March 1920, a warning clearly aimed at providing the DNVP with an alibi in case the coup attempt failed.[10] This had little effect in itself, since von Berger had already been apprised of

---

forced to emigrate. He later became an estate owner and high official in East Prussia. After the failed putsch, Kapp fled to Sweden but returned to Germany in 1922 to appear before the Reich Supreme Court in Leipzig to face an indictment on high treason. He died there while awaiting trial on 12 June 1922.

8. Johannes Erger, *Der Kapp-Lüttwitz Putsch. Ein Beitrag zur deutschen Innenpolitik 1919/1920* (Düsseldorf, 1967); Dietrich Orlow, "Preußen und der Kapp Putsch," *Vierteljahreshefte für Zeitgeschichte* 26 (1978), 191–236; Raffael Scheck, *Alfred von Tirpitz and German Right-Wing Politics, 1914–1930* (Atlantic Highlands, 1998); Winkler, *Weimar*, 120–126; Erich Eyck, *Geschichte der Weimarer Republik*, 4th ed., vol. I (Zürich 1972), 202–208; Hans Mommsen, *The Rise and Fall of Weimar Democracy* (Chapel Hill and London, 1996), 81–88; Hagen Schulze, *Weimar. Deutschland, 1917–1933* (Berlin, 1994), 211–217.

9. Liebe, *Volkspartei*, 57 and 153 (note 268). In East Prussia the governor and the commander of its military district placed themselves at Kapp's disposal.

10. Liebe, *Volkspartei*, 150 (notes 237, 238). In Westarp's literary bequest, which Liebe examined in detail, the warning was interpreted as a precautionary measure, since any complicity in or knowledge of the plot (just as active participation in it) was punishable as high treason.

unrest in the army and chose to do nothing about it.[11] Inside the party, Lindeiner's initiative gave rise to sharp criticism, since a part of the membership considered a military coup against the Republic, accompanied by a possible restoration of the monarchy, as an auspicious new beginning. Former Free Conservatives and Christian Socials supported party chairman Oskar Hergt's attempts to prevail upon General Lüttwitz to exercise caution, whereas most *völkisch* and former DKP members considered an overthrow of the Republic a goal worth fighting for.[12] Since few leading figures of its right wing, mostly East Elbian estate owners, had openly supported the Kapp Putsch, the DNVP as a whole outwardly succeeded in avoiding the impression of open complicity in the events of March 1920. On the other hand, Wolfgang Kapp himself was a DNVP member and well connected in party circles by virtue of his activities as founder and chairman of the Fatherland Party. Gottfried Traub, for example, a member of the DNVP's executive committee, who had been a deputy in the National Assembly and had also served on the executive board of the Fatherland Party, had been appointed Minister of Culture during the putsch.[13]

After the wretched failure of Kapp's attempted coup and the virtually unanimous public condemnation of the undertaking, Hergt (who had personally been against the putsch) and the party leadership took great pains to distance themselves from the whole affair. Among the wider public, however, the impression prevailed that the party had been more deeply entangled than it let on. In the Reichstag elections of 6 June 1920, the DNVP was subsequently punished for its putative involvement, insofar as a substantial section of the electorate that voted for the German People's Party (DVP) might well have opted for the DNVP, had not suspicion of the party's complicity in the putsch prevented them from doing so.[14]

11. Herbert Paul Georg von Berger (1881–1944), the Prussian State Commissioner for the Maintenance of Public Order, a sympathizer of the right, had concealed his knowledge of the impending coup from Prussian and Reich authorities. See Winkler, *Weimar*, 121.

12. Liebe, *Volkspartei*, 54.

13. Gottfried Traub (1869–1956), initially a Progressive People's Party deputy in the Prussian Landtag, was one of the cofounders of the Fatherland Party. After the failure of the putsch, Traub escaped arrest by fleeing to Austria. See Hagenlücke, *Vaterlandspartei*, 306–310; 385–390; Trippe, *Konservative Verfassungspolitik*, 211.

14. In the elections of 6 June 1920 the DVP tripled the number of its voters from 1.345 to 3.919 million, increasing its Reichstag seats from 19 to 65.

Acrimonious intraparty arguments between moderate conservatives and the more radical members of the former DKP, the anti-Semitic parties, and Pan-Germans ensued. In the wake of these conflicts, a group of former Free Conservatives, led by Siegfried von Kardorff, defected to the DVP.[15]

After June 1920, weak Weimar coalition governments confronted a newly roused and increasingly active rightist opposition, which had no qualms about openly showing its colors. Inside the DNVP, fundamentalist radicals were gaining ground over moderates, a process aided by the galloping inflation of 1921 and 1922. In particular the *völkisch* wing began to consolidate its influence due to the influx of impoverished craftsmen, farmers, white-collar employees, and a growing academic proletariat. Supporters of prewar anti-Semitic parties, who had found a political home in the DNVP, now pressed for further radicalization. The party leadership, however, was determined not to abandon the path of legality. Jolted by the Kapp Putsch, it was aware of the danger of radicalization and prepared to counter it by all available means. The inevitable inner-party crisis over the future course of the DNVP, fought out in 1922, resulted in the expulsion of the anti-Semitic wing. The showdown was triggered off by a venomous article about Walther Rathenau published by the DNVP Reichstag deputy Wilhelm Henning, a member of the party's *völkisch* wing.[16] The publication of this article virtually coincided with Rathenau's murder on 24 June 1922, which prompted Chancellor Joseph Wirth (Center Party) to demand that

---

Gains made by the DNVP were moderate by contrast—from 3.121 to 4.249 million votes (from 44 to 71 mandates). See Kolb, *Die Weimarer Republik*, 308–309. Given that the DNVP was the most vociferously anti-Republican party, larger gains had been expected in view of the public disillusionment with the Republic that followed the Versailles Treaty.

15. Siegfried von Kardorff (1873–1945) was the son of Wilhelm von Kardorff, the cofounder of the Free Conservative Party. He had been a Free Conservative deputy in the Prussian Landtag until 1918, when he left his parliamentary faction because he supported the abolition of Prussia's three-class voting system. As DVP deputy he became Vice-President of the Reichstag from 1928 to 1932.

16. "The Real Face of the Rapallo Treaty," *Konservative Monatsschrift* 79 (June 1922). In this article, Henning argued that "the international Jew Rathenau" had sullied German honor because he had failed to mention the murder of the German envoy in Moscow during the Rapallo negotiations (Wilhelm Graf von Mirbach-Horff was murdered on 6 July 1918). Henning's polemic culminated in the phrase, "German honor is not a commodity to be haggled over by international Jews." See Hertzman, *DNVP*, 124–165; Winkler, *Weimar*, 173.

Hergt purge the DNVP of radical elements to avoid having the party as a whole suspected of sanctioning political murder. When Henning, supported by Reinhold Wulle and Albrecht von Graefe, responded to possible expulsion from the party with a sharp attack on the party leadership, an intraparty confrontation had become inevitable.

The DNVP's 1920 party program included an explicitly anti-Semitic passage, and anti-Semitic attitudes were widespread within the party, especially in the Land Associations.[17] Initially anti-Semites in the DNVP were intent on dominating the entire party, whereas the foundation of a separate *völkisch* party was envisaged as a last resort. To organize all those with *völkisch* convictions, a "German *völkisch* study group" was set up within the DNVP in early September 1922 with the goal of "forestalling the imminent danger of an exodus of *völkisch* elements to other political parties."[18] An interesting example of the cross-fertilization between the DNVP and the *völkisch* Nazi party was the election of Wilhelm Kube (who later became notorious as one of the more infamous Nazi *Gauleiter*) to the executive board of this "German *völkisch* study group."[19] The conflict provoked by the Henning-Wulle affair now created a welcome opportunity for the party leadership to cut radical anti-Semites in the party down to size, particularly since it was obvious that their radicalism was harming the DNVP as a whole. Thus, at the October 1922 Görlitz party conference, the confrontation with anti-Semites was high on the agenda. They were quickly thrown on the defensive, since party chairman Hergt and other moderate party notables,

17. Anti-Semitic attitudes of party members and leaders are discussed in chapter 5. When the DNVP was founded in November 1918, anti-Semitism did not play a role in the party's self-image. In the *cause célèbre* of the Republic's early years, Anne von Gierke, daughter of the prominent legal scholar Otto von Gierke (whose wife was Jewish), who had served as a DNVP deputy in the National Assembly in 1919, saw her nomination for a Reichstag seat thwarted by the obstructionism of anti-Semites in DNVP Land Associations, whereupon she and her father left the party.

18. Liebe, *Volkspartei*, 66.

19. Wilhelm Kube (1887–1943) had been a member of Liebermann von Sonnenberg's anti-Semitic German Social Party before 1914, General Secretary of the German Conservative Party in Silesia in 1918, a member of the NSDAP since 1928, *Gauleiter* of the Kurmark, and provincial governor (*Oberpräsident*) of the province of Brandenburg since 1933. In 1941, he was appointed "General Commissar" of "White Ruthenia" in Minsk, where he was assassinated in 1943.

such as Otto Hoetzsch,[20] dominated proceedings at the conference. When Graf Westarp came down on the side of the party leadership, the die was cast: Henning, Graefe, and Wulle left the DNVP and founded the German *Völkisch* Freedom Party in December 1922.

After expelling the extreme anti–Semites, it appeared that the DNVP as a whole might be able to play a more constructive role in Weimar politics, despite the principled opposition of many of its members to the Republic. This opposition would continue to bubble to the surface, however, when it served the party's inter-est to side with a defiant public over matters of national security and foreign policy. The great crises of 1923—the French occupation of the Ruhr, German passive resistance to the occupation, sepa-ratist movements in western Germany, inflation, the widely pub-licized activities of French military courts against Germans who defied the occupier, communist unrest, and all-pervasive political instability—thus reinforced anti-Republican tendencies within the DNVP. Strengthened by internal consolidation after Görlitz, the DNVP advocated intensification of resistance in the Ruhr, cessation of reparation payments, and opposition to the termination of passive resistance advocated by the Stresemann government. Yet, within a year, political conditions and the compelling force of economic in-terests would enjoin the DNVP to abandon policies dictated purely by ideology and to fall in with the political mainstream.

The Dawes Plan

After the disasters of the inflation, the Allied Reparations Commis-sion tried to devise a plan to establish a feasible level of reparations, while making sure that the German budget remained balanced and the currency stabilized. The Dawes Plan, conceived to achieve these goals, was predicated on Germany's economic recovery and the country's actual ability to pay. Payments would begin at the relatively low level of one billion marks, an amount that would be increased

---

20. Otto Hoetzsch (1876–1946), a well-known historian and expert on Rus-sia, professor in Berlin since 1913, member of the Pan-German Association and foreign policy analyst for the *Kreuzzeitung* (1914–1924); since December 1918 member of the DNVP and Reichstag deputy since 1920. Hoetzsch became es-tranged from the DNVP after Hugenberg became chairman. See Gerd Voigt, *Otto Hoetzsch, 1876–1946. Wissenschaft und Politik im Leben eines deutschen Histo-rikers* (Berlin/East, 1978).

to 2.5 billion after 1928. In addition, the Dawes Plan promised the issuing of an American loan designed to help the German economy get back on its feet.[21] The plan, announced to the public at the beginning of April 1924, provided a central campaign theme for the May 1924 elections. From the very beginning, the DNVP came out strongly against the Plan, which it labeled a "second Versailles," objecting, in particular, to the mortgaging of the *Reichsbahn*, the surrender of German sovereignty rights, and the concomitant "enslavement process." The DNVP's success in the elections (5.7 million votes and 95 mandates) appeared to vindicate this campaign strategy.[22] Subsequently, German Nationals drew up a "Seven-Point Program," the fulfillment of which would constitute a precondition for the party's endorsement of the plan.[23] Even though the assent of the SPD, Center, DDP, and DVP had been secured, the passing of the Dawes Plan required a two-thirds majority of those voting in the Reichstag because the plan would alter the status of the *Reichsbahn*. The requisite number of votes could not be attained without the DNVP. But German Nationals had nailed their colors so firmly

21. This was a loan of 800 million marks to satisfy urgent demands for capital and to act as a catalyst for German economic recovery. The total amount of war reparations was not fixed and the conversion of German payments into foreign currency was entrusted to an Allied Reparations Agent, whose duty it was to safeguard Germany's ability to make payments. Germany's national railroad system (*Reichsbahn*) and its national bank (*Reichsbank*) became subject to international supervision. Allied control over the *Reichsbahn* and *Reichsbank* infringed upon German sovereignty rights as did control over the public budget by the Reparations Agent. On the other hand, German industry and agriculture were interested in foreign loans, initial payments were moderate, and the end of the economic division between the occupied and unoccupied areas would offer relief to the population of the Rhineland.

22. Since the DNVP Reichstag faction formed a partnership with the *Landbund* (10 seats), the DNVP now had the largest parliamentary group with 105 seats and was in a position to appoint the president of the Reichstag (Max Wallraf replaced Paul Löbe between May and December 1924, when the SPD again became the strongest party). After the May elections, the weight of economic pressure groups within the DNVP intensified. It was this heightened influence of industrial and commercial circles that partially determined the party's position on the Dawes Plan.

23. *Nationale Rundschau*, 24 July 1924, reprinted in Liebe, *Volkspartei*, 165–166. The DNVP demanded that the German delegation be treated as an equal partner, that those imprisoned during the occupation of the Ruhr be set free, that those expelled be repatriated (more than 100,000), and that "the counter-factual admission of guilt" of the Versailles Treaty be revoked (i.e., Article 231).

to rejection that it was now impossible for them to modify their position without losing face. Shortly before the decisive vote on 20 August 1924, the faction's foreign policy spokesman Otto Hoetzsch reaffirmed the party's disapproval, since none of the seven points had been met during the Dawes Plan deliberations at the London conference. His declaration was supported by the categorical "no" of the entire DNVP Reichstag faction, and further buttressed by the equally uncompromising position of DNVP Land and Kreis (county) Associations.[24] It was at this point, when the fate of the plan seemed virtually sealed, that the influence of industrial and agricultural pressure groups made itself felt. Because of expected foreign loans resulting from the Dawes Plan, both Rhenish industry and the *Reichslandbund*, which could exert direct influence on fifty-two German National deputies, pushed for acceptance.[25] Agriculture was in desperate need of funds and Rural Leagues in the occupied western territories pushed hard for acceptance of the London agreement, while East Elbian Leagues continued to bide their time. In order to give those DNVP deputies organized in the *Reichslandbund* the possibility to represent agricultural interests, the party leadership refrained from imposing party discipline on the faction and allowed a free vote, especially since the Christian Social wing of the union movement and the affiliated Association of German National Shop Assistants had emphatically recommended acceptance. Fear of mass unemployment weighed more heavily than adherence to abstract principles. At the same time, President Friedrich Ebert left no doubt that he would dissolve parliament and call for new elections if the plan failed to pass. For German Nationals, who would then stand accused of sabotaging foreign loans, this meant possible mass desertions of their urban and rural electorate.[26]

The Dawes Plan vote on 29 August 1924 was "one of the most dramatically moving votes ever experienced in the German Reichstag, since the final result remained uncertain up to the very last minute."[27] The ambiguity and vacillation of the DNVP faction had meanwhile become general knowledge, despite all protestations to the contrary. Since the fate of the Dawes Plan would stand or fall with the German National votes, tension reached its height at the beginning of the *Reichsbahn* law discussions, for which deputies had

24. Liebe, *Volkspartei*, 81; Eyck, *Geschichte*, I, 403–430.
25. Liebe, *Volkspartei*, 82.
26. See *Berliner Tageblatt* 406, 27 August 1924; Liebe, *Volkspartei*, 167.
27. *Vossische Zeitung* 412, 30 August 1924.

to dispense with anonymity and vote by name.[28] As the *Vossische Zeitung* reported, initially all that could be seen in the DNVP faction were red "no" ballots; it was only toward the end of the voting process that white cards (signaling assent) began to appear in increasing numbers. Two hundred ninety-four "yes" votes were needed for a two-thirds majority; all told, 314 "yes" votes were registered.

The division within the DNVP over the Dawes Plan vote marked a turning point in the history of the party: fifty-two had stuck to their "no" vote, but forty-eight DNVP deputies voted "yes"; three deputies (among them Alfred Hugenberg) were furloughed due to illness, and two were absent without leave. While the majority of deputies from East Elbian regions (the stronghold of the former DKP) held fast to their unflinchingly negative attitude, and most of the turncoats came from western electoral districts, prominent names such as von Bismarck, Otto Hoetzsch, von Keudell, von Richthofen, von Tirpitz, and Max Wallraf were among the renegades. The mortification of the parliamentary group on account of many deputies' sudden change of heart, heightened by the fact that Socialist, Communist, and Nazi parliamentarians freely heaped scorn and mocking derision upon the DNVP, was surpassed by the dismay of the DNVP party organization and rank and file membership. DNVP Land Associations in northern and eastern Germany publicly attacked the party leadership and Reichstag faction, while resignation letters to East Elbian Associations arrived in droves, demanding that the "yes men" resign their mandates.[29] The reaction from Pan-Germans, who had always been intent on turning the DNVP into a tower of anti-Republican strength, was especially acrimonious. They deprecated politics based on economic interests since this would render cooperation with pro-Republican parties inevitable and corrupt the very principles the DNVP represented.[30] After the disaster of the Dawes Plan vote, Pan-Germans thus decided to consolidate their influence in Land and Kreis Associations by marshalling forces behind their candidate for the party leadership,

---

28. Communists and National Socialists had demanded a vote by name on all bills connected with the Dawes Plan; Social Democrats only for the *Reichsbahn* law. Liebe, *Volkspartei*, 87.

29. Hertzman, *DNVP*, 204–239; Liebe, *Volkspartei*, 88.

30. Regarding the relationship between Pan-Germans and the DNVP, see Michael Stürmer, *Koalition und Opposition in der Weimarer Republik* (Düsseldorf, 1967), 190–196.

Alfred Hugenberg.[31] Though weak in terms of sheer numbers, the influential Pan-German Association had manifold connections to occupants of key positions in the decentralized party organization and could thereby exercise considerable leverage over the selection of Reichstag deputies. In 1927 the Pan-German leader, *Justizrat* (judicial councilor) Heinrich Claß, bluntly affirmed that it was his intention to mobilize the DNVP party organization against the parliamentary faction to make sure that only those who had toed the party line would be supported in the party's selection for its 1928 Reichstag list.[32] Protest from the ranks of former DKP members was equally vociferous: Westarp's literary bequest contains letters from former brothers-in-arms that characterize deputies who voted for the Dawes Plan as traitors to the nation.[33] The conflict, nascent within the DNVP since its foundation, between pragmatists ready to work within the confines of the Republic (if only to safeguard their own interests) and fundamentalists who persevered in their principled opposition to Weimar (regardless of what was at stake) had erupted over the Dawes Plan vote. After August 1924 it became evident that there was an ongoing (if latent) battle between the party organization and Reichstag faction, as well as inside the DNVP Reichstag faction itself. Discord would continue to smolder until, by appointing Hugenberg party chairman in October 1928, the issue was finally decided in favor of uncompromising opposition to Weimar.

From the Dawes Plan to Hugenberg (1924–1928)

The shock to the conservative rank and file occasioned by renegades voting for Dawes Plan acceptance marked a turning point in the history of the DNVP since it galvanized the party's right wing into action. Its members were determined to avoid a second "betrayal" of principles at any cost. Criticism at once focused on Hergt's leadership style: radical forces within the party, and the influential Land Associations of Pomerania, East Prussia, and Schleswig-Holstein,

31. Alfred Kruck, *Geschichte des Alldeutschen Verbandes, 1890–1939* (Wiesbaden, 1954).

32. Stürmer, *Koalition und Opposition*, 193; Thimme, *Flucht in den Mythos*, 43; Claß made it plain that there was no place for deputies who had voted for the Dawes Plan.

33. Reprinted in Liebe, *Volkspartei*, 171 (note 431).

united in demanding his resignation.[34] At an 18 September 1924 meeting of DNVP Land Association chairmen (who demanded his resignation), Hergt consented to relinquish the party leadership if negotiations over DNVP participation in government were to break down. When the failure of these talks became apparent, Hergt resigned on 23 October 1924 both as DNVP chairman and leader of the Reichstag faction.[35] Initially Graf Westarp was considered the most likely successor, given his strong position among former East Elbian DKP members. Yet, since an immediate election of a new party chairman proved impossible (the relevant party agency was unable to meet before the end of the year), a temporary solution was decided upon, and the chairman of the Prussian Landtag parliamentary faction, Friedrich Winckler, was appointed as interim chairman.[36] This had the advantage of keeping the party united for the elections of 7 December 1924 and avoiding further intraparty clashes. Friedrich Winckler was reconfirmed in his position as party chairman on 21 February 1925 and was superseded by Westarp only on 24 March 1926.[37]

In the campaign leading up to the elections of 7 December 1924, the DNVP presented itself even more radically than before, while preserving its emphasis on tradition and the status quo: "Our party remains as it was: monarchist and *völkisch*, Christian and social. Our goals remain the same as our name: German and national. Our glorious colors remain black, white, and red; our resolution is firmer than ever: to create a Germany free of Jewish control and French domination, free from parliamentary intrigue and the populist rule of big capital."[38] As a reaction to the voting behavior in the Dawes Plan ballot, the influence of moderate elements was curtailed, since

34. Hergt himself had voted against the Dawes Plan law, but he refused to impose party discipline on the Reichstag faction since he was aware of the large number of potential dissenters within the party.

35. Winkler, *Weimar, 1918–1933*, 269.

36. A compromise solution was advisable since, apart from Westarp, other candidates were considered: moderates endeavored to put Hergt in charge again; to others the Reichstag president, Max Wallraf, a Catholic, seemed a promising candidate, while agricultural interest groups favored Martin Schiele.

37. Liebe, *Volkspartei*, 99.

38. From *Nationale Rundschau*, 22 October 1924, cited in Liebe, *Volkspartei*, 95; Winkler, *Weimar, 1918–1933*, 269. DNVP handbills exclaimed: "Anyone who does not vote is Juda's slave, France's coolie, calls Bolshevism into the country, sacrifices his children." Cited in Heinrich-August Winkler, *Mittelstand, Demokratie, und Nationalsozialismus* (Köln, 1972), 132.

the party's right wing insisted on choosing its own candidates and did its best to prevent the nomination of former "yes men" when drawing up lists of parliamentary candidates. The election results were surprising in that expected losses failed to materialize. In absolute numbers the DNVP even gained votes (6.2 million in total; and, in union with the *Landbund*, 111 seats); relative to the strength of other parties, however, the election was a setback, since the SPD again became the strongest political force (131 seats). Parties that had supported the Dawes Plan, such as the Center, DVP, and DDP, gained votes, while those that had opposed it (KPD and Nazis) lost ground.

After the elections, Chancellor Wilhelm Marx was replaced by Hans Luther, under whose leadership the German Nationals finally succeeded in attaining their long-coveted inclusion in a "bourgeois bloc" coalition government, comprised of the DNVP, DVP, Center Party, and Bayerische Volkspartei (Bavarian People's Party, or BVP—the Bavarian offshoot of the Center Party).[39] Participation in government, an issue that had been the subject of fierce debate within party circles, appeared to anchor the DNVP more firmly in the Republic, since governmental participation implied at least tacit endorsement of Weimar's political system. Reality would prove more complex. Though the DNVP managed to push through policies that reflected the interests of the party base, tension between pragmatists and fundamentalists again erupted into open conflict when national security issues were at stake. While participation in government compelled some DNVP members to adopt a more moderate stance, the inevitable need to compromise on principles infuriated fundamentalists within the parliamentary faction and Land Associations. During their ten-month stint as part of the coalition, the DNVP assumed a leading role in supporting protective tariffs for agriculture and in the alliance of industrial interests directed against any further

---

39. The DNVP received several portfolios: Martin Schiele, a representative of the Rural League, became Minister of the Interior; Albert Neuhaus, a retired senior official, Minister of Economics; Ministerial Director Otto von Schlieben became Minister of Finance; and the East Prussian estate owner Graf Kanitz, who had been a member of the DNVP until October 1923 and was now without party affiliation, became Minister of Nutrition and Agriculture. Governmental participation lasted from January until 26 October 1925. Winkler, *Weimar, 1918–1933*, 266; Eyck, *Geschichte*, I, 427.

extension of welfare benefits.[40] The party successfully championed the reintroduction of agrarian tariffs (based on the 1902 Bülow tariff), which were represented as a national exigency to protect East German agriculture from cheap imports from Slavic countries.[41] The DNVP had a more difficult time adopting a stance on foreign policy issues that would satisfy both its coalition partners and its restive party organization. Even as part of government, the DNVP proved unrelenting in its struggle against Stresemann's foreign policy, due to pressure from its Land Associations. Controversy over the Locarno Treaty—in which the Reich renounced any claims on Alsace-Lorraine and agreed to recognize the demilitarized status of the Rhineland—was thus inevitable. Never had the chasm between German National Cabinet ministers, who favored acceptance of Locarno, and the party organization, which vehemently rejected it, been deeper. On 23 October 1925 the DNVP executive committee and chairmen of its Land Associations declared that the Locarno Treaty was unacceptable. Resistance from the rank and file membership to Locarno was enormous, and Land and Kreis Associations were inundated with threats of irate party members to resign. By ratifying the Treaty, critics argued, the government acquiesced in the "robbery" of German territory.[42] The DNVP Reichstag faction (against the recommendation of DNVP Cabinet ministers) had already decided that the party should withdraw from the coalition because of Locarno, and at the end of October 1925 the DNVP resigned from the bourgeois bloc government.

Locarno made it clear that fundamentalists within the DNVP were gaining the upper hand over proponents of a more pragmatic approach. In contrast to the Dawes Plan fiasco, German Nationals this time were determined to preserve a united front to the outside.[43]

40. Michael Stürmer, "Die konservative Rechte in der Weimarer Republik," in Oswald Hauser, ed., *Politische Parteien in Deutschland und Frankreich, 1918–1939* (Wiesbaden, 1969), 38–51, esp. 45.

41. See Stürmer, *Koalition und Opposition*, 98–107.

42. Attila Chanady, "The Disintegration of the German National People's Party, 1924–1930," *Journal of Modern History* 39 (1967), 65–91, esp. 74. The Treaty was signed by Chancellor Luther and Stresemann on 16 October 1925; the DNVP ministers' resignation followed on 25 October 1925.

43. See Attila Chanady, "Disintegration," 74–75; Walter H. Kaufmann, *Monarchism in the Weimar Republic* (New York, 1953), 153–156. Locarno was approved on 27 November 1925 by a vote of 300 to 174 (against the votes of German Nationals, National Socialists, Communists, and members of the Wirtschaftspartei).

Since the Locarno Treaty did not require constitutional changes, they were spared the dilemma they had faced over the Dawes Plan: German Nationals could vote unanimously against the Treaty and still be certain that it would pass, since a two-thirds majority was not required for acceptance. This back and forth battle between fundamentalists, who had prevailed over Locarno, and pragmatists, who continued to push for moderation, would continue to have reverberations for the DNVP and the nature of party politics in general. One important interest group within the DNVP that had opposed the decision to leave the bourgeois bloc government in October 1925 was the Rural League. Since the DNVP's resignation from government had been based solely on a foreign policy issue, many close to the Rural League concluded that their interests were being neglected and gradually began to distance themselves (albeit with regional variations) from the DNVP before the 1928 elections.[44] The perception that organized interests were losing influence in determining policy was furthered by the growing power wielded by Alfred Hugenberg's media empire, which had proved to be of decisive importance in the agitation against the Locarno Treaty. With Hugenberg's help, a politics of pure ideology had prevailed over the power of organized interests, which had still been decisive in the Dawes Plan vote. Locarno thus marked a first attempt by fundamentalists to mold the party into an ideologically consistent bloc above particular interests and to create a new dominant party line that made it obligatory to consider intransigent opposition to Republican governments a national duty.

In January 1927, the German Nationals re-entered government with four ministerial portfolios.[45] The DNVP's participation in the governing coalition did not get off to a good start, since the extension of the *Republikschutzgesetz* (Law for the Protection of the Republic), due in 1927, was bound to bring the DNVP into conflict with its own principles. The law had been adopted originally for a five-year period as a reaction to the murder of Walther Rathenau

44. Some founded their own interest groups, such as the Christian National Peasant and Landvolk Party. Pure opposition politics, the argument ran, was detrimental to agricultural interests. See Stürmer, *Koalition und Opposition*, 190; Chanady, "Disintegration," 76.

45. The Fourth Cabinet of Wilhelm Marx, with former party leader Oskar Hergt as Minister of Justice, Walter von Keudell as Minister of the Interior, Martin Schiele as Minister for Nutrition, and Wilhelm Koch as Minister for Transportation.

and was thus clearly directed against the political Right. Article 23a of the law also prohibited the return of the Emperor to Germany, a provision an explicitly monarchist party might find difficult to square with its articles of faith—the restoration of the monarchy was, after all, a central tenet of the DNVP. Yet, when the parliamentary faction voted to prolong the law with virtually no major modifications, it became clear that a significant part of even the party's East Elbian supporters no longer considered the restoration of the monarchy viable.[46] At the next party congress in Königsberg, party chairman Graf Westarp attempted to gloss over contradictions between German National principles and the voting behavior of some of its members.[47] Westarp stressed that the extension of the *Republikschutzgesetz* in no way constituted an endorsement of the republican form of government: now as before, the DNVP was opposed in principle to the *Republikschutzgesetz*, but nonetheless considered it an effective measure to suppress the extreme Left, especially the KPD. Graf Westarp would not be able to play his precarious balancing act for much longer. In October 1927, the still extant but now functionless DKP, which continued to exist in the form of a *Konservativer Hauptverein* within the DNVP, issued a resolution that denounced the Weimar constitution as a product of the betrayal of faith and treason against the nation. Westarp was compelled to react and come out clearly for or against the resolution. In his written response, in which he distanced himself from the attacks against the Republic, Westarp argued that historically outdated, ideological formulas were often major obstacles to successful policies. He stressed that the realization of political goals required realistic judgments and decried the fact that many doctrinaire conservatives insisted on using ideological pronouncements and professions of intransigent principles as a substitute for the give-and-take of practical politics, which resulted in their inability to appraise policy matters in a down-to-earth, realistic way.[48]

These tensions between ideological claims and political reality, under which the party labored during the two periods it formed part of a Weimar governing coalition, often manifested themselves in contradictory policies and a public image that lacked consistency. As a result, German Nationals had alienated many of their

46. On 27 May 1927 the *Republikschutzgesetz* was extended for only two years, which made it more acceptable to the DNVP.
47. Kaufmann, *Monarchism*, 170–173.
48. Stürmer, "Die konservative Rechte in der Weimarer Republik," 46.

middle-class supporters, to whom they owed electoral success in 1924. Losses in the next election were therefore widely anticipated. The DNVP's seesawing between their professed principles, on the one hand, and political expediency, on the other, had also increased disaffection inside the party. Conflicts between mostly younger conservatives, who were prepared to collaborate in Weimar politics, and Pan-German and former DKP members, who considered their own unbending oppositional stance as a source of strength and rejected participation in government as detrimental to German National interests, had intensified in the years after 1924.

In the elections of 20 May 1928, the DNVP lost thirty seats and almost 2 million votes, a defeat that discredited Westarp's half-hearted attempts to steer a course of legality and participate in governing coalitions. Even though party moderates blamed the excessive nationalist rhetoric of the Pan-Germans for electoral defeat, it was clear that now the hour of triumph for radical elements was at hand. Since 1924, Pan-Germans had radicalized political discourse within the DNVP and rendered the party increasingly incapable of compromise. As in every *Weltanschauungspartei* that is pervaded and dominated by "political faith" and dogma, it was easy for ideological diehards to vilify realists as "lukewarm" and injurious to party interests. The regional DNVP Land Associations, which enjoyed considerable influence on financial and organizational matters because of the party's decentralized structure, were particularly unrelenting in their opposition to parliamentary government and the Republic. Their independence (which varied by region) always gained in importance when struggles over the DNVP's political direction threatened party unity. Since the DNVP was dependent upon contributions from industry to maintain the party apparatus and finance election campaigns (membership dues alone were insufficient), financial contributors exercised disproportionate leverage.[49] Alfred Hugenberg capitalized on this dependency. Since the mid twenties his press empire had promoted Pan-German influence, and the effective campaign against Locarno had already provided a foretaste of his influence.[50]

49. Liebe, *Volkspartei*, 103.

50. On Hugenberg's press empire, see Heidrun Holzbach, *Das "System Hugenberg:" Die Organisation bürgerlicher Sammlungspolitik vor dem Aufstieg der NSDAP, 1918–1928* (Stuttgart, 1981); Erich Eyck, *Weimarer Republik*, 4th ed., Vol. II (Zürich 1972), 31–32.

The conflict between the party's two wings, simmering for years and now intensified by election defeat, erupted again in July 1928. The direct cause was an article entitled "Monarchism," written by Walter Lambach, a board member of the Association of German National Shop Assistants,[51] who was sufficiently prominent to occupy second place on the DNVP's Reichstag list.[52] In his article, Lambach argued that with Hindenburg's elevation to the presidency in 1925, the question of a restoration of the monarchy had resolved itself, since Hindenburg's larger-than-life figure far outshone that of any living Hohenzollern. In the eyes of the nation, it was Hindenburg who occupied first place (together with Frederick the Great and Wilhelm I), not the Kaiser. The DNVP's defeat in the May elections, Lambach wrote, was ultimately a defeat for the idea of monarchism, the unpopularity of which had been long apparent. Young voters would continue to shun the DNVP as long as it supported the restoration of the monarchy, which, in any event, could not be realized in the foreseeable future. He called on both monarchists and supporters of the Republic, who opposed a return to monarchy, to join the DNVP.[53] Lambach called for a full transformation of the DNVP; he rejected the idea of a party geared toward the restoration of the monarchy, and championed instead a kind of conservative people's party with a new program and leadership. His initiative unleashed a storm of indignation. The Potsdam II Land Association (to which Lambach belonged by virtue of his residency) expelled him from the party in July.[54] The DNVP legal committee

51. Walter Lambach, "Monarchismus," *Politische Wochenschrift* 4, no. 24, 14 June 1928. Excerpts in English can be found in Kaufmann, *Monarchism*, 182–185. See also Amrei Stupperich, *Volksgemeinschaft oder Arbeitersolidarität. Studien zur Arbeitnehmerpolitik in der Deutschnationalen Volkspartei, 1918–1933* (Göttingen, 1982), 140–146; Larry E. Jones, "Between the Fronts: The German National Union of Commercial Employees from 1928 to 1933," *Journal of Modern History* 48 (1976), 462–482.

52. Eyck, *Geschichte*, II, 215. The Association of German National Shop Assistants was the largest union for white-collar workers (*Angestellte*). It was conservative, nationalistic, and partly anti-Semitic. During the Weimar Republic its membership rose from 147,800 (1918) to 403,000 (1932), and it soon became a rallying point for those inside the DNVP who were hostile to Hugenberg. See Bracher, *Auflösung*, 316.

53. "Monarchists and Republicans, join our ranks! And with this change in our attitude concerning the government, we must also change our program and our party leadership." Kaufmann, *Monarchism*, 183–184.

54. See also Mommsen, *The Rise and Fall of Weimar Democracy*, 257–260; Eyck, *Geschichte*, II, 215–216; Bracher, *Auflösung*, 313–314.

subsequently rescinded his expulsion from the party and chose to reprimand him instead. A short time later, in July 1928, Graf Westarp, whose leadership had come under increasingly severe criticism since the election defeat, resigned as party leader. During his time in office, he had never succeeded in controlling the party's power base—the crucial Land Associations. While Westarp retained his position as Reichstag faction leader, it was clear that his star was on the wane. Inner-party dissent, the steady stream of divisive legislation, the mood within the country, and the shifting foundations of power within the party, all converged to set the stage for a new type of leadership. Alfred Hugenberg's time had now come. At the end of August 1928, in the *Berliner Lokalanzeiger*, Hugenberg outlined his own conception of the DNVP's future, which was diametrically opposed to the ideas of Lambach, and on 20 October 1928 Hugenberg was elected (with no opposing candidates) the fourth chairman of the DNVP.[55] With Hugenberg's election, fundamentalists had won an important victory over their more pragmatic fellow DNVP members. As would soon become apparent, it was a portentous moment both for the German National People's Party and the country as a whole, since Hugenberg's election would change not only the direction of the party itself, but also the political fate of all of Germany.

The End of Conservative Moderation

Hugenberg's position in the party owed little to extraordinary personal or rhetorical abilities. According to Erich Eyck, he came across more "like a vexed subordinate official"[56] than the successful industrial tycoon he actually was. Eyck added, however, that Hugenberg was recognized as an exemplary organizer and a man of great willpower who, with obstinate tenacity, adhered to his principles—a virtue that would ultimately have disastrous consequences for the Republic. Hugenberg hardly ever spoke in the Reichstag; his rare appearances as a speaker caused uproar and laughter. Despised and ridiculed by many, and condemned as a reactionary without substance by those Weimar right-wing intellectuals commonly associated with the "conservative revolution," he was praised by his

55. See Leopold, *Alfred Hugenberg*, 45–55.
56. Eyck, *Geschichte*, II, 216.

Pan-German friends as a visionary and true statesman.[57] On the one hand, his policies helped make Hitler Chancellor; on the other, he was the only one who, time and again, obstinately countered Hitler in Cabinet meetings of the "government of national consolidation."[58] The student of Hugenberg's political maneuverings cannot help but agree with Erich Eyck's dictum that it was ultimately impossible to comprehend Hugenberg's policies as logical or coherent.[59]

Hugenberg's long career was characterized by the transition from posts in the higher civil service to leading positions in industry, a move not uncommon in nineteenth-century Prussia.[60] In the 1890s Hugenberg was one of the cofounders of the Pan-German League, to whose aims he remained committed even as a deputy and chairman of the DNVP.[61] In 1919, he was a member of the Weimar National Assembly, and a year later became a DNVP Reichstag deputy. After 1925, the Pan-German circle around Heinrich Claß[62] repeatedly urged Hugenberg to seek the party leadership. Despite his obvious limitations as a politician, the small but very influential Pan-German group systematically garnered support for Hugenberg in the DNVP Land Associations, where strength and steadfastness of political conviction were held in higher esteem than political ability or rhetorical skill.

---

57. Armin Mohler, *Die konservative Revolution in Deutschland, 1918–1932*, 3rd ed., 2 vols. (Darmstadt, 1990); Kurt Sontheimer, *Antidemokratisches Denken in der Weimarer Republik*, DTV paperback ed. (Munich, 1978).

58. Karl-Heinz Minuth, ed., *Akten der Reichskanzlei. Die Regierung Hitler*, vol. I (Boppard, 1983).

59. Eyck, *Geschichte*, II, 436.

60. Alfred Hugenberg (1865–1951), born in Hannover, began his career in 1889 as an official (Assessor) in Kassel; from 1894–1899 he worked at the *Ansiedlungskommission* in Posen; from 1900 to 1903 he was director of the *Raiffeisengenossenschaften*, following that Privy Counselor in the Prussian Finance Ministry (until 1907) and, from 1909 to 1918, was Chair of the Board of Directors of the Krupp Steel Works. Beginning in 1916, he built up his own companies and newspaper and film enterprises.

61. On the Pan-Germans, see Roger Chickering, *We Men who feel most German* (Stanford, 1982); Kruck, *Geschichte des Alldeutschen Verbandes*; Barry Jackisch, "Not a Large, but a Strong Right: The Pan-German League, Radical Nationalism, and Rightist Party Politics in Weimar Germany, 1918–1933" (Ph.D. Diss., Buffalo, 2000); Rainer Hering, *Konstruierte Nation. Der Alldeutsche Verband 1890 bis 1939* (Hamburg, 2003).

62. Heinrich Claß (1868–1953), a former student of Heinrich von Treitschke, joined the Pan-Germans in 1897 and served as their leader from 1908 until the dissolution of the organization in 1939.

Despite all the contradictions and inconsistencies in Hugenberg's policies, two fundamental trends can be discerned. First, even during his almost five years as party leader, he held fast to the unrealistic goals of overseas expansion and the recovery of German colonies. Secondly, Hugenberg was convinced that a more compact, self-contained political bloc would have a greater impact than a large and heterogeneous party that was divided within itself, a view he put forth in his article *"Party Bloc or Mush,"* published shortly before he became party leader.[63] Over the course of the next two years Hugenberg would act on this conviction, thus undermining his own party and facilitating the Nazis' rise to power. His policies resulted in two major party splits and halved the DNVP's share of the popular vote between 1928 and 1930.[64] In his rejection of Weimar's political system Hugenberg was equally intransigent. When accepting the party leadership on 28 October 1928 he bluntly stated that "the refuse of the Weimar system" would have to be shaken off: "We must free ourselves from this system of committees and commissions, from the fruitless wasting of all strength in speech and counter-speech."[65] Endless jabber in parliamentary faction meetings was a waste of time; it was preferable to construct a solid bloc that embodied the fundamental principles of the party.[66] It soon became obvious that Hugenberg's obdurate intransigence would have consequences for the party by impeding cooperation with other political forces, thereby alienating from the party those more amenable to compromise. Yet, Hugenberg was quite prepared to sacrifice a part of his electorate (as would soon become clear, the larger one) to promote his own conception of the DNVP. In a party circular of July 1931, he went so far as to argue that the entire party might have to be put on the line to escape from the quagmire of democratic compromises to which the DNVP had succumbed between 1924 and 1928.[67] As his policies during the following years would show,

63. "Block oder Brei," *Berliner Lokalanzeiger,* 28 August 1928; Mommsen, *The Rise and Fall of Weimar Democracy,* 256–259.

64. From 14.2 percent (1928) to 7.0 (1930) down to 5.9 (1932). See Kolb, *Weimarer Republik,* 308–309, and Thomas Mergel, "Das Scheitern des deutschen Tory-Konservatismus. Die Umformung der DNVP zu einer rechtsradikalen Partei 1928–1931,"*Historische Zeitschrift* 276 (2003), 323–368.

65. See the party bulletin, *Unsere Partei,* 1928, 340; Hiller von Gaertingen, "DNVP," 547.

66. Schulze, *Weimar,* 312.

67. Bracher, *Auflösung,* 397.

Hugenberg rarely deviated from his self-appointed task of leading Weimar democracy ever closer to the brink of ruin.

With his assumption of the party leadership, Hugenberg demanded greater influence on DNVP policies, thus bringing him into direct conflict with the DNVP Reichstag faction. Even in 1928, the parliamentary faction still harbored a significant contingent of moderate conservatives. To expand the leverage of the new chairman, the party's executive committees were restructured in December 1928: the smallest committee (the *Parteileitung*) was eliminated altogether, while the larger committees (the *Parteivorstand* with about 130 members and the *Parteivertretung* with 260) were retained. Hugenberg also demanded strict party discipline, whereby he would have the authority to make binding decisions for the parliamentary faction without consulting deputies.[68] Although a majority of the Reichstag faction initially opposed this demand, Hugenberg succeeded in pushing the measure through a little later. He thus made the most important political decision of his political career—the DNVP's participation in Hitler's "Cabinet of national consolidation"—without consulting the deputies in the Reichstag faction. Hugenberg also took upon himself the authority to initiate expulsion proceedings against deputies who opposed him and to strike from election lists those who were simply unacceptable to him.[69] The fact that Hugenberg could exert pressure on those deputies who disagreed with his policies would become significant in the two big crises the DNVP faced in 1929 and 1930. The first crucial trial was triggered by the party's reaction to the Young Plan; the second by its stance on Brüning's policies.

The Young Plan

To satisfy the German government's desire for a definitive reparations settlement that would lessen Germany's financial burden (and guarantee her ability to pay), the Allied reparations agent Gilbert Parker attempted to win over Allied governments to a new,

---

68. *Taschenbuch der Deutschnationalen Volkspartei*, published by the Deutschnationale Schriftenvertriebsstelle (Berlin, 1929). Friedrich von Winterfeld, leader of the parliamentary faction in the Prussian Landtag since 1928, and one of Hugenberg's most loyal supporters, demanded this privilege for the party chairman in early 1929.

69. Hiller von Gaertingen, "DNVP," 548.

long-term reparations plan with lower annual payments.[70] The success of this scheme was doubtful from the start since German reparation payments were tied to French and British debts with the United
States,[71] and the new American president Herbert Hoover (elected
on 6 November 1928) rejected debt reduction.[72] After long and difficult negotiations, the commission of experts, which also included
Germans, finally signed the "Young Plan" on 7 June 1929. According to the commission's report, annual payments were to start at
1,707.9 million marks, increase to 2,428 million until 1965–1966,
and then continue, albeit in lower amounts, until 1987–1988.[73]
Foreign control of the German economy, including the *Reichsbahn*
and *Reichsbank*, which constituted the most controversial part of
the Dawes Plan, would end. The so-called "prosperity index," by
virtue of which reparations could theoretically be increased, was
also dropped. Even though annual payments were lower than those
stipulated under the Dawes Plan, the new obligation to pay reparations for almost sixty years provided plenty of fodder for the political Right to agitate vociferously against the Young Plan.[74]

The reaction of the Right was not long delayed. Hugenberg
proposed a national referendum against the Young Plan and, with
this aim in view, established a "*Reichsausschuß* (committee) for the
People's Rebellion against the Young Plan." While negotiations
over the new reparations agreement made only slow progress, the
right-wing press immediately unleashed a storm of indignation
against the new "enslavement treaty," comparing it to a second Versailles and emphasizing the long duration of the payment period.
The anti-Young Plan struggle, characterized as a rescue operation
against the selling out of Germany to the Western Allies, was used
by Hugenberg to concentrate the forces of the entire political Right

70. This happened in the fall of 1928. Under the Dawes Plan, payments for
1928 were raised to 2.5 billion Reichsmark, which strained the country's ability
to pay.

71. Since initial statements from France and Great Britain were not encour-
aging, Stresemann at first even hesitated to recommend the appointment of a
reparations committee to the Reichstag.

72. Werner Link, *Die amerikanische Stabilisierungspolitik in Deutschland,
1921–1931* (Düsseldorf, 1970); Eyck, *Geschichte*, II, 236–245.

73. The liabilities of the inter-Allied debts, which German payments were
supposed to cover, continued until 1987–1988.

74. Under the Young Plan terms the so-called "transfer protection" (*Trans-
ferschutz*) was cancelled, meaning that reparations would have to be paid even in
times of economic hardship.

and polarized domestic politics almost to the point of civil war.[75] His *Reichsausschuß* and his campaign for a national referendum thus amounted to a kind of national counter-parliament. The old slogan of the "national opposition" was revived, even though the DNVP had pointedly renounced this concept after the murder of Rathenau in 1922 to distance itself from radical groups. These groups were now included in the struggle against the Young Plan. In the *Reichsausschuß* the NSDAP was represented as an equal partner; Hitler thus stood alongside Hugenberg, *Stahlhelm* leader Franz Seldte, and the Pan-German Claß at its head, and, with the help of Hugenberg's press, could utilize the political agitation against the Young Plan to make his name known throughout Germany. Hitler had joined the *Reichsausschuß* against opposition from the left wing of his own party, which refused to moderate its polemics against German National "reactionaries."[76] Nazi participation was chiefly responsible for the uncompromising tone and unrealistic demands expressed in the so-called "Law against the Enslavement of the German People," referred to as the "Freedom Law" by the political Right.[77] Any German politician who signed the Young Plan, for example, would make himself liable for punishment under Article IV of this law, President von Hindenburg (who was closer to the German Nationals than to any other party) not excepted.

Not surprisingly, Article IV of the "Freedom Law" soon became the subject of fierce internal debates within the DNVP. The smoldering conflict between moderate conservatives and the German National employee wing, on the one hand, and Hugenberg and the Pan-German wing on the other, erupted once again, whereby Hugenberg's cooperation with the Nazi party constituted the main bone of contention. Hugenberg escalated the conflict by accentuating disagreements, since he was eager to undermine both moderate voices in the party and the strong position of former chairman Graf

---

75. See Schulze, *Weimar*, 310; Mommsen, *The Rise and Fall of Weimar Democracy*, 278.

76. On attacks against the DNVP in Goebbels's *Der Angriff*, see Bracher, *Auflösung*, 317 (note 124). On the opposition to the Young Plan in general, see Otmar Jung, "Plebiszitärer Durchbruch 1929? Zur Bedeutung von Volksbegehren und Volksentscheid gegen den Young Plan für die NSDAP," *Geschichte und Gesellschaft* 15 (1989), 489–510.

77. For the English text, see Jeremy Noakes and Geoff Pridham, *Nazism, 1919–1945. A Documentary Reader* (Exeter, 1996), vol. I, 64–65. Hugenberg circulated the text among his supporters in the summer and finally published it in September 1929.

Westarp, who remained leader of the parliamentary faction and had close connections throughout the entire party. Confrontation had now become inevitable. The rupture within the DNVP that would usher in the disintegration of conservatism as a coherent political force was only a matter of time.

The First Division

In September 1929 four prominent DNVP deputies openly came out against acceptance of the "Freedom Law": former Interior Minister Walter von Keudell, Moritz Klönne (who had defected from the DVP to the DNVP in 1924), the historian Otto Hoetzsch, and former party manager Hans-Erdmann von Lindeiner-Wildau. In addition, a larger group within the Reichstag faction also mobilized against Hugenberg's course. Westarp (whom the moderate wing would have preferred as party leader) expressed his reservations about the "People's Rebellion" before the Reichstag faction in early October 1929, though his attitude remained ambivalent.[78] By and large, Westarp was reluctant to relent to pressure by those DNVP deputies who demanded that he protest against Hugenberg's tactics, since he feared this might create new fissures within the party. It was this reluctance to act, shared by other leading DNVP deputies, such as Oskar Hergt and Martin Schiele, that prompted the group around Lindeiner-Wildau to threaten secession from the party.[79] The now unavoidable split within the DNVP occurred between 27 November and 4 December 1929.[80] After separate meetings of the two camps around Hugenberg and Lindeiner, Hugenberg's supporters insisted on party discipline in the vote on the "Freedom Law." The stalemate was finally broken when a number of deputies hostile to Hugenberg came out with public declarations against their

78. Lindeiner-Wildau was *Hauptgeschäftsführer* until 1921 and, until 1925, political chargé of the party leader. On Westarp's policies, see Bracher, who meticulously evaluated Westarp's literary bequest regarding events in 1929 and 1930, in *Auflösung*, 309–22.

79. Martin Schiele was DNVP Reichstag deputy from 1919 until he left the party in 1930; he held ministerial portfolios in 1925 and 1927–1928 and was president of the Rural League from 1928 to 1930.

80. See Hans von Schlange-Schöningen, *Am Tage danach* (Hamburg, 1946); Weiß and Hoser, eds., *Deutschnationalen*; Denis Paul Walker, "Alfred Hugenberg and the Deutschnationale Volkspartei 1918 to 1930," (Diss. Cambridge, 1976).

own party leader.[81] The initiation of party expulsion proceedings against these deputies, pushed through by Hugenberg in the DNVP executive committee, ushered in developments that led to a first split in the parliamentary faction. At the beginning of December 1929, Gottfried Treviranus, who had never made a secret of his antipathy for Hugenberg, announced his resignation from the DNVP. In cooperation with Hans von Schlange-Schöningen, Treviranus brought together twelve deputies to form an independent "German National Study Group."[82] Their resignation statements from the party followed on 4 December 1929. As a result of these resignations, Westarp relinquished the leadership of the Reichstag faction, since he could no longer claim to represent the will of its members.[83] This was yet another blow to party moderates, since it indicated that Hugenberg remained victorious all along the line in the ongoing struggle within the party, even though the relative strength of the Reichstag faction was diminished as a result. Despite the fact that a much larger number of deputies voted against the controversial Article IV of the "Freedom Law" at the end of November 1929, the initial split remained limited to twelve deputies.[84] Still, the influence of the deputies who had left the party was significant. The "employee" wing, for example, was greatly weakened by the resignation of Reinhard Mumm and Franz Behrens of the Christian Social group; Walter Lambach of the Association of German National Shop Assistants; Emil Hartwig, the leader of the German National *Arbeiterbund*, and the trade union secretary Gustav Hülser.[85]

81. These included Emil Hartwig, leader of the German National *Arbeiterbund*; Walter Lambach, who chaired the DNVP *Reichsangestelltenausschuß*; and the Trade Union Secretary Gustav Hülser; all three were part of the Christian Social wing.

82. Or *Deutschnationale Arbeitsgemeinschaft*. Gottfried Reinhold Treviranus (1891–1971), former officer in the Imperial Navy, DNVP Reichstag deputy since 1924. On Treviranus see Erasmus Jonas, *Die Volkskonservativen, 1928–1933* (Düsseldorf, 1965).

83. Bracher, *Auflösung*, 321.

84. Article IV was the infamous "*Zuchthausparagraph*." According to Eyck, *Geschichte*, II, 282, fifty-five deputies voted "yes"; according to Winkler, *Weimar*, 355, the number was fifty-three. The DNVP received seventy-three seats in the May 1928 elections.

85. Just as prominent in the faction were Hans von Schlange-Schöningen, chairman of the largest Land Association (Pomerania); the Catholic Paul Lejeune-Jung, the factory owner Moritz Klönne, Hans-Erdmann von Lindeiner-Wildau, Walter von Keudell, Otto Hoetzsch, and Gottfried Treviranus, who would soon become chairman of the Konservative Volkspartei. See Bracher, *Auflösung*, 322.

From the entire list of names, only Hans von Schlange-Schöningen and Treviranus had voted against the acceptance of the controversial *Reichsbahn* Law in the Dawes Plan. With few exceptions, then, most deputies remained consistent in their political beliefs. Those closest to the Christian Social wing joined together in December 1929 with the southern German Christlicher Volksdienst to form the Christlich-Sozialer Volksdienst, which would later be led mainly by Gustav Hülser, Emil Hartwig, Walter Lambach, und Reinhard Mumm.[86] The Christlich-Sozialer Volksdienst did not consider itself a *bürgerliche* conservative party and continually stressed that it was at variance with Hugenberg's DNVP.[87] Hans von Schlange-Schöningen joined the Christian National Peasant and Landvolk Party, an agrarian group founded in 1928 that represented peasants in central and southwest Germany, whereas the DNVP predominantly championed the interests of the large estates in the east. During Brüning's government, other German Nationals joined this party, mainly to support Martin Schiele, Nutrition Minister in Brüning's Cabinet.[88]

Those deputies who remained in the "German National Study Group" founded the Volkskonservative Vereinigung on 28 January 1930, which was soon to change its name to Konservative Volkspartei (or "Volkskonservative") after the secession of the Westarp group from the DNVP in July 1930 (see below).[89] Treviranus became the leader of the Konservative Volkspartei, which emerged as the most important of the conservative splinter groups, and other DNVP secessionists, such as Lejeune-Jung, Hoetzsch, Lindeiner-Wildau, and Westarp, would all play important roles in it. The Konservative Volkspartei was significant in that its leading politicians later exerted

86. Siegmund Neumann, *Die Parteien der Weimarer Republik*, 5th ed. (Stuttgart, 1986), 70–72.

87. Its appeal lay primarily in its religious character, although leftist elements strongly stood out: the Volksdienst combined seemingly contradictory elements, such as trenchant criticism of capitalism with emphatic anti-revolutionary attitudes; it rejected the class struggle and pointedly renounced, in contrast to most other Weimar parties, excesses in political propaganda. Adolf Stoecker's Christian Social Movement and Friedrich Naumann, to a certain extent, were held up as models to emulate. See Neumann, *Parteien*, 70–72.

88. Ibid., 65–66.

89. The Konservative Volkspartei was formed on 23 July 1930. Apart from Count Westarp, other wayward DNVP members and deputies, who refused to toe the party line, soon joined its ranks. See Jonas, *Die Volkskonservativen*; Bracher, *Auflösung*, 347–349.

considerable influence on Hindenburg. This type of political group made up of senior civil servants, diplomats, and conservative intellectuals who were prepared to compromise with other parties in order to have a voice in politics, and who repudiated Hugenberg's intransigent attitude, had political predecessors in Prussian history. Its policies were reminiscent of the Wochenblattpartei of the 1850s and the Freikonservative Vereinigung,[90] which continued to support Bismarck after 1866, when the Old Prussian Conservatives had broken with him.[91] Siegmund Neumann emphasizes similarities in the sociological structure, party program, and political origins of the three conservative groups; given the vastly differing political and social conditions between the time of the 1850s and 1860s and the later years of the Weimar Republic, however, such similarities are naturally to be viewed with caution.[92] While there was initial hope that the Association of German National Shop Assistants with its more than 400,000 members might provide a mass basis for the Volkskonservativen, it became clear with the elections of 14 September 1930 that members of the Association tended more toward the Nazi party.[93] The Konservative Volkspartei thus won a mere four seats in the elections of September 1930 and had disintegrated already in February 1931.[94]

Hugenberg did his best to stem the tide of party resignations, which had spread to the Land parliaments and mostly affected deputies who represented agricultural and industrial interests. Nevertheless, it could not be avoided that alongside the DNVP the three newly formed conservative groups entered the ring for the election campaign of September 1930—the Christlich-Sozialer Volksdienst, the Landvolkpartei, and the Konservative Volkspartei. The vehemence and fratricidal fervor with which the various conservative groups fought each other was downright paradoxical: Hugenberg, for his part, slandered the Volkskonservativen as Weimar-loving "Tory-Democrats" without genuine *völkisch* or monarchical bonds,

90. See Michael Behnen, *Das Politische Wochenblatt, 1851–1861. Nationalkonservative Publizistik gegen Ständestaat und Polizeistaat* (Göttingen, 1971).

91. See Beck, "The Changing Concerns of Prussian Conservatism," 86–106.

92. Neumann, *Parteien*, 68–70.

93. Iris Hamel, *Völkischer Verband und nationale Gewerkschaft. Der Deutschnationale Handlungsgehilfenverband 1893–1933* (Frankfurt, 1967); Jones, "Between the Fronts," 462–482.

94. Their four Reichstag deputies were Lambach, Lindeiner, Treviranus, and Westarp.

and former DNVP Reichstag faction leader Graf Westarp had to struggle against attempted interference from hecklers who belonged to the *Stahlhelm* throughout the campaign.[95] Still, from Hugenberg's point of view, the resignation of twelve influential deputies had an advantage insofar as he had now come closer to realizing his goal of a more homogeneous conservative bloc. He had purged the DNVP of a part of the opposition that was directed mainly against himself and his policies, thereby consolidating his position within the party.[96] In the national referendum on the "People's Rebellion against the Young Plan" of 2 December 1929, only 5.825 million votes were cast in favor of the motion, whereas 21 million votes would have been necessary for the protest to be effective.[97] This was an exceedingly poor result given that in the previous national referendum of 20 June 1926 on the expropriation (without compensation) of the property of German princes, which had been supported by the KPD and SPD, a sizeable 15.5 million voters had supported the initiative with their affirmative vote.[98] The colossal fuss generated by Hugenberg over the Young Plan produced two concrete results: Hugenberg's position inside the party was solidified and, on account of the anti–Young Plan campaign, Hitler's name and party had become household words throughout the entire Reich.

Toward a More Authoritarian Republic

After a long tug of war in the Reichstag, the Young Plan was finally accepted on 12 March 1930, by a vote of 265 to 192 with three abstentions.[99] With the signing of a definitive settlement of reparations, the last common denominator in Hermann Müller's Grand Coalition government had disappeared. The next political problem the government would confront—the reform of

95. Bracher, *Auflösung*, 322; Thimme, *Flucht in den Mythos*, 49.

96. It soon became obvious that the bloodletting the DNVP experienced in the September elections of 1930 did not benefit the Volkskonservativen or other conservative groups, but only the NSDAP. The number of DNVP votes fell from 4.381 to 2.458 million; its number of seats from 73 to only 41.

97. This corresponded to only 14 percent of those eligible to vote. Eyck, *Geschichte*, II, 285; Schulze, *Weimar*, 311; Winkler, *Weimar*, 356.

98. Ulrich Schüren, *Der Volksentscheid zur Fürstenenteignung 1926* (Düsseldorf, 1978).

99. Winkler, *Weimar*, 368; Schulze, *Weimar*, 315; Kaufmann, *Monarchism*, 191–195; Jonas, *Die Volkskonservativen*.

unemployment insurance—would shatter this coalition to pieces: already on 27 March, barely two weeks after the Young Plan vote, Hermann Müller tendered his resignation. With him the last government that possessed a majority of the popular vote left office; 27 March 1930 is thus unquestionably a turning point in the history of Weimar. The details of Müller's failure are well known. Elaborate intrigues against his government, prepared mostly by Kurt von Schleicher who, in agreement with Hindenburg, had endeavored ever since the autumn of 1929 to replace Müller's Cabinet with an authoritarian regime more to their liking, certainly played a role in its downfall. But ultimately conflicts within the Grand Coalition were more responsible than outside pressure for the fatal collapse of the last legitimate government.[100] The crises of the previous two years had eroded trust in the government's ability to function: the haggling over the construction of "Battle Cruiser A" exposed the wide chasm between the Social Democratic members of government and the SPD Reichstag faction; street battles in the Berlin *Scheunenviertel* and the working-class districts of Wedding und Neukölln between communists and the Berlin police, who took orders from a Social Democratic magistrate, brought tension between the SPD and KPD to a boiling point, especially since a state of emergency had to be declared in entire city districts to restore order.[101]

---

100. Hagen Schulze, for example, wrote with reference to Schleicher's maneuvers: "These preparations, which did not remain secret, are until this day linked with a persistent republican legend: the stab in the back by reactionaries and industrialists had destroyed the Grand Coalition and brought about the downfall of the Republic. In reality, the events surrounding Hindenburg played no role in Hermann Müller's resignation; rather, he was brought down by his own party." Schulze, *Weimar*, 315. In Winkler's detailed analysis (*Weimar*, 366–374) greater weight is accorded to the role of industrial circles close to the DVP: "The Social Democrats were clumsy enough in the last crisis of the Grand Coalition to be left holding the bag. But the real architects of the change in power sat on the right wing of the government benches or belonged to the extraparliamentary Right." (*Weimar*, 373). Yet, even Winkler concedes that Brüning's proposed compromise, presented literally at the last minute (on the morning of 27 March), was rejected by the SPD faction under the influence of Labor Minister Rudolf Wissell and the union wing of the SPD, whereas the majority of the DVP faction was ready to accept the compromise (*Weimar*, 370–371); see David E. Barclay, *Rudolf Wissell als Sozialpolitiker 1890–1933* (Berlin, 1978).

101. With the Sixth World Congress of the Comintern in the summer of 1928, the united front of the two working class parties (that began in 1924) came to an end. The KPD no longer collaborated with labor unions and Social Democrats, who were now labeled "social fascists," and joint May Day parades

The Sklarek scandal, as a result of which the Lord Mayor of Berlin resigned, cast further doubt upon the credibility of the Berlin SPD.[102] In 1929, a series of bombings against administrative offices (*Landratsämter*) in Schleswig-Holstein and tax offices in the state of Oldenburg, as well as widespread tax strikes in northern and central Germany, had focused general attention on the plight of agriculture.[103] This surfeit of political problems and economic crises (in the face of which the government appeared helpless), along with the unproductive haggling over the Young Plan, lent weight to a widely held view that the unstable coalition, led by the well-meaning but lackluster and phlegmatic Chancellor Hermann Müller, was not up to the task of solving the nation's problems.[104] At this point in time the reverberations of the world economic crisis had become evident in Germany as well: in February 1930 unemployment figures shot up to 3.3 million,[105] the entire agricultural sector (not only large East Elbian estates) found itself mired in problems, and reduced demand, as well as a general slump in sales and the threatening financial ruin of many towns, led to mass dismissals of employees in the economy and the local civil service. The position of civil servants on all levels had, in any case, been weakened by the Inflation, and even the very substantial salary raises of the previous years had been unable to undo its nefarious financial effects.[106] Officials had always played a formidable role in German life and in the economy and

---

were no longer permitted. See Siegfried Bahne, *Die KPD und das Ende von Weimar* (Frankfurt, 1976); Ossip K. Flechtheim, *Die KPD in der Weimarer Republik* (Frankfurt, 1969).

102. Arthur Rosenberg, *Geschichte der Weimarer Republik*, new ed. (Hamburg, 1991), 200–201.

103. Gerhard Stoltenberg, *Die politischen Strömungen im Schleswig-Holsteinischen Landvolk 1918–1933* (Düsseldorf, 1962), 125–128; Rudolf Heberle, *Landbevölkerung und Nationalsozialismus. Eine soziologische Untersuchung der politischen Willensbildung in Schleswig-Holstein 1918–1932* (Stuttgart, 1963), 156–160; and Hans Fallada's novel, *Bauern, Bonzen, und Bomben* (Berlin, 1931).

104. Hermann Müller (1876–1931) suffered from liver and gallbladder diseases and died in March 1931. On Müller's government, see Martin Vogt, ed., *Akten der Reichskanzlei. Das Kabinett Müller II*, 2 vols. (Boppard, 1970–1971).

105. Harold James, *Deutschland in der Weltwirtschaftskrise, 1924–1936* (Stuttgart, 1988), 451, cites an unemployment figure of 3.366 million for February 1930.

106. Rainer Fattmann, *Bildungsbürger in der Defensive. Die akademische Beamtenschaft und der 'Reichsbund der höheren Beamten' in der Weimarer Republik* (Göttingen, 2001).

administration of the country, so that their own insecurity greatly enhanced the feeling of general uncertainty and instability.

This seemingly hopeless situation, in which one social group blamed another for its own misery,[107] created a climate of opinion in which undemocratic, authoritarian measures, which were believed to facilitate decisive and effective solutions, gained ground. Even men known and esteemed for their democratic convictions, such as Theodor Wolff (1868–1943), journalist, editor of the *Berliner Tageblatt*, and cofounder of the DDP, and Emil Ludwig (1881–1948), whose fame was based on his biographies of Goethe, Napoleon, and Bismarck, were of the opinion that the Weimar Republic could well take some lessons from fascist Italy. Both made it clear, though at different points in time, that the Republic's political crisis had occasioned a fundamental alteration in their political beliefs. Both were convinced that, given the political situation of the early 1930s, the temporary establishment of an authoritarian regime, based on the model of fascist Italy, might offer a way out of Germany's political predicament.[108]

Given this changed climate of opinion regarding more authoritarian political solutions, Heinrich Brüning's government, which was based on Hindenburg's emergency decrees and not on parliamentary majorities, began its tenure under relatively favorable auspices. The former front-line officer was ascetic, personally unassuming, and a

107. This point is made by Harold James, "Economic Reasons for the Collapse of the Weimar Republic," in Ian Kershaw, ed., *Weimar: Why did German Democracy Fail?* (New York, 1990), 30–58. "In Weimar Germany employers believed that they had been obstructed by over-powerful trade unions. Unions believed that employers had embarked on a combination of economically senseless investment projects and political counter-revolution. The state's fiscal crisis led to farmers thinking that they paid high taxes to subsidize unemployed (and idle) workers and bankers who needed state bailouts when they failed as a result of their own mistaken policies. Workers thought that their real wages were too low because of the limitless greed of German agriculture." (Ibid., 46).

108. Theodor Wolff and Emil Ludwig originally counted among the critics of the Italian dictator. Wolff's interview with Mussolini (documenting his own political change of heart) appeared on 11 May 1930, and Emil Ludwig's book, which enjoyed even international success, was published in 1932. Both drew a clear line between Mussolini's fascism and that of his German emulators. See Wolfgang Schieder, "Der Faschismus als Vorbild in der Krise der Weimarer Republik," *Historische Zeitschrift* 262 (1996), 73–125, esp. 85–87; and Wolfgang Schieder, "Fatal Attraction: The German Right and Italian Fascism," in Hans Mommsen, ed., *The Third Reich between Vision and Reality. New Perspectives on German History 1918–1945* (Oxford & New York, 2001), 39–59, esp. 43.

man of few words. His superb formal education (including studies
in philology, jurisprudence, history, and economics before receiving
his doctorate in 1915), his expertise in economic and financial matters, and the dogged perseverance with which he translated plans
into action, made him one of the most exceptional Chancellors of
the Weimar Republic. It was Brüning's patriotism, his professional
competence, and the general respect accorded to him as faction
leader of the Center Party that recommended him to the group
around Hindenburg and Kurt von Schleicher. To Schleicher, who
headed the *Ministeramt* of the Reichswehr Ministry—a political liai-
son between the armed services and the Reich ministries—Brüning
seemed the right choice to preside over a presidential Cabinet and
tackle the gargantuan task of putting state finances back on their
feet.[109] During Brüning's chancellorship, the executive was no longer subject to parliamentarian control. The more than two years
of Brüning's government thus witnessed a gradual erosion of parliamentarian rule: the number of days the Reichstag was in session
decreased from 94 (1930) to 42 (1931), and then down to 13 (1932).
While the Reichstag managed to pass 98 laws in 1930, that number fell to 34 in 1931 and a mere 5 in 1932. On the other hand,
the number of laws enacted as emergency decrees by Hindenburg
rose from 5 in 1930 to 44 in 1931, and finally to 66 in 1932.[110]
After Brüning's appointment, the administrative machinery gained
ground on all fronts and the relative autonomy of the state apparatus
increased, in turn enabling the executive to push through important decisions even if they ran counter to the wishes of influential
pressure groups. In the 1950s and 1960s the nature of Brüning's
government became the subject of heated debate between Werner
Conze and Karl-Dietrich Bracher: Conze argued that the crisis of
the parliamentarian system rendered the transition to an authoritarian presidential Cabinet virtually inevitable, while Bracher contended that even under the conditions of 1930 a more democratic
solution could have been attempted. According to Bracher, such attempts were never made because the circle around Hindenburg had
prepared the transition to a presidential Cabinet well before the collapse of the Grand Coalition. Bracher thus assessed Brüning's time

109. Gordon Craig, *The Politics of the Prussian Army, 1640–1945* (Oxford,
1964), 436–453.
110. Kolb, *Die Weimarer Republik*, 135; Some historians, such as Arthur
Rosenberg, considered Brüning an "unconstitutional dictator", *Geschichte der
Weimarer Republik* (Hamburg, 1991), 211.

in office as a first fateful stage in the process of the dissolution of the Republic, whereas Conze judged Brüning more favorably as the "Chancellor above party strife."[111]

The Second Division

Brüning's economic policies soon led to irreconcilable differences of opinion in the DNVP Reichstag faction and triggered a second wave of intraparty secession. Initially, Brüning's minority government that took office on 30 March 1930 was supported by the Center, the BVP, DVP, and DDP.[112] Those responsible for planning Brüning's presidential Cabinet had counted on support from the moderate and pragmatic forces in the DNVP. Correspondingly, Brüning's new Cabinet members had more of a conservative than a liberal background. In addition to the former Free Conservative Johann Viktor Bredt of the Economic Party (Wirtschaftspartei), these included Gottfried Treviranus and Martin Schiele, the leader of the *Reichslandbund*, who laid down his mandate as a DNVP deputy when taking up a Cabinet position under Brüning, as well as the

111. See Werner Conze, "Die Krise des Parteienstaates in Deutschland 1929/30," *Historische Zeitschrift* 178 (1954), 47–83; Werner Conze and Hans Raupach, *Die Staats- und Wirtschaftskrise des Deutschen Reiches, 1929–1933* (Stuttgart, 1967), 176–252; Bracher, *Auflösung*; Bracher, "Parteienstaat, Präsidialsystem, Notstand," in Gotthard Jasper, *Von Weimar zu Hitler 1930–1933* (Köln and Berlin, 1968), 58–72. For Conze, Brüning's policies were a last attempt to save the Republic; see also his "Brünings Politik unter dem Druck der großen Krise," *Historische Zeitschrift* 199 (1964), 529–550. For Bracher, by contrast, the presidential Cabinets of Brüning, Papen, und Schleicher were all part of the prehistory of the Third Reich. Brüning's own vision, as published in his posthumous memoirs, initially seemed to support Bracher's point of view, since Brüning portrayed himself as a monarchist and opponent of the Republic, who hoped for support from the anti-republican right. Yet reservations were soon voiced about the reliability of the memoirs; see Rudolf Morsey, *Zur Entstehung, Authentizität und Kritik von Brünings "Memorien 1918–1934"* (Opladen, 1975). The question remains whether Brüning, counting on the support of moderate conservatives and convinced that the President would support him, rejected the possibility of cooperation with the SPD too easily.

112. In contrast to Hermann Müller, who needed five weeks to form his "Cabinet of personalities," Brüning formed his government in two days (Schulze, *Weimar*, 305), a feat that was made easier for him since he retained eight of the twelve Ministers from Müller's Cabinet. Bracher, *Auflösung*, 326.

politically independent Wilhelm Groener as Reichswehr Minister.[113] Encouraged by Hindenburg, Schiele submitted an ambitious agrarian program, designed especially to accommodate East Elbian estate owners, that was enthusiastically welcomed by the agrarian wing of the DNVP. It was thus clear from the very beginning that Hugenberg's intransigent stance, one bound to lead to a confrontation with Brüning, would result in a further split in the DNVP Reichstag faction. Predictably, the Social Democrats vociferously opposed the preferential treatment accorded to big landowners and responded to Brüning's inaugural speech (*Regierungserklärung*) on 1 April 1930 by sponsoring a motion of no confidence. The success or failure of this motion depended entirely on the DNVP faction, thus bringing Hugenberg's predicament to the fore sooner than expected. Hugenberg himself was hostile to Brüning's Cabinet and his press empire freely gave vent to this animosity. But since Brüning's government promised urgently needed assistance to East Elbian estate owners, Hugenberg had good reason to fear that many deputies would desert him if he backed the SPD's motion of no confidence. Once again, Hugenberg's actions were marked by self-defeating inconsistency: in order to prevent a further fragmentation of his party, he opposed the vote of no confidence before his parliamentary faction (which thanks to the DNVP was rejected by a vote of 253 to 187), but then proceeded to attack Brüning in an exceedingly critical speech that stood in marked contrast to his official position.[114] But Hugenberg's criticism of Brüning was not enough to appease the Nazis, who considered his opposition to the vote of no confidence as a betrayal of the national interest and promptly reneged on their former collaboration with the DNVP in the "Reich Committee for the People's Rebellion."

On 12 April 1930, the Reichstag was called upon to decide on the draft appropriations bill for the 1930 Reich budget, which the Reichstag had already approved on 24 March during the Müller

---

113. Winkler, *Weimar*, 377; Bracher, *Auflösung*, 326.

114. According to Erich Eyck, Hugenberg's speech was drowned out by laughter in the Reichstag (*Geschichte*, II, 324). In court hearings after 1945, Hugenberg, inconsistent as always, claimed that he had saved Brüning's Cabinet in the vote of 3 April 1930 by rejecting the motion of no confidence. As Eyck points out, Hugenberg was prudent enough not to include a copy of his Reichstag speech. See also Joseph Borchmeyer, ed., *Hugenbergs Ringen in deutschen Schicksalsstunden*. 2 vols. (Detmold, 1951), 11; Eyck, *Geschichte*, II, 324–326; Winkler, *Weimar*, 377–378; Bracher, *Auflösung*, 326.

government. The agricultural program that was so attractive to estate owners was now tied to the appropriations bill in a package deal. Both could thus come into effect only in tandem, a strategy designed to exert pressure on German National deputies to induce at least a part of the faction to support Brüning. Subsequently, both bills were approved by a narrow majority of 217 to 206 votes. Hugenberg had insisted on rejecting the package deal, but only a minority of twenty-three deputies had been prepared to follow him. Six DNVP deputies did not vote on 12 April, while thirty-one deputies, led by Graf Westarp, voted in favor of the budget appropriations bill and thus helped the government attain its slim majority.

The simmering crisis in the DNVP now once again threatened to erupt. At its meeting of 25 April, the DNVP executive board (*Vorstand*) came down on the side of Hugenberg, thus making it clear that in the event of another division, control of party finances and organization would remain with the wing loyal to Hugenberg. The executive board sharply criticized those deputies who had voted in favor of Brüning, demanded party discipline both inside the party and parliamentary faction when it came to decisive votes, and committed the future course of the party to fundamental opposition to Brüning's policies.[115] This put an end to Westarp's hopes for close cooperation with Brüning, just as it thwarted the hope of the Chancellor and Treviranus of expanding their support base to the right. A further party split now appeared inevitable. Westarp's supporters, who rebelled against Hugenberg's dictatorial party tactics, had an interest in bringing about a break as soon as possible, for it was evident that Brüning's controversial program would soon result in the dissolution of the Reichstag and new elections. If this were to happen, the Hugenberg-controlled party apparatus would undoubtedly ensure that all those inimical to the chairman would no longer be put up as candidates.[116] To preempt further splits and a consolidation of the various groups of German Nationals that had left the DNVP, Hugenberg encouraged a speedy dissolution of the Reichstag, especially since he was well aware of the seething discontent in the Reichstag faction and knew that further ruptures were only a question of time.

115. Bracher, *Auflösung*, 327.
116. Westarp was well aware of the weak position in which a new conservative party without a party organization would find itself. See Bracher, *Auflösung*, 329, note 178.

In mid June 1930, Brüning's government was mired in its first major crisis. Financial difficulties had induced Finance Minister Paul Moldenhauer to face reductions in civil servants' salaries (*Reichshilfe der Festbesoldeten*) against vehement opposition from his own party, the DVP.[117] Because of the stubbornly high level of unemployment, the appropriations resolutions of April were no longer sufficient to satisfy the Reich's financial needs. The difficulty of rallying a parliamentary majority for an amended appropriations bill soon became obvious. Before the decisive ballots of 16 and 18 July 1930 it had also transpired that the government had little hope of winning over the larger part of the DNVP faction.[118] With Hindenburg's announcement on 16 July that the appropriations program would be pushed through using Article 48 if necessary, it became clear that the establishment of a regime based on emergency decrees could no longer be prevented. In the crucial ballot of 16 July 1930, the government was clearly defeated by a vote of 193 to 256 (with opposing votes from the KPD, SPD, NSDAP, and a majority of DNVP deputies). Brüning responded by imposing his program using emergency decrees. The following day, the SPD initiated another motion of no confidence against his government. Since discussions between Hugenberg and Brüning on 17 July failed to produce the desired result—Hugenberg's promise to support Brüning—the Reichstag session on the following day was the last for the parliamentary body that had been voted in on 20 May 1928. In that critical session of 18 July 1930, the renewed division in the DNVP became apparent: DNVP faction leader Ernst Oberfohren voted against the Brüning program, while his predecessor, Graf Westarp, voted for Brüning and against the no confidence motion. Since a majority of DNVP deputies voted for the no confidence measure, however, it passed by a relatively narrow margin of 236 to 222 votes. As a result, Brüning proclaimed the dissolution of the Reichstag, and reenacted (in more severe form) the emergency legislation that had just been annulled by a Reichstag resolution, a decision that rendered it all too plain

117. Heinrich-August Winkler, *Der Weg in die Katastrophe. Arbeiter und Arbeiterbewegung in der Weimarer Republik 1930 bis 1933* (Berlin & Bonn, 1987), 123–187.

118. Already on 7 July, Ernst Oberfohren, who had taken over the position of faction leader from Graf Westarp in December 1929, spoke out against the government's tax proposals. The SPD also rejected the government's tax program, albeit for different reasons. See Bracher, *Auflösung*, 337–338; Winkler, *Weimar*, 378–380; Winkler, *Der Weg in die Katastrophe*, 123–187.

that the Chancellor was fully prepared to venture into hitherto un-explored constitutional territory.[119] Just before the decisive vote on 18 July, Westarp issued a statement on behalf of twenty-five deputies endorsing Brüning's emergency legislation.[120] The second division implied in this announcement was formally confirmed on 24 July by a resolution of the party executive committee, which condoned Hugenberg's attitude and condemned the members of the Westarp group for the way they had voted.[121] Those deputies expelled from the DNVP for supporting Brüning were partly absorbed by the Konservative Volkspartei, the Christlich-Sozialer Volksdienst, and the Landvolk. These splinter parties continued to back Brüning's government, though they became ever more worn down, marginal-ized, and deserted by their voters because of the increasing radical-ization of the political struggle. Only the Volksdienst would survive the July 1932 election. The dissolution of the fourth Reichstag, elected in May 1928, compelled Brüning to call for new elections that had to be held within 60 days. Many consider it tragic that Brüning failed to come to an understanding with the SPD, since the more favorable majority ratios of the fourth Reichstag might have remained in place until May 1932 had the dissolution of parliament been avoided. This view, however, does not sufficiently account for the fact that, because of Hindenburg's (and Brüning's) bias against the SPD, an agreement with the Social Democrats would hardly have been feasible.

119. In his appropriations bill for the reform of state finances, Brüning pur-sued a rigorous deflationary policy: reduction of public spending; tax increases, especially on high incomes; and an "emergency contribution" for those with guaranteed incomes (*"Notopfer der Festbesoldeten"*). Since Brüning had apparently counted on obtaining a sufficient number of votes from DNVP renegades (ac-cording to Winkler, *Weimar*, 380, Brüning needed at least 39 DNVP votes), he eschewed the possibility of sounding out a compromise with the SPD, which might have been a viable option. (Kolb, *Weimar*, 133–35). According to SPD deputy Wilhelm Keil, even minor modifications in Brüning's spending reduc-tion program would have sufficed to win SPD support. See Wilhelm Keil, *Erleb-nisse eines Sozialdemokaten*, vol. II (Stuttgart, 1948), 335–337.

120. Hiller von Gaertingen, "DNVP," 552, mentioned the number of twenty-five deputies. In a meeting on the evening of 17 July, a majority of thirty-four to twenty-one votes was established for the SPD's no confidence motion (according to Winkler, *Weimar*, 380).

121. Bracher, *Auflösung*, 349–351. After the split, Graf Westarp defended his group of renegades by castigating Hugenberg's dictatorial leadership style. Be-ginning in early 1929, Hugenberg had allegedly used pressure and threats of ex-pulsion from the party to keep deputies in line.

The DNVP and the Rise of Nazism

The elections of 14 September 1930 fundamentally changed Weimar's political landscape as the NSDAP swept into the position of second strongest party after the SPD.[122] Election results even had international repercussions, as French banks withdrew their short-term credit from Germany in reaction to Nazi successes, leading to an aggravation of the economic crisis and shortages of foreign currency in German banks.[123] The DNVP was cut down to 7 percent and 41 seats, whereas the NSDAP now had, with 18.3 percent of the vote, 107 seats at their disposal. The balance of power between the two parties had reversed itself—a trend that would become even more accentuated in coming years. The stagnation of the DNVP at a low level, eventually even a further decrease to 5.9 percent and 37 seats in the elections of 31 July 1932, contrasted sharply with the apparently inexorable advance of the NSDAP over the next two years.[124] The DNVP and NSDAP shared a number of important ideological common denominators, from extreme nationalism to anti-parliamentarianism and opposition to the Republic, but at its core the DNVP remained a *bürgerliche Partei*, while the identity of the Nazi party was distinctly anti-*bürgerlich* and radical, with revolutionary overtones in its public pronouncements and propaganda. How did Hugenberg's DNVP react to the ascendant threat on the political far Right?

122. This did not happen completely unexpectedly since the NSDAP had made substantial gains in elections to Land parliaments in 1929. Whereas the NSDAP had attained only 2.6 percent in the Reichstag vote of 20 May 1928 (and only 1.8 percent in the Prussian Landtag vote on the same day), the party's electorate rose to 3.4 percent in elections in Lippe on 6 January 1929; 5.0 percent in Saxony on 12 May 1929; 4.1 percent in Mecklenburg-Schwerin on 23 June 1929; 7.0 percent in Baden on 27 October 1929; 8.1 percent in Lübeck on 10 November 1929; 11.3 percent in Thuringia on 8 December 1929, and finally to 14.4 percent in a second election in Saxony on 22 June 1930.

123. Eyck, *Geschichte*, II, 354–355; Schulze, *Weimar*, 346–347.

124. In the Bremen elections on 30 November 1930: NSDAP 25.4 percent; DNVP 5.7 percent; in Schaumburg-Lippe on 3 May 1931: NSDAP 27 percent; DNVP 10.1 percent (in 1928, the DNVP gained 16.6 percent); in Oldenburg on 17 May 1931: NSDAP 37.2 percent; DNVP 4.8 percent; in Hamburg on 27 September 1931: NSDAP 26.2 percent; DNVP 5.6 percent (in 1928, the DNVP received 13.7 percent); finally in Hesse on 15 November 1931: NSDAP 37.1 percent; DNVP 1.4 percent. See Jürgen Falter, Thomas Lindenberger, and Siegfried Schumann, *Wahlen und Abstimmungen in der Weimarer Republik. Materialien zum Wahlverhalten, 1919–1933* (Munich, 1986), 89–113.

After Hugenberg had assumed the party leadership and succeeded in expelling his main opponents from the party organization and Reichstag faction, the DNVP moved closer to the NSDAP. With its rigorous "blockade politics" and constant stonewalling, the DNVP now appeared fully prepared to work toward the collapse of the Weimar Republic, thereby inching closer to Hitler's policies. Yet, even after the dramatic reversal of fortune at the ballot box, Hugenberg continued to treat the NSDAP as a junior partner that, he believed, could be used for his own ends, even though Nazi propagandizing against the "Reaction" and "reactionaries"—big capital and the bourgeois establishment (which the DNVP represented)—continued unabated. Seemingly blinded to the dangers, Hugenberg would continue underestimating the dynamics inherent in National Socialism until it was too late.[125] On the surface, the year 1931 appeared to be a time of increased collaboration between the two parties of the far right. When the Reichstag voted to adopt proposals curtailing excessive politicking in parliament by Nazis and communists in February 1931, German National deputies walked out of the Reichstag building together with their NSDAP colleagues. The DNVP's 1931 party conference in Stettin (19–20 September) was built up as a demonstration of unity. Trying to emulate Nazi successes, the DNVP eagerly imitated National Socialism by declaring that the party would strive to become a "Hugenberg movement" and attempting to integrate the "leadership principle" into inner-party practice. In a vain effort to create its own storm troopers or at least some kind of substitute SA, the DNVP now enlarged and expanded the hitherto-neglected *Kampfstaffeln* (fighter squadrons) that had grown out of the *Bismarckbund*.[126] DNVP members, who advocated the transition from a political party to a movement like National Socialism, failed to consider that Nazi successes could not be easily replicated. In the spring of 1931, another joint action of the Right brought together the DNVP, DVP, NSDAP, Wirtschaftspartei, and

125. Jones, " 'The Greatest Stupidity of My Life,' " 63–87.
126. Hiller von Gaertingen, "DNVP," 553–556. The name varied: they were also referred to as *Kampfgemeinschaft* and *Kampfring*. The DNVP was not alone in adopting the "leadership principle." Most conservative groups in the late Weimar Republic subscribed to it as an effective political strategy. See Kurt Sontheimer, *Antidemokratisches Denken in der Weimarer Republik* (Munich, 1978), 214–24; Klemens von Klemperer, *Germany's New Conservatism* (Princeton, 1957); Armin Mohler, *Die Konservative Revolution in Deutschland, 1918–1932*, 3rd ed. (Darmstadt, 1989).

the *Stahlhelm*. This was the organization of a referendum to bring about the dissolution of the Prussian Landtag, the last stronghold of the SPD and Center Party. The referendum held on 9 August 1931 failed, however, even after the KPD had joined in the attempt, since only 9.8 million votes (36.9 percent of the electorate; 13.2 million votes were needed) were cast in favor of dissolution.[127] In Prussia, Otto Braun's government thus won a little breathing space until the next regularly scheduled elections on 24 April 1932.

Perhaps the best-known cooperative venture of the Right was the meeting of the "National Front" in Bad Harzburg on 10 to 11 October 1931. Held at Hugenberg's initiative, the *Harzburger Front* brought together most political forces inimical to the Republic (except for the KPD), though it was ultimately more an expression of will and a façade without great political significance. Bad Harzburg in the northern German state of Braunschweig was intentionally selected as the meeting place since both the DNVP and NSDAP were represented in its state government, and Weimar's political opponents could safely gather there, out of reach of the clutches of the Prussian police, who were under the authority of the hated Social Democrats. On the eve of the Harzburg meeting, President von Hindenburg received Hitler and Göring for the first time, thereby strengthening the NSDAP's position in Harzburg. In addition to German Nationals and Nazis, the gathering included monarchists from the officer corps and the patriotic leagues, members of the DVP, Pan-Germans, the leadership of the *Reichslandbund*, retired officers such as the former head of the Reichswehr, Hans von Seeckt, and industrialists and financiers such as Fritz von Thyssen and Hjalmar Schacht.[128] Those present had little in common except for their animosity toward the Republic. National Socialists in attendance were especially intent on maintaining their independence and pointedly steered their own course. Before the beginning of official functions, the NSDAP Reichstag faction held a separate gathering, where faction leader Wilhelm Frick emphasized that any alliance with the German Nationals would be based on purely tactical motivations. In

127. Kolb, *Weimarer Republik*, 135.

128. On the *Harzburger Front*, see Gerhard Schulz, *Von Brüning zu Hitler. Zwischen Demokratie und Diktatur*, vol. III (Berlin, New York, 1992), 554–560; Brüning, *Memoiren*, 425–428; Bracher, *Auflösung*, 407–415; Winkler, *Der Weg in die Katastrophe*, 432–435. Winkler noted that Brüning's sharpest critics from the camp of industrialists and employers seemed to hold back, and representatives of heavy industry and the DVP turned out only in small numbers (p. 432).

his Berlin newspaper *Der Angriff,* Goebbels equally made no bones about the fact that tactical considerations were decisive in the (only temporary and instrumental) alliance with the German Nationals, since a legal assumption of power would be possible only through the formation of a coalition government.[129] As if consciously trying to provoke indignation, Hitler very demonstratively left the VIP stand after his SA formations had marched past.[130] Though Hugenberg presided over most of the sessions, he made concession after concession, as Bracher wrote, "with the indulgence born of assured arrogance that is fed by the certainty of being in command."[131]

By the time Brüning resigned office on 30 May 1932, merely eight months before the Nazi seizure of power, Weimar's political landscape had fundamentally changed: the public increasingly had become accustomed to the idea of authoritarian solutions; the bureaucracy had gained in significance as the executive organ that implemented Brüning's emergency decrees, the Reichstag had been effectively eliminated from political decision making, and the army leadership, as well as the president, had come to hold the key positions. In the formation of the successor government to Brüning, Franz von Papen's "Cabinet of Barons," Hugenberg was ostentatiously passed over in the selection of ministerial posts. His uncompromising obduracy and steadfast obstructionism had long been a thorn in Hindenburg's side, with the result that other conservatives received ministerial portfolios in Hugenberg's place, such as Wilhelm Freiherr von Gayl as Minister of the Interior and Franz Gürtner as Minister of Justice.[132] In the elections of 31 July 1932, the DNVP was reduced to 5.9 percent and thirty-seven seats, its worst showing ever. Given the election results, there now existed the theoretical possibility of a coalition between Nazis and the Center/Bavarian People's Party, which together held an absolute majority of 53 percent. Following the breakdown of negotiations between Hitler, Papen and Schleicher on 13 August 1932 over the entry of the

---

129. "Von Harzburg nach Braunschweig," *Der Angriff,* 21 October 1931; "Die nationale Opposition," *Der Angriff,* 19 December 1931; and Bracher, *Auflösung,* 413.

130. Theodor Duesterberg, *Der Stahlhelm und Hitler* (Wolfenbüttel and Hannover, 1949).

131. Bracher wrote: "mit der Nachgiebigkeit des führungsgewissen Hochmuts." In *Auflösung,* 410–411.

132. Ulrike Hörster-Philipps, *Konservative Politik in der Endphase der Weimarer Republik: Die Regierung Franz von Papen* (Cologne, 1982).

NSDAP in Papen's cabinet, Hitler called off his truce with Papen. After the—to outward appearances—grandiose success in the July elections, in which the NSDAP had become the strongest party by far with almost 38 percent of the vote, Hitler claimed, among other things, the office of Chancellor for himself. He felt duped by Schleicher and Papen when Hindenburg (in what Hitler considered to be humiliating attendant circumstances) pointedly refused to entrust the office to his care.[133] As a result of the 13 August meeting, Hitler and his party fought the DNVP, Papen's main parliamentary supporter, tooth and nail. Hugenberg, in fact, staked everything on Papen's "New State"—an authoritarian, anti-parliamentary system that was closer to dictatorship than democracy—and stressed his party's role as the "political army of the New State."[134] On 12 September 1932, the Nazi party supported a communist no-confidence motion against Papen to overthrow his government. Despite Papen's attempt to dissolve the Reichstag immediately (he carried Hindenburg's dissolution order with him), Hermann Göring, the newly elected speaker of house, overrode him and went ahead with the vote. The result of 512 to 42 votes against Papen, who was supported only by the DNVP and DVP, was disastrous for the Chancellor in that it laid bare the exceedingly slim basis on which his government was built. The subsequent elections of 6 November, though increasing the number of DNVP deputies by fifteen, left the overall picture unaltered.[135] Thus, after Papen again had vainly tried to secure Nazi support for his government, Schleicher forced the President (who had conceived a liking for Papen) to act and dismiss the Chancellor by demonstrating that Papen's scheme of authoritarian government without popular backing might well result in a civil war that would be beyond the capacity of the police and Reichswehr

133. Josef Becker, "Prälat Kaas und das Problem einer Regierungsbeteiligung der NSDAP 1930–1932," *Historische Zeitschrift* 196 (1963), 74–111. Hitler was offered merely the unattractive post of Vice-Chancellor, and Hindenburg upbraided him like a schoolboy for his refusal to continue supporting Papen's government.

134. Bracher, *Auflösung*, 529–559.

135. The NSDAP lost two million votes and thirty-four seats; the DNVP gained about 800,000 votes and fifteen seats; the SPD and Center had slight losses of twelve and five seats respectively; and the KPD became the third-strongest party in the Reichstag with almost six million votes and a hundred seats. See Kolb, *Weimarer Republik*, 308–309.

to contain.[136] With extreme reluctance, Hindenburg relented and, in a tearful interview, parted from his preferred Chancellor. On 2 December 1932, Schleicher emerged from behind the scenes and assumed the post of Chancellor himself.

In the autumn of 1932, during the run-up to the 6 November Reichstag elections, the relations between the Nazi party and the DNVP reached their absolute nadir. The DNVP and the Papen government became the principal targets of a Nazi propaganda machine at its most slanderous and offensive. German Nationals noted indignantly that "the pact with us has been torn apart," while Goebbels's Berlin paper, *Der Angriff*, called for a "Reckoning with the *Hugenzwerg*."[137] The Nazi press poured disdain and derision over Hugenberg, suggesting that he had to be a magician, since he hoped to turn "an insignificant heap of reactionaries" into a people's movement. In September, Nazis broke up German National election meetings with stink bombs and tear gas; they accused the prominent German National deputy Axel von Freytagh-Loringhoven of being a traitor to the fatherland, since he allegedly fought against Germany as a czarist officer; and, in the Prussian Landtag, Nazi deputies heckled a German National deputy and called him "Jew boy," as the socialist *Vorwärts* gleefully reported.[138] And so it continued. Helene Freifrau von Watter, a German National deputy and physician by profession, was threatened with a beating by NSDAP deputies for calling Nazis in the Prussian Landtag *"Schweine"*; Wilhelm Kube, leader of the NSDAP faction in the Prussian Landtag and himself

136. In a war game commissioned by Schleicher, it was convincingly demonstrated that the government did not have sufficient forces at its disposal to master such a contingency. See Thilo Vogelsang, *Reichswehr, Staat und NSDAP* (Stuttgart, 1962), 316–317; Eyck, *Geschichte*, II, 483–549; Winkler, *Weimar*, 477–521; Ulrike Hörster-Philipps, *Konservative Politik in der Endphase der Weimarer Republik. Die Regierung Franz von Papen* (Cologne, 1982); Franz von Papen, *Der Wahrheit eine Gasse* (Munich, 1952), 215–253.

137. A play on words: "Berg" means mountain; "Zwerg" means dwarf. BA Berlin-Lichterfelde, "Pressearchiv Reichslandbund, NSDAP and DNVP," R 8034, II, no. 9030, 7–8.

138. BA Berlin-Lichterfelde, "Pressearchiv Reichslandbund," ibid., 9–10. Axel von Freytagh-Loringhoven (1878–1942), a member of a prominent Baltic German family and, though ethnically German, a Russian subject, was a professor of constitutional law at the University of Dorpat (present-day Tartu in Estonia) during the war and was exempt from military service. Before 1911, he had served as a cavalry officer in the Russian army. He was known to be one of the more anti-Semitic DNVP deputies.

a former member of the DNVP from 1919 to 1923, emphasized the need to "fight the DNVP to the death"; and on 27 September 1932, National Socialists, in an attempt to break up a German National meeting in Breslau, seriously injured seven people (mostly *Stahlhelm* members). Following this incident, another German National meeting was prohibited by the police for fear that it might be stormed by Nazis.[139] At the end of September 1932, Goebbels's *Angriff* accused Hugenberg and the German Nationals of "conceit, megalomania, and caste spirit," and Goebbels issued a party order not to read the "bourgeois national press," whereupon Hugenberg and his Scherl publishing house sued him. Faced with an injunction to pay 300,000 marks, serve a six-month jail term, or rescind the ban, Goebbels was prevailed upon to choose the latter.[140]

But even after the 6 November elections, when a coalition between the NSDAP and the Center/Bavarian People's Party would no longer result in an absolute majority, relations between German Nationals and National Socialists did not improve. In the Reichstag sessions of 6–9 December 1932, for example, Nazi deputies still mocked and derided Hugenberg openly. The leader of the DNVP had been named *Schriftführer* (recording clerk) of parliament. At each mention of Hugenberg as the "leader" (*Führer*) of the German Nationals, the Nazi deputies broke out into deafening heckling, yelling "*Schrift*führer!"[141] It was in this mutually hostile, poisoned, and bitterly resentful atmosphere that the fateful alliance between the German National People's Party and Hitler came into being.

German National Assessments of Nazism before 1933

How did the *bürgerliche* DNVP assess the Nazi party in the two years after the Nazi breakthrough at the polls in September 1930? This

---

139. BA Berlin-Lichterfelde, "Pressearchiv Reichslandbund," ibid., 14–15, 17, 19. On the Breslau incident see "Stahlhelmpogrom in Breslau. Stahlhelmer viehisch mishandelt," *Vorwärts*, 28 September 1932; "Nationalsozialistischer Versammlungsterror in Breslau," *Deutsche Allgemeine Zeitung*, 28 September 1932.

140. BA Berlin-Lichterfelde, "Pressearchiv Reichslandbund," ibid., 16, 26. See also "Ein Jahr nach Harzburg. Nationalsozialistische Stinkbomben gegen Deutschnationale. 'An den Galgen mit Hugenberg,'" *Morgenpost*, 29 September 1932; "Hugenberg gegen Goebbels," *Vorwärts*, 30 September 1932.

141. Meaning: He may be a leading clerk but no "leader." See Hiller von Gaertingen, "DNVP," 566.

relationship can best be illuminated from statements in the German National local press, since local party newspapers reacted more bluntly to the political upheavals of the day than the larger Berlin conservative dailies, such as the *Kreuzzeitung* or *Der Tag*. The German National press response to political events in which the Nazis showed their true colors (and which also provided a foretaste of what was in store for Germany once Hitler was in power) are revealing with regard to German National attitudes about their future coalition partner.[142] Analyzed in the local context, German National reactions can be directly compared with those of other *bürgerliche* presses, namely Center Party publications and liberal mainstream urban mass circulation dailies. The southern German university town of Freiburg im Breisgau, a city with about 100,000 inhabitants and several daily papers in 1933, offers a productive field of investigation in this endeavor.[143] The dailies were mostly *bürgerlich* in orientation: the liberal *Freiburger Zeitung* (close to the DVP) had the highest circulation by far, followed by the Center Party newspaper, *Freiburger Tagespost*, and the German National *Breisgauer Zeitung*.[144]

In the last two years of the Weimar Republic the Nazis made few bones about their ultimate goals and, on several occasions, clearly indicated by their actions what the German population could

142. In 1927 there were 444 DNVP newspapers. Of these, 341 appeared six times per week and thirty-nine even had a Sunday edition and appeared seven times weekly. Among this latter group counted the large conservative daily, *Der Tag*, which belonged to Hugenberg's *Scherl Verlag* and had a circulation of about 100,000. Maximilian Müller-Jabusch, *Handbuch des öffentlichen Lebens*, 5th ed. (Leipzig, 1929), 664.

143. Even though Freiburg was demographically not typical for the Reich as a whole: two-thirds of Freiburg's population was Catholic (as opposed to 32.5 percent for Germany in 1933) and, compared with the Reich average, Freiburg had a larger proportionate share of civil servants and *Angestellte* (white-collar employees) and fewer blue-collar workers. Public service, trade, and commerce were overrepresented, the industrial sector underrepresented. See Statistisches Amt Freiburg, ed., "Die wichtigsten Ergebnisse der Volks-, Berufs- und Betriebszählung vom 16. Juni 1933 in Freiburg," *Beiträge zur Statistik der Stadt Freiburg* 7 (Freiburg, 1937), 18, 32, 37, 56, 68, 75.

144. Otto Haffner, "Geschichte und Entwicklung der Freiburger Tagespresse," *Zeitschrift für Geschichtsforschung von Freiburg* 34 & 35 (Freiburg, 1919–1920). On the structure of the German press before 1933, see Oron Hale, *The Captive Press in the Third Reich* (Princeton, 1964), 1–15. For more information on Freiburg's local press, see Hermann Beck, "Lokalpresse und Aufstieg der NSDAP. Eine Studie anhand bürgerlicher Freiburger Tageszeitungen," M.A. thesis (Freiburg, 1981).

expect in the event of a National Socialist takeover. In this context, the "Boxheim documents" offered a foretaste of what was to
come after stirring the public in the wake of the November 1931
Hessian Land elections, as did the murder in the Silesian town of
Potempa during Papen's tenure in office on 10 August 1932. The
Boxheim documents (named after a manor house in Southern Hesse
near Lampertheim), prepared by Werner Best, legal advisor to the
Hessian NSDAP, were detailed contingency plans for a response to
an anticipated communist coup.[145] Best's plans were indeed astonishing: after crushing the communist revolt (which hypothetically
had resulted in the removal of traditional state authorities), all power
was to pass into the hands of the SA. Any noncompliance with SA
orders would be met with the death penalty.[146] Civil servants and
public employees who refused to resume their regular duties were
to be shot "without trial, on the spot." Private property was to be
abolished until further notice. Only those who performed their
duty by taking part in a national labor service would be guaranteed
food stamps. In Best's conception, those who were to be excluded
from labor service and food stamps, such as "non-Aryans," were
condemned to starvation. After the Boxheim documents had been
made public, it was generally expected that drastic measures would
be taken to curb National Socialist activities. The Nazi leadership
protested its innocence, asserting that the documents were drawn
up by Hessian National Socialists alone and thus wholly unknown
to them. Besides, they argued, they were based on the premise that
a communist rebellion had taken place, so that the proposed measures should be judged solely as a reaction to such an event. These
excuses carried considerable weight: despite the insistence of Prussian Interior Minister Carl Severing, the Attorney General (*Oberreichsanwalt*) refrained from initiating criminal proceedings based on
the charge of "high treason" against the Nazis. Nevertheless, at the

---

145. Schulz, *Von Brüning zu Hitler*, 604–610; Ulrich Herbert, *Best: Biographische Studien über Radikalismus, Weltanschauung und Vernunft 1903–1989*, 2nd
ed. (Bonn, 1996), 112–119; Bracher, *Auflösung*, 431–435; Winkler, *Der Weg in die
Katastrophe*, 448–451. For the text of the document, see Wolfgang Michalka and
Gottfried Niedhart, eds., *Deutsche Geschichte 1918–1933. Dokumente zur Innen-
und Aussenpolitik* (Frankfurt, 1992), 203–206.

146. During the Second World War, Werner Best became *Reichskommissar*
for Denmark. He was sentenced to death in 1948, but then pardoned in 1951.
See Herbert, *Best*, as well as Hermann Weiß, ed., *Biographisches Lexikon zum
Dritten Reich*, 2nd ed. (Frankfurt, 1998), 39–41.

end of November 1931, the case of the Boxheim documents dominated the front pages of every large and small (non-Nazi) paper in
the Reich.

The reaction of the Freiburg liberal mainstream and Center Party
press ranged from indignation to horror. Commentators on the
Boxheim documents denounced the intended infringement upon
private property, drew comparisons between Nazis and Communists, condemned forced labor and other propositions that smacked
of dictatorship, and raised the burning issue that a National Socialist Germany might resemble the blueprint so clearly laid out in the
documents.[147] The German National *Breisgauer Zeitung*, on the other
hand, downplayed the whole incident by arguing that "a racket
about high treason was artificially staged against the Right" and by
appearing convinced that the National Socialist leadership had been
oblivious to the events in Hesse. The *Breisgauer Zeitung* merely commented: "Something as immature as this playing around with dictatorship (*Diktaturspielerei*) is absolutely inconceivable . . ."[148] After
Boxheim, anyone could easily see the clear writing on the wall
about the goals and methods of the Nazi party. Yet, this potential
warning to beware of future alliances with the NSDAP was all too
quickly swept under the carpet by the German Nationals. The facts
are obvious: the Boxheim documents did indeed constitute a "blueprint" of a future Nazi dictatorship, a blueprint that was discussed
in every corner of the German Reich in the late fall of 1931, since
countless daily papers made the documents the object of intense
reporting and detailed commentary. There are two possible explanations as to why the Boxheim affair was not taken more seriously
as a general warning of things to come: the claim that responsibility
lay only with the Hessian National Socialists, not the NSDAP as a
whole, and, perhaps more significantly, the general misery and all-
pervasive corrosion of social mores and political culture that characterized the last years of the Weimar Republic. This decline was
not limited to palpable problems, such as continually climbing unemployment rates, lack of prospects for the future, and rising crime
and suicide rates. A less tangible, but equally potent danger resulted

147. "NSDAP in Hessen," *Freiburger Zeitung*, 27 November 1931; "Das Boxheimer Dokument," *Freiburger Tagespost*, 30 November 1931; "Zum Boxheimer
Skandal," *Freiburger Tagespost*, 2 December 1931. On the whole, the Center Party
press did not react as sharply as may have been expected, because Brüning hoped
to drive a wedge between the DNVP and NSDAP after the Harzburg meeting.
148. "Die Bilanz von Boxheim," *Breisgauer Zeitung*, 1 December 1931.

from the erosion of long-standing political practices and traditions: election campaigns dominated by murder and deadly beatings; the unending accumulation of well-publicized political corruption cases that made the public wary of the parliamentary system's ability to function at all; and, finally, an inflation of outrageous and radical political opinions of all kinds that knew no bounds, to the extent that newspaper readers no longer took warnings of coming catastrophes very seriously.

Meanwhile, there was no shortage of warnings. The summer of 1932 saw a second and equally ominous portent of things to come that was connected with the escalating political violence. Street battles between paramilitary organizations of the Left and the SA had become increasingly acrimonious during the July 1932 election campaign. Especially after Papen's government lifted the ban on uniforms (part of the price Papen paid for the NSDAP's toleration of his Cabinet), an atmosphere akin to civil war descended upon the streets of many Prussian cities. The most notorious example was the "bloody Sunday" in Altona where, on Sunday, 17 July, the SA, marching through a working-class quarter of the city, got caught in a communist ambush.[149] The street battle that followed claimed more than fifteen lives.[150] Directly following the elections of 31 July, the Nazis took bloody revenge on their communist enemies in the east Prussian capital Königsberg. In order to put a stop to the spiral of ever-intensifying political violence, Papen's government issued an ordinance on 9 August 1932 that made "deadly assaults" upon political opponents punishable by the death penalty. The sentencing of political crimes would be executed in summary trials by special courts.[151]

149. On street violence in 1932, see Richard Bessel, *Political Violence and the Rise of Nazism. The Storm Troopers in Eastern Germany, 1925–1934* (New Haven, 1984); Peter Merkl, *Political Violence under the Swastika. 581 Early Nazis* (Princeton, 1975); Wehler, *Gesellschaftsgeschichte, 1914–1949*, vol. IV, 495–588; Mommsen, *Rise and Fall of Weimar Democracy*, 438–490; Winkler, *Weimar*, 477–521; Schulze, *Weimar*, 372–391.

150. At that time Altona was part of the Prussian province of Schleswig-Holstein. Papen used the events of 17 July 1932 as a pretext for his *"Preußenschlag"* of 20 July 1932, when he declared a state of emergency in Prussia and removed the Braun government. Karl-Heinz Minuth, ed., *Akten der Reichskanzlei. Das Kabinett von Papen*, Vol. I (Boppard, 1989), 248–316.

151. The 9 August decree threatened the death penalty for those who "in the passion of political struggle undertook a deadly attack on their opponents out of

The Potempa murder was as telling as the Boxheim documents in predicting future Nazi actions. On the night of 10 August 1932, in the small upper Silesian town of Potempa, five uniformed SA men forced their way into the lodgings of the communist laborer Pietrzuch, clubbed and trampled him to death in front of his mother's very eyes, and severely injured his brother through similar abuse. In accordance with the new ordinance, all five SA men were sentenced to death by a special court in Beuthen on 22 August. The murder in Potempa caused an immense sensation in the press throughout the Reich. The scandal was further intensified when it became known that Hitler sent a telegram to the condemned SA men, in which he assured them of his solidarity with their actions and declared: "My comrades, faced with this most monstrous blood judgment I find myself joined with you in unbounded loyalty. From this day, your freedom has become a question of our honor."[152] In the Nazi *Völkischer Beobachter* Hitler turned, in threatening posture, on Papen: "Herr von Papen, I now know your bloody objectivity well. . . . We will liberate the concept of 'national-mindedness' from the clutches of an 'objectivity' whose inner essence sets the judgment of Beuthen against nationalist Germany. Herr von Papen has thereby engraved his name with the blood of national warriors on German history."[153] This undisguised public threat might have served Papen and the DNVP as an unmistakable warning and ought to have convinced them to do everything possible to prevent Hitler from coming to power. In his proclamation to Papen, Hitler clearly hinted at the disdain for legal practices in a future National Socialist dictatorship and dropped the deceptive mask of legality he had heretofore obligingly adopted.

Freiburg's Center Party press struck up an unambiguously anti-Nazi tone, despite coalition negotiations between the Center Party and the NSDAP, and raised general concerns about legal practices in a future Nazi state, pointing to Hitler's double standards and comparing Nazi legal practice "to the Bolshevik concept of law as one

---

anger and hatred, even if no premeditation was involved." See Schulz, *Von Brüning zu Hitler*, 958–961.

152. Eyck, *Geschichte*, II, 515–516.

153. Ibid. Hitler knew well enough that he could justify himself by referring to the fact that the murdered worker Pietrzuch had fought on the Polish side for the inclusion of Upper Silesia into Poland after World War I. This branded him as a traitor to the German national cause.

reduced to a mere servant of politics in the total state."[154] The liberal mainstream *Freiburger Zeitung* cautiously pointed to the severity of the sentence for this "bloody deed," arguing that one would
have "to go far back in German legal history to find a comparable
case of mass execution," while the German National *Breisgauer Zeitung* unapologetically mentioned that the "dead man of Potempa,"
whose life was "now to be atoned for with five death sentences"
had after all "fought on the Polish side as an insurgent against his
fatherland."[155] The *Breisgauer Zeitung* conspicuously held back criticism and even expressed understanding for "calling this traitor to
the fatherland to account,"[156] despite the fact that relations between
the DNVP (which remained the political pillar of Papen's government) and the Nazis were at a low ebb in the late summer of 1932.

Given that German Nationals were prepared to make allowances
for Nazi murder and freely condone other breaches of the law at a
time when their relations were strained, it was unlikely that they
would exert an effective moderating influence on Nazi excesses
under the very different conditions prevailing during the period of
the Nazi seizure of power, especially after entering a formal coalition with the NSDAP. The following six chapters focus on the relationship between the DNVP and the conservative establishment it
represented, on the one hand, and the Nazis, on the other, from 30
January 1933—the day Hindenburg transferred the chancellorship
to Hitler—to mid July of that year when, with a ban on all political
parties other than the NSDAP, the first phase of the Nazi revolution
came to an end.

154. "Sturmzeichen," *Freiburger Tagespost*, 25 August 1932. Those on the nationalist side, the paper continued, were to be spared, even if they committed
heinous crimes.

155. "Gnade für Recht," *Freiburger Zeitung*, 24 August 1932; "Ohlau und
Beuthen," *Breisgauer Zeitung*, 24 August 1932.

156. "Ohlau und Beuthen." In another article, "Wiederaufnahme" of 25 August, the *Breisgauer Zeitung* wrote that different yardsticks applied when crimes
against "national-minded Germans" were committed, indicating that a retrial
was in order.

Chapter II

UNEASY PARTNERS

The Relationship between the DNVP
and the Nazis, 30 January–5 March

The immediate events surrounding Hitler's appointment to the
Chancellorship have been the subject of much detailed recent
scholarship so that, in the context of the present study, it will suf-
fice to emphasize a number of salient points.[1] (1) The transient
character of Schleicher's Chancellorship was apparent from the
first, not least because Schleicher remained in the Ministry of Defense at the Bendlerstrasse, while Papen resided in close proximity to Hindenburg in the Ministry of the Interior and continued
to enjoy privileged access to the president. The failure of Schleicher's grand design—to create a government based on the support of trade unions and the left wing of the Nazi party—became

---

1. Turner, *Hitler's Thirty Days to Power* offers the most up-to-date and
detailed account. The German translation of Turner's study, *Hitler's Weg zur
Macht. Der Januar 1933* (Munich, 1996), contains the "Moscow Document,"
Schleicher's thoughts on the occasion of a dinner on 13 January 1933. See also
Broszat, *Die Machtergreifung*; Eyck, *Geschichte*, II, 549–597; Gordon Craig, *Ger-
many 1866–1945* (Oxford, 1978), 565–569; Winkler, *Weimar*, 557–594. On the
role of the DNVP see Otto Schmidt-Hannover, *Umdenken oder Anarchie* (Göt-
tingen, 1958), 317–343; Hiller von Gaertingen, "DNVP," 567–576; Leopold,
Alfred Hugenberg, 127–139; Weiß and Hoser, eds., *Die Deutschnationalen*; Larry E.
Jones, "'The Greatest Stupidity of My Life,'" 63–87; and Larry E. Jones, "Nazis,
Conservatives, and the Establishment of the Third Reich, 1932–34," *Tel Aviver
Jahrbuch für Deutsche Geschichte: Nationalsozialismus aus heutiger Perspektive* (1994),
41–64.

apparent after only a few weeks.[2] (2) The Nazi party rose to power
at a time when its fortunes seemed on the wane. Not only had the
NSDAP lost two million votes, about 15 percent of its electorate, in the November elections, it also suffered further losses at
local elections in Thuringia, thus reinforcing the impression of an
unstoppable downward trend.[3] At the beginning of the new year,
Weimar's democratic press rejoiced that the Nazi movement now
seemed inexorably relegated to the rubble heap of history.[4] And
the feeling that Nazi support had peaked out was not confined
to Hitler's opponents. When, in early December 1932, on top of
election defeats, Gregor Strasser resigned his position as NSDAP
Reichsorganisationsleiter (party manager), panic spread throughout
the entire party: the opportune moment for gaining a foothold
in government seemed to have been missed, a realization accompanied by mass desertions of members and vociferous criticism
by party veterans. Financially the party seemed on the verge of
collapse. (3) The relationship between Hugenberg's DNVP and
the Nazi party had reached a nadir in the autumn of 1932. It had
never been free of tension, even during the phony unity of the
Harzburger Front. The fact that Nazi propaganda had heaped abuse
on the "reactionaries" during the November election campaign
and concentrated its foul invectives on Hugenberg's short stature
("*Hugenzwerg*") and embonpoint deepened the rift. The German
National press responded by attacking the Nazis for their socialism, street violence, and the "economic experiments" that might
be in store for Germany if Hitler came to power. While Hugenberg could not be brought to support Schleicher, partly because of
the Chancellor's unwillingness to entrust him with the Ministries
of Agriculture and Economics in Prussia and the Reich,[5] his first
meeting with Hitler in the new year, on 17 January 1933, remained
frosty despite the fact that the DNVP had refrained from attacking

2. Gregor Strasser, who favored Nazi participation in government, was
soon forced to abandon this scheme. He resigned from his party offices without
even making an attempt to divide the party, while trade union leaders, after first
welcoming Schleicher's initiative, were soon warned by members of the SPD
leadership (Breitscheid) not to trust Schleicher, who had acquired a reputation
for duplicity. See Craig, *Germany*, 565–569; Winkler, *Der Weg in die Katastrophe*,
810–857; Volker Hentschel, *Weimars letzte Monate. Hitler und der Untergang der
Republik* (Düsseldorf, 1978).
3. Broszat, *Die Machtergreifung*, 156.
4. Turner, *Hitler's Thirty Days to Power*, 1–2.
5. Broszat, *Die Machtergreifung*, 165.

the Nazi party during the elections in Lippe on 15 January.[6] (4) When, on 20 January, the reopening of parliament was scheduled for Tuesday, 31 January, it became clear that Schleicher might well be faced with a no-confidence motion that could result in yet another dissolution of parliament—accompanied by a new round of elections or possibly an adjournment *sine die*. On 23 January, the Chancellor had to admit to Hindenburg that he had been unable to procure any parliamentary backing. He suggested, therefore, to dissolve the Reichstag for longer than the sixty-day limit stipulated in the constitution, a scenario very much like the one Papen had propounded in November (and which, since it harbored the danger of civil war, had led to his downfall). Hindenburg gave Schleicher to understand that he was unwilling to envisage any breach of the constitution. (5) Papen had been in contact with Hitler ever since their 4 January meeting in the house of the Cologne banker Kurt von Schröder. To overcome Hindenburg's continued strong reluctance to accept a presidential Cabinet under Hitler's leadership,[7] Papen now tried to win over the DNVP and the ex-servicemen's organization *Stahlhelm* (with close to 500,000 members including affiliated organizations). The *Stahlhelm* leader, Franz Seldte, was easily persuaded, but his co-leader Theodor Duesterberg, a candidate in the first round of the 1932 presidential elections who knew Nazi methods from bitter personal experience, balked at the idea. Hugenberg was initially equally intransigent. Not only did he demand for himself the Ministries of Agriculture and Economics, which Schleicher had already refused him, but he also adamantly opposed the idea of entrusting Hitler with the position of Reich Commissar for Prussia, since this would mean putting the Nazis in charge of the Prussian police.[8] When Hitler himself spoke with Hugenberg on Friday, 27 January, the interview ended in an éclat and Hitler, who felt that he might again be fobbed off with less

6. There, the Nazis gained 39,064 of 99,812 votes cast, which exceeded their performance in November and thus marked an end to the downward trend, but still fell short of their July 1932 results.

7. Hindenburg's closest advisors, his Undersecretary of State Otto Meissner and his son Oskar von Hindenburg, had met Hitler in Ribbentrop's villa on 22 January, when Hindenburg's son had a long conversation with Hitler, after which he seemed more amenable to the idea of a Hitler Cabinet.

8. During Papen's Chancellorship, the Prussian government had been taken over by the Reich under the pretext that it was unable to maintain order on its territory (see chapter 1).

than his due, had to be talked out of returning to Munich. At this point, Hindenburg was still not won over to the plan of appointing Hitler as Chancellor in a presidential Cabinet, while his advisors— his son and Meissner—already seemed reconciled to the idea. (6) On the morning of Saturday, 28 January, a mere three days before the opening of the Reichstag, Papen, together with Meissner and Oskar von Hindenburg, finally succeeded in dispelling the lingering doubts of the old President, explaining that the successful formation of a new government depended on Hitler becoming Chancellor. At noon, following Hindenburg's meeting with Papen, Schleicher submitted the resignation of his Cabinet. In the early afternoon of that day, in yet another meeting with Papen (Meissner and Oskar von Hindenburg were also present), the President finally gave his reluctant consent to appoint Hitler.[9] (7) After debates between Papen, Göring, and Hitler, the latter was reconciled to the idea of having Papen appointed as Commissar for Prussia (with Göring as Minister of the Interior and thus in charge of the police) and handing over the Ministries of Agriculture and Economics in Prussia and the Reich to Hugenberg. Papen was careful not to mention to Hugenberg that Hitler insisted on new elections, since he correctly anticipated that Hugenberg would reject this outright. (8) With all obstacles seemingly overcome, the designated Cabinet met in Meissner's office on the morning of Monday, 30 January to be sworn in by Hindenburg (the ceremony was scheduled for 11 a.m.), when Hugenberg, now finally acquainted with Hitler's demand for new elections, got into an argument with the Chancellor-designate that put the formation of the new government in jeopardy. Even Hitler's "word of honor" to leave the composition of the government unchanged, no matter what the outcome of the elections, did not placate Hugenberg. According to Henry Turner, Papen, who had become fearful that his grand

9. One of Hindenburg's old Junker friends, Elard von Oldenburg-Januschau, had urged Hindenburg in the same direction. Franz von Papen would serve as Vice-Chancellor, and members of Schleicher's Cabinet, Foreign Minister Konstantin von Neurath, Minister of Finance Lutz Graf Schwerin von Krosigk, Minister of Justice Franz Gürtner, and Postal and Transportation Minister Paul von Eltz-Rübenach, would stay on under Hitler. The *Stahlhelm* leader Franz Seldte was put in charge of the Ministry of Labor, and Hugenberg obtained the coveted portfolios of Economics and "Agriculture and Nutrition" for both the Reich and Prussia. General Werner von Blomberg, Hindenburg's own choice, would be in charge of the Reichswehr.

scheme might fall apart, indignantly confronted Hugenberg as to how he could possibly doubt the "solemnly given word of honor of a German man."[10] But Hugenberg, whose acumen for once was not at fault, remained unyielding. It was only Meissner's breathless exhortation at 11:15 a.m. that Hindenburg could no longer be kept waiting that brought Hugenberg back into line. Less than half an hour later, Hitler was made Chancellor of the Reich.

Papen was clearly the driving force behind the formation of the new Cabinet, even though he initially meant to replace Schleicher with a government led by himself and buttressed by Nazi support. Ironically, among those involved in forming the government or participating in it—Papen, Hugenberg, and the *Stahlhelm* leader Seldte—no one wanted Hitler as Chancellor, and Hindenburg's aversion to the "Bohemian corporal" was legendary.[11] From within the DNVP, Hugenberg was strongly advised to give preference to a Papen government, a *"Kampfkabinett Papen-Hugenberg,"* but if he were to enter a Cabinet under Hitler's leadership, he was urged to ascertain that neither the Prussian police nor the Reichswehr were to fall under Nazi command.[12] Even though, as his biographer John A. Leopold stressed, "Hugenberg was not included in all of the meetings and schemes that went on in the background," he was, in principle, prepared to accept "a Hitler Chancellorship, but not a Nazi dictatorship."[13] When Ewald von Kleist-Schmenzin, the most diehard opponent of Nazism among German Nationals, tried to prevail upon Hugenberg to deny rumors that he was ready to be part of a Hitler government, Hugenberg refused, claiming that this might be the last opportunity to remedy Germany's plight.[14] Was it ambition or rather the conviction that he could decisively influence Germany's economic fate in a "government of national consolidation" that made him shove aside scruples and act against what must have been his better judgment that a pact with Hitler was bound to have fateful implications? In the final analysis, it is impossible to ascertain the precise factors that made Hugenberg swallow his pride and disregard the personal attacks, insults, and invectives the Nazi press had poured over him so liberally. Hiller

10. Turner, *Hitlers Weg zur Macht*, 206–209.
11. Weiß and Hoser, eds., *Die Deutschnationalen*, 226.
12. Weiß and Hoser, eds., *Die Deutschnationalen*, 227, note 16; Thilo Vogelsang, *Reichswehr, Staat und NSDAP*, 376–380.
13. Leopold, *Alfred Hugenberg*, 135.
14. Hiller von Gaertingen, "DNVP," 571.

von Gaertingen argued that it may have been a combination of fear that a Hitler Cabinet could be formed without him, and the belief that he alone was capable of salvaging the economy and the agricultural sector.[15] On 30 January he got all he wanted: the Reich Ministries of Agriculture and Economics, coupled with the Prussian Ministries of Agriculture and Commerce, as well as the post of Reich Commissar for Eastern Relief (*Osthilfe*) and the Department of Social Policy and Labor that had been transferred from the Ministry of Labor to his responsibility.[16] But already on the day after the swearing in of the new Cabinet, Hugenberg confessed to Carl Goerdeler, *Oberbürgermeister* of Leipzig and a leading conservative politician: "I have just committed the greatest stupidity of my life; I have allied myself with the greatest demagogue in world history."[17] Yet, as Larry Jones correctly points out, if Hugenberg "had indeed committed 'the greatest stupidity' of his life by joining the Hitler Cabinet on 30 January 1933, then this was the result of a strategy that he had conscientiously pursued ever since his election to the DNVP party chairmanship in October 1928. . . . The aim of this strategy was nothing less than the destruction of Weimar democracy and the establishment of a new system of rule that no longer rested upon the will of the people, but sought to restore the dominance of Germany's traditional elites . . ."[18] These traditional elites would soon be in for a rude awakening, for on 30 January 1933 they would get something far different than they had bargained for.

15. Ibid., 570–571. This, Hiller von Gaertingen continues, might explain "why in the end he made a decision, without having the consent of any German National we know of." Ibid., 571.

16. Jones, " 'The Greatest Stupidity of My Life,' " 63–87.

17. Jones, " 'The Greatest Stupidity of My Life,' " 63; and Gerhard Ritter, *Carl Goerdeler und die deutsche Widerstandsbewegung*, DTV paperback ed. (Munich, 1964), 65–66.

18. Jones, " 'The Greatest Stupidity of My Life,' " 79. Jones also points out that "a handful of Hugenberg's own colleagues desperately tried to sabotage the negotiations with Hitler," (ibid., 80) but that events had assumed a momentum of their own that could not be halted. Jones rightly emphasized the divisions within the German right on the eve of the Nazi assumption of power: "It would be a serious misreading of events that led to the formation of the Hitler Cabinet in January 1933 to assume that Hugenberg's gambit enjoyed the full or unequivocal support of even one of his known supporters." Ibid.

The Impact of 30 January

In contrast to every other significant date in German history, 30 January 1933 would have a profound impact on the life of every German. Other important historical events, no matter how far-reaching and dramatic, usually left the private sphere of life intact. Sebastian Haffner illustrated this vividly: "We gained experience, acquired convictions, but remained basically the same people. However, no one who has, willingly or reluctantly, been caught up in the machinery of the Third Reich can honestly say that of himself."[19] Haffner notes that historical events encompass varying degrees of intensity. An historic event can leave the lives of private individuals virtually untouched or it can wreak such havoc that nothing is left standing: "The usual way in which history is written fails to reveal this. '1890: Wilhelm II dismisses Bismarck.' Certainly, a key event in German history, but scarcely an event at all in the biography of any German outside his small circle of protagonists. Life went on as before. No family was torn apart, no friendship broke up, and no one fled his country. Not even a rendezvous was missed or an opera performance cancelled. Those in love, whether happily or not, remained so; the poor remained poor, the rich remained rich. Now compare that with '1933: Hindenburg sends for Hitler.' An earthquake shatters 66 million lives."[20]

In the first days after 30 January 1933, the tremendous impact this date would indeed have on the life of every German was not apparent to everyone. The Bonn theologian Karl Barth,[21] member of the SPD since 1931 and forced to leave Germany in 1935 after refusing to take the required oath of allegiance to Hitler, wrote on 1 February 1933 that he did not think Hitler's appointment would change much of anything, since he was convinced that "the German body politic is too inert, both in domestic and foreign affairs" and that it "has too little of that *élan vital* and dynamism that is required to establish either a regime like Mussolini's or engage in a

19. Haffner, *Geschichte eines Deutschen*, 12; English translation: *Defying Hitler* (New York, 2003), 6.
20. Haffner, *Geschichte eines Deutschen*, 12–13; *Defying Hitler*, 7.
21. Karl Barth (1886–1968), one of the most influential Protestant theologians of the twentieth century, joined the SPD to demonstrate his opposition to National Socialism. He was Professor of Theology in Bonn from 1930–1935; thereafter in Basel until 1962.

counterrevolution."[22] Theodor Eschenburg, later to achieve prominence as a political scientist, who had harbored the worst fears when
Hitler was appointed Chancellor, characterized the general mood in
early February as follows: "The course of events seemed to prove me
wrong. For the moment, nothing changed. Rather, a certain calm
set in. In their Monday editions newspapers no longer reported the
number of dead and wounded of the street battles from the week-
end. At most, people shook their heads over the seemingly inane
exultation of the Nazis."[23]

On the left, fears were allayed by the comforting thought that the
conservatives in the Cabinet ultimately set the tone and that Hugenberg and Papen had effectively contained Hitler and used him for
their own purposes. On 7 February, the pacifist editor of the *Weltbühne,* Carl von Ossietzky,[24] wrote that it was the German Nationals who would reap benefits for their people, whereas "the National
Socialists will reap nothing but hatred."[25] Kurt Schumacher, SPD
Reichstag deputy and the chairman and moral conscience of the
West German SPD after the Second World War, a man who would
spend several years of his life in concentration camps like Ossietzky,
was even more blinded by ideological considerations.[26] In a speech
in Augsburg on 4 February 1933, Schumacher claimed that Hitler was merely a "decoration piece":[27] "The Cabinet has Hitler's
name on the masthead, but in reality the Cabinet is Alfred Hugenberg. Adolf Hitler may make the speeches, but Hugenberg will act."
Schumacher mockingly noted that Hitler was the first Chancellor
who had to be accompanied by his vice-Chancellor when meet-

22. Klaus Scholder, *Die Kirchen und das Dritte Reich,* vol. I (Frankfurt, Berlin, 1977), 280.

23. Eschenburg, *Letzten Endes meine ich doch,* 11.

24. Carl von Ossietzky (1889–1938). The leftist weekly *Weltbühne* was critical of the militarist and nationalist tendencies in the Weimar Republic. From
1933 to 1936, Ossietzky was imprisoned in various concentration camps; in 1936
he was awarded the Nobel Peace Price in absentia. Ossietzky died in 1938 as a
result of his confinement.

25. Carl von Ossietzky, "Kavaliere und Rundköpfe," *Sämtliche Schriften,* VI
(Hamburg, 1994), 468.

26. Kurt Schumacher (1895–1952) spent more than ten years in Nazi concentration camps. See Willy Albrecht, *Kurt Schumacher. Ein Leben für den demokrati-
schen Sozialismus* (Bonn, 1985).

27. Quoted in Josef and Ruth Becker, eds., *Hitlers Machtergreifung. Dokumente
vom Machtantritt Hitlers 30. Januar 1933 bis zur Besiegelung des Einparteienstaates 14.
Juli 1933,* 2nd rev. ed (Munich, 1992), 45–49, esp. 45.

ing with the President. And where, Schumacher added sarcastically, was the promised terror: "These people have been in power for five times 24 hours, but the long knives still remain sheathed." Reality was very different from these first fleeting impressions of Nazi rule in the early days of February, a fact that would become obvious all too soon.

The more pessimistic mood among conservative groups reflected more accurately the actual political situation. Hugenberg's longtime confidant, the DNVP deputy Reinhold Quaatz, who had crossed the floor from the DVP to the DNVP in 1924, noted in his diary on 1 February: "Hugenberg, who normally phones daily or arranges to have me fetched, has been silent since the night before last."[28] Quaatz noted with anxious concern that the DNVP was bound to lose its flexibility and clout if the Center Party were to enter into a coalition agreement with the Nazis.[29] The trained political observer Quaatz immediately noted the fact that Hitler had "occupied all key positions with his own people—the Interior Ministries in both Prussia and the Reich, the police, schools, universities, wireless stations. We are in charge of the economy, for which the sixty-eight year old Hugenberg is solely responsible."[30] Quaatz soon realized that Hugenberg was not up to the job. Hindenburg's *Staatssekretär* Otto Meissner voiced concern already on 7 February that Hugenberg had taken on too much.[31] On 9 and 10 February, vociferous protest erupted across the entire party because Hugenberg, following a suggestion from Papen, insisted that the DNVP should enter the campaign for the upcoming elections, scheduled for 5 March 1933, jointly with Papen and the *Stahlhelm* under the programmatic name of the old Imperial colors "Battlefront Black-White-Red." Ernst Oberfohren, Graf Westarp's successor as DNVP Reichstag faction leader, formerly one of Hugenberg's closest allies, now disagreed with the direction his party had taken since its alliance with

28. Weiß and Hoser, eds., *Die Deutschnationalen*, 231.

29. Quaatz, diary entry of 1 February 1933, ibid., 231. Even after 30 January, there was a chance of renewed talks between the NSDAP and Center, but this was soon nipped in the bud by Hitler. Already in the summer and early fall of 1932, the NSDAP and Center/ Bavarian People's Party were engaged in coalition talks that were anxiously monitored by the DNVP.

30. Ibid, 231–232. The formerly close relationship between Quaatz and Hugenberg had become strained because Hugenberg had seemingly been unable (or unwilling) to obtain a government post for Quaatz.

31. Quaatz, diary entry of 7 February 1933, ibid., 233.

the NSDAP, and subsequently whipped up inner-party opposition
to Hugenberg. Ultimately this proved unsuccessful and would later
destroy Oberfohren and not Hugenberg.[32] As Quaatz reported,
negative assessments of Hugenberg began to accumulate: "In the
country he is not popular. Since I am considered his intimate, most
people avoid talking about him to me. What one does hear is unfavorable. He lacks charisma. Most worrisome is the concern voiced
earlier by Meissner: Will he be able to cope with the manifold
burdens he has taken on?"[33] By early March, Quaatz feared that
"Hugenberg is losing ground not only to Hitler and Göring, but
also to Papen" and that the consistent burden of work was taking its
toll: "On top of everything there are health problems. In addition
to the flu, he suffers from renal colic. He needs rest, especially since
he has already come through two bouts of pneumonia."[34] So much
for the "Leader" of the German National People's Party, the title he
had donned with pride since the 1931 Stettin party conference, and
the man meant to stop the Nazis in their tracks by helping to push
Hitler—to use Papen's famous phrase—"so far into the corner that
he'll squeak."[35]

The DNVP was faring almost as badly as its leader. Since Hugenberg was fully occupied with his various ministerial portfolios, the
deputy party chairman, Friedrich von Winterfeld, who had been
a member of the Prussian Landtag since 1921 and chairman of the
parliamentary faction of the Prussian DNVP since 1928, effectively
assumed the leadership of the party and its organizations, a task for

32. Quaatz, diary entries of 8 to 10 February 1933, ibid., 233; see also chapter 6 below.
33. Quaatz, diary entry 17 February 1933, ibid., 235: "Everybody just
shrugs their shoulders about this experiment: attempting to manage five ministries, one party, and a film and publishing house."
34. Quaatz, diary entry of 4 March 1933, ibid., 237. Despite critical comments, Hugenberg and Quaatz remained on a familiar footing, and Quaatz continued taking an intense interest in party matters.
35. Craig, *Germany 1866–1945*, 570. In his memoirs, Theodor Eschenburg
recounted the short, but telling, impression he received of Hugenberg. Looking for a free corner seat while traveling on a train, Eschenburg passed a compartment with a single passenger: "I had almost passed him when I suddenly
thought: 'How does this village school teacher get into first class?' But the face
looked somehow familiar. Only after I had found a seat, I suddenly remembered:
it was Hugenberg, whom I knew from photographs. He looked so utterly insignificant with his crew cut and twirled moustache, totally unprepossessing and
petty bourgeois in appearance, a little like a retired porter." Eschenburg, *Letzten
Endes meine ich doch*, 9.

which he was woefully unprepared.[36] So it was without much enthusiasm that a defensive Winterfeld presented his report on the
most recent political developments to a DNVP party meeting on 5
February 1933.[37] Even though the DNVP had consistently fought
the parliamentary system since Hugenberg had assumed the party
leadership, the ratio of power in the coalition between DNVP and
NSDAP now prompted Winterfeld to assert that "ultimate control
rests with parliament." Winterfeld was caught in an inescapable predicament: he could not countenance parliamentary rule, yet he was
unprepared to throw over parliamentary control altogether. While
the DNVP considered itself an anti-parliamentary party that believed in "executive authority" and not party politics, Winterfeld
was aware that some measure of parliamentary control could be a
protection against an overbearing alliance partner. According to
Winterfeld, Hugenberg's decision to join the Hitler Cabinet was ultimately correct, since the country "was on the edge of a precipice."
He thus presented the formation of the "government of national
consolidation" not as a stroke of genius, but as an act of desperation born out of dire need: "Therefore no more time was to be lost,
which is why we joined the government."[38]

At Papen's urging but against strong resistance from within the
DNVP, it was finally decided on 8 February after long debate that
the DNVP would fight the March election campaign in alliance
with Papen and the *Stahlhelm* as "Battlefront Black-White-Red."[39]
Many on the non-Nazi right were obviously convinced that a concentration of all conservative forces would constitute a more effective political check on the increasingly imperious and high-handed
Nazi movement. In the DNVP, on the other hand, longtime members were reluctant to endorse such a united conservative front for
fear that the party might lose its identity. In his letter to Hugenberg,

36. In early February Winterfeld became "permanent deputy leader" (*stän-
diger Vertreter*) of the party leader, since Hugenberg withdrew from party-related
work after entering the Hitler Cabinet.

37. BA Berlin-Lichterfelde, "Pressearchiv Reichslandbund, DNVP Partei-
tage," R 8034 II (formerly 61 RE I) no. 4334, 53; *Mitteilungen der Deutschnationalen Volkspartei*, 7 February 1933.

38. Ibid.

39. Quaatz, diary entry of 8 February, in Weiß and Hoser, eds., *Die Deutschnationalen*, 233: "In the afternoon, hour-long discussions about, and then with,
Papen. As he is afraid of Hindenburg, he declines to be a direct candidate with
us and demands that we change our name for him and go together with more
moderate forces to blend into some mish-mash combination party."

Papen justified his demand by arguing that "the party shackles of pre-war Germany" must be broken, for they had become too confining for a nation "welded together in the firestorm of the World War."[40] Papen claimed further that the Catholic segment of the population would find its legitimate interests represented in the "Battlefront Black-White-Red," thereby implying that the memory of the old Imperial colors conjured up by the name "Black-White-Red" would exert a strong appeal to those Catholics who might otherwise be turned off by the primarily Protestant character of the DNVP. The National Socialist press, for its part, was affronted that the German Nationals claimed the heritage of Imperial Germany to be theirs alone. A few days after the official proclamation of the "Battlefront" on 11 February, the Nazi press emphasized that "the flag of Bismarck's Reich" should not be turned into a "party banner": "The spirit of frontline soldiers and Black-White-Red are above parties . . . one must not sign electoral pacts with the blood of two million dead."[41] Goebbels, on the other hand, expressed little concern. On 11 February, he noted in his diary: "Hugenberg, Papen, and Seldte speak on the radio. They have set up a battle-bloc Black-White-Red, but this is certainly only a fleeting phenomenon."[42]

Meanwhile, Hugenberg was anxious to evoke the unity of the nationalist front. In his opening speech for the Reichstag election campaign on Saturday, 11 February before a "jam-packed" (according to the DNVP press) Berliner Sportpalast, he heralded the ascendancy of Germany.[43] Hugenberg's speech was reminiscent of a Germanic epic: "Once upon a time there existed a great, rich and noble people. Then disaster happened upon them. Their neighbors had forced war upon them. Standing united, they kept their countless enemies far away from their borders. But then the people succumbed to hunger. They became divided into party factions and fell victim to internal discord . . ." Now that domestic strife had been

40. "Vice Chancellor von Papen to Reichsminister Hugenberg," *Kreuzzeitung*, 13 February 1933; and Hiller von Gaertingen, "DNVP," 635.

41. 14 February 1933 at BA Berlin-Lichterfelde, "Pressearchiv Reichslandbund, Parteileben Deutschland: Nationalsozialismus und DNVP," R 8034 II, no. 9030, 172. The *Preußischer Pressedienst der NSDAP* took exception to the name change of the DNVP pamphlet *Unsere Partei* to *Der nationale Wille*, arguing that the will of the nation ran counter to that of the DNVP. See ibid., 169.

42. Josef Goebbels, *Vom Kaiserhof zur Reichskanzlei. Eine historische Darstellung in Tagebuchblättern, Januar 1932 bis zum Mai 1933* (Munich, 1940), 261.

43. See "Kampffront Schwarzweißrot marschiert," *Der Tag*, 12 February 1933, for the complete text of the speech.

transcended by the formation of a "government of national consolidation," Hugenberg contended, the resurrection of the nation could begin anew, though everything depended on all partners living up to the spirit of the "Pact of Trust and Faith" that nationalist forces had concluded on 30 January 1933. There was no need to be more explicit. Hugenberg's audience knew all too well exactly which of the two partners might not live up to the spirit of the Pact. Correspondingly, he was quick to point out that any breach of faith would result in "chaos" and "German Bolshevism"; in sum, Germany's destruction. Hugenberg admitted that, although he had been opposed to calling for yet another round of national elections, he also had been determined not to let the election issue destroy the formation of the "government of national consolidation." Finally, he avowed that from this point on, he would concentrate primarily on his duties as Cabinet minister, since it was now more important "to work, rather than speak and campaign."

While Hugenberg emphatically conjured up a unity whose validity he must have doubted himself, the opposition press did its best to accentuate potential areas of conflict and contradictions inherent in the pact of the unequal partners. The SPD paper *Vorwärts* published a list of past and present disagreements between DNVP and NSDAP under the headline "Memories of Harzburg,"[44] highlighting the murder of *Stahlhelm* members by Nazi storm troopers and Goebbels's personal abuse of Hugenberg. A slew of articles concentrated on Nazi attempts to undermine the legitimacy of the German Nationals.[45] Reports about fissures in the alliance were well-founded, as evidenced by a letter from Major Hans Nagel, DNVP executive board member in charge of party affairs, to Hans Heinrich Lammers, Undersecretary of State (*Staatssekretär*) in Hitler's Chancellery, in which Nagel passed on a complaint from Dr. Paul Bang, DNVP *Staatssekretär* in the Reich Economics Ministry. NSDAP Reichstag deputy Schrader had allegedly threatened that after the elections, Hugenberg would have to disassociate himself from his German National Undersecretaries of State Rohr and Bang, "otherwise he

---

44. BA Berlin-Lichterfelde, "Pressearchiv Reichslandbund, Parteileben Deutschland," R 8034 II, no. 9030, 170; "Harzburger Erinnerungen. Wie sie sich lieben," *Vorwärts*, 1 February 1933.

45. "Maulwurfskrieg," *Vorwärts*, 7 February 1933; "Frank II gegen Hugenberg," *Vorwärts*, 3 February 1933. The latter focused on a Nazi speech that vilified the national-minded bourgeoisie: "The bourgeoisie, which today shakes the Führer's hand, betrayed Germany to Marxism in 1918."

will be thrown out as well." In his response, Lammers promised to bring the complaint to Hitler's attention and expressed his conviction that "the Reich Chancellor will surely disapprove of this."[46]

The freedom of the press to criticize and deride the government would soon become a thing of the past. As a reaction to the KPD's call for a general strike on 31 January 1933, Hindenburg was prevailed upon to enact the emergency ordinance "For the Protection of the German People," which facilitated the banning of newspapers and public meetings that "abused, or treated with contempt, organs, institutions, authorities or leading officials of the state." This decree, which had already been drafted by Hitler's predecessors in the Chancellor's office during the turbulent final phase of the Weimar Republic, furnished the government with far-reaching powers to silence the opposition press. Even though it was theoretically possible to lodge a complaint with the Reich Supreme Court in Leipzig, the likelihood of a successful appeal had vanished by the end of February.[47] Thus, Frederick M. Sackett, the American Ambassador to Berlin from 1930 to April 1933, reported to Secretary of State Stimson on 27 February 1933: "In the course of this month, approximately 150 newspapers have been suppressed, most of which are Social-Democratic or Communist organs, though a large number of Centrist organs have also been suppressed for publishing an election appeal by leading Catholic associations. . . . The prohibition of many Left journals in Prussia is being daily rescinded by the Supreme Court, but the work of suppression continues unabated. Accurate descriptions of existing conditions in Germany appear only in the foreign press."[48]

The famed Prussian Rechtsstaat, that is, government and administration based on the rule of law, had ceased to function long before the elections.[49] In contrast to leftist and Center Party press organs, which were viewed as antagonistic to the government, DNVP newspapers continued to appear freely. In the first stages of the

46. 3 March 1933 "Nagel to Lammers," 4 March 1933 "Lammers to Nagel," in BA Berlin-Lichterfelde, "DNVP: Politischer Schriftwechsel 1933," R 8005, no. 19, 170–171.

47. Broszat, *Der Staat Hitlers*, 88; Thamer, *Verführung und Gewalt*, 239; Karl-Dietrich Bracher, *Die Stufen der Machtergreifung* (Tübingen, 1974), 92–93.

48. 27 February 1933: "Sackett to the Secretary of State," in *Foreign Relations of the United States*, vol. II (Washington, 1949), 199.

49. Already on 1 February Hindenburg had agreed to Hitler's request to dissolve the Reichstag (something he had previously refused to Schleicher), which indicated that Germany would continue to be governed by emergency decrees.

election campaign, the DNVP portrayed itself as the "strong central pillar of a new phalanx, on one side of which stands *Stahlhelm* leader Minister of Labor Seldte, with the largest German ex-servicemen's organization, and on the other Vice Chancellor Papen as figure-head of all independent conservative forces."[50] During the DNVP party congress of 11 to 12 February 1933, Hugenberg was portrayed as the great charismatic leader of "tough Westphalian stock," who made one feel that "this man is made of granite," though with "a warm heart beating in his breast."[51] With their campaign rhetoric clearly borrowed from the well-tested style of the Nazis, German Nationals strenuously tried to emulate the atmosphere of somber and heroic gravity they had come to admire in Nazi assemblies. In practice, DNVP rhetoric was even more bereft of substance than that of the Nazis. In an age of mass unemployment and widespread misery, nationalist platitudes, such as "Just as Bismarck created the Reich of our Fathers, so must we create the Nation,"[52] sounded un-convincing and devoid of emotional appeal when promulgated by a party that represented the establishment. To distinguish themselves from the Nazis, German Nationals continually warned of "socialist experiments" and employed slogans such as "Social yes—Socialist no." They contended that strong German National influence within the government was essential to fortify the ethos of Christian con-servatism, protect the German people from socialist experiments, re-establish an incorruptible state, rein in factionalism and partisan-ship, and, finally, provide the necessary backing for Hugenberg.[53] German National propaganda desperately tried to represent Hugen-berg as "social": Hugenberg's true goal as Minister of Economics and Agriculture, election pamphlets emphasized, was "to master the economic crisis and eliminate the hardships of unemployment."[54]

50. BA Berlin-Lichterfelde, "Pressearchiv Reichslandbund, DNVP Partei-tage," R 8034 II, no. 4334, 3. The militant campaign rhetoric of the German Nationals ("phalanx," "campaign battle") was partly a sign of the times, partly a reflection of the acrimony of the election campaign.

51. Ibid., 4.

52. Ibid., 4; see also Richard E. Frankel, *Bismarck's Shadow. The Cult of Lead-ership and the Transformation of the German Right, 1898–1945* (Oxford, New York, 2005).

53. *Der Nationale Wille*, 11 February 1933, 69–70; Hiller von Gaertingen, "DNVP," 580.

54. BA Berlin-Lichterfelde, "Pressearchiv Reichslandbund, DNVP Partei-tage," R 8034 II, no. 4334, "Hugenbergs Sozialprogramm," in *Mitteilungen der Deutschnationalen Volkspartei*, 1–2.

It was sheer calumny to brand Hugenberg a "social reactionary," to claim that he was a "representative of capital," and to assert that he had no heart for the common man. In reality, the opposite was true: Hugenberg had a distinct social program, he fought against the "arbitrariness of unsocial entrepreneurs," and was interested in preserving, not dismantling, social insurance. Hugenberg favored the "ruthless elimination" of international capital, and nothing could be further from the truth than his wish "to accumulate riches."[55] These arguments did not convince many voters. The introverted, awkward Hugenberg, generally introduced to the public as "Privy Councilor" (*Geheimrat*), was known, after all, as the exceedingly prosperous owner of publishing and film interests, a former director of the Krupp steelworks, and a man with manifold connections in industrial and business circles. It would have been very difficult for even the most adroit of propagandists to sell him as a politician with a social conscience.

Even though the DNVP leadership (*Parteivertretung*) had formally approved Hugenberg's decision to join the Hitler Cabinet at the beginning of the party congress on 11 February, cracks in the carefully preserved facade of unity soon became apparent, especially since it was obvious that little except their common enmity for the "system" of Weimar held the DNVP and NSDAP together. Ewald von Kleist-Schmenzin,[56] since 1928 chairman of the *Konservativer Hauptverein* that saw itself carrying on the tradition of the old German Conservative Party, announced his resignation from the DNVP on 13 February. In a detailed letter to Hugenberg, Kleist declared that he did not want to see one kind of party rule substituted by another.[57] He argued that while most people might have the impression that the DNVP and NSDAP were basically in agreement, Hugenberg must have known only too well that this was not the case: driven by fear that the formation of a rightist government

55. Ibid., 1–2.

56. Ewald von Kleist-Schmenzin (1880–1945) rejected Hugenberg's policies of cooperation with the Nazi party from the start. In 1932 he had published a pamphlet with the programmatic title "National Socialism—a Danger," and in January 1933 he had done his utmost to prevent Hitler's appointment as Chancellor and to win over Hindenburg, Papen, and Hugenberg for a rightist Cabinet without Hitler. He was executed in April 1945 because of his close contacts to Goerdeler.

57. 13 February 1933: "Ewald von Kleist-Schmenzin an Reichsminister Hugenberg," reprinted as document no. 9 in Hiller von Gaertingen, "DNVP," 635–637.

might fail, frank discussions about the true goals of both parties had
been consciously avoided. According to Kleist, the national-minded
part of the population had a genuine desire for internal unity, and
once they became aware of the deceit, the resulting disillusionment
would be terrible: "When our followers, who have been allowed to
lose themselves in understandable euphoria, realize the groundless-
ness of their joy, they might easily lose trust in their entire current
leadership."[58] Kleist bluntly told Hugenberg that the DNVP and the
Nazis were no more united on 30 January than they had been in the
fall of 1932. To form a government in these circumstances, Kleist
charged, amounted to nothing but a dishonest truce and was therefore a fraud committed against national-minded voters.

Many nationalist voters from the ranks of the *Bürgertum*, like the
Hamburg teacher Luise Solmitz, indeed rode high on a wave of
euphoria.[59] At the beginning of February, Solmitz was overjoyed
that the "fratricidal strife that caused us so much distress" had finally been settled. Now the mood was reminiscent of the enormous upsurge in national unity that characterized August 1914.[60]
Solmitz enthusiastically welcomed Hitler's programmatic speech in
the Berlin *Sportpalast* on 10 February, in which Hitler expressed the
belief that "even if millions still curse us now, they will be marching behind us one day."[61] And on 14 February she wholeheart-
edly endorsed Göring's "cleansing actions" of the upper echelons of
the Prussian bureaucracy, whose victims included numerous police
presidents and provincial governors: "The iron broom cleaning out
Prussia! Finally."[62]

The reaction of the shrunken remainders of the liberal democratic *Bürgertum* was very different. A representative example of
the liberal *haute bourgeoisie* that would soon be extinct is the author
Erich Ebermayer, son of the judicial scholar and Attorney General at

---

58. Ibid., 636.

59. The diary of Luise Solmitz (born 1889) was published in extracts in
Werner Jochmann, *Nationalsozialismus und Revolution. Ursprung und Geschichte der
NSDAP in Hamburg, 1922–1933* (Frankfurt, 1963), 400–433. According to Joch-
mann, the diary epitomizes the "mood, hopes and fears of a part of the German
Bürgertum." Ibid., x–xi.

60. Entry of 6 February 1933, Jochmann, *Nationalsozialismus und Revolution*,
422–423.

61. Jochmann, *Nationalsozialismus und Revolution*, 424–425. Solmitz was impressed with Hitler's claim that all great men of German history would support
his movement in spirit.

62. Jochmann, ibid., 425.

the Supreme Court in Leipzig, *Oberreichsanwalt* Ludwig Ebermayer, who interpreted Hitler's *Sportpalast* speech very differently: "The man visibly grows with the task proffered to him. Toward the end he seems to begin praying and closes with the word 'Amen.' Just the right mix for his audience: brutality, threats, swanking muscleman antics and then again humility before the much quoted 'Almighty.'"[63] Ebermayer knew his bourgeois world well and sensed instinctively the haplessness of its rarified culture in opposing the Nazis' all-inclusive arrogation of power that, as Hitler's speech intimated, encompassed the entire nation. At an evening soirée at the house of Max Brockhaus, the chairman of the Leipzig *Gewandhaus*-Society, which was attended by "a good part of Leipzig's intellectual and musical elite," Ebermayer registered a "certain ironic reserve toward the new age" and noted that people were determined "to brave any cultural revolution in Leipzig."[64] At the same time, however, he became conscious that those in attendance were not entirely dissatisfied with the new regime: "Resurgence, the rise of the nation, an economic boom, the struggle against communism and, within reason, also against Eastern Jews—all this seems quite palatable to Leipzig patricians." On the other hand, it was the prevailing opinion at the soirée that "the anti-Semitism in Hitler's program, should it be implemented at all, would certainly exempt the great artistic and intellectual personages, and be it only to avoid embarrassment abroad."[65] This assumption that the "unreasonable" elements of the Nazi program would be tempered by bourgeois sensibilities showed all too clearly that the traditional *Bürger* failed to understand the Nazi mindset. It was reasonable in the context of a bourgeois *mode de raisonnement* not to alienate, let alone expel, the most prominent citizens of one's country, who were respected throughout the world. The majority of the *haute bourgeoisie* present could not comprehend that an apparently deeply patriotic Nazi

63. Erich Ebermayer, *Denn heute gehört uns Deutschland. Persönliches und politisches Tagebuch. Von der Machtergreifung bis zum 31. Dezember 1935* (Hamburg, Vienna, 1959), 21–22; diary entry of 11 February 1933.

64. Entry of 13 February, Ebermayer, *Denn heute gehört uns Deutschland*, 23. In addition to Max Brockhaus, those present included Leipzig's Lord Mayor Carl Goerdeler, the President of the Reich Supreme Court Dr. Bumke, and Detlef Sierck, "the highly talented young director of the municipal theater" (of Hollywood fame and better known by his American name Douglas Sirk).

65. Ibid., 24. This point was made when the discussion touched upon Bruno Walter, the famous conductor of the *Gewandhaus* orchestra. Everyone expected (wrongly, as it happened) that Bruno Walter would remain in Leipzig.

movement was quite prepared to injure the interests of the fatherland and was resolved to pursue its goals at any cost, even to the detriment of Germany. Those learned and sophisticated members of the bourgeoisie could not fathom that National Socialist ideas and actions were based on assumptions and goals inimical to their own pragmatism, that they were in effect driven by an uncompromising ideology that had little connection with reality. The mindset of the remaining remnants of the *haute bourgeoisie* was too different from that of the Nazis to appreciate the true monstrosity of what was actually their own bitterest enemy, and not, as many thought, their fellow nationalist ally. Four days after that soirée, Ebermayer noted resignedly in his diary: "Do all these people really understand that this is the dawning of a truly new era, one that, with the victor's sneering grin, will triumphantly trample underfoot their vested and inviolable rights?"[66]

Opposition to Nazi Repression and Increasing Terror

Even if one ignored Nazi threats about the establishment of a dictatorship, uttered long before their accession to power, informed political observers must have been aware by mid February that a fundamental break with Weimar was under way. German Nationals had repeatedly emphasized that, as far as they were concerned, the March elections were to be the last for years to come, thus indicating their preference for a long-term authoritarian presidential Cabinet, and Hitler himself, while professing to attain power legally, had made no bones about the fact that, once he was at the helm, the Weimar "system" with its more than thirty parties would be ruthlessly cast aside. Göring's merciless "cleansing" of the Prussian administration, higher police force, and upper ranks of the civil service that began in February made it all too plain that a new force was at work and that, as Luise Solmitz had put it, an "iron broom" was now sweeping out all of Prussia.[67] After failing to dissolve

66. Ebermayer, *Denn heute gehört uns Deutschland*, diary entry of 17 February, 26.

67. Even though Papen, as Reich Commissar, was nominally in charge of Prussia, the Prussian police came under Göring's jurisdiction as *kommissarischer* (temporarily appointed) Minister of the Interior. Prussia was far and away Germany's largest state: in the borders of 1933, Germany had 468,799.58 square kilometers; Prussia's 292,771.65 km² accounted for 62.54 percent of German

the Prussian Landtag by regular means, Prussian Reich Commissar Papen obtained an emergency ordinance from Hindenburg on 6 February "to establish a well-ordered government in Prussia,"[68] by transferring all power and authority still vested in Otto Braun's former government to Papen and Göring.[69] Now nothing stood in the way of calling new elections in Prussia, which were scheduled together with the general elections on 5 March 1933. The dissolution of provincial, county, and community legislatures, as well as other local representative bodies, had already been ordered on 5 February, and new elections set for 12 March.[70] Following his *Preußenschlag*, the *coup d'état* of 20 July 1932, Papen had begun to purge the Prussian administration: the Commissioner of Berlin police Albert Grzesinski[71] was dismissed from his post and personnel changes were effected on all levels, particularly among provincial and district governors (*Oberpräsidenten* and *Regierungspräsidenten*), whereby the victims were primarily Social Democrats.[72] Göring energetically continued this purge, which now also affected members of other democratic parties.[73] In February 1933 alone, fourteen police commissioners of larger Prussian cities as well as other senior officeholders, including district governors (*Regierungspräsidenten*) and

territory. Out of a population of 65,335,879 (16 June 1933), Prussia's 39,958,073 amounted to 61.15 percent. See Statistisches Reichsamt, ed., *Statistisches Jahrbuch für das Deutsche Reich*, 52 (Berlin, 1933), 5.

68. See Broszat, *Der Staat Hitlers*, 88–97. A motion by the Nazi parliamentary faction for self-dissolution of the Landtag had been rejected by parliamentary majority.

69. Papen's *coup d'état* against the Prussian government of 20 July 1932 had not been completely successful since—in response to a complaint of the unseated Braun government—the Supreme Court ruled on 25 October 1932 that while the President had the authority to appoint a Reich Commissar, the Braun government would be allowed to retain some vestiges of governmental authority and the right to represent Prussia in the *Reichsrat* (statehouse).

70. Broszat, *Der Staat Hitlers*, 89; 443–444.

71. Albert Grzesinski (1879–1947) was Commissoner of Berlin police in 1925–1926 and 1930–1932, and served as Prussian Minister of the Interior from 1926 to 1930. In this position he advanced the democratization of administration and police, favoring SPD members for high administrative posts.

72. See Wolfgang Runge, *Politik und Beamtentum im Parteienstaat. Die Demokratisierung der politischen Beamten in Preußen zwischen 1918 und 1932* (Stuttgart, 1965), 237–240; Broszat, *Der Staat Hitlers*, 90. Franz Bracht, the Reich Commissar appointed by Papen, replaced five *Oberpräsidenten*, eight *Regierungspräsidenten* and, by consolidating counties, seventy *Landräte*.

73. Broszat, *Der Staat Hitlers*, 90–91; Bracher, *Stufen der Machtergreifung*, 90–97.

Landräte (in charge of counties), as well as the provincial governor of Westfalia (who was a member of the Center Party), were forced into retirement. Most of them were replaced by conservative landowners, former officers or industrial managers who were politically close to the DNVP, a practice Franz Bracht had followed already after 20 July 1932.[74] Conservative professional experts were chosen because National Socialist candidates lacked the necessary qualifications.[75] SS *Gruppenführer* Kurt Daluege was empowered as "commissar for special tasks" to dedicate himself to the political purging of the Prussian police in February and March 1933 before he was appointed to head the police department in the Prussian Interior Ministry in April 1933.[76] All these measures had been initiated by Göring in his capacity as provisional Minister of the Interior. His blunt, direct language, his innate unscrupulousness, and the fact that—as he once boasted—his measures "were not emasculated by undue concerns for legality,"[77] made him an effective hatchet man for Hitler in eliminating potential enemies of the Nazi cause. In his "shooting order" of 17 February, Göring instructed the Prussian police in unambiguous language to be lenient toward members of nationalist associations, such as the SA, SS, and *Stahlhelm*, and avoid prosecuting them for their offenses, but to use strong measures in countering the actions of "subversive" organizations, including

74. Franz Bracht (1877–1933), a member of the Center party's right wing, began his career as a public prosecutor before becoming a high administrative official. In 1923–1924 he was *Staatssekretär* in the Reich Chancellery; from 1924 to 1932 Lord Mayor of Essen; and after Papen's *coup d'état*, deputy Reich Commissar and *kommissarischer* Minister of the Interior (the identical position later occupied by Göring). In Schleicher's short-lived Cabinet he held the post of Interior Minister.

75. Broszat, *Der Staat Hitlers*, 91.

76. Kurt Daluege (1897–1946) joined the NSDAP in 1923 after meeting Hitler and cofounded the Berlin SA. In 1928 he transferred to the SS; after Heydrich's assassination in 1942, he became deputy Reich Protector for Bohemia and Moravia and was responsible for the Lidice massacre and other executions. He was himself executed on 23 October 1946 after being sentenced by a court in Prague.

77. In a speech in Frankfurt am Main on 3 March 1933. See Hermann Göring, *Reden und Aufsätze*, ed. by Erich Gritzbach, 8th ed. (Munich 1943), 27. In the first phase of the *Machtergreifung*, Göring, not Reich Interior Minister Frick, was the real engine behind the "National Socialist revolution." Bracher, *Machtergreifung*, 117.

the "unsparing resort to firearms."[78] Undoubtedly Göring's order weighed heavily on Prussian police officers, especially as it was accompanied by palpable threats to prosecute those officers who failed to carry out their duties with the required severity. Few high-ranking police officers with large families would have dared to countermand or oppose those instructions. It thus came as no surprise that the Prussian police remained largely inactive when confronted with the outrages of Nazi storm troopers, such as the severe wounding of the prominent Center party politician Adam Stegerwald by the SA in Krefeld, as reported by the appalled American Ambassador.[79] In another decree dated 22 February, SA, SS, and *Stahlhelm* members were entrusted with the function of auxiliary police, though only one-fifth of these could be recruited from the ranks of the *Stahlhelm*; the SA contributed more than one-half, and the SS the remaining third.[80] From now on, it would become increasingly dangerous to take a stand against the rising tide of Nazi power.

Nonetheless, in the second half of February there were still instances of vociferous protest against arbitrary Nazi measures, though protests of non-Marxist parties remained confined to the Catholic Center and the remnants of the former DDP (now Staatspartei). A 17 February election appeal by Catholic organizations warned against Hitler's rule by referring to political developments since Hindenburg's re-election as a "national disaster."[81] The government was accused of "substituting arbitrariness and partisanship for the rule of law and special interests for the common weal" and of creating "Bolshevism in a nationalist cloak."[82] The language was so uncompromising that a part of the Catholic press in Baden, fearful their papers might be banned, published the appeal only in excerpts.[83] In his speech in Würzburg on 18 February former Reich

78. Broszat, *Der Staat Hitlers*, 93; Bracher, *Machtergreifung*, 90–119; Bracher, *Die deutsche Diktatur*, 295–315; Thamer, *Verführung und Gewalt*, 232–258; Evans, *The Coming of the Third Reich*, 310–328.

79. *Foreign Relations of the United States. Diplomatic Papers 1933*, vol. II (Washington, 1949), 198; Goebbels, *Vom Kaiserhof zur Reichskanzlei*, entry of February 13.

80. Bracher, *Stufen der Machtergreifung*, 116–117. These auxiliary police were equipped with pistols and rubber truncheons.

81. Bernhard Stasiewski, ed., *Akten deutscher Bischöfe über die Lage der Kirche 1933–1945*, vol. I (Mainz, 1968), 3–6.

82. Ibid, 3–4.

83. Hugo Stehkumper, ed., *Der Nachlaß des Reichskanzlers Wilhelm Marx*, I (Cologne, 1968), 150.

Chancellor Brüning upbraided the government for banning Center Party papers and urged that newspaper bans and other undemocratic measures be met with vigorous resistance.[84] On 23 February the Center Party politician and president of the Prussian State Council (*Staatsrat*, the representative body of the Prussian provinces), Konrad Adenauer, lodged a protest in the name of this body against Göring's emergency decrees as incompatible with the Reich Constitution and petitioned Hindenburg to rescind all decrees enacted since 4 February.[85] Adenauer's opposition to Nazism went so far that, on the occasion of a campaign stop Hitler made in Cologne on 19 February, he arranged to have the lights along the Rhine River turned off and swastika flags removed. The reaction of the Nazi press left no doubt that, in future, Adenauer would have to pay for such actions.[86]

On the other hand, no opposition was to be expected from the DNVP. Göring's purge of the police and higher Prussian administration was in the German Nationals' own interest, since they profited by filling some positions with their own candidates.[87] The very parties now under attack as "system parties"—Social Democrats, Center, and the former Democratic Party—had been the enemies of the DNVP, so that German Nationals could only welcome threats to their existence. Regarding terror against Communists, protest from the ranks of German Nationals could hardly be expected, since they considered themselves as staunchly anti-communist as the Nazis themselves. Initially, the DNVP thus evinced little concern for Nazi acts of terror that were gathering momentum in the second half of February, since political violence was directed almost exclusively

84. Becker and Becker, eds., *Hitlers Machtergreifung*, 75–79. Brüning himself wrote: "For my speech in Würzburg on 18 February, I was already under strong police protection. The mood was still very pugnacious—more than I had expected." Brüning, *Memoiren*, 650.

85. Cuno Horkenbach, ed., *Das Deutsche Reich von 1918 bis heute*, vol. IV (Berlin, 1935), 68; Becker and Becker, eds., *Hitlers Machtergreifung*, 93–94. Konrad Adenauer (1876–1967), West German Chancellor from 1949 to 1963, was Oberbürgermeister of Cologne from 1917 to 1933 and president of the Prussian State Council from 1921 to 1933.

86. "Adenauer und der Nationalsozialismus," *Westdeutscher Beobachter*, 21 February 1933; reprinted in Becker and Becker, eds., *Hitlers Machtergreifung*, 86–87.

87. Martin Broszat maintained that conservatives profited greatly from the purges since new positions were often filled by German National experts, which, in turn, prevented a more thorough nazification of the Prussian bureaucracy. Broszat, *Der Staat Hitlers*, 91.

against their political enemies. This would change abruptly in the second half of March 1933, as the German Nationals themselves became victims of Nazi attacks. With hindsight, it is barely comprehensible how blindly German Nationals rushed headlong into ruin. The violent overtones of Nazi propaganda and the attacks directed against the DNVP in the autumn of 1932, as well as street fights between the SA and members of the *Stahlhelm*, should have served as a reliable indicator of what was in store for them.

The way the Nazis conducted their election campaign against the SPD, Center, and the liberal parties was far from peaceful. As Brüning recounted,[88] Center Party meetings were regularly disrupted and injuries were not uncommon. In southern Germany, the Nazis broke up campaign rallies of the Württemberg DDP and its chairman, Reinhold Meier, to the point where the DDP complained in a telegram to Hindenburg that the Nazis ran their campaign like an "open civil war."[89] When it came to the SPD, disruptions were so massive that even seasoned politicians like the former Prussian Interior Minister and President of the Berlin police, Albert Grzesinski, simply gave up. In a letter to SPD party secretaries of northern and western German cities, Grzesinski complained that several of his campaign rallies had been brutally broken up and many participants suffered major injuries. Without sufficient police protection he was completely at the mercy of the SA and SS, and therefore asked party officials to be excused from staging any more campaign rallies.[90] Grzesinski mentioned that the Nazis were out for his blood because in a February 1932 speech in Leipzig he had demanded that Hitler

---

88. Brüning, *Memoiren, 1918–1934*, 651. During one of Brüning's campaign meetings on 20 February, for example, shots rang through the hall. According to Brüning, complaints lodged with Hindenburg were to no avail. Brüning constantly needed police protection for fear of violent attacks, and he frequently had to take detours to reach appointed campaign stops.

89. Waldemar Besson, *Württemberg und die deutsche Staatskrise 1928–1933. Eine Studie zur Auflösung der Weimarer Republik* (Stuttgart, 1959), 335. Reinhold Meier (1889–1971) had been chairman of the DDP in Stuttgart since 1924, and in 1930 Minister of Economics in Eugen Bolz's Center Party-led government. The Württemberg DDP retained its old name even after the founding of the Staatspartei. After the war, Meier became the first *Ministerpräsident* of the newly created state of Baden-Württemberg; from 1957 to 1960 he was chairman of the Free Democratic Party (FDP).

90. 24 February 1933: "Grzesinski to party secretaries Franz Klupsch (Dortmund), Paul Röhle (Frankfurt/Main), Paul Bugdahn (Altona) and Richard Hansen (Kiel)," in Matthias and Morsey, *Das Ende der Parteien*, 234–235.

be driven out of Germany with a horsewhip. During the election campaign, violent attacks by gangs of SA men on innocent bystanders, the liberal use of firearms, and breaches of the peace by members of Nazi organizations became commonplace. The perpetrators justified their use of violence by claiming that its ultimate goal was the extirpation of Marxism.[91]

The decisive and dramatic change in Germany's political climate came in the wake of the Reichstag fire during the night of 27 to 28 February, one week before the elections of 5 March. The Nazis used the Reichstag fire as a coveted opportunity to seize the political initiative once and for all. "The first event that sent chilling fright through our bones was the Reichstag fire. A premonition went through Germany: Now things are getting dangerous," Theodor Eschenburg wrote in his memoirs.[92] Erich Ebermayer also sensed the dawning of a new era and had similar forebodings: "Just now, last night, the revolution has begun in earnest."[93] On the morning following the fire, Eschenburg traveled by train from Berlin to Hamburg together with a distant relative and discussed with him "the brown plague." His companion "turned around with a worried glance at the compartment door. This was the first time I saw the 'German gaze.'"[94] Regardless of who was ultimately responsible for the fire, it provided the Nazis with a welcome excuse to suspend parts of the constitution and declare a state of emergency, both of which they used to break any real and potential opposition to their rule. Goebbels's diary entries, the memoirs of Franz von Papen and Otto Meissner, and the Nuremberg protocols of Göring's interrogation all indicate that the rulers themselves were surprised by the fire, though post-factum justifications and manipulations of the evidence were naturally in their own best interest.[95] Göring conceded that arrest lists had been compiled for later use, and quite independently of the fire, the timing of which had been highly

---

91. 26 February 1933 at BA Berlin-Lichterfelde, "Akten der Reichskanzlei, NSDAP," R 43 II, no. 1195, "Richard Moeller, Staatsminister a.D. an Hindenburg," 20. Moeller also points out that many Nazi party members had, until recently, been members of communist organizations; see also 23 February 1933 at *Foreign Relations of the United States*, vol. II (Washington, 1949), 198.

92. Eschenburg, *Letzten Endes meine ich doch*, 13.

93. Ebermayer, *Denn heute gehört uns Deutschland*, 33.

94. Eschenburg, *Letzten Endes meine ich doch*, 13. Eschenburg used the term "den deutschen Blick."

95. On Göring's interrogation, see Bracher, *Stufen der Machtergreifung*, 516–517.

inconvenient since, on account of Hitler's insistence that arrests be made without delay, he was forced to act in haste before preparations had been completed. Hans Mommsen also emphasizes this element of surprise.[96]

The Nazi press depicted the Reichstag fire not as the act of an individual (the Dutch communist Marinus van der Lubbe, who made a full confession after being arrested on Reichstag premises), but as a widespread communist conspiracy in which Social Democrats had also participated. The innate senselessness of the act, and the implausibility of any collaboration between the deeply hostile camps of Communists and Social Democrats, contributed to the widespread assumption of the better part of the French, British, and American press that ultimately the Nazis were to blame for the fire. This presupposition became even more convincing when the Nazis quickly proceeded to exploit the proffered opportunity by responding with an unprecedented spate of arrests.[97] The Prussian police had already ransacked the KPD's Berlin headquarters, the Karl Liebknecht Haus, on 23 and 24 February, though the announced release and publication of evidence indicating high treason, ostensibly unearthed during the search, never materialized.[98] The Nazis were the principal beneficiaries of the Reichstag fire, for not only did it provide them with a long-coveted pretext for the elimination of the KPD, but it also furnished a compelling theme for the remainder of the election campaign: the dreaded specter of an imminent Communist takeover. In his comprehensive study of the Reichstag fire published in the early 1960s, Fritz Tobias provides a vast amount of evidence that van der Lubbe was the sole perpetrator, thus triggering a controversy

96. Hans Mommsen, "The Reichstag Fire and its Political Consequences," in H.W. Koch, *Aspects of the Third Reich* (New York, 1985), 62–96.

97. Extensive preparations had been made to crack down on the KPD after the elections. Broszat estimated that in Prussia alone at least ten thousand people were taken into custody by 15 March. Reports from twenty-four (of thirty-four) Prussian *Regierungsbezirke* (administrative districts) cite 7,784 arrests by 15 March based on the Reichstag fire decree (Broszat, *Staat Hitlers*, 101–102). Already on 31 January, Goebbels confided to his diary (published during the Third Reich): "In discussions with the Führer, we establish guidelines for the fight against the Red terror . . . The Bolshevik attempt at revolution needs to flare up first. We will then crush them at the right moment." See Goebbels, *Vom Kaiserhof zur Reichskanzlei. Eine historische Darstellung in Tagebuchblättern* (Munich, 1940), 254.

98. Reports mentioned "many hundredweights of treasonable material." Bracher, *Stufen der Machtergreifung*, 123–124.

that continues to this day.[99] Despite the clarification of a multitude of details, it is unlikely that historians will ever come up with an explanation that will satisfy everyone.

At Hitler's direction, Göring ordered the arrest of all KPD deputies and other leading Communist functionaries during the very night of the Reichstag fire. This was followed by an immediate ban on the entire communist press.[100] After preliminary discussions in the Prussian Interior Ministry and two short debates in the Cabinet, Hindenburg signed the emergency decree on "The Protection of the People and the State," which had been drafted by Nazi Interior Minister Wilhelm Frick (who used parts of an older draft ordinance of July 1932), on 28 February.[101] This quickly cobbled-together provisionary arrangement became the unacknowledged "basic law" of the Third Reich. The decree terminated a number of fundamental rights that were subject to temporary suspension under Article 48.[102] In addition, the Reich government was authorized to usurp the power and rights of individual Land governments, if these failed to take measures necessary for the "Re-establishment of Public Order

99. Fritz Tobias, *Der Reichstagsbrand. Legende und Wirklichkeit* (Rastatt, 1962); Uwe Brackes et al., *Reichstagsbrand: Aufklärung einer historischen Legende* (Munich, 1986); Ulrich von Hehl, "Die Kontroverse um den Reichstagsbrand," *Vierteljahreshefte für Zeitgeschichte* 36 (1988), 259–280; Jürgen Schmädecke, Alexander Bahar, and Wilfried Kugel, "Der Reichstagsbrand in neuem Licht," *Historische Zeitschrift* 269 (1999), 603–651. Many doubted that the fire was the lone act of Marinus van der Lubbe, given the different sources of the blaze—from the ground floor to the cupola of the Reichstag building—which lent weight to the assumption that several arsonists were involved. A connection to the KPD leadership could never be proved, and the trial at the Supreme Court in Leipzig in December 1933 ended with the acquittal of the four communist codefendants for lack of evidence. See also Wolfgang Benz, ed., *Legenden, Lügen, Vorurteile*, 2nd ed. (Munich, 1992), 177–179.

100. Broszat, *Der Staat Hitlers*, 100.

101. Minuth, ed., *Akten der Reichskanzlei*, 128–131. Göring even ordered the temporary closure of museums and castles in Prussia. According to Frick, this decree was based on a 20 July 1932 Decree on the Re-establishment of Public Order and Safety in Greater-Berlin and Brandenburg. There were two short debates about the law at 11 a.m. and at 4:15 p.m. on 28 February; Hugenberg was absent on both occasions.

102. According to Article 48 of the Weimar Constitution, the fundamental rights set out in Articles 114 (personal freedom); 115 (inviolability of the home); 117 (confidentiality of postal and telegraph service); 118 (freedom of speech); 123 (freedom of assembly); 124 (freedom of association); and 153 (inviolability of personal property) could be temporarily suspended.

and Safety."[103] What was more, the Decree on the Protection of the People and the State was not accompanied by detailed guidelines from the Interior Ministry that specified how exactly the law was to be applied, as was the usual legal practice. The actual interpretation and enactment of the decree thus remained within the purview of the different Länder. Accordingly, it was interpreted and implemented differently in Prussia than in those Länder where the Nazi party was not yet part of the governing coalition.

Perhaps the greatest benefit the Nazis reaped from the Reichstag fire was of a psychological nature, for they succeeded in spreading a wave of fear and resentment against communism in all social classes, with the exception of the urban proletariat. Since 1918, newspapers, journals, and the entire multifaceted print media of the Weimar Republic had been publishing detailed reports of horrors perpetrated in the Soviet Union since the Revolution, reports that were confirmed by tales of Russian emigrants who had found temporary exile in Berlin and other German cities.[104] As far as average Germans were concerned, anything was preferable to Communist rule in their own country. What made the communist danger real, palpable, and eminently believable was the fact that the KPD had greatly improved its electoral standing on 6 November 1932 to become the third strongest party. With one hundred deputies and almost 17 percent of the vote, it was still behind the NSDAP and SPD, but far ahead of the Center and the DNVP. It was generally known that the KPD was controlled and directed by Moscow and that its ultimate goal was the establishment of a communist regime that would bring the dreaded conditions prevailing in the Soviet Union

---

103. Minuth, ed., *Akten der Reichskanzlei*, 132. Papen's last-minute effort to modify the ordinance in such a way that Hindenburg would have to make the decision whether or not to send a Reich Commissar to a particular Land was blocked (by Minister of Defense Blomberg, among others).

104. Oron Hale, *The Captive Press in the Third Reich* (Princeton, 1964). Hale has high praise for the German print media of the Weimar years: "During the 1920s, 7,000 periodicals in all fields of interest and knowledge, approximately 4,000 daily and weekly newspapers, and 30,000 books were published annually in Germany" (ibid., 1). He stressed the fact that the German press was decentralized and argued that "the German press surpassed that of any other country as an educational and cultural medium . . . In the amount of printed materials offered to subscribers, the German journals outdid all others" (2). In 1932, there were 4,703 daily and weekly newspapers; "52% of these were classified as independent or non-partisan." Ibid., 4.

to Germany. After the Reichstag fire, to many Germans only one party and its leading politician seemed willing and able to take the drastic measures required to avert this mortal danger—Hitler and the NSDAP.

The *Bürgertum* was particularly apprehensive. The deeply patriotic Luise Solmitz, who took the Nazis' exaggerated fearmongering about the communist threat at face value, epitomized bourgeois reactions and considered Hitler to be the only protection against mortal danger.[105] Solmitz blindly swallowed the tales of impending communist putsches and coup attempts, though she conceded that "it would sound like a cock-and-bull story, were it not for Russia, which has experienced Asiatic methods of torture and orgies of violence . . ." Government press reports about communist plans for an imminent overthrow, as related by Solmitz, sound farfetched: "Hostages from the bourgeoisie, wives and children of police officers as human shields, destruction of all cultural values as in Russia: castles, museums, churches. . . . They wanted to send armed mobs into villages to commit murder and plunder, while terror was to take possession of the larger cities, denuded of police, in the meantime. Poison, boiling water, everything from the most sophisticated to the most primitive tool was to be turned into a weapon."[106] It would be wrong to assume that credulity and blind faith in government propaganda were confined to certain sections of the population. Even members of the political and cultural elite believed that the communist danger was real. In a conversation with Cardinal Michael Faulhaber on 1 March 1933, an account of which was written up by the Cardinal, Papen reported on the police raid of the communist Liebknechthaus and recounted similar stories, which he obviously believed himself: that communist revolutionaries had relinquished their former practice of storming government buildings, but were now intent on wearing down the people by setting fire to farmsteads, ripping up railroad tracks, kidnapping the children of officials on their way home from school to use them as human shields in strikes, poison food, break into houses

105. Reprinted in Jochmann, *Nationalsozialismus und Revolution*; entry of 28 February 1933, 426: "All thinking and feeling of most Germans is dominated by Hitler, his fame rises to the stars, and he is the savior in an evil, sad German world."

106. Jochmann, *Nationalsozialismus und Revolution*; entry of 1 March, 427–428.

and shoot the doorman and the staff, and so on. Faulhaber seemed to have considered the information reliable and entered it into his files accordingly.[107]

German National propaganda was also modified in the remaining days between the Reichstag fire and the 5 March election, though it avoided the hysterical tone of the Nazis. The official party bulletin with the headline "Save the People and the Fatherland," published after the fire, left no doubt where it stood: "Bolshevism and its breeding grounds" had to be "annihilated root and branch" to make room for a new "Christian conservative state ethos."[108] In his last important speech before the election, Hugenberg argued in the same vein that "the firebrand that Bolshevism had thrown into the German Reichstag" constituted a "declaration of war by Communists" and their Social Democratic accomplices. He spoke of the necessity of "draconian measures" and use of the death penalty.[109] Still, Hugenberg's language is more measured than Göring's, who seemed to have convinced himself of the imminence of the communist danger and worked himself up into a rage when shouting: "Here I do not have to practice justice; here I only have to destroy and exterminate, nothing else."[110] Ultimately, such hate-filled passion made his rhetoric more effective, as his audience undoubtedly perceived it as a deeply felt anger about a political situation that profoundly affected them. Under these conditions, Erich Ebermayer noted resignedly, there would be "a resounding victory for the Nazis and the Battlefront Black-White-Red. The bourgeoisie, which, for a while, had been vacillating and repelled by the roughness and lack of polish of the Nazis, have now been frightened and won over by the Reichstag fire."[111] For Ebermayer, the *Bürgertum's* abdication of responsibility is the most humiliating and shameful fact of the period. The Nazis, he argued, could not be blamed for capitalizing on their victory; they were, after all, an "anti-*bürgerliche*, revolutionary

107. Ludwig Volk, ed., *Akten Kardinal Michael Faulhabers 1917–1945*, vol. I (Mainz, 1975), 651–653; reprinted in Becker and Becker, eds., *Hitlers Machtergreifung*, 113–114.

108. "Rettet Volk und Vaterland," *Mitteilungen der Deutschnationalen Volkspartei*, 4, at BA Berlin-Lichterfelde, "Pressearchiv Reichslandbund, DNVP Parteitage," R 8034 II, no. 4334, 64a.

109. "Hugenberg–Papen–Seldte im Endkampf um die Entscheidung für die Nation," *Süddeutsche Zeitung*, 2 March 1933.

110. Göring, *Reden und Aufsätze*, 27–28.

111. Ebermayer, *Denn heute gehört uns Deutschland*, 34, entry of 5 March.

party" and had never made any bones about that fact:[112] "Weak, cowardly, and inclined to any betrayal and compromise is always only the *Bürgertum*—that is, my, our social class. That part of the *Bürgertum* that now helps the Nazis to achieve total power and assists them in the 'legal' implementation of their revolution, bears the real guilt for everything that may yet happen to us."[113]

112. Ibid., 34.
113. Ibid., 35.

Chapter III

CONSERVATIVES AND THE NSDAP DURING THE "NATIONAL REVOLUTION" OF MARCH 1933

After the Reichstag fire and the 5 March 1933 elections, the "*Nationale Erhebung*" (national awakening) turned into the "national revolution."[1] In the ministerial discussions of 7 March, Hitler declared before his Cabinet that he considered "the events of 5 March . . . [to be] a revolution."[2] And on 8 March, Goebbels noted in his diary: "The German revolution marches steadfastly on and cannot and will not be halted."[3] The journal *Die Hilfe* used the term "cataclysmic change of power" to describe post-election events: after 5 March the Nazis usurped power in those German states not yet ruled by National Socialist governments. Ministers, mayors, and high officials were forcibly removed from their positions, personally humiliated, and in some cases even physically manhandled. The central characteristic feature of the period between 5 and 20 March was the boundless, willful, and unevenly distributed violence against

1. The political journal *Die Hilfe* wrote on 18 March 1933: "Theorists of revolution may debate whether an election can constitute a 'revolution' or belongs to the sphere of 'evolution.' That the concomitant phenomena of the cataclysmic change of power [*Machtumwälzung*] present a picture typical of revolutionary actions, as we well remember from the winter of unrest 1918/19, is clear to everybody." In *Die Hilfe* 39 (1933), 165; see also Becker and Becker, eds., *Hitlers Machtergreifung*, 146.
2. Minuth, ed., *Akten der Reichskanzlei*, 160.
3. Diary entry of 8 March 1933, in Joseph Goebbels, *Vom Kaiserhof zur Reichskanzlei. Eine historische Darstellung in Tagebuchblättern* (Munich, 1940), 277.

everything and everybody that stood in the path of the Nazi take-over. Very few dared to resist actively. In some regions of Germany, openly confronting the SA could be tantamount to suicide. Random Nazi violence was often accompanied by the settling of old scores. Some of those considered a thorn in the side of local Nazi functionaries or the SA, or those who had once run afoul of them in the past, were murdered outright.[4] Even though, on the whole, no detailed "master plan" existed, the violence was not always spontaneous; the Berlin SA, for instance, had compiled lists with names of their Communist adversaries well before 28 February. Violent behavior and aggression toward political enemies varied regionally and also depended on the local SA, Nazi party officials, and the heads of the local police. While in the three East Prussia *Regierungsbezirke* (governmental districts) of Königsberg, Gumbinnen, and Allenstein a total of 421 persons were taken into "protective custody" in March and April 1933, the number was almost ten times as high (3,818) in the Düsseldorf *Regierungsbezirk* in the Rhine province, where SS *Gruppenführer* Weitzel was acting police commissioner (*Polizeipräsident*); the Trier *Regierungsbezirk*, in contrast, reported only seventy-eight cases of protective custody for the same period.[5] These numbers do not include all those prisoners languishing in the torture cellars and so-called "wild" (extra-judicial) concentration camps of the SA that are so vividly described by Rudolf Diels, the first head of the Gestapo.[6]

4. See, for example, Martin Broszat, Elke Fröhlich, Falk Wiesemann, eds., *Bayern in der NS-Zeit. Soziale Lage und politisches Verhalten der Bevölkerung im Spiegel vertraulicher Berichte* (Munich and Vienna, 1977), vol. I, 432.

5. Martin Broszat "Nationalsozialistische Konzentrationslager 1933–1945," in Martin Broszat, Hans-Adolf Jacobsen and Helmut Krausnick, *Anatomie des SS-Staates*, vol. II, 5th ed. (Munich, 1989), 21. Fritz Weitzel (1904–1940), originally active in the Socialist Youth Movement, a member of the SS since 1926, and SS *Gruppenführer* since 1931; he became commissioner of the Düsseldorf police at the age of 29. See Weiß, ed., *Biographisches Lexikon zum Dritten Reich*, 484.

6. Rudolf Diels, *Lucifer ante Portas. Es spricht der erste Chef der Gestapo* (Stuttgart, 1950); see especially the chapter "Prügelstätten und Konzentrationslager," 187–197: "I was now able to enter the torture chamber with police squads. There the floors of a few empty rooms used by the torturers were covered with straw. The victims we encountered were close to death by starvation. For days they had, in standing position, been locked into narrow closets to extort 'confessions.' 'Interrogations' had begun and ended with beatings, whereby a dozen ruffians battered victims with iron bars, rubber truncheons and whips at hourly intervals. The suffering was evidenced by knocked-out teeth and broken bones. As we entered, these living skeletons lay there in rows with festering, suppurating

The violence of the "national revolution" exempted absolutely no one: social position, political prominence, international reputation, services rendered to the nation, scientific achievements, or literary prominence offered no protection. All Germans were potential victims of house searches and confinement to concentration camps. On 21 March 1933, for example, the British Ambassador reported on searches at the house of Siegfried von Kardorff, a prominent former Free Conservative deputy in the Prussian Landtag between 1909 and 1918, later a DVP Reichstag deputy and Reichstag Vice President from 1928 to 1932.[7] The Nazis searched the house of the widow of Friedrich Ebert (Hindenburg's predecessor as Reich President) for republican flags and ransacked Albert Einstein's home, looking for explosives.[8] In their fervor to eliminate the movement's imagined, potential, and real enemies, members of the SA and other Nazi organizations shunned any form of rational thought or utilitarian calculation of what was in Germany's best short- and long-term interests. Indifferent to the harm done to Germany's reputation abroad and to the immense losses in all spheres of art, science and technical expertise, the Nazis threatened, and many times persecuted, those who had once been outspoken in their criticism of Nazism or who now seemed likely to swell the ranks of potential enemies. The constant fear generated by house searches and arrests that hung like a Damocles sword over the population proved to be an effective deterrent: people were afraid to speak their minds, let alone resist Nazi aggression actively. Untold numbers may have felt like Theodor Eschenburg, who addressed the issue in his memoirs: "I do not recall any personal acquaintances who were in concentration camps, but one often heard of beatings with canes and truncheons or of whippings, mistreatment by punching and kicking, deprivation of food or sleep. Torture was committed behind closed doors, but it was correctly calculated that rumors would make the rounds and set people's tongues wagging, to instill fear and thereby

---

wounds on rotting straw. There was not one whose body was not covered from head to foot with blue, yellow, and green bruises that bore witness to the inhuman thrashing visited upon them."

7. Siegfried von Kardorff (1873–1945). Free Conservative Party deputy in Prussia (1909–1918), then deputy for the DNVP in 1919; crossed the floor from the DNVP to the DVP after the Kapp Putsch; Vice-President of the Reichstag from 1928–1932.

8. *Documents on British Foreign Policy*, 1919–1939, 2nd series, vol. IV (London, 1950), 472.

ensure submission and obedience. I personally was always in fear of the torture and corporal punishment that had permeated our consciousness."[9] The Nazis' violent usurpation of power in Germany's remaining Länder, and the fear generated by their sometimes arbitrary, sometimes systematic violence illustrated beyond the shadow of a doubt that after 5 March 1933 a new era had dawned upon Germany. This did not mean, however, that the whole country descended into chaos or complete lawlessness. In fact, one defining characteristic of this period was the coexistence of legality and illegality. Unbridled SA violence and terror often went hand in hand with the continued smooth functioning of the rule of law in certain spheres of public life. Since Nazi aggression took place within the confines of some form of established legal order (though regional differences were significant), many Germans learned to live with the violence and assumed that only those who actively opposed the rising fortunes of National Socialism had anything to fear from the movement's thugs. Since Germans had become unwillingly accustomed to political violence from the election campaigns of the early 1930s, during the course of which hundreds were killed and thousands seriously injured, large sections of the middle classes may genuinely have perceived the seizure of power as a less tumultuous period than the last years of the Weimar Republic, in particular since the "patriotic" majority largely endorsed the brutal suppression of the Left and chose to ignore Nazi lawlessness. In fact, to many, Nazi terror appeared less as an instrument of repression than an unconventional, but welcome, means to restore order. The combination of violence and legality led to vastly different interpretations of the "revolution": opponents viewed it as a violent, illegal overthrow of an unstable but constitutional political system; supporters saw it as an orderly, systematic, and thoroughly legal takeover of power to save the nation from the results of what they considered the disastrous political experiment of Weimar.

Becoming Obsolete:
The Outcome of the March Elections

Given the advantages the NSDAP and the DNVP had enjoyed over their opponents during the election campaign, the electoral success

---

9. Eschenburg, *Letzten Endes meine ich doch*, 16.

of the governing coalition was less than overwhelming,[10] and hardly a reason for the loudly professed enthusiasm of Nazi leaders.[11] Despite its temporary name change into "Battlefront Black-White-Red," designed to appeal to a wider cross section of patriotic Germans in the March elections, the DNVP barely matched the 8 percent of the vote it received in the 6 November 1932 elections. The anticipated influx of national-minded Catholic voters to whom the all-inclusive label "Black-White-Red," intentionally reminiscent of the old Imperial colors, was meant to appeal did not materialize. In the elections for the Prussian Landtag, also held on 5 March 1933, the DNVP gained approximately 2 percent compared to their poor showing on 24 April 1932.[12] The NSDAP, on the other hand, managed to improve its results from 33.1 percent to 43.9 percent, a gain of 92 seats (from 196 to 288) in an election with a voter turnout of 88.8%.[13] The intangible factor in the outcome was the element of intimidation and the psychological pressure on voters to mark "Liste 1" and vote for the NSDAP, especially in small towns rife with rumors that the confidentiality of the vote might not be guaranteed.

10. The French Ambassador André François-Poncet noted that apart from the prohibition of opposition newspapers, "the public was subject to systematic pressure . . . intimidation and . . . a kind of hypnosis. This pressure was evident in the dismissal of officials, through instances of individual violence, the use of radio solely on behalf of the government . . . through the elevation of brownshirts to the ranks of regular police." Becker and Becker, eds., *Hitlers Machtergreifung*, 127.

11. Hitler interpreted the election result as "a revolution," and Goebbels, in his published diary, waxes equally enthusiastic: "Then the first results come in. One victory followed by another, fantastic and unbelievable. As we returned to the Reich Chancellery after the performance, the glorious triumph has become reality, more stunning in its magnitude than any of us would have dared to hope." Goebbels, *Vom Kaiserhof zur Reichskanzlei*, entry of 5 March 1933, 275.

12. Edgar J. Feuchtwanger, *From Weimar to Hitler. Germany 1918–1933*, 2nd ed. (New York, 1995), 329; Falter, et al., *Wahlen und Abstimmungen in der Weimarer Republik*, 101. In comparison to the April 1932 elections, the DNVP gained 600,000 votes in Prussia and improved its showing from 6.9 percent to 8.8 percent, or thirty-one to forty-three seats.

13. This was the highest voter turnout since 1919, and an increase of almost five percent over the July 1932 elections (84.1 percent). The voter turnout for Reichstag elections had been high throughout the Republic, never falling below 75 percent. The lowest voter turnout was registered for the elections of 20 May 1928 (75.6 percent), while 83 percent turned out for the elections to the National Assembly in January 1919, and 82 percent for the decisive elections of 14 September 1930. Kolb, *Weimarer Republik*, 308–309.

Otherwise there were no major fluctuations from the pattern established by recent elections. The relative strength of the Catholic parties remained mostly unchanged: the Center gained four seats and obtained seventy-four mandates, though its percentage share fell from 11.9 percent to 11.2 percent, while the Bavarian People's Party lost two seats for a total of eighteen seats with its percentage share falling from 3.1 percent to 2.7 percent; the small *bürgerliche* and liberal parties disappeared almost entirely, so that the DVP was left with a mere two seats, the Christlich-Sozialer Volksdienst with four, and the Staatspartei with five seats and 0.9 percent of the popular vote. Among the leftist parties the SPD suffered only slight losses from 121 to 120 seats and 20.4 percent to 18.3 percent of the popular vote, while the Communists held on to 81 seats with 12.3 percent of the popular vote, though all Communist mandates were subsequently repealed and the party's deputies arrested. Since, therefore, only 566 of the elected 647 delegates would take their seats in the new Reichstag, the NSDAP alone enjoyed an absolute majority with its 288 deputies. German National deputies were now no longer needed to obtain simple majorities, a fact that was not without repercussions on the Nazis' comportment and their tenor of discourse toward what now seemed an increasingly dispensable alliance partner.

It is difficult to determine the precise impact of the Reichstag fire and its aftermath on the outcome of the elections, since there is no way of knowing what the results would have been without it. But it is clear that the fire and its consequences had a significant impact, as the French Ambassador André-François-Poncet[14] aptly explained: "The unassuming, naïve masses in the provinces saw in this event the full confirmation of the charge that order and security in the country were threatened not just by Bolshevik conspiracies, but in general by the politics of leftist parties, who were at the least guilty of weakness and blindness. A feeling of fear and loathing spread among the people, coupled with feelings of gratitude and enthusiasm for those who had demonstrated such energy and saved Germany, thanks to the boldness of their decisions and the steadfastness of their actions."[15] In the eyes of many Germans,

14. André François-Poncet, 1887–1978, French Ambassador in Berlin 1931–1938, Rome 1938–1940, and, after the war, first Allied High Commissioner in West Germany, 1949–1953, Ambassador in Bonn, 1953–1955.
15. Documents Diplomatiques Français 1932–1939. Première Série, Vol. II (Paris, 1966), 744–745; reprinted in Becker and Becker, eds., *Hitlers Machtergreifung*, 127–128.

this energy and resolve had often been missing during the fourteen years of the Weimar Republic. Frequently, during the crisis-ridden early years and especially during the permanent instability following 1929, wide sections of the population longed for politicians with the ruthless resolve to take drastic action and to make sometimes unpopular decisions. Since the political left was blamed for most domestic problems, it is hardly surprising that the bulk of the middle classes did not object to "settling the score with Marxism," even if this involved unfettered violence. The suppression of the KPD was, for the most part, generally welcomed. This was especially true for Hitler's German National coalition partners: In fact, Hugenberg himself had first proposed a general ban on the KPD during the first Cabinet meeting of the Hitler government on 30 January 1933, insisting that a ban was preferable to new elections. He had to be restrained by Hitler and other Cabinet members, who pointed out that the time had not yet come for such a step.[16]

The momentum the Nazis received from the Reichstag fire, the resulting emergency legislation, and the complete elimination of their most obdurate opponent, the KPD, together with the party's success in the 5 March 1933 elections were now all put to good use in the takeover of those state governments that still eluded Nazi control. In the relatively short period between 30 January, when Hitler became Chancellor, and 14 July, when the NSDAP was declared to be the sole legitimate party, the speedy and virtually unobstructed takeover of those non-Prussian states not yet in Nazi hands may well have constituted the single most significant success on the road to establishing dictatorial rule. Two elements greatly facilitated this takeover: (1) The Nazi rank and file played a central role in the conquest of the non-Prussian Länder by applying pressure from below through assemblies and marches and virtually setting itself up as herald of the people's will. The state governments had no choice but to react to the ensuing "disorder" which, in turn, gave Berlin the opportunity to step in, since the Decree on the Protection of the People and the State, passed after the Reichstag fire, permitted the takeover of states if they proved unable to maintain law and order. Local Nazi authorities then took over the police force so as to completely control the state executive. (2) Already during the last days of February the very real threat of having a "*Reichskommissar*" imposed on them hovered starkly over several Länder, since

---

16. See Minuth, ed., *Die Regierung Hitler*, 2–4.

the state governments of Bavaria, Württemberg, Hesse, Saxony, and Hamburg had only acting minority governments, so that it could be claimed with some justification that they were inherently unstable.[17] The Nazis thus succeeded in their bid to usurp Länder governments by a combination of self-engendered "populist support" and strong-arm tactics to seize and maintain power that was partly backed up by the emergency legislation of 28 February.

Rife with symbolism, the takeover of the state governments began with a "flag war." On 5 March, the National Socialists among Hamburg police department officials raised the swastika flag on police barracks and buildings to force the surrender of the police department to a Nazi chief of police. The government of the Hanseatic city, the Hamburg Senate, had already been weakened by the resignation of three Social Democratic senators, including Hamburg's chief of police, *Polizeisenator* Schönfelder, on 3 March. The Lord Mayor of the city-state, Dr. Carl Petersen, a prominent member of the Staatspartei who had long and successfully served as mayor of his native city, thereupon offered his resignation. At this point, the now leaderless rump Senate showed characteristic reluctance to order its mostly non-Nazi police officers and squads, the vast majority of whom were loyal to the Hamburg government, to take down the swastika flags. In the meantime, Nazi Interior Minister Wilhelm Frick, apprised of events by the Nazi *Gauleitung* in Hamburg, took advantage of the indecision of the Senate. Citing the Reichstag fire emergency legislation, he ordered the appointment of a provisional head of the Hamburg police on the evening of 5 March, asserting that "public safety" in the Hanseatic city could not be guaranteed.[18] The takeover of the political apparatus in the city-state of Bremen on 6 March followed much the same pattern. Here too, when confronted with the hoisting of the swastika flag that so ostentatiously flew in the face of the legally elected democratic government, the Senate could not bring itself to utilize its own police to force the Nazis back into line. Instead, to protest the Nazi action, all SPD senators resigned. A similar system of wresting power from non-Nazi governments was practiced in other Länder as well, in particular in the state capitals of Darmstadt, Stuttgart, and Munich, where "victory marches" of Nazi supporters organized

17. Broszat, *Der Staat Hitlers*, 132.

18. Broszat, *Der Staat Hitlers*, 130–140; Karl Dietrich Bracher, *Stufen der Machtergreifung*, 190–202; Henning Timpke, ed., *Dokumente zur Gleichschaltung des Landes Hamburg* (Frankfurt, 1964); Thamer, *Verführung und Gewalt*, 258–265.

in revolutionary processions, together with military-like threatening parades and ostentatious marches by the SA and SS, did their bit to exert pressure on the respective Land governments to hand over power to the NSDAP. In all of this, the raising of the swastika flag at town halls and other public buildings heralded the imminence of the Nazi takeover and often triggered off unrest.[19] Thus, in the few days between 5 and 9 March 1933, the Nazis succeeded in imposing National Socialist Reich Commissars not only on Hamburg and Bremen, but also on Lübeck, Schaumburg-Lippe, Hesse, Baden, Württemberg, Saxony, and Bavaria; this was quickly followed by the formation of National Socialist governments in those states. The combined population of those Länder in which the Nazis had usurped power between 5 and 9 March 1933 exceeded 21 million.[20] These tremendous Nazi successes found no equivalent in comparable German National political gains. On the contrary, the Nazi coalition partner had hardly been given due consideration when it came to dividing up the political spoils that accrued as a result of the swift takeovers.[21] During the course of March, German Nationals looked on powerlessly as the Nazis filled the posts of provincial governors (*Oberpräsidenten*) in Prussia (with the exception of the western provinces) with their own *Gauleiter* or with SA *Gruppenführer*.[22] Protests were to no avail, though the DNVP leadership expressed its concern that, contrary to Hitler's professions, National Socialists had consistently filled *Oberpräsidenten* positions with untrained personnel, and not civil servants with professional expertise.[23]

This almost effortless takeover of Germany's non-National Socialist Länder clearly showed that the fate of Weimar democracy was sealed and that the battle had been fought and won by the Nazis. On 9 March the American Ambassador summed up the prevailing sentiment in his report to Secretary of State Hull: "Democracy in Germany has received a blow from which it may never recover. Germany has been submerged under a huge Nazi wave. The much

---

19. Martin Broszat, *Der Staat Hitlers*, 135.
20. See Table 2 in Appendix.
21. Broszat, *Der Staat Hitlers*, 140.
22. See Table 3 in Appendix.
23. Peter Thiele, "NSDAP und allgemeine innere Staatsverwaltung. Untersuchungen zum Verhältnis von Partei und Staat in Dritten Reich." Diss. Phil., (Munich, 1967); see also Broszat, *Der Staat Hitlers*, 445.

heralded Third Reich has become a reality."[24] The opposition, in particular the leaders of the SPD, realized that they had missed the time and opportunity for resistance.[25] At the same time, SPD members began to leave the party in droves, especially civil servants who feared for their careers.[26] National Socialists, on the other hand, could barely fend off the stream of new applicants. Nazism had succeeded in putting itself forward as capable of offering a better alternative for the future, just as potential political opponents to Nazism faltered and caved in without resistance or defected to the Nazis out of opportunism, fear, or—quite often—genuine conviction. In public perception (as in reality) the "national revolution" of March 1933 had been pushed through solely by the Nazi party and its organizations, without any meaningful participation on the part of their DNVP coalition partner. In contrast to the National Socialist party base, the average DNVP member had not participated in the massive political changes that swept through Germany in March 1933. Soon many German Nationals would be forced into the role either of victims, and thus actual targets of attack, or disbelieving onlookers with no resources at their disposal other than indignant letters of protest to Papen's Vice Chancellery (soon to be known as the Reich Complaints Office)[27] and the DNVP headquarters in Berlin. Both offices were natural contact points for voices of protest against Nazi violations of the law, though both were in effect connected with the

24. *Foreign Relations of the United States. Diplomatic Papers 1933*, Vol. 2 (Washington, 1949), 209.

25. Hagen Schulze, ed., *Anpassung oder Widerstand? Aus den Akten des Parteivorstandes der Deutschen Sozialdemokratie 1932–1933* (Bonn and Bad-Godesberg, 1975), 161–180. In his *Germany: Jekyll & Hyde* (Berlin, 1996), a book originally written only seven years after these events, Sebastian Haffner argued that the potential and the will to resist did exist in the mass organizations of those Germans who initially opposed the Nazis, but that their leaders feared to shoulder the responsibility to initiate such a momentous step and basically left their followers in the lurch.

26. For revealing examples of resignation statements see Erich Matthias, "Die Sozialdemokratische Partei Deutschlands," in Matthias and Morsey, eds., *Das Ende der Parteien 1933* (Bonn, 1960), 101–278, esp. 239–241. A typical resignation statement of 10 March 1933 read as follows: "Due to prevailing political conditions, I see myself compelled, in consideration of my family's well-being, to declare my resignation from the party. I am presently unable to provide additional reasons. W.L., (Stadtbaumeister)." Ibid., 240.

27. The term *Reichsbeschwerdestelle* is used by (among others) Norbert Frei, *Der Führerstaat. Nationalsozialistische Herrschaft 1933–1945*, 6th ed. (Munich, 2003), 26.

government. Still, in the eyes of many, these were two of the remaining political offices whose members tried to salvage remnants
of the swiftly fading Rechtsstaat.

The floods of correspondence arriving at the offices of the Vice
Chancellery and the DNVP party headquarters bore vivid testimony to the deep bewilderment of conservative Germans, who
initially had enthusiastically embraced the Hitler government and
were now left dumbfounded by the daily upheavals. This tumultuous course of events was not how they had envisioned the longed-
for national awakening. Walter Baerwolff,[28] party manager of the
Bavarian DNVP, wrote a detailed letter of protest to Papen along
these lines on 10 March 1933. The events in Munich on the night
between 9 and 10 March, he reported, could be compared only with
those of the revolution of 1918: "Forcible liberation of SA members
who were incarcerated under suspicion of arson and whose trials are
impending, arbitrary arrest and maltreatment of the leader of the
Jewish religious community, then of Interior Minister Dr. Stützel
and a further 500 people; some of these arrests are personal acts of
revenge by individual SA troopers."[29] In these circumstances, Baerwolff argued, cooperation between the DNVP and NSDAP was
absolutely impossible in Bavaria. Given these Nazi actions, he urged
Papen to ensure that power in Prussia be apportioned fairly in order
to safeguard the "endangered authority of the Reich President."[30]
A similar letter arrived from Regensburg on 10 March, reporting
SA outrages and terror in that city and urging Papen to make sure
that "justice and the rule of law" be restored in Regensburg.[31] The
conservative establishment sensed how power was inexorably slip-
ping from its hands.

Given the more than modest results the DNVP attained in the
March elections, and the simple truth that the party was no longer needed to obtain a parliamentary majority, the Nazi party's

28. Walter Baerwolff (born 1896); Chairman of the Bavarian DNVP
1920–1933; member of the Bavarian State Parliament 1924–1932, and the
Reichstag 1932–1933. See Weiß and Hoser, eds., *Die Deutschnationalen*, 246; and,
for more details on his correspondence, "Institut für Zeitgeschichte," Munich,
"DNVP in Bayern, 1921–1934," ED 714/1-2.

29. 10 March 1933 at BA Berlin-Lichterfelde, "Stellvertreter des Reichskanzlers, Kanzlei von Papen," R 53, no. 71 "Allgemeine Politische Angelegenheiten," 115.

30. Ibid., 116.

31. Ibid., 134.

treatment of its small coalition partner now changed apace. After all, the elections had added 5,540,000 votes to the National Socialists' total, while the DNVP had gained a mere 177,000 votes, despite the fact that 3,896,000 more voters had gone to the polls.[32] Referring to the election results, the National Socialist *Schlesische Tageszeitung* commented unequivocally on 6 March: "The German people looks to the future, not the past. It stands behind Adolf Hitler and his vision and not behind the forces of reaction that are personified in Hugenberg."[33] An incident on 10 March 1933 clearly demonstrated that even established conservative politicians such as Düsseldorf Lord Mayor Robert Lehr were totally at the mercy of the Nazis when confronted with National Socialist violence.[34] On that day, a group of Nazi ruffians forced their way into the office of the mayor, who was in conference with the municipal councilor Dr. Haas. In the course of the ensuing altercation, Haas was repeatedly hit in the face with a leather whip, while the mayor and other councilors were forcibly prevented from rendering assistance.[35] Even though Haas was politically affiliated with the nationalist Right, Nazis accused him of failing to resist French pressure energetically enough during the occupation of the Ruhr in 1923 and of supporting the separatist tendencies encouraged by the French. Though this was demonstrably false, Mayor Lehr was compelled to furlough Haas.[36] Now finally in power, Nazis could at random dole out "retribution" wherever and whenever they saw fit, even for "offenses" long past. Considering that even a German National mayor in the capital city of Prussia's most populous province had to stand by helplessly as

32. Numbers of Nazi votes rose from 11,737,000 to 17,277,000; those of the DNVP from 2,959,000 to 3,136,000, corresponding to a rise from 33.1 percent to 43.9 percent for the NSDAP, while the DNVP declined (due to higher voter turnout) from 8.3 percent to 8.0 percent. On 6 November 1932 a total of 35,758,000 valid votes had been cast; on 5 March 1933 the total was 39,654,000. Kolb, *Weimarer Republik*, 308–309.

33. 6 March 1933 in *Schlesische Tageszeitung* at BA Berlin-Lichterfelde, "DNVP, Politischer Schriftwechsel 1933," R 8005, no. 19, 167.

34. Robert Lehr (1883–1956), German National mayor of Düsseldorf, 1924–1933.

35. Repeated reference was made to this incident in the files; see BA Berlin-Lichterfelde, "DNVP, Politischer Schriftwechsel," R 8005, no. 19, 165–166; and "Reichskanzlei, NSDAP" R 43, II, no. 1195, "Telegramm von Lehr an Hitler," 55.

36. BA Berlin-Lichterfelde, "DNVP: Politischer Schriftwechsel," R 8005, no. 19, 165.

Nazi ruffians ransacked his offices and threatened city officials, one might ask how the average German could defend himself or lend assistance to others when confronted with SA terror.[37]

Crusades against Bourgeois Corruption and Special Interests

Incidents of Nazi terror and the ensuing futile and enraged indignation of conservative and national-minded Germans, who had initially welcomed the DNVP-NSDAP coalition government, were legion and reports of them abound in the files. In letters of protest sent to the DNVP's Berlin headquarters that were addressed to Hugenberg's deputy, Friedrich von Winterfeld, or the party manager, Major Hans Nagel, conservative citizens vented their dismay and consternation.[38] It now gradually dawned upon the average rank and file member of the DNVP that, due to Nazi ascendancy in all spheres of politics, their traditional way of life was about to change fundamentally. They seethed with impotent fury over the impertinence and lack of respect shown by gangs of young Nazi thugs, who displayed flippant indifference and dragged everything that was dear to them through the mud: public order, a well regulated life, morals, decency and decorum, experience, the sanctity of property, respect for achieved rank, reputation, Bildung, and traditional lifestyles. DNVP member Karl Hoffmann, chairman of the *Kriegerverein* (warrior's league) in the small town of Schlichtingsheim in the Grenzmark Posen-Westpreußen, lodged a vehement protest over a National Socialist rally held on Friday 10 March, where speakers insulted the middle-class citizenry (*Bürgerschaft*) and accused Hoffmann of "embezzling welfare funds."[39] "Young thugs" had abused female German National delegates nominated for the

37. In 1933, Düsseldorf had a population of 498,600. Nazi voters in the March elections in this industrial and overwhelmingly Catholic city accounted for only 29 percent. The Rhine province had 7,627,117 inhabitants in 1933, more than any of the other German states, including Bavaria. Thamer, *Verführung und Gewalt*, 258, and *Statistisches Jahrbuch für das Deutsche Reich*, 5.

38. Friedrich von Winterfeld (1875–1949) was a member of the Prussian Landtag from 1921 to 1933 and Chairman of the parliamentary faction of the DNVP (1928–1933); then "permanent deputy" of the party leader since February 1933.

39. BA Berlin-Lichterfelde, "DNVP: Politischer Schriftwechsel," R 8005, no. 19, 159. According to Hoffmann's letter of 31 March, these charges were

town council in a "particularly vile manner" and threatened to depose the German National mayor without the least cause.[40] Like most other complaints, Hoffmann's appeal to the DNVP leadership had no effect whatsoever.

There was an underlying purpose behind Nazi accusations of misappropriation of funds, embezzlement, and corruption. These were frequently used and very effective tools to incriminate the bourgeoisie, especially since there was often truth in the accusation that members of the *Bürgertum* engaged in special-interest politics. This very suspicion of complicity in abusing class privileges aroused by the Nazi press and in party rallies was usually sufficient to discredit the bourgeoisie and its *bürgerliche Interessenpolitik* and feed into popular resentment of entrenched interests. Among the ranks of the bourgeoisie, it had long been a traditional custom to pass contracts to each other, a practice from which the socially less prominent Nazis were excluded. In the economic cosmos of small and medium-sized towns, the public sector, dominated by traditional "bourgeois" sensibilities, had an important role to play in granting contracts to private firms. In this milieu, nepotism, cronyism, and "irregularities" of all kinds were nothing unusual. There was an inexorable link between this economically advantageous position of the conservative middle classes in the small towns of Pomerania, East Prussia, and in parts of Brandenburg and Silesia, and their strong political influence that predominated until 1933.[41] By alleging misuse of economic privileges, the Nazis directed the limelight to, and thereby cast aspersions on, the political representatives of the supposedly privileged *Bürgertum*—including their own coalition partner—hoping to shatter the nexus of political and economic power. Here two interesting general points emerge: (1) National Socialist propaganda used anti-bourgeois attacks to gain populist support, and this strategy proved very successful. The attacks on the bourgeoisie were sold to the public as a kind of rebellion against class privileges, which naturally resonated with the average simple

---

fabrications, and he lodged a complaint with the public prosecutor's office against slander.

40. Ibid., 159–160. Hoffmann was especially indignant that such young louts would dare to "throw dirt at national-minded German women" without being punished for it. Hoffmann thought that Hugenberg should report these incidents directly to Hitler, since the Reich Chancellor "so firmly espoused propriety in public life."

41. See Table 4 in Appendix.

citizen, who was excluded from the tight circle of special bourgeois interests. The success of this strategy explains in part the "positive" support for Nazism during the *Machtergreifung*, as opposed to the "negative" support that arose from the National Socialists' more coercive tactics. (2) The Nazis used their attacks on the *Bürger*[42] to demonstrate that the bourgeoisie and, after the inexorable decline of the liberal parties, their last remaining political representative, the DNVP, tried to protect special interests, while the Nazis stood for "universal" values and vowed to fight for the universal interests of the national community as opposed to the particular interests of a privileged class.

A case in point is an incident in the Pomeranian district town of Köslin, where German Nationals were subjected to acrimonious Nazi attacks during the week following the elections of 5 March.[43] In a Nazi rally for the local elections to be held on 12 March, National Socialist speakers bluntly declared that the (Imperial) "Black-White-Red" flag should not be a "flag for a clique of special interests."[44] Nazi Landtag deputy Czirnick, who had traveled from the provincial capital Stettin for the purpose, fiercely attacked German Nationals, shouting that "the selfish special interest politics of individual occupational groups" must finally be brought to an end and calling for a clean sweep among the "upper ten thousand." In future, no city councilor should ever be able to procure contracts without tendering public bids. This was a clear allusion to practices among German National councilors, who had been too free with the public purse.[45] Czirnick further railed against the "corruption mentality" of the *Bürgertum* and their nepotism, cronyism, backscratching, and interlacing of political and business interests, of

42. In the German context, the term refers to a member of the entrenched middle classes; it is here equated with "bourgeois," though "bourgeois," in the original French and traditional Marxist meaning of the term, refers to the *haute bourgeoisie* (*Großbürgertum*), whereas the *Bürgertum* also includes certain sections of the *petite bourgeoisie*, such as master craftsmen and middle-ranking officials.

43. Köslin, population of 28,812 (1925); *Statistisches Jahrbuch*, 52 (Berlin, 1933), 12.

44. 11 March 1933 at BA Berlin-Lichterfelde, "DNVP, Politischer Schriftwechsel 1933," R 8005, no. 19, 146–153, esp. 148.

45. The National Socialist *Kreisleiter* of Köslin pointed to financial irregularities between the town bank and the DNVP town councilor Krause and accused councilors of using free tram tickets to go sailing in Grossmöllen (on the nearby Baltic). German National city councilors (and businesspeople) were also said to have enriched themselves through contracts with public authorities.

which the German Nationals had also been guilty.[46] The NSDAP, most of whose members had themselves been excluded from the privileges enjoyed by the entrenched Pomeranian *Bürgertum*, naturally had an economic interest in eliminating the conservative *Bürgertum*'s dominance over economic life. This also served their political interests by undermining the political representatives of bourgeois economic power. As a counterpoint to bourgeois selfish interest politics and corruption, the Nazis artfully cast their own subjective economic and political interests as furthering the collective interest and common good of the German nation. In the Pomeranian party rally, Czirnick contrasted the "corruption" and "special interest politics" of the German Nationals (whom he accused of betraying Stein's ideal of self-government) with the Nazis' "organic community" and their "positive values," such as "serving the common good and the whole of the nation." In the last elections, he continued, National Socialism had, after all, rallied the masses of the people behind them, while "they [the German Nationals] achieved nothing."[47] National Socialists, who had heretofore been invested in local politics to only a limited degree, could thus offer themselves as an unspent, fresh, and uncorrupted force that would end bourgeois sleaze and fraud and act disinterestedly for the entire German nation.[48]

Nazi Attacks Prepare the Takeover

Already in the first few weeks after the election, detailed reports of National Socialist violations of the law, various and sundry transgressions, and not least physical attacks, were sent to the DNVP headquarters from all regions of the Reich. On the morning of 9 March, for example, the SA raided the police department of Hohenstein-Ernstthal in Saxony and deposed the German National

---

46. 11 March 1933 at BA Berlin-Lichterfelde, "DNVP, Politischer Schriftwechsel 1933," R 8005, no. 19, 148 and 151. In Pomerania, the DNVP, as the strongest party during the 1920s, had been the main rival of the NSDAP. The campaign rally was thus directed mainly against the DNVP.

47. Ibid., 152.

48. On the enormous extent of National Socialist corruption, see Frank Bajohr, *Parvenüs und Profiteure: Korruption in der NS-Zeit* (Frankfurt, 2001).

mayor, who was replaced by an SA leader.[49] Armed SA men, who were not wearing auxiliary police armbands, searched the premises of a café opposite the *Gedächtniskirche* in the center of Berlin close to midnight on 10 March without bothering to identify themselves. The powerless proprietor and guests watched the illegal search with uneasy anxiety.[50] Earlier on that day, National Socialist ruffians had blocked the entrance to one of Berlin's large department stores, the *Kaufhaus des Westens* at the Wittenbergplatz in the western section of the downtown, and bullied pedestrians.[51] Concurrently, the Reich Chancellery was flooded with complaints that gave testimony to the immense number of infringements perpetrated by National Socialist organizations.[52] In spite of Hitler's repeated exhortations to maintain peace and order, and to control "provocative elements . . . [that operate] under the cloak of the party," so that Germany's reputation abroad would not be harmed, the attacks did not abate.[53] Archival files reflect the huge number of illegal acts and provocations, as well as the chaos and lawlessness of the weeks following 5 March 1933.

This multitude of infringements can be divided into roughly three categories. First there was a whole host of attacks against foreign citizens and foreign embassies. On 7 March, for example, a group of Nazi thugs forced their way into the Polish legation and raised the

49. 10 March 1933 at BA Berlin-Lichterfelde, "DNVP, Politischer Schrift-wechsel," R 8005, no. 19, 163–164.

50. 13 March 1933 at BA Berlin-Lichterfelde, "DNVP, Politischer Schrift-wechsel," 156–157.

51. 10 March 1933 at BA Berlin-Lichterfelde, "DNVP, Politischer Schrift-wechsel," 158.

52. BA Berlin-Lichterfelde, "Reichskanzlei, NSDAP," R 43, II, no. 1195; see also chapter 5.

53. "Ermahnungen des Reichskanzlers," in BA Berlin-Lichterfelde, "Reichs-kanzlei, NSDAP," R 43, II, no. 1195, 13 (of 22 February 1933) and 61–62 (of 11 March 1933). Hitler's appeal to the SA and SS of 11 March 1933 read as follows: "Party members, SA and SS men: Germany has undergone an immense cataclysm. It is the result of the most acrimonious battles, the most tenacious perseverance, but also of the highest discipline. Unscrupulous elements, mostly communist spies, are trying to compromise the party through isolated actions that bear no relation to the great feat of the national awakening, but instead besmirch and debase our struggle. In particular, by harassing foreigners in cars flying foreign flags, they attempt to bring the Party and Germany into conflict with foreign powers. SA and SS men! You must stop and detain such creatures immediately and call them to account. Hand them over to the police immediately, no matter who they may be."

swastika flag without permission;[54] this was followed by repeated harassment and bullying of American, British, Indian, and Yugoslav citizens as well as the mistreatment of a French official. Reich Chancellery files abound with complaints from the British, Italian, and Dutch embassies and legations concerning attacks on their citizens,[55] and Foreign Minister Neurath himself provided a comprehensive list of these incidents.[56] The second category of complaints related to the disruption of the economy, such as the forced closure of retail shops and harassment of their owners,[57] or the SA's threat to shut down the Berlin Stock Exchange, as reported by the appalled *Staatssekretär* Paul Bang, who feared that any interference with the stock market might jeopardize the nascent economic upswing.[58] The third category of attacks referred to anti-Semitic attacks, such as the Magdeburg SA's raid on a Jewish restaurant, in which the Swiss citizen Willy Guggenheimer was injured.[59] Frequently the SA focused their attacks on Polish, American, or Czech Jews living in Germany; these incidents made their way into the files through the detailed complaints registered by their respective diplomatic missions.[60] In the course of one of these anti-Semitic attacks in Dresden on the evening of 18 March, the police officers summoned to the scene asserted that "police duties do not include the protection of Jews."[61] In addition to SA attacks, which were marked by such extreme violence that victims often had to be hospitalized, there was also wanton destruction of valuables and property on a considerable scale.[62] The sheer number of attacks on foreign Jews alone indicates that there may well have

54. BA Berlin-Lichterfelde, "Reichskanzlei, NSDAP," R 43, II, no. 1195, 23–24.

55. Ibid., 24; 30–53, with numerous cases listed, and 67–79.

56. Ibid., 30–60.

57. 13 March 1933 at BA Berlin-Lichterfelde, "Reichskanzlei, NSDAP," R 43, II, no. 1195, 82.

58. 9 March 1933, BA Berlin-Lichterfelde, "Reichskanzlei, NSDAP," R 43, II, no. 1195, 88. Dr. Paul Bang, born 1879; *Oberfinanzrat*, leading member of the *Alldeutscher Verband* and rabid anti-Semite; DNVP Reichstag deputy, 1928–1933; from February to June 1933 *Staatssekretär* in the Reich Economics Ministry.

59. 11 March 1933 at BA Berlin-Lichterfelde, "Reichskanzlei, NSDAP," R 43, II, no. 1195, 67–70.

60. BA Berlin-Lichterfelde, "Reichskanzlei, NSDAP," R 43, II, no. 1195, 99–112.

61. Ibid., 201.

62. Ibid., 203. In an open-air market in Hamhorn, for example, an unknown offender knocked over a basket with five hundred eggs for no apparent reason.

been a comparable number of attacks on German Jews that went unrecorded, since German citizens were in no position to seek protection from foreign missions and may have been very reluctant to call in the police. For the most part, DNVP members and leaders were mere onlookers in all of this; they watched uneasily from the sidelines, but dared not interfere, partly because they felt too deeply compromised by their coalition with Hitler.[63]

By mid March 1933, political life had changed to such an extent that the German Rechtsstaat was a thing of the past. Though largely unregulated, chaotic, and often in opposition to the directives of the Reich government, the unchecked violence of the SA, with its countless accompanying illegal actions, was not wholly unwelcome to the Nazi leadership. In a certain sense, the "revolutionary anarchy" of March and April 1933 proved to be indirectly beneficial to their ultimate goals, since it became increasingly obvious to potential opponents that everyone who resisted the advance of National Socialism—in speech, action, or writing—put their own lives at risk. Too many had already vanished in the torture cellars of the SA for the passive opponent of Nazism to contemplate open opposition lightly. Nazi leaders quickly discovered how to channel the widespread fear fostered by wanton SA acts of violence into a tool of "revolutionary" change beneficial to their needs. March 1933 was also a time when old accounts were settled without any consideration of legal or social proprieties. The politician, journalist, or private citizen who had in the past been too outspoken in his opposition to Hitler, now had reason to be concerned about more than simply his career. The tradesman who had been a member of the SPD might see his shop closed down from one day to the next, and with the enactment of the Law on the Restoration of a Professional Civil Service of 7 April, even those deemed formerly untouchable, such as German civil servants, became victims of Nazi retribution. From mid March onwards, as the archival evidence makes very clear,[64] conservatives of all shades, including the Nazis' own German National coalition partner, were next in line. The conservatives, still legalistic in their thinking, would have found it impossible to answer violence spontaneously with counterviolence, even if the

---

63. On the DNVP's reaction to anti-Semitic violence, see chapter 5.

64. After 5 March, numerous complaints to the Reich Chancellery were concerned with attacks on members of the DNVP or their paramilitary organization, the *Kampfringe*; BA Berlin-Lichterfelde, "Reichskanzlei, NSDAP," R 43, II, no. 1195, 207, 213–231; 233–235.

relative ratio of physical power (which was heavily weighed against them) had made such action feasible. In any case, they and others like them could no longer appeal to higher judicial authorities, as these had ceased to exist: the police chose to ignore Nazi attacks, the Reich Interior Ministry failed to follow up on complaints, and young Nazi judges soon gained ascendancy over the court system.[65]

Conservative Bastions under Attack

The files containing the DNVP's political correspondence for the months of March to May 1933 constitute a repository for the flood of complaints from all regions of the Reich about attacks against their own members and organizations. The distinctiveness of these complaints lies in the fact that the bulk of them originated from conservative, extremely national-minded Germans (many of whom were members of the DNVP), who at first had enthusiastically welcomed the advent of the coalition government between the DNVP and the Nazi party. Most of them had initially embraced the formation of a long-awaited "national" government, in which the DNVP would play a central role, even though it had come at the price of an alliance with Hitler. Confronted now with Nazi terror or acts of sheer revenge directed against "upright" conservative and patriotic DNVP members, as well as uninvolved third parties, they reacted with bewilderment, indignation, and hapless fury. As their letters testify, they saw themselves lured into complicity and now ensnared in a trap, with their earlier collusion rendering protest difficult, if not impossible. No higher constitutional authority remained to hear appeals, for the legal safeguards of the Old Prussian and Imperial *Rechtsstaat* had been destroyed and German Nationals themselves had had a helping hand in destroying it. The sole recourse left was to lodge protests with the DNVP party leadership, since it was known that Hugenberg was too preoccupied with his ministerial posts to lend succor. If this was to no avail, they could turn to the Reich Chancellery in the vague hope that Hitler might interfere or complain to Papen's Vice Chancellery.[66]

65. For a vivid description of young Nazi judges in the courts, see Haffner, *Defying Hitler.*
66. BA Berlin-Lichterfelde, "DNVP, Politischer Schriftwechsel 1933," R 8005, no. 19; "Akten der Reichskanzlei," R 43 II no. 1195 "NSDAP" (on microfilm); "Stellvertreter des Reichskanzlers, Kanzlei von Papen," R 53.

By the late winter and early spring of 1933, the DNVP had thus begun to reap the fruits of what it had sown, and—in countless local incidences—the party and its members began to turn from the victors of 30 January into the powerless victims or bewildered bystanders of March. In the course of the Prussian elections for the district and provincial parliaments of 12 March, for example, the SA confiscated 3,000 DNVP campaign leaflets and later reprints of the same leaflets in the small town of Züllichau (county of Schwiebus in the Neumark). Protests addressed to the *Oberpräsident* (governor) of the province had no effect.[67] During the same campaign, the speaker for the Nazi party in Delitzsch, a town in the Prussian province of Saxony, uttered the plain threat that Hugenberg and Papen would be thrown out of the government at the next best opportunity.[68] From Munich the prominent former DNVP deputy Gottfried Traub, one of the founders of the Vaterlandspartei, a participant in the Kapp Putsch, and now publisher of the Hugenberg-owned paper *München-Augsburger Abendzeitung*, reported on the chaos and multitude of Nazi attacks and voiced his fears that German Nationals would soon no longer be needed there, since the Nazis might form a coalition government with the Bayerische Volkspartei.[69] Because of these apprehensions, he indicated his willingness to overlook the Nazis' worst excesses and to try to repair cracks in the alliance by continuing to cooperate with them. On 17 March, the chairman of the DNVP's local chapter in Berlin-Wilhelmshagen, Dr. Schulze, complained about a National Socialist city councilor, who had publicly labeled Hugenberg a traitor and *Stahlhelm* leader Franz Seldte a megalomaniac, and demanded that both of them be gotten rid of.[70] The overall mood within the Wilhelmshagen NSDAP, Schulze lamented, was, as far as he could tell, very much in keeping with such statements. Complaints abounded about the inactivity and powerlessness of the police, as well as their avoidance of conflicts with

67. 11 March at BA Berlin-Lichterfelde, "DNVP, Politischer Schriftwechsel," R 8005, no. 19, 145. The NSDAP fought the election campaign mainly against its own coalition partner.

68. BA Berlin-Lichterfelde, "DNVP, Politischer Schriftwechsel," R 8005, no. 19, 141–143. In Torgau, Nazi speakers made it clear that the German Nationals would have to be removed as soon as possible.

69. 13 March 1933 at BA Berlin-Lichterfelde, "DNVP: Politischer Schriftwechsel," R 8005, no. 19, 136–139. Death threats had also been made against the chief Rabbi of Munich's Jewish community.

70. 17 March 1933 at BA Berlin-Lichterfelde, "DNVP, Politischer Schriftwechsel 1933," R 8005, no. 19, 130.

the SA. Reports came in from Magdeburg on 18 March that the police had literally stood aside and watched as the SA demolished the furnishings of the *Magdeburger Volksstimme*, an SPD newspaper, and then continued to spread terror in the streets: "The police did not intervene because they were physically threatened by the SA."[71] In a dispatch from Breslau, bank manager Waldemar Wadsack recounted his arrest on 17 March on the baseless charge that he had been a member of the "Black Front" and his subsequent conveyance to SA headquarters, where SA men lashed him with horsewhips, cruelly manhandled him for hours, and finally confiscated his property. Though trying to be helpful, the police had been unable to recover his property, despite all their efforts.[72] From the Waldeck district in Kurhessen dispatches reached DNVP headquarters that the SA had arrested approximately one hundred people, mostly Jews and members of the Left, through 25 March. They had been interrogated and then submitted "to prolonged and monstrous beatings" that were administered "with bestial brutality" in a dark side room.[73] The victims were then unceremoniously thrown out, some being forced to seek medical assistance at a Kassel hospital. The report stressed that the entire population of the Waldeck district was in a state of great agitation and consternation since no one could henceforth feel safe from mistreatment; even *Stahlhelm* leaders, who were disliked by the SA, considered themselves to be in danger.[74] In Reichenbach in lower Silesia the SA stormed the *Dienstwohnung* (official residence) of the mayor at 11:30 p.m., roused him from bed, and conducted a search of the premises on the day following the 12 March local elections. No incriminating materials were found in the home of the "politically centrist mayor" who was, according to the report of the DNVP Lower Silesian Land Association, a "sound

71. 18 March 1933 at BA Berlin-Lichterfelde, "DNVP, Politischer Schrift-wechsel 1933," R 8005, no. 19, 131–133, esp. 131.

72. 28 March 1933 at BA Berlin-Lichterfelde, "DNVP, Politischer Schrift-wechsel 1933," R 8005, no. 19, 126–128. The "Black Front" was a militant group of revolutionary National Socialists led by Otto Strasser that united remnants of the abortive SA Stennes revolt with disillusioned National Socialists and Communists in the summer of 1931, when it adopted the name "Black Front." This group of *völkisch* conservatives with social revolutionary ideas never counted more than five thousand members; banned in February 1933, its members were depicted as dangerous terrorists by Nazi propaganda.

73. 28 March 1933 at BA Berlin-Lichterfelde, "DNVP, Politischer Schrift-wechsel," R 8005, no. 19, 120–121.

74. Ibid., 121.

and experienced local politician," though "the mental strain of the attack left him with a nervous breakdown. He is now gravely ill and bedridden."[75]

The chaos, mayhem, and disorder of March 1933 were so all-encompassing that there were even clashes in the camp of the victor, that is, among Nazi organizations themselves. As reported by the DNVP Hannover-South Land Association (the southern part of present-day Lower Saxony), there were open conflicts between the NSDAP's political leadership and the SA. In Hameln, for example, the NSDAP county leader and top candidate in the local election was "grossly abused and molested by his own people."[76] But discord and clashes among Nazi organizations were by no means tantamount to a reprieve for the German Nationals: "Incursions and encroachments by the National Socialists increase hour by hour. There seems to be a method in how they burn their bridges to the DNVP," reported the DNVP Posen-Westpreußen Land Association in Schneidemühl[77] to DNVP headquarters on 1 April; an ominous prognostication followed: "We are here getting ever closer to anarchy. No administrative or governmental body seems to have the courage to confront the terror in the street." Nazi hoodlums vigorously pursued their own goals and, in the words of the Schneidemühl DNVP: "[U]nless these undisciplined and raging hordes are disarmed immediately, we will have here unadulterated Russians conditions . . . ,"[78] referring to the fact that several of the most violent Nazis had once been notorious Communists. Brawls between the SA and the German National *Kampfringe* were already a daily occurrence.[79] These

75. 13 March 1933 at BA Berlin-Lichterfelde, "DNVP, Politischer Schrift-wechsel 1933," R 8005, no. 19, 140. In the local elections of 12 March the NSDAP attained an absolute majority of votes in Reichenbach.

76. 15 March 1933 at BA Berlin-Lichterfelde, "DNVP, Politischer Schrift-wechsel 1933," R 8005, no. 19, 144. In opposition to party orders, the SA occupied the town hall on 14 March and closed down all Jewish shops. The NSDAP party leadership noted that this was the handiwork of lower SA leaders.

77. Schneidemühl, in the Grenzmark Posen-Westpreußen, had a population of 37,520 (1925).

78. 1 April 1933 at BA Berlin-Lichterfelde, "DNVP, Politischer Schrift-wechsel 1933," R 8005, no. 19, 104–104 verso. Here, too, the comment is made: ". . . but the police do not dare to intervene."

79. 31 March 1933, "Anruf von Herrn Krämer, Schneidemühl," at BA Berlin-Lichterfelde, "DNVP, Politischer Schriftwechsel," R 8005, no. 19, 105. Due to the SA's vastly superior numbers, members of the German National *Kampf-ringe* regularly came off worse.

complaints from the Grenzmark Posen-Westpreußen in the Reich's eastern regions were matched with those from the west. In a dispatch from Verden an der Aller in the province of Hannover, for example, it was reported that the NSDAP intended to marginalize the German Nationals to the point that invitations to the *Vaterländische Vereine* were sent only to the *Stahlhelm* and assiduously ignored the German Nationals. Disillusioned, the Hannover-East Land Association chairman wrote to Berlin on 29 March: "The tendency to eliminate the DNVP appears to be prevalent everywhere."[80] Already on 10 March, Walter Baerwolff, the party manager of the Bavarian DNVP, had maintained that the Nazi party's brutal attacks rendered any collaboration between the NSDAP and DNVP impossible, comparing Nazi lawlessness with "the events during the revolution of 1918."[81] But even this comparison did not go far enough, for it soon became clear that the events of March 1933 would have far more debilitating repercussions for German conservatives than those of November 1918.

Violent clashes with Nazi organizations, such as those described above, greatly affected the spirit of the DNVP's leadership and rank and file alike—both became increasingly aware of their own powerlessness. Since complaints about Nazi encroachments had been directed mostly to the DNVP central office in Berlin, party leaders and deputies knew of the multitude of attacks. But even those who were not familiar with the details had experienced the momentous transformation of political climate in all its ramifications, first in the days following the Reichstag fire and then in the weeks after the elections. They all were keenly aware that the DNVP was hardly in a position to stop the triumphal march of Nazism or channel it into different directions. Already on the eve of the opening of the new Reichstag, the so-called Day of Potsdam on 21 March, and the passing of the Enabling Act two days later, the DNVP party organization and members were, to a certain extent, broken. They had certainly lost much of their former confidence. The rank and file membership throughout the Reich had also experienced the seemingly unstoppable upswing of National Socialism with all its attendant consequences: now the wind of revolution was blowing in their faces and not at their backs. They had been

---

80. 29 March 1933 at BA Berlin-Lichterfelde, "DNVP, Politischer Schriftwechsel 1933," R 8005, no. 19, 108–109.
81. 10 March 1933 at BA Berlin-Lichterfelde, "Stellvertreter der Reichskanzlei, Kanzlei von Papen," R 53, no. 71, 115–116.

stunned at the ease and rapidity with which their own inveterate foes, the KPD and SPD and all their organizations, had disappeared from the streets, were repressed, and rendered mute. Within the DNVP itself, voices urging that the party merge with the NSDAP, while it was still taken seriously as a political force, grew louder.[82] Hugenberg and most of the party leadership did their best to steer an independent course and preserve the DNVP's autonomy, though they knew all too well that calls within the party to fuse with the NSDAP, along with the increasing dominance and popularity of Nazism, were bound to undermine their own position. The political developments of the next few months cannot be understood without taking into account the changed climate of politics, the enormous popularity that Nazism and some Nazi leaders, especially Hitler, had acquired with their seemingly resolute actions following the Reichstag fire, the seventeen million votes cast for the NSDAP on 5 March, the effortless takeover of the Länder, and the ever-swelling army of *Märzgefallenen*—the "casualties of March"—who now clamored to join the Nazi party while it was still accepting applicants. Given the new distribution of power, which was based more on the widespread popular sense that everything and everyone was contributing to the steadily growing torrent of Nazism than on the NSDAP's actual parliamentary strength, the DNVP leadership believed it had no alternative but to put a good face upon events and go along with Nazi policies. Certainly no one had expected that the DNVP would run out of viable political alternatives less than two months after Hitler became Chancellor of Germany.

The Last Hurdle: Potsdam and the Enabling Act

The immense spectacle at Potsdam on the occasion of the new Reichstag was, to all outward appearances, a significant step toward the revival of a traditional, conservative Germany—and thus of the DNVP—since it seemed as if Hitler ostentatiously tried to merge his National Socialist movement with the tradition of Prussian simplicity, decency, and order. He made sure to pay deferential respect to the old field marshal, President Hindenburg, who embodied all

---

82. Some parts of the DNVP were prepared to merge with the Nazis as early as March; see chapter 6.

of these qualities.[83] In immense posters, Nazi propaganda had postulated an implicit line of descent from Frederick the Great on to Bismarck, Hindenburg, and then Hitler.[84] The images penetrated deeply into the consciousness of millions of Germans, who longed for a radically changed future as long as it was anchored firmly in the achievements of the past. Viewed superficially, the Nazism presented at Potsdam gave the impression of being tamed, seemingly verifying the old elite's calculations that the attempt to domesticate Hitler and his movement had succeeded after all. Nothing could have been further from the truth. The actual impact of the "Day of Potsdam" was very different—as it was intended to be. The Nazis set out to co-opt the traditional symbols of Prussian conservatism for their own radical ends. They had no intention of supporting the goals of German conservatism, but only used German conservatism as a means to establish a foothold in power. Once their place was secure, the Nazis could dispense with the pretense of allying with the German Nationals as national-minded brothers-in-arms. Their successful fusion of Prussian and National Socialist symbols of power and national pride, as well as the seamless inclusion of Hitler into an unbroken chain of Prussian-German historical continuity, would soon render the DNVP superfluous as the exclusive representative of German national history and traditional values. With their ingeniously stage-managed display of national unity in Potsdam, the Nazis scored a clear victory over the German Nationals in their ongoing struggle over who would be the rightful heir to the national heritage. The conflict had previously erupted on the occasion of local festivities, such as the 120th anniversary of the onset of

83. The date of the opening coincided symbolically with the anniversary of the first opening of the Reichstag of the Second Reich on 21 March 1871. See also Bracher, Sauer, Schulz, *Die nationalsozialistische Machtergreifung*, 144–152; Werner Freitag, "Martin Luther, Friedrich II und Adolf Hitler—der Tag von Potsdam im neuen Licht," in Volkshochschule "Albert Einstein," ed., *Preußen und der Nationalsozialismus. Das Land Brandenburg und das Erbe Preußens* (brochure), (Potsdam, 1992), 15–33.

84. Postcards that showed Frederick the Great, Bismarck, and Hitler next to each other had existed since 1931 (Hindenburg was then left out); see also Manfred Schlenke, "Das 'Preußische Beispiel' in Propaganda und Politik des Nationalsozialismus," *Aus Politik und Zeitgeschichte* 27 (1968), 16–23; Manfred Schlenke, "Nationalsozialismus und Preußen/Preußentum," in Otto Büsch, ed., *Das Preußenbild in der Geschichte* (Berlin, 1981), 247–264; Wolfgang Wippermann, "Nationalsozialismus und Preußentum," *Aus Politik und Zeitgeschichte* 52/53 (1981), 13–22.

the Wars of Liberation against Napoleon.[85] Now it was elevated to
the national stage, where the seemingly successful symbiosis of traditional Prussian conservatism and National Socialism manifested a
reconstituted national unity and a vigor that appealed not only to
sympathizers of National Socialism, but in some ways even to those
who viewed it very critically. Erich Ebermayer, who had supported
the DDP during the Republic and remained consistently critical of
the Nazis even during the height of "national awakening" in March
1933, wrote in his diary:

> What masterful mise-en-scène by the stage manager Goebbels!
> The procession of Hindenburg, the members of the government and
> the deputies passes from Berlin to Potsdam through tightly packed
> rows of jubilant millions. Tout Berlin seems to be in the street.
> Members of government and deputies walk from the Nikolai to the
> Garnison church. Ringing of bells and firing of canons. Hinden-
> burg enters the Garnison church side by side with Hitler. The radio
> announcer's voice suffused with emotion. Then Hindenburg reads
> his message. A straightforward, strong message, emanating from a
> simple heart and thus appealing to simple hearts. Just the fact that
> here is a man who unites generations of German history in his own
> person, who took part in the fighting in 1866, was present at the
> Imperial coronation at Versailles in '71 and rose to become the na-
> tional hero of 1914–18; whose popularity with our strange people
> remains undiminished by any lost battle or lost World War, whose
> stature, on the contrary, grew in defeat into mythical proportions,
> and who then, as octogenarian, took the helm of the Reich for a
> second time; not out of vanity or lust for power, but doubtless from
> a Prussian sense of duty—and now here, only steps away from his
> grave, he executes the fusion of his world with the newly rising one
> that is represented by the Austrian corporal.

> Then Hitler speaks. No use denying: he has grown. The demagogue
> and party leader, the fanatic and rabble-rouser seems to be develop-
> ing—to the puzzlement of his opponents—into the true statesman.
> A genius after all, whose mysterious and unknown soul harbors an
> unsuspected and immense potential?. . . . Hindenburg lays down
> wreaths at the tombs of Prussian kings. To the lance corporal of
> the World War the aged field marshal holds out his hand. The lance

85. See Chapter VI below.

corporal inclines his head deeply over the hand of the field marshal. Cannon thunder over Potsdam—over Germany. No one can hide his emotion. Even father is deeply impressed. Mother is moved to tears.[86]

If the politically aware and liberal-minded Ebermayer could be so affected by the symbolism of the moment, what could now prevent a large part of the national-minded bourgeoisie from supporting the dynamic leader of a large Volkspartei rather than the pedantic and lackluster Hugenberg?

The widespread enthusiasm generated by Potsdam, where the Nazi Party affected a symbiosis between the youthful energy of their National Socialist movement and the grandeur of the Prussian past, produced an auspicious atmosphere for the introduction of the Enabling Act. Two days after the Potsdam spectacle, when the Reichstag assembled in Berlin's Kroll Opera house (directly across from the fire-damaged Reichstag building), it was clear from the start that the DNVP would vote for the Enabling Act, especially since the party had also been instrumental in bringing the "Law on Relieving the Suffering of Nation and Reich" to the Reichstag floor.[87] Former Chancellor Heinrich Brüning claimed that some DNVP members had approached him to draft an amendment to the Enabling Act that would "guarantee civic and political freedoms." According to Brüning, this issue of legal safeguards had been discussed in Hugenberg's home on the evening of 21 March, when it was agreed that for tactical reasons the DNVP should bring this amendment to the Reichstag floor. Just before the second reading of the bill, DNVP deputy Otto Schmidt-Hannover passed Brüning and, in a tense atmosphere and ringed by SA and SS troopers,

86. Ebermayer, *Denn heute gehört uns Deutschland*, 46–47. Ebermayer's father, Dr. Ludwig Ebermayer, an eminent legal scholar, was *Oberreichsanwalt* (the highest prosecutor of the Reich) during the Weimar Republic, and an obdurate opponent of the Nazis. He died on 30 June 1933.

87. In the three parliamentary deliberations of this *Gesetz zur Behebung der Not von Volk und Reich* the Speaker (*Reichstagspräsident*) of the Reichstag, Hermann Göring, referred to it as the motion put forward by the NSDAP and DNVP parliamentary faction leaders (". . . Beratung des von den Abgeordneten Dr. Frick, Dr.Oberfohren u. Gen. eingebrachten Entwurfs . . ."). See Rudolf Morsey, *Das Ermächtigungsgestz vom 24. März 1933. Quellen zur Geschichte und Interpretation des 'Gesetzes zur Behebung der Not von Volk und Reich.'* (Düsseldorf, 1992), 55, 64.

managed to whisper to him: "We have been taken for a ride."[88] On
the following day, Brüning discovered that an intraparty rebellion
of twenty-two DNVP deputies, led by Martin Spahn and Eduard
Stadtler, had allegedly sabotaged the amendment by threatening to
leave the DNVP and join the Nazi party if it were put forward.[89]
Brüning's various versions of this incident are so riddled with inconsistencies and contradictions that the massive criticism of his
account by other contemporary political actors hardly comes as a
surprise.[90] Whatever the case, the passing of the Enabling Act com-

88. "Wir sind hereingelegt worden." See Morsey, *Das Ermächtigungsgesetz*,
142, note 3.

89. In a letter of 20 August 1946 to Hans Bernd Gisevius, Brüning wrote
that Ernst Oberfohren (who was then still DNVP parliamentary faction leader)
and Otto Schmidt-Hannover (who would soon become his successor) organized
a meeting between Brüning and Hugenberg "on the day after the opening of
the Reichstag" (22 March), in which legal safeguards against the Enabling Act
were discussed. In another letter, published in the *Deutsche Rundschau* in 1947,
that meeting had been moved to 21 March. In his memoirs, where the events
surrounding the passing of the Enabling Act are discussed in detail [Brüning,
Memoiren, 652–662], the meeting date given is again 21 March. In the accounts
of 1946 and 1947, Brüning mentioned that he was approached by Ernst Oberfohren, who suggested that he meet with Hugenberg. Given that Oberfohren
and Hugenberg were on very bad terms just then, to the point that Oberfohren
was actively plotting against Hugenberg (see chapter 6 below), this is extremely
unlikely. Even less plausible is Brüning's claim in his 1946 account that Hugenberg was going to approach Hindenburg to bring about "the release of arrested
SPD members." Given Hugenberg's intense dislike of the SPD, he was the last
person to work toward their release. There are further, albeit minor, respects
in which the three accounts do not tally. The letters from 1946 and 1947 are
reprinted (with minor omissions) in Morsey, *Das Ermächtigungsgesetz*, 138–144;
quotations 138, 139.

90. When he first heard of Brüning's letter in 1947, Thomas Esser, former
Center Party deputy and Vice-President of the Reichstag (deputy speaker), flatly
refused to believe in the existence of such a document and, in a letter to the
editor of the *Deutsche Rundschau*, freely spoke of ". . . the fairy tale of the allegedly agreed-upon amendment with Hugenberg that was never put forward . . ."
When he was forced to concede the authenticity of the letter, Esser admitted
that it destroyed "much of the halo still surrounding Brüning's personality" (reprinted in Morsey, *Ermächtigungsgesetz*, 144). DNVP deputy Edmund Forschbach,
writing in 1978, cast doubt on both Hugenberg's participation in advancing such
an amendment and Spahn's and Stadtler's threat to defect with other deputies to
the NSDAP. Since both did indeed leave the DNVP for the Nazi party later in
the spring—a prelude to the final downfall of the party (see chapter 7 below)—
Forschbach surmised that Brüning confused the date of their rebellion. Forschbach's statement is reprinted in Morsey, *Ermächtigungsgesetz*, 177–180.

pletely freed Hitler from any restrictions that Hindenburg, as President, might have imposed upon him, since presidential approval was now no longer required to pass legislation. In fact, the Enabling Act only gave official sanction to an already extant political reality, since the "party-revolution from below" had long since revolutionized the distribution of power at the top.[91] The affirmative votes of the Center, BVP, Staatspartei, DVP, and other splinter parties have to be seen in this light. Even members of the SPD, whose remaining ninety-four deputies were the only ones to vote "no," conceded after the war that a no-vote from the Center Party would ultimately have been to no avail, even though it would have thwarted Hitler's determination to consolidate his hold on power through legal means.[92] Most of the deputies of the above-mentioned parties later justified their affirmative vote by arguing that non-acceptance would only have led to an outbreak of further Nazi violence and bloody anarchy.[93] The thousands of armed, threatening, leering and jeering SA and SS troopers outside as well as inside the meeting hall added a very visible element of threat and coercion, despite the presence of foreign diplomats.[94] This aspect of sheer physical menace was not without effect. Among the parliamentary faction of the SPD, some of whose deputies had already been arrested, it was debated prior to the meeting whether it might be better not to attend at all. It took the moral outrage of the seemingly more fearless female SPD deputies, such as Luise Schröder, and the insistence of Otto Wels and Kurt Schumacher for the others to attend the Reichstag session, despite threats to life and limb.[95] In addition to physical threats and the fact that a no-vote might well have proven futile, another powerful factor that compelled deputies of the Center and liberal splinter parties to vote affirmatively was the forceful current in the

91. The term "party revolution from below" is used in Broszat, *Der Staat Hitlers*, 108.

92. Wilhelm Hoegner, *Der schwierige Außenseiter* (Munich, 1959), 93–94. The government needed a two-thirds majority for the law to pass, which was possible only if the Center Party voted in favor of the Act.

93. See, for example, the 1947 statements of Center Party deputies Joseph Ersing and Franz Wiedemeier before an investigative committee of the Württemberg-Baden Landtag, reprinted in Morsey, *Ermächtigungsgesetz*, 129–130.

94. These observers duly noted the threats. See the observations of the French ambassador André François-Poncet in Morsey, *Ermächtigungsgesetz*, 184–185.

95. See the statement of SPD deputy Josef Felder in Morsey, *Ermächtigungsgesetz*, 172–175.

popular mood during the second half of March 1933 that practically demanded consent. After the war, few of those who had voted "yes" dared to own up to the intangible pressure exerted by the *vox populi*, though it occasionally appears through the cracks in their statements. The Württemberg Center Party deputy Johannes Groß admitted in 1947 that ". . . the people had grown tired of bickering among the parties in the Reichstag. . . . Things had to change. This, I should say, played a role with everyone back then. I also have never been attacked because of my affirmative vote to the *Ermächtigungsgesetz*, in any political assembly."[96] Hermann Dietrich of the Staatspartei put it even more bluntly: "I have suffered many discomforts and shouldered unpopular duties in my life, difficulties of all kinds; I have been scolded and praised. But in my whole life I have never experienced such ostentatious manifestations of consent, especially in writing, as on the occasion of this vote, the Enabling Act . . ."[97] In the immediate postwar climate, when people still remembered the popular mood of spring 1933, it was probably easier to spell out the plain truth that a vast majority of Germans wanted the Enabling Act, even many of those who had voted for the Center and the Staatspartei. Yet this truth had become too unpleasant to utter after a second World War, the genocidal murder of millions carried out on the basis of abstract principles, and the realization that those who voted for the Enabling Act had facilitated Hitler's assumption of total power, and thus indirectly war and the Holocaust. Thus, in later statements this element of acting in accordance with the popular mood (even against one's better judgment) is notably missing.

After the virtually complete elimination of the leftist opposition and the willingness of the Center Party to collaborate with the NSDAP, a willingness further underlined by the pro-government declaration of Catholic bishops on 28 March,[98] National Socialism could even more freely show its true face and turn against what it perceived to be another dangerous opponent: the conservative bourgeoisie. This antagonism between Nazism and what was left of the *Bürgertum* and its way of life is often overlooked in the history of

96. Statement reprinted in Morsey, *Ermächtigungsgesetz*, 130.

97. Like the Center Party deputies Joseph Ersing and Franz Wiedemeier, Hermann Dietrich also spoke before an investigative committee of the Württemberg-Baden Landtag in a hearing held between 5 February and 27 March 1947, more than two years before the foundation of the West German state.

98. See chapter 7 below.

the Nazi seizure of power. As Hitler had ominously called out in his rejoinder to the speech of the SPD leader Otto Wels: "Do not mistake us for the *bürgerliche Welt*,"[99] a clarion call that seemed to herald a reckoning to come. The following chapter addresses the conflict between this *bürgerliche Welt* and National Socialism, as the day of reckoning drew inevitably closer.

99. The significance of this short sentence in the rapidly delivered torrent of Hitler's seemingly *ex tempore* riposte to Wels, one of his greatest rhetorical triumphs, was not lost on Erich Ebermayer. See *Denn heute gehört uns Deutschland*, 48.

Chapter IV

THE NAZIS AND THE CONSERVATIVE *BÜRGERTUM*

A Clash of Worlds

After the elections of 5 March and especially after the Enabling Act of 23 March, the Nazis made no bones about the fact that their conservative alliance partner had become completely expendable. The role of the DNVP as the stirrup holder for the Nazis had played itself out. Already in the course of the takeover of state governments, violent attacks against conservative dignitaries had become so prevalent that the Bavarian DNVP deputy Walter Baerwolff, indignantly and with great dismay, equated Nazi iniquities and law-breaking with ". . . the events during the revolution of 1918."[1] For the conservative establishment, however, the events of winter and spring 1933 would prove even more "revolutionary" than those of 1918, so often conjured up by conservatives as the nightmarish turning point in Germany's fortunes. The "revolution" proclaimed by Hitler after the election success of 5 March (even though it fell pitifully short of the expectations of Nazi leaders) carried in its wake sweeping and all-encompassing transformations whose social impact was greater than anything that came in the wake of 1918.[2]

---

1. 10 March 1933 at BA Berlin-Lichterfelde, "Stellvertreter der Reichskanzlei, Kanzlei von Papen," Rep. 53, no. 71, 115.
2. On social change after 1933, see Wehler, *Deutsche Gesellschaftsgeschichte*, vol. IV, 771–781; Dieter Ziegler, ed., *Großbürger und Unternehmer* (Göttingen, 2000); Tim Mason, *Social Policy in the Third Reich* (Oxford and New York, 1993); Thomas Saunders, "Nazism and Social Revolution," in Gordon Martel, ed., *Modern Germany Reconsidered, 1870–1945* (London and New York, 1992),

The flood of conservatives' complaints about their alliance partner was initially tempered by the hope that the countless violent Nazi attacks of the winter and spring of 1933 were exceptions rather than the rule. There was, after all, one great common denominator shared by conservatives and National Socialists that transcended their manifold differences: extreme nationalism. Both were united in their categorical rejection of the Versailles Treaty and their adamant opposition to the "war guilt lie," and both had fought side by side in the "People's Rebellion" against the Young Plan. With respect to foreign policy, both promoted an uncompromisingly extremist course, placing the greatest priority on the resurgence of Germany's former political might and military glory. Both rejected the Republic, vowing to replace it with a more authoritarian form of government, and both stood united in their hatred of democracy, parliamentary politics, and the political Left. These commonalities had brought together the unequal partners in the (albeit tenuous) *Harzburger Front* of October 1931, and helped spawn the Hitler Cabinet of January 1933. In Bad Harzburg, as well as on 30 January 1933, Hugenberg and his DNVP had hoped to harness the vast mass movement of National Socialism for their own conservative ends. For the Nazis, on the other hand, the alliance with the DNVP served as their badly needed passport to respectable society. The pact conferred respectability to National Socialism.

Hidden under the cloak of unity lurked barely veiled conflicts. The most fundamental and irreconcilable of these revolved around their respective visions of society. Despite inflation, its concomitant impoverishment, the world economic crisis, and the sharp decline in national income that came in its wake,[3] the DNVP remained the party of the conservative middle and upper classes, the Protestant notables in small towns in northern and eastern Germany (even though they were but a shadow of their former selves economically),

---

159–178; Jeremy Noakes, "Nazism and Revolution," in Noel O'Sullivan, ed., *Revolutionary Theory and Political Reality* (London, 1983), 73–100; David Schoenbaum, *Hitler's Social Revolution. Class and Status in Nazi Germany, 1933–1939*, 2nd ed. (New York and London, 1980).

   3. Between 1929 and 1933 the gross national product fell on average 7.2 percent per annum; over the twelve-year period from 1913 to 1925 it had decreased slightly by 0.4 percent p.a. Between 1928 and 1932 national income had fallen sharply from 75.373 million Reichsmark to 45.175 million Reichsmark and the unemployment rate (1932) stood at 29.9 percent. See Dieter Petzina, Werner Abelshauser, and Anselm Faust, *Sozialgeschichtliches Arbeitsbuch III. Materialien zur Statistik des Deutschen Reiches 1914–1945* (Munich, 1978), 78, 102, 119.

the East Elbian aristocracy, the upper echelons of the bureaucracy, and of the ever-dwindling remnants of the *Bildungsbürgertum*. Politically it was the DNVP, more than any other party, that represented all those remnants of *Bürgerlichkeit*, the fragile relics of a bourgeois lifestyle weakened by the privations of war, inflation, and the Great Depression. After 1928, the voters of the once influential workers' wing of the DNVP had turned to other parties, and the Association of German National Shop Assistants, with its more than 400,000 members, had defected, for the most part, to the Nazi camp.[4] Due to Hugenberg's uncompromising policies since 1929 and an ever-deepening economic crisis, the DNVP had increasingly become the party of the Establishment, more so than it had been at any time during the 1920s.

Before 1933, members of Nazi organizations, notably the SA, which had been responsible for the bulk of violent attacks, were by contrast often of lower and lower middle class background.[5] Since civil servants had been banned from joining the Nazi party in Prussia, the party lacked any significant following in the bureaucracy before the Nazi seizure of power.[6] After the elimination of the leftist parties, many Nazis, who felt disadvantaged, turned their spite against the DNVP. In the words of a well-known Nazi song, the conservatives were the "brittle bones" of a lifeless world, the *"Reaktion"* that had promulgated a reactionary politics of interest and repressed the younger generation and their new ideas. In Nazi eyes, the DNVP was the embodiment of the *bürgerliche* world (as they understood it), a despised cosmos of rules and conventions that excluded those who had not imbibed them with their mothers' milk; a universe of entitlement (*Berechtigungsscheine*, as the Nazi press disparagingly called it)

4. Amrei Stupperich, *Volksgemeinschaft oder Arbeitersolidarität. Studien zur Arbeitnehmerpolitik der Deutschnationalen Volkspartei, 1918–1933* (Göttingen, 1982).

5. Peter Longerich, *Geschichte der SA* (Munich, 1989); Richard Bessel, *Political Violence and the Rise of Nazism*; Conan Fischer, *Stormtroopers*; Hilde Jamin, *Zwischen den Klassen. Zur Sozialstruktur der SA-Führerschaft*; Michael Kater, "Zum gegenseitigen Verhältnis von SA und SS in der Sozialgeschichte des Nationalsozialismus von 1925 bis 1939," *Vierteljahresschrift für Sozial-und Wirtschaftsgeschichte* 62 (1975), 339–379. Yet beginning in 1932, parts of the upper middle classes in the wealthier suburbs of Germany's larger cities increasingly voted for Hitler, as Richard F. Hamilton, *Who Voted for Hitler?* (Princeton, 1982), points out.

6. In particular among higher echelons of the bureaucracy. By the mid 1930s the social composition of the NSDAP had undergone a profound change since professionals and members of the civil service had joined the party in large numbers (especially between February and 1 May 1933).

that required formal education, standardized tests, and schooling—
Mittlere Reife, Abitur, and university studies—as preconditions for social advancement.[7] It runs counter to the often implied community
of interests between Nazis and their conservative allies that Nazis—storm troopers and intellectuals alike—hated the conservative
bourgeoisie with consuming passion. The Nazis evinced a venomous hatred for the *Bürger* and his way of life, continually attacked the
traditional hierarchical order upheld by conservatives (who profited
by its existence), and employed revolutionary rhetoric with its threat
of a "second" revolution accompanied by menacing violence, which
conservatives were ill-equipped to counter. In political propaganda,
the conservative establishment was execrated as the standard-bearer
of Germany's class-ridden society, branded as indecisive, lukewarm,
and at least partially to blame for Germany's misfortunes since 1918.
In the charged atmosphere of the late winter and spring of 1933,
permeated by widespread acts of violence, a multitude of clashes
occurred that ushered in far-reaching, radical upheavals, wreaking
havoc on the traditional world of the German bourgeoisie by eroding hitherto accepted norms of political and social behavior.

Nazi "Revolutionary Fervor" in Action

An incident characteristic of the social upheavals occurred on 8
March 1933 in the Prussian Ministry of Finance, an agency (*Be-
hörde*) that, like all Prussian ministries, was characterized by its rigid
hierarchical structure. *Ministerial-Amtsgehilfe* (office assistant) Blume,
a low-ranking civil servant whose official position clearly placed
him on the lower end of the official hierarchy and one of the very
few Nazis in the ministry, raised the swastika flag on the Ministry of Finance building. The hoisting of the swastika flag had been
an almost daily occurrence during the Nazi takeovers of the non-
National Socialist Länder governments (such as Hamburg, Bremen,
and Bavaria), which followed the election of 5 March and usually
passed unchallenged. The head of the Prussian Finance Ministry,

7. Of central importance in the three-tiered German school system was
the *Abitur* (which required nine years of *Gymnasium*) as a prerequisite for admission to university studies. The different classes of the German civil service were
structured according to education: for entry into the *höhere Dienst* of the civil
service, a completed course of study at a German university was indispensable.

Johannes Popitz, a right-wing conservative and monarchist,[8] immediately ordered that the flag be taken down, whereupon, according to official records, the lowly office assistant Blume retorted: "No—the flag stays raised."[9] It was only after another prominent National Socialist in the Prussian Interior Ministry instructed him "not to make an affair of State out of this issue" that Blume agreed to lower the flag.[10] On the following day Popitz issued a written order to Blume, "effective immediately," requiring that the office assistant be suspended and leave the Ministry that same day.[11] Given the immense audacity of the incident—namely, that a mere office assistant had the nerve to counter his Minister directly—it is astonishing that Popitz's overall reaction was exceptionally forbearing. In his expulsion letter, Popitz showed himself disinclined to impose the (by the standards of Prussian officialdom) well-deserved disciplinary measures against the office assistant, and even promised to ensure Blume's transferal to a comparable position in another Ministry. The conservative Minister clearly meant to pre-empt a counterreaction on the part of the Nazis when he tried to rationalize the unauthorized hoisting of the flag in his letter to Blume: "Your understandable enthusiasm over the fact that the national movement which you have served has won a great victory in the elections may render your behavior in part excusable." Paradoxically, Popitz's letter emphasized extenuating circumstances in Blume's transgression: "I fully take into account that you have suffered during the war and more than done your duty for the fatherland."[12] Nevertheless, the counterreaction was not long in coming.

8. Johannes Popitz (1884–1945), a high-level administrator, had worked since 1919 in the Reich Finance Ministry, where he became Ministerial Councilor (*Ministerialrat*) in 1921. In Schleicher's Cabinet he was Minister without portfolio and provisionary head of the Prussian Ministry of Finance; on 21 April 1933 he was officially appointed Prussian Minister of Finance. The resignation from this post, which he submitted in 1938, was not accepted since, as a leading specialist in financial matters, he was considered indispensable. He later became active as a member of the opposition against Hitler.

9. 9 March 1933 at BA Berlin-Lichterfelde, "Reichskanzlei, NSDAP," R 43 II, no. 1195, 136.

10. Ibid., 136. Blume spoke with his fellow Nazi party member, SS *Gruppenführer* Kurt Daluege, the future head of police in the Prussian Interior Ministry.

11. Ibid., 138.

12. Ibid., 138. Blume had been wounded and partially disabled during the war.

On 9 March 1933, the very date of Popitz's letter to Blume, the secretary-treasurer of the National Socialist faction in the Reichstag who was also in charge of civil service-related matters, Dr. Hans-Eugen Fabrizius, sent a letter to Hermann Göring (in early March still provisional head of the Prussian Interior Ministry) in which he lodged a complaint against the Finance Minister. Fabrizius requested that the disciplinary action against the office assistant be rescinded, especially since Blume was one of the "most faithful and active National Socialist civil servants in Prussia" who had had "the courage to declare his support for National Socialism at a time when Prussian civil servants were banned from joining the NSDAP."[13] Since Göring, as provisional Interior Minister, was hardly in a position to issue instructions to his opposite number in the Finance Ministry, the case was referred to the Reich Chancellery. The Finance Minister, a man undoubtedly well-versed in the power relations of the Prussian civil service, having held leading positions in the Ministry of Finance for more than a decade, must have received an indelible impression of changes within the power structure when, in the second half of March, a letter from the Reich Chancellery reached his desk. In it, the Chief of Staff of Hitler's Chancellery, *Staatssekretär* Hans Heinrich Lammers, let Popitz know in no uncertain terms (if couched in polite language) that he should refrain from taking any "well-founded disciplinary action" against Blume.[14] Lammers's otherwise respectfully worded letter concluded with an open threat: "I have not yet had the opportunity to report the present case to the Reich Chancellor," though, he went on, there could be no doubt that Hitler "would express the desire to ignore a gaffe borne out of the first blush of enthusiasm over the success of the national uprising and the general excitement of the times."[15] Confronted with Lammers's threat to involve Hitler in the matter directly, Popitz had no alternative but to comply. With Lammers's letter, the lines

13. Ibid., 136 verso. In a second letter on 11 March Fabrizius claimed "that in the Prussian Ministry of Finance one is intent on keeping the National Socialists out or casting aspersions on them" (141).

14. BA Berlin-Lichterfelde, "Reichskanzlei, NSDAP," R 43 II, no. 1195, 144–144 verso; date illegible (either 20 or 25 March). Hans Heinrich Lammers (1879–1962) was a judge before entering the Reich Ministry of the Interior. In 1931, disciplinary proceedings were initiated against him for his participation in the *Harzburger Front*. In February 1932, he left the DNVP to join the Nazi party. On 30 January, he became Secretary of State and Chief of Hitler's Reich Chancellery.

15. Ibid., 144–144 verso.

of authority had been made clear and the case was closed. It is likely that never before in Prussian history had a simple office assistant caused such trouble to a Minister of Finance. Perhaps already here we find the roots of Popitz's disillusionment with the National Socialist state.[16] Eventually this would lead him into active opposition during the war. The extent to which the Nazis—in the hierarchically structured Prussian world—looked after their own people remains astonishing. And it was entirely novel that members of all social classes—provided they were members of the Nazi Party—felt free to lodge complaints against the authorities. In a land of "status formalization," as Ralf Dahrendorf once characterized Germany,[17] it was virtually unheard of for an office assistant to turn to an elected representative for help in a matter relating to his own bureaucratic department, and unthinkable to appeal to the head of government in a matter as trifling as the transfer of a low-ranking civil servant.

The "revolution" of March and April 1933 upset all norms that had hitherto governed public life. A characteristic example of this is the case of *Oberschulrat* (Chief Schools Inspector) Dr. Theodor Bohnert, a high ministerial official who supervised secondary schools, whose very livelihood was threatened by an unavoidable professional difference of opinion (a matter of a simple grade) with a member of the Nazi movement. As Bohnert's case made amply clear, anyone who had once dared to cross swords with a member of the NSDAP, regardless of his social class, now had cause for concern.

On 16 March 1933 Chief Schools Inspector Dr. Bohnert appealed to former Chancellor Franz von Papen, now Vice-Chancellor and Reich Commissar for Prussia, whose personal acquaintance he had once made as a member of the DDP in the Prussian Landtag.[18]

---

16. Popitz, who was held in high esteem as a financial expert throughout the entire Reich, played an important role in the *Mittwochs-Gesellschaft* ("Wednesday Society"), founded by Johann Gustav Droysen in 1863, which brought together sixteen illustrious personalities from the scientific, administrative, cultural, and military communities who met every second Wednesday. Other members of the conservative opposition who belonged to the *Mittwochs-Gesellschaft* included the diplomat Ulrich von Hassel and Ludwig Beck, Chief of the German General Staff. See Klaus Scholder, ed., *Die Mittwochs-Gesellschaft. Protokolle aus dem geistigen Deutschland 1932–1944* (Berlin, 1982).

17. On the concept of "*Statusformalisierung*," see Ralf Dahrendorf, *Gesellschaft und Demokratie in Deutschland* (Munich, 1968; first published in 1965), 86–107.

18. Franz von Papen (1879–1969). Before becoming Chancellor, Papen had been a member of the Prussian Landtag from 1920 to 1928 and from 1930–May 1932 for the right (and monarchist) wing of the Center Party; see Larry E.

Bohnert reported that in 1930 he had "to intervene in his capacity as Chief Schools Inspector in an *Abitur* examination which resulted in a complaint that was politically motivated."[19] Confronted with this complaint, the Schools Inspector now saw his family's livelihood put in jeopardy and feared "expulsion from a position in which I have honestly endeavored to give my best."[20] On 24 February 1933 Nazi Party member Werner Repke, *Abitur* class of 1930 and employed as a *Postaushelfer* (postal assistant), wrote to the Reich Commissar for the Prussian Ministry of Culture, Bernhard Rust, demanding that Rust exact justice "in a matter that has hitherto overshadowed—nay, devastated—my whole life."[21] In a self-absorbed letter pervaded by wounded pride and perceived injustice, Repke revealed the following facts: the "democratically oriented" (close to the DDP) Schools Inspector Dr. Bohnert had ruined Repke's *Abitur* with a bad grade in German. Another teacher, also a member of the left-liberal DDP, had denounced Repke as a Nazi. What was more, Repke claimed that he had not been the only victim of political intrigue. The teacher Lindemann, a political conservative who taught German literature, had been temporarily suspended from his position because of his "right-wing radicalism and convictions inimical to the state." Lindemann, suspended for his nationalist views, was another martyr for the national cause and had also suffered because of Bohnert's political preferences.[22] Seen in perspective, Repke's complaint lacked firm grounding: his overall *Abitur* grades were low, barely above passing level, reflecting the fact that he had been a poor student all along.[23] This, in turn, made it possible for Bohnert to argue that Repke's lack of professional success was due not to his bad grade in German but to his poor overall *Abitur* performance. The conservative teacher

---

Jones, "Franz von Papen, the German Center Party, and the Failure of Catholic Conservatism in the Weimar Republic," *Central European History* 38 (2005), 191–217.

19. 16 March at BA Berlin-Lichterfelde, "Stellvertreter des Reichskanzlers, Kanzlei von Papen," R 53, no. 71, 182–182 verso.

20. Ibid., 182 verso. This is reminiscent of the predicament of the fictional Director of Berlin's Königin Luise Gymnasium, Alfred François, in Lion Feuchtwanger's novel, *The Oppermanns*.

21. "Stellvertreter des Reichskanzlers," R 53, no. 71, 192–195, esp. 192. Bernhard Rust (1883–1945) became Commissar for the Prussian Ministry of Culture on 4 February 1933.

22. Repke mentioned Lindemann's suspension, well knowing that this was bound to prejudice Rust against the democratic Schools Inspector.

23. Ibid., 187.

Lindemann had himself assigned a low grade to Repke's *Abitur* essay, so that, in the final analysis, the only charge the Nazi Repke could level against the Schools Inspector was that Bohnert was a democrat. Repke's demand that Bohnert be chased from office for being "unsuited to serve as a model to students, let alone teachers, because of the insufficient moral qualities he had exhibited,"[24] could thus be grounded only in political, not professional, considerations. An overview of the correspondence leads to the obvious conclusion that Repke had used the Nazi seizure of power to better his *Abitur* grades and take revenge on an *Autoritätsperson* whose political convictions gave him a welcome pretext for taking action. Bohnert's nine-page letter in his own defense strikes the modern reader as awkward, especially the clumsy effort to stress his nationalist credentials and patriotic convictions.[25] As concerns the actual grounds for Repke's bad German grade, Bohnert's arguments are convincing.[26] In any case, Bohnert's long-winded letter of justification corroborates the fact that, on the eve of the Third Reich, even secondary schools in Germany were politicized to the point that the ideological orientations of the teachers were widely known. To Repke, this state of affairs was self-evident (if only intuitively), inducing him to take advantage of the Nazi seizure of power for his own, very personal, ends.

The incident with the Schools Inspector illustrated the erosion of traditional authority in the wake of the Nazi seizure of power. After the elections of 5 March (already viewed by contemporaries as the decisive caesura it would come to represent in political history), another dike had broken, and those who felt shortchanged in life could now take advantage of this all-pervasive politicization to

---

24. Ibid., 194.

25. BA Berlin-Lichterfelde, "Stellvertreter des Reichskanzlers, Kanzlei von Papen," R 53, no. 71, 183–191. Bohnert stressed the fact that he had been principal of the German School in Rome for seven years and that his entire family "had worn itself out in the service of Germans living abroad—his father in Cameroon and his brothers at Japanese universities." Bohnert, in his exalted position as *Oberschulrat*, was hardly accustomed to having to defend himself in the matter of a simple *Abitur* grade. In his haplessness, the good Republican in him complains about the widespread anti-Republican mood at Repke's *Gymnasium*, which could be construed to lend weight to Repke's charge that the low *Abitur* grade was politically motivated.

26. It would have been easy for Bohnert to let Repke fail the *Abitur* altogether due to overall low grades. Bohnert did not want to fail Repke because of the latter's disadvantaged social background.

further their own ends. In doing so they called into question the traditional social order. By the standards of the age, the idea that a Chief Schools Inspector had to fear for his position because of one (perfectly justifiable) *Abitur* grade just so a former student, seeking revenge for a putative politically motivated injustice, could better his grade and his current lowly position as a "postal assistant," was difficult to comprehend.

Traditional Hierarchies and Conservative Values on the Line

The National Socialist drive to challenge existing hierarchies, and to hold accountable those in positions of influence, was understandable since, up to this point, most members of the Nazi movement had largely been prevented from partaking in the spoils of power. In the upper echelons of the civil service, where political preferences usually lay with the German Nationals, this challenge gave rise to a deep-seated uncertainty, since the authority of civil servants, as representatives of the state, was called into question.[27] The Nazis' endeavor to destroy traditional hierarchies would gradually come to pervade all spheres of life, even conservative strongholds.

An interesting case in point was a complaint of the Osnabrück DNVP to the party's Berlin Head Office on 12 April 1933. At the Osnabrück *Land- und Amtsgericht* (District Court), according to the charge, "three lowly employees, standing under a swastika flag, had held forth on the establishment of a National Socialist complaints office where any civil servant would be in a position to lodge a complaint against judges and other superiors."[28] All *mittlere Beamte* (middle-ranking officials) at the Osnabrück District Court had been requested to attend the speech and were thus encouraged to exert a measure of control over their own superiors. Quite obviously, these particular Nazis were trying to tap into feelings of jealousy or even hatred toward higher-ups, and clearly counted on low- and middle-ranking bureaucrats proving more receptive to Nazi ideas than those in the upper ranks of the civil service, who were considered natural

27. On the civil service, see Rainer Fattmann, *Bildungsbürger in der Defensive. Die akademische Beamtenschaft und der "Reichsbund der höheren Beamten" in der Weimarer Republik* (Göttingen, 2001).

28. 12 April 1933 at BA Berlin-Lichterfelde, "Politischer Schriftwechsel, DNVP," R 8005, no. 19, 6.

supporters of the DNVP.[29] The striking phenomenon here, characteristic for the social change of the period, was the fact that "three low-ranking officials" considered themselves in a position to issue instructions to their middle-level superiors. And Osnabrück was no exception. A similar incident was reported by the Vice President of the Frankfurt *Oberlandesgericht* (Circuit Court) to the DNVP Berlin Head Office on 3 April 1933. According to the report, the notorious Nazi judge Roland Freisler had delivered "a rabble-rousing speech to all of the 1,500 officials and employees" of the Frankfurt law courts: "He emphasized that from now onwards no more distinctions would be made between higher and lower ranking court officials and that law courts would no longer mete out justice according to objective standards but to service the needs of the German people (which can only mean the needs of the NSDAP)."[30]

This social and ideological struggle against conservative strongholds was relentlessly pursued in all regions of the Reich. As a concerned report from the DNVP office in Liegnitz (Lower Silesia) related on 23 March 1933, local Nazis had made it unambiguously clear that "the national revolution will be followed by the National Socialist revolution and, concurrently, the struggle against 'Reaction'."[31] The report highlighted the speech by the Liegnitz *Kreisleiter* (Nazi county leader) Klieber, who openly threatened that "no one should make the attempt to steer our National Socialist revolution into bourgeois waters"; otherwise, the Nazis would make sure that "the national revolution will find its natural conclusion in the National Socialist revolution."[32] This anti-bourgeois thrust, observable in Nazi behavior throughout the Reich in the spring of 1933, is often buttressed by the open threat: "Those who believe they can disrupt our work of reconstruction will be carted off to

29. It was characteristic of the uncertainties of the time that the Osnabrück German Nationals had no idea whether an official decree establishing a "National Socialist Complaints Office" had been issued or whether it was all based on an initiative of the local Nazi party.

30. 3 April 1933 at BA Berlin-Lichterfelde, "Politischer Schriftwechsel, DNVP," R 8005, no. 19, 63 v.

31. 23 March 1933 at BA Berlin-Lichterfelde, "Politischer Schriftwechsel, DNVP," R 8005, no. 19, 122. The report stressed the economic consequences: "The prospect of an impending second revolution with completely unforeseeable economic results has exerted such a paralyzing effect that virtually all sectors of the economy of Lower Silesia are affected by it." (ibid., 122).

32. Ibid., 123. The *Kreisleiter*'s speech was reprinted in the *Liegnitzer Tageblatt* on 23 March 1933.

concentration camps, where they can ponder our radicalism."[33] The unabashed threat to use open violence fewer than eight weeks after the Nazi seizure of power remains astounding. The concentration camp at Dachau had been opened on 20 March with some fanfare; the existence of a number of so-called "wild" concentration camps and torture cellars of the SA was widely known, as was the fact that neither police nor law courts could offer protection. Every German citizen, regardless of social position, found himself at the mercy of the terror of the SA. Just days after the Reichstag Fire Decree, at the very latest after the elections of 5 March, German citizens were no longer protected by the rule of law. Even prominent Germans with reputable conservative and nationalist pedigrees could hardly hope to be spared if they openly voiced their displeasure with the regime. The bands of SA thugs would be stopped by neither name nor rank, all the more so since they knew only too well that their criminal acts would go unpunished. Violent daily attacks, even on uninvolved bystanders and respectable citizens, often nipped in the bud any criticisms of Nazi actions. At times, attacks had no apparent political foundation; rather, revenge, robbery, pillaging, looting, and the wish for personal enrichment lay at the heart of National Socialist assaults.[34] But these, too, served the purpose of inducing fear and stifling criticism. The question remains, of course, whether it was solely the threat of physical violence, that is, the very real danger of being attacked by bands of SA thugs or landing in a concentration camp that accounted for the absence of significant protest.

As long as the main victims of Nazi violence remained confined to members of the political Left, German Nationals intuitively countenanced Nazi aggression, as it suited their purpose to see their inveterate political foes finally humiliated and broken. This tacit collusion in the Nazi terror against the Left undermined the position of conservatives when political violence later came to be trained upon them. The protection once offered by the Rechtsstaat of Weimar, which had remained theoretically in place throughout February, broke down with the Reichstag Fire Decree. Political violence, or even the mere threat of it, played a key role in the social upheavals of the winter and spring of 1933. If possible, the victims avoided speaking about violent encroachments, partly for fear of reprisals

33. Ibid., 123.
34. One example of many at BA Berlin-Lichterfelde, "Stellvertreter des Reichskanzlers, Kanzlei von Papen," R 53, no. 184, "Überfall in Köln."

and partly because the very fact of victimization was humiliating in itself. In addition, the steady stream of daily degradations, such as bands of SA men rattling their collection boxes under the noses of passersby, had their inevitable numbing effect. And who would voluntarily own up to throwing money into the coffers of the SA because he felt intimidated by its members' threatening behavior? Most victims remained quiet and sought refuge in a hapless rage.

After the elections of 5 March 1933 had rendered the DNVP redundant as ally and coalition partner, National Socialists employed revolutionary rhetoric with the very conscious intent of undermining the position of German Nationals. A typical example of the anti-conservative and anti-bourgeois thrust of Nazi propaganda is an appeal of 20 March in the *Oberlausitzer Frühpost*, published in Görlitz.[35] The language in this appeal to "German peoples' comrades" was blunt: "The national revolution will and must be followed by the National Socialist revolution! Our comrades-in-arms have not died for the resurrection of a reactionary nationalism, our storm troopers have not gotten themselves bloodied and crippled for the return of economic conservatism; they have struggled and suffered for the creation of a true National Socialism." The Nazi paper predicted that this National Socialist revolution would be pushed through "without allies" since the German Nationals were bound to consider a second revolution to be "directed against their own interests and thus unnecessary." The *Oberlausitzer Frühpost* further admonished its readers "to see the reactionary evil behind the smiling mask"[36] and reminded them that "nationalistic reactionaries" ultimately constituted "obstacles and recalcitrant opponents," who "would have gladly snuffed the life out of our movement during its difficult years." What a second revolution might have meant for the economy is reflected in a complaint by Friedrich Wilhelm Diegse, Vice President of the *Reichsbank* Directorate.[37] According

35. BA Berlin-Lichterfelde, "Politischer Schriftwechsel, DNVP," R 8005, no. 19, 125. Görlitz in the province of Lower Silesia, 91,702 inhabitants (1926). See *Statistisches Jahrbuch für das Deutsche Reich* 1933, 11. This appeal is representative of countless similar proclamations.

36. Ibid., 125. Nazi supporters were instructed to subscribe solely to National Socialist (and not to right-wing bourgeois, nationalist) papers to avoid watering down the movement.

37. 5 May 1933 at BA Berlin-Lichterfelde, "Akten der Reichskanzlei, NSDAP," R 43 II, no. 1195, 296. Given its urgency, Diegse's complaint was submitted by telephone.

to Diegse's report, a National Socialist *Reichsbank* employee named Tönnies had demanded to be appointed to the Executive Board of the Dresdner Bank. The Board of Directors, while refusing to bow to this demand, had—to accommodate Tönnies—created a place for him on the *Börsenvorstand*, the Executive Board of the stock market, by arranging for the withdrawal of another candidate.[38] Tönnies, nevertheless, continued to insist on his immediate inclusion on the Bank's Executive Board, and even threatened to force admission by violent means with the help of the SA. Even though the records indicate that Tönnies was subsequently reprimanded and "expelled from the party,"[39] this apparently minor incident is telling because of the anxiety caused by Tönnies's otherwise laughable demands, and the desperate efforts to appease him. Prussia's traditional social order, whose hierarchical structure had evolved over generations, had become brittle and began to disintegrate within the course of a few months after 30 January. These cracks in the traditional social edifice were deepened by pressure from the street, since many Nazis, inebriated by the ease and completeness of their victory, delighted in making sport of the desecration of all that was sacred and inviolable to conservatives. A typical example of such provocative debasing of conservative values occurred in a hotel in Glauchau (Saxony) in the middle of April 1933.[40] According to the report of the incident, local Nazis claimed that the "national revolution" had in reality been a "socialist" revolution, that the Kaiser "was a coward who had furtively absconded in the middle of the night," and that it was foolish to dream of the return of the Hohenzollern, because it would only mean that once again "a first born idiot would take the throne."[41]

Members and supporters of the DNVP, on the other hand, clung to the vision of unity with their overbearing alliance partner. In April and May 1933, the German Nationals went so far as to conjure up external dangers and a threatening stranglehold of hostile powers around the Reich to stress the need for domestic unity and internal

---

38. Ibid., 296.
39. Ibid. (This was done "by order of the Reich Chancellor.")
40. 12 April 1933 at BA Berlin-Lichterfelde, "Politischer Schriftwechsel, DNVP," R 8005, no. 19, 8. Glauchau, in the *Regierungsbezirk* Chemnitz in Saxony, was a town with 29,135 inhabitants (1925).
41. Ibid.

cohesion in their increasingly tenuous coalition with the Nazis.[42] In style and content, German Nationals feverishly attempted to bring their party in line with the more successful NSDAP: German National combat squadrons were structured along the lines of the SA, the "German National People's Party" was renamed the "German National Front" at the beginning of May, there was increased emphasis on the leadership principle, and German Nationals did not even shy away from aping the Nazi salute, turning "Heil Hitler!" into "Front Heil" and "Heil Deutschland."[43] To this unreflective imitation of their own style, the Nazis responded with scorn and derision, all the more so since they increasingly set themselves apart from the German Nationals in their own propaganda and public self-portrayal. After the KPD had been declared illegal, the SPD neutralized, the Center willing to cooperate with the Nazis in the Enabling Act (if only out of political calculation and fear), and the liberal parties reduced to utter insignificance, it had become clear that the DNVP was the only party that stood between the Nazis and absolute power. After the passing of the Enabling Act on 23 March 1933, it was next in line.

Anti-Bourgeois Ideology and Rhetoric

In Nazi eyes, German Nationals were still a factor to be reckoned with given that DNVP members and sympathizers still held central positions in the economy, administration, and local politics, and also participated in the governments of Prussia and the Reich. The increasingly anti-bourgeois slant of Nazi propaganda, therefore, can be explained partially with reference to expediency. Throughout April and May the Nazis unleashed a stream of criticism directed at the conservative establishment that highlighted the alleged moral weakness of the bourgeoisie and emphasized its inherent corruption, thereby buttressing the claim that German Nationals had forfeited their share in power. Anti-bourgeois epithets, over and above their use in the heated atmosphere of daily politics, had a long tradition

42. BA Berlin-Lichterfelde, "Reichslandbund Pressearchiv, Organisiertes Bürgertum," R 8034 II, no. 9021, 9. Conservative papers warned that in view of external enemies, "we national parties" had better stick together.

43. Many letters to the DNVP Berlin head office were signed "Front Heil" or "Heil Deutschland," as a sign of the writers' solidarity with the German National cause.

with National Socialists. The anti-bourgeois undertone of Nazi propaganda had developed during the Weimar Republic, when German Nationals were often combatted as rivals at the election box. In the ideological mouthpiece of the NSDAP, the *Nationalsozialistische Monatshefte*,[44] in which mostly issues of principles were discussed, Ernst Graf von Reventlow disparaged the bourgeoisie and its lifestyle as early as 1930.[45] Reventlow, who was held in high esteem in party circles because he had brought north German *völkisch* groups into the NSDAP, was one of the few Nazis with an impeccable upper-class pedigree.[46] According to Reventlow, the bourgeoisie had forsaken its initially liberal political orientation and appropriated conservative politics, so that "conservatism in Germany increasingly fell prey to embourgeoisement."[47] Reventlow believed that the bourgeoisie "by virtue of its very nature could never comprehend that life presents man with an uncompromising 'either-or'."[48] This reproach of political vacillation, indecision, and opportunism pervaded Nazi assessments of the bourgeoisie. Reventlow ended his diatribe with the characteristic wish: "The *Bürger* and the bourgeoisie in its past and present form will and must not be allowed to return. May both disappear as quickly as possible, [to be] ruined by money—their false god—as well as by their irresoluteness, lack of strength, and the insipidness of their self-satisfied philosophy of life."[49] In that same issue of the *Nationalsozialistische Monatshefte*, Goebbels, in an article

---

44. The *Nationalsozialistische Monatshefte* was frequently used to hold forth upon ideological issues that went beyond the more mundane issues of day-to-day politics.

45. Ernst Graf von Reventlow, "Nemesis über dem Bürgertum," *Nationalsozialistische Monatshefte*, 1. Jahrgang (1930), 5–11.

46. Ernst Graf von Reventlow (1869–1943), a former naval officer and descendant of the Schleswig-Holstein nobility, was one of the few outwardly respectable figures of the NSDAP in the 1920s. Before the First World War, he had attracted attention as an uncompromising critic of Wilhelmine Germany. In the Republic, he became a champion of *völkisch* ideas and, for a while, even of a united *völkisch*–communist front. In 1927, he went over to the NSDAP and took the greater part of the "German-*Völkisch* Freedom Party" with him. See Otto-Ernst Schüddekopf, *Linke Leute von rechts. Die nationalrevolutionären Minderheiten und der Kommunismus in der Weimarer Republik* (Stuttgart, 1960); Stephan Malinowski, *Vom König zum Führer. Deutscher Adel und Nationalsozialismus* (Berlin, 2003).

47. Reventlow, "Nemesis über dem Bürgertum," 8.

48. Ibid., 10 (as exemplified by the "attitude of the German Nationals toward the Dawes Plan").

49. Reventlow, "Nemesis über dem Bürgertum," 11.

on the "patriotic bourgeoisie," uses even more pointed language.[50] Like Reventlow, he found fault with the *Bürger's* all-too-ready willingness to compromise and his lack of fighting spirit: "He lacks that kind of exclusivity that covets something either completely or not at all."[51] The German Nationals had compromised the very idea of conservatism in the minds of the people, since they contented themselves "to conserve what already exists, irrespective of its value and of whether it should be preserved or discarded."[52] That is why the German Nationals could only be considered "reactionary," since they balked at any imperative progress in the lifeblood of German politics.[53] Goebbels became quite specific: "The three-class franchise classifying voters along property lines, the 'pittance' legislation [social welfare], the *'beschränkter Untertanenverstand'* [limited comprehension of the subject], the 'lord-of-the-manor' way of thinking, the industrial capitalistic firebrands—all of these are typical fabrications of conservative reactionaries who, being fully alive to their own incompetence and inability to foster creativity, enviously suppress achievement and progress by others . . ." With contemporary German Nationals the "true conservative element" had thus shrunk to complete insignificance, as all political activity had been dwarfed by economic concerns.[54] Expressions of shared interest with the German Nationals should thus be taken with a grain of salt, and temporary alliances considered but marriages of convenience: "There can be absolutely no doubt that a deep ideological chasm yawns between us and them, a fact that needs to be pointed out all the more clearly, the more often we are compelled to form alliances with bourgeois forces in order to attain our tactical goals. They are

50. Joseph Goebbels, "Das patriotische Bürgertum," *Nationalsozialistische Monatshefte*, 1. Jahrgang (1930), 221–229.
51. Ibid., 222. Given their *raison d'être*, bourgeois parties were bound to oppose National Socialism: "As absurd as this may sound, the front that opposes us stretches from Westarp to Thälmann [conservatives to communists]; what lies in between differs only in nuance, not in essence." (225).
52. Ibid., 225. The true conservative, by contrast, would defend "the eternal values of blood and *Volk*" in the interest of his people and, if he considered these values in jeopardy, would turn into a rebel out of a "conservative sense of duty." (225).
53. Ibid., 225. Goebbels freely gave vent to his hatred for the conservative bourgeoisie, based on the charge that in November 1918, they had abandoned Germany to "international adventurers," thereby leaving "the fate of the nation completely to chance." (226).
54. Ibid., 226.

captives of their own bourgeois mindset."[55] The Nazi "mindset" was clearly different.

Long before 30 January, National Socialists thus emphasized deep-seated differences in ideology and reasoning between themselves and German Nationals. After 30 January 1933, this philosophical-ideological chasm became deeper. The programmatic article "Our Commitment to German Socialism," by Walther Schmitt, is revealing with respect to the distinct anti-bourgeois slant of the NSDAP immediately following the *Machtergreifung*.[56] Schmitt argued that for National Socialism the catastrophe of 1918 hardly had the same meaning as it did for the "reactionaries,"[57] who were, after all, as much to blame for the downfall of Germany as the Marxists. It had been mainly the belief in the emergence of a new Germany that rendered bearable the untold sacrifices and deprivations of the war for millions of German soldiers, not the war aims of "patricians and patriotic privy councilors."[58] The sacrificial death of so many hundreds of thousands of loyal Germans imposed upon National Socialists the obligation of constructing a new Germany based on the principle of a "German" socialism. The most grievous offense of the bourgeois epoch was its legacy of a deep social divide, "which defrauded the German state of millions of its best people,"[59] who, alienated from their national community, were driven into the camp of the Marxist parties. For this reason, the "brown battalions of the swastika" were equally opposed to "the caste spirit and conceit of the *Bürger*" as to "the rabble-rousing class-oriented propaganda of Marxism." The author made no distinction between Marxists (and leftists of all persuasions), on the one hand, and the conservative bourgeoisie, on the other, as the undisputed enemies of National Socialism. Neither the left nor the conservative bourgeoisie, Schmitt emphasized, belonged in the new Germany. In the final analysis, Schmitt argued, the central issue was not the reorganization of the German state but the creation of a new German *Mensch* (man).[60] To bring this off,

55. Ibid., 226–227. According to Goebbels, the concept of "bourgeoisie" as a remnant of a class-based way of thinking had now been overcome.

56. Walther Schmitt, "Unser Wille zum deutschen Sozialismus," *National-sozialistische Monatshefte*, Heft 35 (Februar 1933), 82–86.

57. Ibid., 82.

58. Ibid., 83.

59. Ibid., 84.

60. The creation of this "new German man" was indispensable, since the legacy of the revolution could be safeguarded only by reorienting the values and expectations of every individual.

the *Bürger* had to be transcended, for the new German man of the future had to be free of snobbery, conceit, and class hatred. Schmitt used unambiguous language to characterize the political situation in the winter of 1933: "Even today this new German generation finds itself in a struggle for survival since it must also fight against those members of the bourgeoisie who have chosen the NSDAP as their political mouthpiece. In the revolutionary conflict between generations, it is inevitable that people of the old order seek to make the new age serve their own purposes to safeguard their own position. Temporarily, they may even attain leadership positions, but the dynamic strength of the movement's young warriors will soon sweep them away."[61] Put plainly, even if conservatives managed to attain positions of power by dint of their alliance with Hitler, they would soon be cast aside by the revolutionary dynamic of the Nazi movement.

Another concern of the author—and a central theme of Nazi propaganda in the months after 30 January—was the elimination of the "*Berechtigungswesen* (entitlement character) of the bourgeois state."[62] This was an attack on the barriers and limitations established by the German educational system that had to be overcome for acceptance into "good society" and which implicitly discriminated against the lower and lower-middle classes: without the nine-year stint at a Gymnasium, there was no *Abitur*; without the *Abitur* there was no possibility for university study, and without a university degree there was no chance to enter the higher civil service. To counter this injustice, the "entitlement character" of bourgeois society thus had to be abolished in order to promote "the social rise of natural leaders, even if they were the sons of peasants and workers."[63]

Here the attack on the *Bürger* and his lifestyle turned into a fully fledged assault on bourgeois society and its class barriers, which prevented outsiders from joining the ranks of the upper crust and partaking of its privileges. Needless to say, in February 1933 a majority of Nazis were still outsiders. The propelling force behind this leveling and equalizing anti-bourgeois instinct was the understandable desire to destroy bourgeois class-ridden society (which, after all, blocked Nazi ambitions), even if this desire was cloaked in the veil of high-minded idealism—for example, that the *Bürger* had betrayed

61. Ibid., 85.
62. Ibid.
63. Ibid.

Germany. But in the end, very concrete interests lay behind the anti-bourgeois posture of National Socialism, which was further accentuated by the newcomer's spite for the establishment. During the early months of 1933, the necessity of tearing down class barriers was stressed time and again, even by the National Socialist Interior Minister Wilhelm Frick himself. The "meaning of our Age," wrote Frick, lies "in the surmounting of differences between classes and estates," as well as "in the incorporation of the fourth estate—the German worker—into the state as a citizen with equal rights."[64] The second central theme, one already touched upon in Walther Schmitt's article about "German Socialism"—the simultaneous struggle against the conservative bourgeoisie and the concept of class struggle inherent in Marxist ideology—also became a leitmotif of Nazi propaganda after 30 January. In June 1933, Goebbels thus bemoaned the "giant burden of an unprecedented political two-front war" against the "conceit of the Right" and the "class consciousness of the Left."[65] Even the hierarchy of values drawn up for the (yet to be created) new man of National Socialism, with the characteristic title "Moral Requirements of National Socialism," implicitly passed judgment on the conservative bourgeoisie.[66] This became especially clear when "Condemnation of Self-Interest" was elevated to the level of a moral imperative. The contemporary reader was thus instinctively reminded of the corruption scandals of the winter and spring of 1933, which implicated leading representatives of the bourgeoisie and which were heralded with great glee and fanfare in the National Socialist press. In light of the countless violent Nazi attacks in the winter and spring of 1933, it is ironic that "Respect for the Individual," the "Imperative of Truthfulness," and "Readiness to Lend Succor" occupy pride of place in the ranks of the promulgated cardinal virtues.[67]

64. Wilhelm Frick, "Der Sinn unserer Zeit," *Nationalsozialistische Monatshefte*, Heft 39 (June 1933), 245–246.

65. Joseph Goebbels, "Die deutsche Revolution," *Nationalsozialistische Monatshefte*, Heft 39 (June 1933), 247–248. The "German Revolution," as Goebbels referred to the Nazi seizure of power in the winter and spring of 1933, had been the "least bloody revolution in world history." (248).

66. F.O. Bilse, "Die sittliche Forderung im Nationalsozialismus," *Nationalsozialistische Monatshefte*, Heft 39 (June 1933), 263–276.

67. The "moral imperatives" of National Socialism were: "Self-interest as a Curse," "Respect for the Individual," "The Imperative of Truthfulness," "A Sense of Honorable Behavior," "A Sense of Duty," "Preparedness to Help Others," and "The Führer as the Model."

The "Demise" of the *Bürger*

The more the German Nationals, in their powerlessness and impotence, tried to blur all differences between themselves and the Nazis (while paradoxically insisting on the autonomy of their party), the more National Socialists emphasized the differences between themselves and the "reactionaries," whom they dismissed with contempt. Nazi speakers and the Nazi press accentuated the discrepancies in values and conceptions of society between themselves and the German Nationals, to the point where the contemporary reader could not help but get the impression that the sharpest dividing line in the German party system ran between the Nazis and German Nationals—rather than between either of them and the Left. The Nazis concentrated their fire most directly on the conservatives' outmoded conception of society. So, for example, an official of the National Socialist Factory Cells argued in a speech on the basic principles of National Socialism entitled "The German Nationals and Us":[68] "In Germany, class conceit is the fundamental evil. In Adolf Hitler's German workers' state it is of no consequence whether somebody is a street cleaner or a chief executive. We will see to it that in the future brains and not bags of money will be decisive." At the same time, it was made clear in no uncertain terms that the conservatives were no longer regarded as a serious opponent. Reacting to critical remarks of the German Nationals during the Danzig election campaign, the Nazi press was quick to point out that "the revolution has been strong enough to exercise generosity where appropriate, but it will also be strong enough—on the road toward building German Socialism—to shove aside the smoldering heap of rubble that calls itself the national bourgeoisie."[69] Here the Nazis presented themselves as a movement of protest and rebellion against the entire bourgeois way of life (which seemed, in any case, anachronistic in an age of

68. 1 June 1933 at BA Berlin-Lichterfelde, "Pressearchiv Reichslandbund," R 8034 II, no. 9030, "Parteileben Deutschland: Nationalsozialisten und DNVP," 185.

69. Ibid. "Unsere Geduld ist am Ende. Front gegen deutschnationale Angriffe." In the Danzig election of 24 May 1933, the NSDAP received 50.03 percent of the vote and 38 of 72 seats in the Danzig parliament, the *Volksrat*. See Eckhard Jesse, "Hermann Rauschning—Der fragwürdige Kronzeuge," in Ronald Smelser, Enrico Syring, and Rainer Zitelmann, eds., *Die braune Elite II* (Darmstadt, 1993), 193–206; esp. 194.

economic depression and mass unemployment), thereby distancing themselves markedly from their conservative alliance partner.

In the Nazi party and its organizations this "anti-bourgeois" ideology was widespread and all-pervasive. The National Socialist Students' Association, for example, which had won absolute majorities in elections among German university students long before 1933, were imbued with a deep-seated, vociferous, and almost violent anti-bourgeois attitude. The *Bürger* epitomized the enemy per se: "We see him as that eternal element of decomposition that is responsible for our national misery and domestic strife. We want to give him the name he deserves. We want to label him and brand him for all time; we want to throw all our boundless contempt and disgust into this one word: *"Bürger."*[70] Here the venomous language makes it plain that many Nazis rebelled against what they considered the self-satisfied and complacent bourgeois lifestyle that was blamed for Germany's misfortunes. This deep-seated aversion to the bourgeoisie was also found in the press of student organizations, whose members, aspiring to successful careers, might be expected to admire and emulate rather than to disparage bourgeois lifestyles. Here the *Bürger* is characterized as the "epitome of the spiritless man, lacking in revolutionary fervor—insipid, lackluster, hidebound, and mediocre." He is viewed as "conventional and efficient, but by no means heroic, for the courage to face the absolute is alien to a *Bürger*, whose *raison d'être* lies in the safety of his own material security."[71] In National Socialist Student Associations, these anti-bourgeois and anti-capitalist tendencies went hand-in-hand with a rejection of the traditions associated with the *Bildungsbürgertum*, a paradoxical sentiment in those who would come to embody the educational elite. A former functionary of the National Socialist German Student Association, Joachim Haupt, gave a much-quoted speech on this very theme in September 1933,[72] in which he differentiated between a

---

70. Quoted from "Schlagt die Reaktion, wo ihr sie trefft," *Der Heidelberger Student*, no. 3 (June 22, 1934), 1, cited in Michael Grüttner, *Studenten im Dritten Reich* (Paderborn, 1995), 248. See also Geoffrey Giles, *Students and National Socialism in Germany* (Princeton, 1985).

71. "Nationalsozialistische Kulturpolitik," *Der Turnerschaftler* 50 (1933/34), 167, cited in Michael Grüttner, *Studenten*, 249. Here again, the roots of anti-bourgeois revulsion are traced back to the First World War: "In the World War we see the initial impetus and in the National Socialist revolution the final implementation of the liquidation of the bourgeoisie" (Ibid.).

72. Joachim Haupt, born in 1900, NSDAP member since 1922, 1927–1928 leader of the Kiel Student Association; after 1928, teacher in Kiel and other

"tedious" and an "interesting" National Socialism:[73] "The 'tedious' National Socialism, which is presently gaining ground in Germany, endeavors to restore the good old ways: indecent books are again banned, nightclubs are again closed, and once again people observe traditional proprieties. The 'tedious' National Socialism is tantamount to the restoration of bourgeois morals." According to Haupt, an essential element of the new, "interesting" (and not "tedious") National Socialism was the rejection of "West European civilization," especially "the absolute disdain for so-called *Bildung*." Haupt maintained that "[a]nyone who is taken in by the hollow claptrap of *Bildung* will never be receptive to the ideas of National Socialism."[74]

A barrage of all-embracing accusations against the bourgeoisie appeared in the Nazi press upon the death of Ernst Oberfohren, the former head of the German National parliamentary faction, who had opposed the alliance with Hitler after 30 January, and who finally resigned his party positions at the end of March.[75] Oberfohren was found shot to death in his home on 7 May 1933. The official cause of death—suicide—was quickly called into question, though it was never conclusively proved that murder had actually been committed.[76] Under the characteristic title "The End of the *Bürger*," the Nazis portrayed Oberfohren's death as symptomatic of "the serious political crisis in which the bourgeoisie has found itself for many years."[77] For a long time, the author of the article argued, the bourgeoisie had been unable to keep pace with the overall development of society, to the point where the bourgeois way of life had lost its legitimacy: "Past ages have placed the *Bürger* at the center of events,

---

towns in Schleswig-Holstein; dismissed from state employment in 1931 because of his pro-Nazi activities; 1932–1933 NSDAP deputy in the Prussian Landtag; 1933–1935 *Ministerialrat* in the Prussian Ministry of Culture (see Grüttner, *Studenten*, 508).

73. "The 'interesting' National Socialism includes all its socialist elements, the nationalization of banks, sports as part of military training (*Wehrsport*), and much else besides." In Joachim Haupt, "Die Erziehung der Studentenschaft," *Deutsche Studentenschaft*, 9 October 1933, 2–3, cited in Grüttner, *Studenten*, 249.

74. Ibid., and Grüttner, *Studenten*, 250.

75. On Ernst Oberfohren, see *Neue Deutsche Biographie* 19 (Berlin, 1999), 384, and chapter 6 below.

76. For more details, see chapter 6 below.

77. 9 May 1933 at BA Berlin-Lichterfelde, "Pressearchiv Reichslandbund," R 8034 II, no. 9030, "Parteileben Deutschland, Nationalsozialismus und DNVP," 183.

have upheld bourgeois respectability as the aim of all desires toward which everyone strove but which only few could attain. Between start and finish, barriers had been erected, walls put up, and ditches dug that could be overcome only by those who, by virtue of birth, property or education, had the tools at their disposal necessary to surmount these obstacles."[78] The bourgeoisie was largely blamed for the political misery and failure of the Republic: "The *Bürger* has failed politically. Not only did he no longer possess the strength to prevent chaotic developments, but rather he promoted and abetted . . . chaos."[79] As illustrated by a string of corruption scandals, now even the last bastion of the bourgeoisie had collapsed—"absolute uprightness and integrity, the clean escutcheon without a blot, the stainless reputation." In this connection, bourgeois dignitaries were singled out—Lord Mayors who had allegedly lined their pockets by defrauding the public purse, as well as conservatives caught in (at least partially fabricated) corruption scandals. In the bourgeois age, now relegated to the past, "too much was made of technical expertise, specialized knowledge and outward form, but people failed to realize that in the end it was personality and character that mattered most. These, of course, were traits one could not acquire from books or etiquette manuals. People had focused too exclusively on outward appearances, devoted all their energies toward mastering formalities, so that no time was left to cultivate one's conscience, one's honor, and one's character."[80]

The Anti-Bourgeois Thrust of the Nazi Social Revolution

During the *Machtergreifungszeit* there was no confluence of national-bourgeois and National Socialist values and interests. As Goebbels had written, the Nazis were fighting "an unprecedented political two-front war" and it remains astonishing how National Socialism, fighting against so many political factions in society, could succeed at all. Violent opposition to communism and socialism had been the

---

78. Ibid. In contrast to the German Nationals, the Nazis also rejected the Second Empire as a whole.

79. Ibid.

80. Ibid. Here again the "moral imperatives" of National Socialism are sharply contrasted with the lukewarm neutralism of the bourgeoisie, who, it was alleged, lacked moral fiber.

mainstay of their program from early on, and vociferous opposition to political Catholicism emerged in the struggles of the late Weimar Republic. But their passionate loathing of the conservative bourgeoisie and its ways fully came to the fore only after the seizure of power. Only then did the break with the past—the extent to which they abominated the old Imperial Germany—become fully evident. The gulf that divided them from a conservative bourgeoisie accused of vacillation, the debasement of conservative values, indecision, opportunism, and the lack of the uncompromising fighting spirit required by the new age, now opened wide. The "new man" of National Socialism who refused to acknowledge class barriers and was bent on stamping out the bourgeois *Berechtigungswesen*— the manifold hurdles from educational prerequisites to behavioral codes—considered the *Bürger* his main enemy. The catalogue of values for this "new man" passed judgment on the *Bürger* and found him wanting; the specter of a "second revolution" threatened to undercut his very livelihood.

Concrete interests clearly lay behind this anti-bourgeois posture of National Socialism: the campaign against "class conceit," the ridiculing of bourgeois forms of life, and the attempt to undermine hierarchical structures was fed by the outsider's proverbial resentment against those in power. The immense social dynamism of the period after the March elections was directed against the old elites, especially the conservative bourgeoisie. The members of the conservative establishment, who had facilitated Hitler's rise to power, were among the main social victims of his rapid success. This anti-bourgeois thrust of Nazism, though undoubtedly effective as a political device, was also a genuine and sincere expression of personal disgust. The very fact that it was heartfelt, that it gave vent to deeply held beliefs in unaffected language, rendered it all the more effective as a propaganda weapon. This dynamic of pent-up resentment directed against traditional authorities, values, and beliefs was bound to have dramatic consequences. Karl Dietrich Bracher spoke in this context of a "verbal social revolution,"[81] but what happened in the late winter and spring of 1933 was more than that. As the evidence

---

81. See Bracher, *Die deutsche Diktatur*, 483. In my opinion, Bracher puts too much emphasis on the element of conscious manipulation: "Es vollzog sich eine verbale 'Sozialrevolution,' in deren Zeichen sowohl der alte Antikapitalismus wie die vielschichtige neue Anhängerschaft manipuliert werden konnten." He goes on to argue that the regime had contributed to "dismantling the structures of social consciousness."

shows, the immense political upheaval that followed 30 January carried wrenching social and psychological reverberations in its wake. The almost obsequious letter of a Prussian Minister trying to excuse the unauthorized flag-raising of an "auxiliary" official in the Ministry, followed by blatant insubordination and the open refusal to obey his Minister's order to lower the flag, is a banal incident in itself, but it reveals a revolution in the world of Prussian officialdom—and one that, to be sure, would also be unthinkable in contemporary British or French Ministries. The palpable fear of a Chief Schools Inspector, a high official who supervised Prussian *Gymnasien*, resulting from the flak over a—to all intents and purposes well justified—*Abitur* grade he had given to a student, speaks to the rapid erosion of time-tested standards of social authority. In Weimar Germany, the mere idea that a student complaint might possibly be cause for concern to a *Schulrat* would have been preposterous. The Nazi attempt to institute a "Complaints Office" against high-ranking judicial officials at the Osnabrück and Frankfurt law courts, impossible in the Weimar Republic, illustrates the rebellion of underlings against the entrenched positions of their formerly unassailable superiors.[82] Times had now changed. All those in positions of dependency, provided they could claim affiliation with the Nazi Party, were suddenly in a position to exert a measure of control that they had not possessed before.[83] In an odd sense, then, the Nazi state promised to be more

82. Mostly, these politically motivated "Complaints Offices" led nowhere, and Nazis in the civil service were soon relegated to their initial station though, for reasons of opportunism, the percentage of Party members among officials rose dramatically after 1933. Overall, the social status of civil servants declined after 1933; within the bureaucracy one observes a leveling trend as the distance between different grades of officials shrank. See also Hans Mommsen, *Beamtentum im Dritten Reich* (Stuttgart, 1966), 20–22.

83. To speak in this context of "modernization" with its implied positive connotation—as, for example, Michael Prinz and Rainer Zitelmann, eds., *Nationalsozialismus und Modernisierung* (Darmstadt, 1991)—may well lead to misunderstandings because it ignores the inhuman aspect of the regime: any potential "modernization" of a regime based on terror with anachronistic aims came at such a high price that it automatically outweighed any "modernizing" benefits. As Michael Burleigh and Wolfgang Wippermann put it: ". . . the word 'modern' only fits the Third Reich if one strips it of all connotations of 'betterment' or 'improvement' to an extent which renders it utterly meaningless . . ." See Michael Burleigh and Wolfgang Wippermann, *The Racial State: Germany 1933–1945* (Cambridge, 1991), 2. As long as the term "modern" is governed by the positive implications it usually carries in the literature, its application to Nazism will remain problematic. The literature on the issue is immense; for an

"democratic" for those who supported it than the Weimar Republic had ever been. Undoubtedly, this contributed in no small measure to the popularity of the regime: a mood of a new awakening, of fundamental change, hung in the air. A radically new departure seemed imminent, one that promised a better future, more in tune with the spirit of the crisis-ridden age, and one that seemed prepared for a radical break with the dusty bourgeois world that was pervaded by the foul smell of unrepentant failure.

Since the old bourgeois order was disparaged by the new government, discredited and questioned "from above," that is, with official sanction, the social consequences were immediate. It cannot be denied that the omnipresent threat of violence, the very real possibility of being thrown into a concentration camp, and the unabashed use of terror accelerated political and social change.[84] Whether one refers to this as a social revolution, like Ralf Dahrendorf or David Schoenbaum in the mid 1960s,[85] as a "verbal social revolution" like Karl Dietrich Bracher,[86] or as a process by which "the old elites were pushed aside," like Thomas Nipperdey,[87] the fact remains that even before the war a social restructuring and psychological revolution with respect to social class took place. It was, of course, only a partial displacement of the old elites and not their complete

---

overview see Norbert Frei, "Wie modern war der Nationalsozialismus," *Geschichte und Gesellschaft* 19 (1993), 367–387; and Hans Mommsen, "Noch einmal: Nationalsozialismus und Modernisierung," *Geschichte und Gesellschaft* 21 (1995), 391–402.

84. The latent, but omnipresent, threat of terror was one explanation for why there was little resistance to Nazism from the beginning. To law-abiding Germans there were few possibilities of defense against Nazi thugs. The police were unwilling to protect citizens, whose ability of self-defense was further curtailed by the fact that SA thugs were obviously acting in the name of the state.

85. Dahrendorf, *Gesellschaft und Demokratie in Deutschland*, 415–432; David Schoenbaum, *Hitler's Social Revolution. Class and Status in Nazi Germany 1933–1939* (New York, London, 1980, first published in 1966).

86. Bracher, *Die deutsche Diktatur*, 483. Bracher points to the paradoxical fact that the Nazis spoke of the equality of all "Volksgenossen in einem Atemzug mit einer scharf gegliederten Kommandostruktur, militärisch-aristokratischer Art . . ." Ibid., 485.

87. Thomas Nipperdey, "Probleme der Modernisierung in Deutschland," in Nipperdey, *Nachdenken über die deutsche Geschichte* (Munich, 1986), 44–60, esp. 57. Nipperdey argued that the "de facto" abdication of the old elites was a truly "revolutionary event." German fascism, he held, ". . . has leveled and equalized German society . . ." and he asserted emphatically that "a 'brown revolution' had really taken place."

dispossession. After the dissolution of the German National Front on 27 June 1933, and especially after Hitler had made it clear that he considered the revolution ended—first on 6 July and then again on 14 July 1933—he did his best to secure the active support of Germany's conservative elites in order to pursue shared goals in the realms of economic and foreign policy. But the fact that the very foundations of their lifestyle were called into question, together with their "character" and integrity, made it clear that from 1933 onwards, even if they remained in positions of power, they would have to play the game by the rules of the new masters.

Chapter V

BETWEEN THE DICTATES OF CONSCIENCE AND POLITICAL EXPEDIENCY

The DNVP and Anti-Semitism

The scope and intensity of Nazi anti-Semitic attacks during the last years of the Weimar Republic had made it clear that the lives of the 525,000 German Jews[1] were bound to take a turn for the worse after the 85-year-old President Paul von Hindenburg appointed Hitler Chancellor. For years, Hitler and his lieutenants had levied barrages of hate-filled charges against Jews, blaming them for the devastation of the First World War, the debilitating 1918 armistice, the Treaty of Versailles, the 1923 inflation, Marxism, and world communism as a whole. Yet few recognized the urgency of the problem during the first days of Hitler's rule, even though public discrimination of German Jews began in February and the SA's violent attacks started on a large scale after the 5 March 1933 elections. Random attacks turned into more systematic abuse when the Nazi Party organized a nationwide boycott of Jewish-owned shops on 1 April. That month,

---

1. For figures, see Friedländer, *Nazi Germany and the Jews*, 15, 328. Friedländer estimates that about 25,000 Jews left Germany between January and June 1933. Since 1880, the percentage of Jews in the German population had been declining steadily, due partly to a lower birthrate compared to the rest of Germany and an ongoing assimilation process. The percentage figure fell from 1.09 percent in 1880 to 0.76 percent in June 1933. Between 1925 and June 1933 there was even a decline in absolute figures from 568,000 to about 500,000. For more statistical information, see Karl A. Schleunes, *The Twisted Road to Auschwitz* (Chicago and London, 1970), 37–40; on anti-Semitic violence before 1933, see Dirk Walter, *Antisemitische Kriminalität und Gewalt. Judenfeindschaft in der Weimarer Republik* (Bonn 1999).

a series of laws excluded German Jews from the upper echelons of the civil service (7 April), banned large numbers of Jewish judges, public prosecutors, and attorneys from practicing law (11 April), excluded Jewish doctors from the *Krankenkassen*, the national health insurance organization (22 April), and introduced rigid quotas for Jewish *Gymnasium* and university students (25 April).[2] The latter restriction would make it impossible for many Jewish students to obtain their secondary-school graduation certificate, the *Abitur*, a prerequisite for attending a German university, and thus meant that they would be prevented from entering the professions. Thanks to Hindenburg's intervention, the "Aryan paragraph" in the April laws excluded from the prohibitions those German Jews who had actively participated in the First World War, those whose fathers or sons had been killed in action, and those who had held office already on 1 August 1914. The high number of German Jews who participated in the war reflected the fact that more than 60 percent of Jewish lawyers and 50 percent of judges and prosecutors initially remained in place, though the majority of professionals and high-ranking civil servants were still subject to the humiliating and abusive measures of the April laws.[3] To which political forces could German Jews turn for help in this desperate situation?

Germany's Rechtsstaat, the state based on the rule of law and due process that had been firmly established since the late eighteenth century, had traditionally acted as a counterweight to Germany's weak democratic tradition by providing legal redress to instances of abuse.[4] In the past, German Jews were able to seek restitution for wrongs committed against them by appealing to courts or political parties to act in their interest, using the institutions and processes of the authoritative Rechtsstaat. The two parties that had occasionally intervened on behalf of German Jews during the Weimar Republic,

---

2. On the boycott of 1 April and the April legislation, see Schleunes, *Twisted Road*, 62–115; Friedländer, *Nazi Germany and the Jews*, 17–73; Uwe Dietrich Adam, *Judenpolitik im Dritten Reich* (Düsseldorf, 1972); and Herbst, *Das nationalsozialistische Deutschland*, 73–80.

3. See Herbst, *Das nationalsozialistische Deutschland*, 78. For Hitler's revealing response to Hindenburg's intercession of 4 April regarding the Law on the Restoration of a Professional Civil Service, see *Akten zur Deutschen Auswärtigen Politik, 1918–1945*, Serie C, 1933–1937, vol. I, part 1 (Göttingen, 1971), 253–255.

4. Martin Broszat emphatically stresses this point in *Der Staat Hitlers*, 403.

the DDP and the SPD, were now, however, powerless.[5] The trans-muted DDP had, in any case, changed its name to Staatspartei in 1930, after which it developed anti-Semitic tendencies, and the SPD itself became subject to so much Nazi persecution that all its ener-gies were devoted to its own survival. After January 1933, the only political force in any position to uphold the Rechtsstaat tradition in the face of Nazi transgressions, including the potential power to counter anti-Semitic attacks, seemed to be Hitler's alliance partner, the conservative German National People's Party. As part of Hitler's governing coalition, the DNVP was the sole political force that had the potential to fight for the rights of German Jews in the face of Nazi attacks. Even months after 30 January 1933, prominent Ger-man Jews, such as Georg Bernhard, the former editor of the liberal *Vossische Zeitung*, were convinced that "in the long run German Na-tionals are bound to constitute an obstacle for the implementation of Nazism's racial idiocies."[6] Yet, overall, the party was a most unlikely champion of Jewish interests, given the anti-Semitic background of some of the groups that made up its core constituency. The DNVP was imbued with both a tradition of anti-Semitism and a conserva-tive allegiance to the rule of law. How did the German National-als reconcile the tension between their own latent anti-Semitism and their tradition of supporting the Rechtsstaat? More importantly, what implications did this have for the hundreds of thousands of German Jews under Nazi attack?

A Contradictory Record: Previous Research on the DNVP and Anti-Semitism

Some of the existing literature on the DNVP addresses the nature of the party's anti-Semitism (in contrast to that of the Nazis) and

5. According to Saul Friedländer, who refers to studies by Ernest Ham-burger, Peter Pulzer, and Arnold Paucker, more than 80 percent of Jewish voters supported either the SPD or DDP (Friedländer, *Nazi Germany*, 356, note 87), and representatives of both parties also spoke out against anti-Semitism. After the DDP turned into the Staatspartei, the SPD increasingly attracted Jewish votes. For detailed information on voting patterns in electoral districts in Berlin, Hamburg, and Frankfurt, see Peter Pulzer, *Jews and the German State. The Politi-cal History of a Minority, 1848–1933* (Oxford, 1992), 291–324.

6. Georg Bernhard, *Die deutsche Tragödie. Der Selbstmord einer Republik* (Prague, 1933), 25.

its renunciation of terror. Studies refer to the DNVP's "moderate" anti-Semitism, but offer little systematic analysis of what this means. Monographs that deal with the DNVP in the Weimar Republic either skirt the issue or exclude it altogether because their focus of investigation lies elsewhere.[7] Studies on German anti-Semitism treat the DNVP's role in an equally cursory fashion. We thus know relatively little about the precise attitudes and behavior of German Nationals toward Jews during the Weimar Republic and next to nothing about the DNVP's policies during the Nazi seizure of power between 30 January 1933 and mid July 1933, when Hitler declared the "revolution" ended. This chapter seeks to help fill the void by offering evidence of the DNVP's position toward German Jews and Nazi anti-Semitic measures during this six-month period as a way to analyze more substantively the implications of the party's role.

There is a strong tacit assumption in the literature that the DNVP, by virtue of its position as the Nazis' coalition partner, exerted a moderating, even restraining influence on Hitler and the SA, the organization responsible for most of the anti-Semitic outrages during the winter and spring of 1933. Bernd-Jürgen Wendt, for example, asserts that initially Nazis had "to curtail their own urge for action" out of consideration for, among others, "their conservative-bourgeois coalition partner . . ."[8] In the same vein, Karl Schleunes maintains that as of mid March 1933 Hitler was still putting a brake on anti-Semitic measures since he was reluctant "to defy openly the wishes of the coalition partners."[9] These assessments, as will be shown in this chapter, are based more on conjecture and lack of information than historical reality, since the Nazis' conservative

---

7. Thimme, *Flucht in den Mythos*, refers to anti-Semitism only in passing. Main exceptions are Liebe, *Volkspartei*, 61–74, and Hertzman, *DNVP*, 124–165, who discuss the party's anti-Semitism in some detail, since both deal with the 1922 Görlitz party congress, when the extreme anti-Semites were forced out of the party. Other monographs, where anti-Semitism is occasionally mentioned, include Dörr, "Die Deutschnationale Volkspartei," Gisbert J. Gemein, "Die DNVP in Düsseldorf 1918–1933" (Ph.D. diss., Cologne, 1969); Reinhard Behrens, *Die Deutschnationalen in Hamburg 1918–1933* (Ph.D. diss., Hamburg, 1973); Denis P. Walker, "*Alfred Hugenberg and the DNVP 1918–1930*" (D.Phil., Cambridge, 1976); Holzbach, *Das "System Hugenberg"*; Leopold, *Alfred Hugenberg*; Stupperich, *Volksgemeinschaft oder Arbeitersolidarität*.

8. Bernd-Jürgen Wendt, *Deutschland 1933–1945. Das Dritte Reich* (Hannover, 1995), 166.

9. Schleunes, *Twisted Road*, 76.

coalition partner gave little evidence of any moderating action. The faulty assumption about the DNVP's willingness to restrain Nazi excesses may derive from the nature of the party's anti-Semitic orientation, which was (usually) more temperate and inconsistent than that of the NSDAP.

A general consensus has emerged in surveys of Weimar and Nazi Germany (insofar as the issue is mentioned at all) that the DNVP stood for "a moderate anti-Semitism, though in its treatment of the 'Jewish question' its policies were not uniform."[10] Helmut Berding, while stressing the inconsistencies of the DNVP's ideology, also notes the continued existence of what he refers to as the "Protestant-anti-Semitic element of traditional conservatism."[11] Berding underscores the party's rejection of violence and terror and speculates that ". . . if the DNVP had ever come to power it would have pursued a system of apartheid, though not a policy of extermination."[12] Avraham Barkai's passing references to the DNVP in his detailed history of the *Centralverein* suggest an assessment of the party's brand of anti-Semitism that is close to Berding's in indicating that the DNVP might have preferred separation. The DNVP, he notes, favored the Zionists because they advocated Jewish emigration to Palestine.[13]

10. Herbst, *Das nationalsozialistische Deutschland*, 53.

11. Helmut Berding, *Moderner Antisemitismus in Deutschland* (Frankfurt, 1988), 213. According to Berding, its exponent was Gottfried Traub, a member of the party's executive committee and DNVP Reichstag deputy, who continued the Christian Social tradition of Adolf Stoecker. Wehler reiterates this point in the chapter on Weimar anti-Semitism; see *Deutsche Gesellschaftsgeschichte*, IV, 503.

12. Berding, *Moderner Antisemitismus*, 214. In this context, Berding cites Christoph Dipper, "Der deutsche Widerstand und die Juden," *Geschichte und Gesellschaft* 9 (1983), 349–380, though the assumption originally went back to George Mosse, "Die deutsche Rechte und die Juden," in Werner Mosse, ed., *Entscheidungsjahr 1932. Zur Judenfrage in der Endphase der Weimarer Republik*, 2nd rev. ed. (Tübingen, 1966), 227. Wehler adopts it virtually verbatim: "If one were to speculate, as rulers of the country the German Nationals would certainly have been capable of initiating an anti-Jewish policy of apartheid, though not physical elimination." *Gesellschaftsgeschichte* IV, 503–504.

13. Avraham Barkai, *'Wehr Dich!' Der Centralverein deutscher Staatsbürger jüdischen Glaubens, 1893–1938* (Munich, 2002), 114–115; 406, note 29. Barkai makes a few references to the DNVP in his contribution to Michael Meyer, ed., *German-Jewish History in Modern Times. Renewal and Destruction, 1918–1945*, vol. IV (New York, 1998), where he points out that "a small number of upper class Jews supported the German People's Party (DVP) . . . a yet smaller minority endorsed the right-wing radical views of the anti-Semitic German National People's Party (DNVP) . . . ," 109.

Werner Jochmann and George Mosse provide the most detailed information on German National attitudes toward Jews in their long essays from the 1960s and 1970s.[14] Focusing on the years before 1923, Jochmann maintains that, for reasons of opportunism, the DNVP leadership initially avoided taking a clear stance on the "so-called Jewish question" for fear of alienating the various factions within the party that had been fed by tributaries of former Free Conservatives, German Conservatives, Christian Social, and *völkisch* elements, the latter three of which brought with them a tradition of anti-Semitism.[15] Indeed, the DNVP's anti-Semitic record is contradictory. On the one hand, the party began to exclude Jews from membership while, at the same time, some of its more prominent members protested against anti-Semitic policies. In the run-up to the 1920 elections, for example, Anna von Gierke, DNVP deputy and daughter of the famous legal scholar Otto von Gierke, was not renominated by her local party organization on account of her Jewish ancestry, thus excluding her candidacy.[16] Even the party's expulsion of its most extreme anti-Semitic members after the murder of Walther Rathenau did not seem to amount to a significant reorientation of its overall policy.[17] George Mosse also stresses the increasing inner-party anti-Semitism of the DNVP during the Weimar Republic.[18] Already by 1923, six important DNVP *Ortsgruppen* (local groups) refused membership to Jews. The party leadership was reluctant to overrule the local groups and by 1929, according to the DNVP party manual, Jews were to be denied admission to the party

14. Werner Jochmann, "Die Ausbreitung des Antisemitismus," in Werner Mosse, ed., *Deutsches Judentum in Krieg und Revolution, 1916–1923* (Tübingen, 1971), 409–511, esp. 487–492; Mosse, "Die deutsche Rechte und die Juden," 183–247, esp. 226–238.

15. Jochmann, "Die Ausbreitung des Antisemitismus," 487.

16. Ibid., 489; Pulzer, *Jews and the German State*, 237. Subsequently, she and her father left the party.

17. In Jochmann's estimation in "Die Ausbreitung des Antisemitismus," 492–493. But Jochmann also mentions protests in DNVP party circles against both anti-Semitic transgressions and the "language of swine herds" (*Sauherdenton*) used in the *völkisch* gutter press (491). Donald L. Niewyk, *The Jews in Weimar Germany* (Baton Rouge and London, 1980), 49–51, also refers to conflicting views on anti-Semitism in the DNVP.

18. Mosse, "Die deutsche Rechte und die Juden," 227. Mosse asserted that the "history of the DNVP is one of stimulus and response between the old conservative tradition and the radical völkisch impulse" and pointed to a radicalization of the party during the Weimar Republic.

altogether. As Mosse points out, throughout the election campaigns of the 1920s, local DNVP election posters and pamphlets appealed to anti-Semitic prejudices, especially as a means to attack the DDP.[19] On the other hand, several leading German Nationals decried the anti-Semitic stance of their party. Peter Pulzer argues that the initial DNVP leadership group in the Weimar National Assembly, including Graf Arthur von Posadowsky-Wehner, Clemens von Delbrück, and Adalbert von Dühringer, all former high-ranking civil servants, were "averse to all demagogy and found anti-Semitism distasteful."[20] Some other prominent German Nationals, such as Friedrich von Oppeln-Bronikowski, a frequent contributor to *Der Nationaldeutsche Jude*, the press organ of the Association of National German Jews, and, as Mosse emphasizes, Alfred Hugenberg, party leader since 1928, who never made an anti-Semitic remark in any of his speeches, showed few signs of anti-Semitism.[21] On the other hand, Hugenberg's *Staatssekretär* in the Ministry of Economics after 30 January 1933, Paul Bang, was a rabid anti-Semite and author of lurid anti-Semitic tracts.[22]

To sum up, the available secondary literature on the German Nationals and anti-Semitism highlights two main differences between their anti-Semitism and that of the Nazi Party: (I) Ideologically, DNVP anti-Semitism never acquired the all-encompassing preeminence it had for the NSDAP. In Saul Friedländer's terminology,

19. Mosse, "Die deutsche Rechte und die Juden," 229. Pulzer, in *Jews and the German State*, 237, also stresses that anti-Semitic themes were explicit in German National attacks on the DDP in charges that the party "was led by Jews and dependent on Marxism." The DNVP was also strongly opposed to the emigration of Eastern Jews to Germany, a feeling shared by the Association of National German Jews, an organization that had some common political ground with the DNVP. See Carl J. Rheins, "The Verband Nationaldeutscher Juden, 1921–1933," *Leo Baeck Institute Yearbook*, 25 (1980), 243–268; Niewyk, *The Jews in Weimar Germany*, 165–178.

20. Pulzer, *Jews and the German State*, 216.

21. Carl J. Rheins, "The Verband Nationaldeutscher Juden, 1921–1933," 265–266; Mosse, "Die deutsche Rechte und die Juden," 231–232. Mosse characterizes Hugenberg's viewpoint as "pragmatic," and mentions that he "held his protective hand" over some men with Jewish ancestry, such as Reinhold Quaatz and *Stahlhelm* leader Theodor Duesterberg.

22. Under the alias of Wilhelm Meister, Bang published an obscene anti-Semitic tract, *Judas Schuldbuch. Eine Deutsche Abrechnung* (Munich 1919). See Saul Friedländer, "Die politischen Veränderungen der Kriegszeit und ihre Auswirkungen auf die Judenfrage," in Werner Mosse, ed., *Deutsches Judentum in Krieg und Revolution*, 65.

the DNVP's anti-Semitism was thus not "redemptive,"[23] but rather an extension, albeit a radicalized one, of traditional conservative anti-Semitism. (II) The DNVP remained opposed to any form of public terror in its abstract commitment to the Rechtsstaat. As late as March 1933, the party proclaimed that it opposed "in principle terrorizing any segment of the population."[24] What the existing literature fails to tell us is that in the course of the winter and spring 1933, it quickly became clear that this opposition was purely theoretical and did not compel the party leadership to oppose actively anti-Semitic acts of terror. This reluctance to intervene, combined with the fact that differences between the German National and Nazi brands of anti-Semitism had little impact on actual policies, helped seal the fate of German Jews.

This chapter investigates the plight of German Jews during the Nazi seizure of power in 1933 and, in particular, how the leadership and members of the DNVP reacted to Nazi transgressions and violence. The first section sets out the problem: the plethora of violent attacks on Jewish-owned businesses and individual Jews following the 5 March 1933 elections and the reaction of the German authorities. The second section traces the relationship between German conservatives and Jews, in particular the conservatives' predicament as upholders of law and order on the one hand, and their anti-Semitic leanings on the other. The third section highlights the DNVP's reaction to the dilemma of national-minded German Jews, a large number of whom fought for Germany in the First World War. Despite the overall faithfulness of these men to the conservative ideal of how national-minded Germans should behave in an hour of national crisis, conservative protest against anti-Semitic measures, empathy, or help were rarely forthcoming. The fourth section examines the few cases of conservative protest and attempted help, and the fifth section highlights the more numerous cases of rejection and disapprobation. The sixth section discloses the often contradictory reactions of local DNVP associations and the head office in Berlin when baptized Jews or half-Jews applied for party membership. The conclusion reviews the spectrum of inconsistent, conflicting, and at times outright contradictory reactions that the DNVP displayed toward German Jews during the Nazi

---

23. Friedländer, *Nazi Germany and the Jews*, 73–113, esp. 86–90.
24. Mosse, "Die deutsche Rechte und die Juden," 227. The evasive German formulation used was *"irgendwelcher Volkskreise."*

seizure of power. History in the making is rarely consistent, logical, or likely to fit into preconceived patterns. This investigation reveals the full range of conservative reactions to the inherent plight of German Jews in the winter and spring of 1933. As will be shown below, the DNVP completely failed to live up to its professed ideals, thereby undermining the very principles to which its members so tenaciously clung and setting the stage for the further erosion of the rights of German Jews.

Anti–Semitic Violence

An enormous wave of violence, emanating from SA troopers (many wearing armbands of the auxiliary police) and ordinary members of the Nazi Party who wanted to settle old scores, engulfed Germany in the days and weeks after the elections of 5 March 1933.[25] The number of anti–Semitic attacks multiplied. These attacks were not orchestrated from above, officially sanctioned, or elaborately planned. They emerged from a kind of "grassroots" violence surging from the local level, mostly from local SA units and other discontented elements of Nazi organizations. Reich Chancellery records of March 1933 are full of reports from Berlin's foreign delegations that complain of violent, often brutal, attacks perpetrated against their citizens.[26] Among these are reports from the Polish, French, Yugoslavian, Swiss, American, and Soviet embassies about acts of provocation and violence, directed mostly against Jewish citizens of these countries.[27] On the whole, these reports concerned Jews from abroad who had either lived in Germany for some time because they were married to Germans, or who found themselves in the country temporarily on short business trips. The attacks included events like raids on Jewish restaurants (in Magdeburg one Swiss and six Italian

25. See also chapters 3 and 6. On SA violence in general, see Richard Bessel, *Political Violence and the Rise of Nazism. The Storm Troopers in Eastern Germany, 1925–1934* (New Haven and London, 1984); Eric Reiche, *The Development of the SA in Nürnberg, 1922–1934* (Cambridge, 1986); Peter Longerich, *Die braunen Bataillone. Geschichte der SA* (Munich, 1989).

26. BA Berlin-Lichterfelde, "Akten der Reichskanzlei, NSDAP," R 43 II, no. 1195; see especially 29–53; 67–97; 91–112; 113–120; 150–161; 164–204.

27. BA Berlin-Lichterfelde, ibid., 150–161. A possible exception were the complaints from the Soviet embassy. Here, it was mostly hatred of communism and not only anti–Semitism that lay at the root of the attacks on Soviet citizens.

citizens were injured during an incursion), the smashing of shop windows of businesses owned by Polish Jews, and assaults on cafes, whose proprietors were ordered to shut down operations under the threat of repeat attacks.[28] In 1933 there were an estimated 150,000 Eastern Jews in Germany, many of whom had been in the country for decades without having been given German citizenship.[29] The methods used in the attacks differed from those of ordinary organized crime only insofar as they were carried out mostly in broad daylight. Destruction, extortion, and gang-related violence often took place in full public view. Yet this increased exposure had little impact, given the pervasive atmosphere of fear and intimidation that had set in immediately after the Reichstag Fire Decree. Newspapers, for example, failed to report most of the incidents. Conservative newspapers (those least in danger of being banned) were so cowed that they reported attacks on their own members (which became more frequent as the spring wore on) only in abridged form. Attacks were so "public" that passersby and neighbors, equally intimidated, often consciously averted their eyes in order not to become unwitting eyewitnesses.

A second category of attacks was directed against foreign Jews who had lived for a long time in the Reich, were well known in their neighborhoods, and now became victims of personal acts of revenge.[30] Germans who were involved with foreign Jews in lawsuits

28. BA Berlin-Lichterfelde, "Akten der Reichskanzlei, NSDAP," R 43 II, no. 1195, 67–73; 76–77. Swiss citizen Willy Guggenheim was on a business trip in Magdeburg, where he was attacked in a Jewish restaurant (on 8 March); two Dutch Jews were ordered to close their fur shop in Charlottenburg. The police declared that they could do nothing and were unable to spare any police officers for protection (ibid., 74–75;113–120).

29. Schleunes, *Twisted Road*, 110–111. As Schleunes pointed out, the difficulties of becoming a naturalized German were immense, since each state government had the right to veto any application for citizenship, so that most Jewish refugees from eastern Europe, even if they had raised families in Germany, retained the citizenship of the country from which they had fled. This did not change significantly during the Weimar Republic. Thus, thousands of Jews whose grandparents had settled in Germany remained citizens of foreign states. See also Jack Wertheimer, " 'The Unwanted Element'—East European Jews in Imperial Germany," *LBIYB* 26 (1981), 23–46.

30. For example, a Czechoslovakian Jewish couple, the Leistners, were attacked by an SS-Commando in the street on 11 March in Berlin-Mariendorf. The husband was dragged off to an SA facility. Even though the incident was reported, the police did nothing. It was suspected that the assault originated with a neighbor of the Leistners who had lost a court case with the husband

or who owed them money now used the triumph of National Socialism to take revenge on their adversaries or force cancellation of debts.[31] Victims were usually attacked by gangs of SA men, often brutally battered (to the extent that some required a long hospital stay) or robbed in their homes. Entry was forced under the pretext that "the police" were at the door[32]—and which law-abiding citizen would dare refuse to comply in these circumstances? Cash and jewelry invariably went missing. In the rare case that the police were called in and actually showed up, they took no subsequent action. On one occasion, five uniformed men forced their way into the apartment of a Polish rabbi in Dresden and beat him up with rubber truncheons. According to the Polish Embassy report, policemen summoned to the scene explained that: "It is not the obligation of the police to protect Jews."[33] In another attack in Dresden that involved a direct threat (armed, uniformed men had previously, on several occasions, attempted to assault the proprietor of a draper's shop), the police justified their inaction by stating that they were "not in a position to provide any help."[34] At the scene of another attack on a hotel in Magdeburg on 8 March, the police (according to another report of the Polish Embassy) refused ". . . to record the

---

and threatened revenge. BA Berlin-Lichterfelde, "Akten der Reichskanzlei, NSDAP," R 43 II, no. 1195, 109.

31. BA Berlin-Lichterfelde, "Akten der Reichskanzlei, NSDAP," R 43 II, no. 1195, 170. Often criminal extortion was used, as in the case of the American Julian Fuchs (ibid., 96–98; 106–107).

32. See, for example, BA Berlin-Lichterfelde, "Akten der Reichskanzlei, NSDAP," R 43 II, no. 1195, 99–101. On 10 March 1933, uniformed men forced their way into the apartment of the Klauber family in Munich. When the family asked the reason for this action (Frau Jean Klauber was an American citizen) they were told: "Jews! We hate you! We have waited for this for fourteen years and tonight we are going to string up the lot of you." (100). In the records, one frequently encounters sentences such as: "The riot squad, notified by phone, failed to appear" (e.g., ibid., 108). For numerous other cases of robbery, see ibid., 113–120.

33. BA Lichterfelde, "Akten der Reichskanzlei, NSDAP," ibid., 201. In this report from the Polish legation (199–204), incidents from throughout the Reich are listed. In Hamborn, for example, an unknown assailant overturned a basket with five hundred eggs belonging to a Polish grocer and swore at him in the "middle of the marketplace," that is, in a very public spot (203). In those cases where victims themselves went to the police to report attacks, they soon had to realize that no action would be taken.

34. Ibid., 202.

incident and take down the statements of Polish citizens."[35] It was thus certain that no assistance could be expected from the police, reports of which fact had doubtless spread far and wide to victims and potential victims alike.

The attacks—criminal provocations that sprang chiefly from personal hatred, vindictiveness, or the search for enrichment—were not welcomed, for the most part, by the NSDAP-DNVP government. This became clear with the number of Hitler's appeals to put an end to the "independent actions."[36] Formal complaints providing details of what had actually occurred were sent from the embassies mostly to the Foreign Office. From there, the concerned Foreign Minister Konstantin von Neurath (who had good reason to fear the potential damage of these attacks on the reputation of the Reich) circulated the complaints to Reich Interior Minister Wilhelm Frick, Prussian Minister of the Interior Hermann Göring, and Heinrich Lammers, Hitler's *Staatssekretär* in the Reich Chancellery. In this way, von Neurath wanted to ensure that as many Ministries as possible, and especially the Reich Chancellor himself, would endeavor to put an immediate end to the transgressions.[37] Hitler relentlessly admonished

35. 18 March 1933 at ibid., 173. This report (165–174) covers incidents from throughout the Reich. The first wave of attacks coincided with the Nazi takeover of those German states in which the Nazis were not already in government (5–11 March 1933). In 1900, 7 percent of the Jews in Germany came from eastern Europe; by 1933, the percentage of *Ostjuden* had risen to almost 20. They were concentrated mostly in the larger cities of central and eastern Germany: in 1925, eastern Jews represented 25.4 percent of Berlin's Jewish population, 60 percent of Dresden's, and more than 80 percent of Leipzig's. See Friedländer, *Nazi Germany and the Jews*, 353; and, for further details, Esra Bennathan, "Die demographische und wirtschaftliche Struktur der Juden," in Werner Mosse, ed., *Entscheidungsjahr 1932*, 87–135.

36. BA Berlin-Lichterfelde, "Akten der Reichskanzlei, NSDAP," R 43 II, no. 1195, 61. See also the *Berliner Lokalanzeiger*, 11 March 1933: "Hitler gegen Einzelaktionen" (ibid., 63). In Cabinet meetings, Hitler maintained that the attacks had been committed mainly by communists in SA uniforms (ibid., 84).

37. BA Berlin-Lichterfelde, "Akten der Reichskanzlei, NSDAP," R 43 II, no. 1195, 67, 33, 29–32, 91–94. Reich Interior Minister Frick thereupon dispatched "express letters" to other Reich Ministers, in which he urged the recipients "in the interest of public security and order . . . to counter these attacks most vigorously and to take the necessary steps to do so" (ibid., 82). Already on 3 March, Neurath had made a point of stressing to Lammers that the use of the auxiliary police for the protection of foreign missions and embassies was to be avoided (ibid., 33). When violent transgressions did not abate by the second half of March, Neurath expanded the list of recipients of his express letters to include the police superintendents of the Berlin districts.

his SA and SS to stop the attacks and catch the guilty parties, "no matter whom they may be," to call them to account, and "deliver them without delay to the police." In this he seemed to be entirely sincere, since widespread random violence could serve only to undermine his government.[38] Frick, von Neurath, and Lammers also made repeated efforts to tackle the problem. Despite all this, no one succeeded in flushing out the perpetrators of the attacks. The wall of silence remained firmly in place. On 3 May, almost two months after the onset of the attacks, *Staatssekretär* Lammers sent another circular, reproachful in tone, to the Cabinet ministers.[39] In spite of the Reich Chancellor's desire to resolve the problem of the attacks, he had "up to now received no report whatsoever about handling, answering, or clearing up the facts of the matter."

The SA, SS, and auxiliary police formations that were implicated in the criminal acts clearly knew how to obfuscate factual findings and thus avert punishment for the attacks. This would hardly have been possible without the collusion of senior SA leaders. Hitler's admonitions, the efforts of the bureaucracy, and even those of the Nazi Interior Minister to shed light on the incidents had been futile. Here it should be taken into consideration that attacks on foreigners, including Jews, non-Jews, and even diplomats, inevitably caused harm to the foreign policy interests of the Reich.[40] The (carefully edited) published selection of Reich Chancellery records likewise contains a large number of documents pertaining to violent attacks on foreign diplomats, members of German National associations, the DNVP, trade unions, economic associations, and members of

38. Schleunes (among others) pointed out that if party radicals and the SA seemed to be getting the upper hand, Hitler's own position might be jeopardized. While Hitler welcomed terror in general since it reduced the capacity of his communist and socialist opponents to organize, it had to be clear that he was firmly in control. If his grasp on government appeared to be tenuous, excessive terror by the SA could only be harmful to his own standing. Schleunes, *Twisted Road*, 68–69.

39. 3 May 1933 at BA Berlin-Lichterfelde, "Akten der Reichskanzlei, NSDAP," R 43 II, no. 1195, 177.

40. With respect to the damage, see the explanations of the *Staatssekretär* in the Foreign Ministry, Bernhard von Bülow, concerning the deterioration of German–Soviet relations, which had been caused principally by countless Nazi attacks. Von Bülow left no doubt that he considered Soviet complaints legitimate. See Minuth, ed., *Akten der Reichskanzlei*, 836–838.

other bourgeois parties.[41] From the perspective of the perpetrators, attacks on German Jews probably carried an even smaller risk than those on foreign Jews and were even less likely to be prosecuted by the authorities. Furthermore, potential attackers could not help but notice that the press, for the most part, deliberately turned a blind eye to the attacks. The German National Party press, which could air its views with relative freedom, as it was least affected by bans and suppressions, contained few denunciations of the numerous anti-Semitic acts of violence. This did not necessarily signal sympathy with the perpetrator but was more likely due to self-interested indifference, preoccupation with the party's own affairs, or simply the fear that extensive reports of criminal provocations might fall in the category of *Greuelpropaganda* (basically unfounded inflammatory propaganda) and thus be interpreted as fouling one's own nest.

German Jews were thus caught in an inescapable predicament. They could appeal to the police, but no help would be forthcoming. Even a visceral physical reaction—self-defense provoked by threat to life and limb—already not very promising in light of the superior numerical strength of the attackers, was out of the question. Most German Jews were fully assimilated German citizens (in the Empire, they were already strongly represented in the middle and upper middle classes as well as forming a small wealthy elite),[42] and,

41. Minuth, ed., *Akten der Reichskanzlei*, 191–193; 195–197; 207–208; 260–261; 395–398; 563–564; 593–595.

42. Thomas Nipperdey, *Deutsche Geschichte 1866–1918, Arbeitswelt und Bürgergeist* (Munich, 1990), 396–414; esp. 399. In 1910, twenty-nine Jews were among the one hundred wealthiest men in Prussia. Many were considered pillars of the community who made generous public endowments, such as spas, libraries, and hospitals. In 1905, for example, the Jewish population of Berlin, which amounted to 5.1 percent, carried 30.7 percent of the tax burden; in Mannheim the Jewish population of 3.2 percent paid 28.7 percent of the taxes; and in the small Baden city of Bruchsal the Jewish population of 1.1 percent paid 17.6 percent of the taxes (Nipperdey, *Deutsche Geschichte*, 399). According to Peter Pulzer, the average amount of tax paid by Jews was seven times as high as that paid by Catholic Germans and three and a half times as high as that paid by Protestants. An important population shift during the Empire was from the countryside to the city and the east-west migration of German Jews. In 1933, over 70 percent of German Jews lived in large cities; about 160,000 lived in Berlin, 26,000 in Frankfurt, 20,000 in Breslau, almost 17,000 in Hamburg, 15,000 in Cologne, 11,500 in Leipzig, and more than 7,000 in Nuremberg. See Thamer, *Verführung und Gewalt*, 258; Schleunes, *Twisted Road*, 39; Peter Pulzer, "Die jüdische Beteiligung an der Politik" in Werner Mosse, ed., *Juden im Wilhelminischen Deutschland 1890–1914*, 2nd ed. (Tübingen 1998), 143–241, esp. 189.

like other Germans, they were accustomed to paying heed to the state authorities and submitting to their directives. If terror was exercised in the name of the state (by way of SA members in auxiliary police uniforms)—even if it proved life-threatening—Germans, Jews and non-Jews alike, found themselves caught in a hopeless psychological dilemma, since there was no effective defense against an abuse of state power. No one had reckoned with the possibility that, practically overnight, the police or those acting in their name would be transformed from a shield of protection to an instrument of terror.[43]

In their distress, many unprotected and abandoned German Jews, left to the mercy of the attackers, turned to the one authority that appeared to retain at least a semblance of influence in the face of the all-pervasive domination of the National Socialists—the DNVP. This was a problematic choice, since the party itself had a past tinged with anti-Semitism.

Conservatives and Anti-Semitism

During the German Empire, the German Conservative Party (many of whose supporters later joined the DNVP) had entertained close ties to the Christian Social Party of the anti-Semitic Court Chaplain Adolf Stoecker in hopes of gaining new classes of voters and creating a mass base in the urban lower middle classes.[44] At the height of the Christian Social Party's success in the early 1890s, anti-Semitism even found its way into the new Conservative Party program, the so-called "Tivoli Program" of 1892. Against the opposition of influential conservative circles, the Tivoli Program railed

---

43. Even during the Kaiserreich, the conservative Prussian state apparatus constituted a protective barrier against "rabble-rousing anti-Semitism" (*Radau-antisemitismus*). See Gerhard Hoffmann, Werner Bergmann, and Helmut Walser Smith, eds., *Exclusionary Violence* (Ann Arbor, 2002); Berding, *Moderner Anti-semitismus in Deutschland*.

44. This strategy was not new. In the 1860s, Hermann Wagener had attempted a similar strategy with his "Prussian *Volksverein*" with some success. In the struggle against freedom of trade (*Gewerbefreiheit*), Wagener attempted to win over the urban lower middle classes to the conservative cause. See also Werner Jochmann, "Strukturen und Funktion des deutschen. Antisemitismus," in Mosse, ed., *Juden im Wilhelminischen Deutschland*, 389–479; Peter Pulzer, *The Rise of Political Anti-Semitism in Germany and Austria*, rev. edition (Cambridge, Mass., 1988).

against the ". . . aggressively pushy, demoralizing and subversive Jewish influence on the life of our people."[45] In 1875, the Conservative Party's main press organ, the *Kreuzzeitung*, aimed at settling scores with Bismarck's liberal policies of the 1870s in the so-called *"Ära Artikel,"* and denounced the policies of the Reich as *Judenpolitik* and the "liberalism of Jewish-led bankers."[46] After Stoecker's forced resignation from the German Conservative Party in 1896 and the decline of the Christian Social Party, the Agrarian League assumed the twin tasks of developing a mass base and mobilizing voters for the Conservative Party. Anti-Semitic rhetoric and ideology played a significant role in this endeavor.[47] On the other hand, it was clear that Conservative Party dignitaries were opposed to any kind of rabble-rousing anti-Semitism, the populist-revolutionary elements of which threatened their own position. Stoecker's following had, in any case, been far too "leftist" for conservative East Elbian landowners, especially since they feared that the social policy efforts of

45. Felix Salomon, *Die neuen Parteiprogramme mit den letzten der alten Parteien zusammengestellt*, 2nd ed. (Leipzig & Berlin, 1919), 23; Beck, "The Changing Concerns of Prussian Conservatism, 1830–1914," 86–106. The "Tivoli Program" superseded the 1876 program and remained in force until 1918. Despite anti-Semitic program points, German Jews voted occasionally for Conservative Party candidates in runoff elections, especially in the German-Polish province of Posen, where the Jewish community generally supported the German side in nationality questions. In a runoff election in 1908, for example, the larger part of the Jewish population of Posen supported the Conservative Party candidate Kuno Graf von Westarp (who had assured the Jewish community that the Conservative Party would acknowledge their full equality) against a candidate of the Catholic Center party, supported largely by the Polish population. With the help of the Jewish vote, Westarp carried the election. See Peter Pulzer, "Die jüdische Beteiligung an der Politik."

46. See Thomas Nipperdey, "Antisemitismus: Entstehung, Funktion und Geschichte eines Begriffs," in Nipperdey, *Gesellschaft, Kultur, Theorie* (Göttingen 1976), 113–133, esp. 119. The *"Ära Artikel"* referred to the "era of Bleichröder-Delbrück-Camphausen," blaming economic crisis, materialism, and the decline of moral and ethical standards on Bismarck's alliance with liberal Jews. See Fritz Stern, *Gold and Iron: Bismarck, Bleichröder, and the Building of the German Empire* (New York, 1977).

47. James Retallack, *Notables of the Right. The Conservative Party and Political Mobilization in Germany, 1876–1918* (London and Boston, 1988); Geoff Eley, *Reshaping the German Right: Radical Nationalism and Political Change after Bismarck*, 2nd ed. (Ann Arbor, 1992); Puhle, *Agrarische Interessenpolitik*; Thomas Nipperdey, *Machtstaat vor Demokratie. Deutsche Geschichte 1866–1945*, II (Munich, 1992) 536–541; Wehler, *Deutsche Gesellschaftsgeschichte III*, 835–838; 1060–1063; Hans-Peter Ullmann, *Interessenverbände in Deutschland* (Frankfurt, 1988), 85–94.

the Christian Social party might come to include their own agricultural laborers, an undertaking that could prove quite costly.[48] Radical anti-Semites, such as the "Hessian peasant king" Otto Böckel or Hermann Ahlwardt, conducted their election campaigns with slogans such as "Against Junkers and Jews."[49] This "radical populist-democratic anti-Semitism," as Nipperdey calls it, with its social revolutionary, egalitarian, and anti-elitist elements and invectives against "Junkers, parsons, and Jews," was deeply suspect to Conservatives. As staunch supporters of law and order, they abhorred the lawless, plebian, revolutionary elements of radical anti-Semitism, which they considered distasteful and potentially dangerous. The Conservative Party sanctioned anti-Semitism as a tool of electoral campaigning but opposed it as an instrument of dangerous social agitation.[50] In short: if the Conservative Party opposed anti-Semitism, it was because it had the potential to disrupt social order, upset the status quo of social organization, and encourage populist feelings to overtake the rational functioning of social and political institutions. There is no evidence of any concern by the Conservative Party that anti-Semitism was wrong in itself—its opposition to anti-Semitism was instrumental and not based on moral considerations.

From its inception, the DNVP, heir to the conservative parties of the Empire and various anti-Semitic splinter groups, was equally tainted with the brush of anti-Semitism. Initially, conciliatory tones prevailed in the DNVP's "Appeal to Reason" of 27 December 1918: "We demand respect and consideration for every kind of religious feeling, institution, and community."[51] By 1920, when the DNVP published its *Grundsätze* (principles), this had changed radically. Now there is talk of the struggle ". . . against any subversive, un-German spirit, whether it emanates from Jewish or other circles. We emphatically oppose the increasingly disastrous predominance of Judaism in government and public life, which has come to the

---

48. Nipperdey, *Machtstaat vor Demokratie*, 336–337.

49. Nipperdey, "Antisemitismus," 430, note 81. On Böckel (1859–1923) and Ahlwardt (1846–1914), see Pulzer, *The Rise of Political Anti-Semitism*.

50. Nipperdey, *Machtstaat vor Demokratie*, 289–311; esp. 306–307. "By raising a tamed anti-Semitism and nursing it, Conservatives also prepared the ground for radical anti-Semitism." Ibid., 307; and Berding, *Moderner Antisemitismus*, 107.

51. Wilhelm Mommsen und Günther Franz, eds., *Die deutschen Parteiprogramme 1918–1930* (Leipzig and Berlin, 1931), 20; this was also designed to include Catholics.

fore since the revolution."[52] Even though the extreme anti-Semitic wing was pushed out of the DNVP at its Görlitz party Congress in October 1922, the party's anti-Semitism remained in place during the life of the Republic.[53] At the same time, it was continually influenced by countervailing traditions. Many conservatives were rooted in the *Altpreußentum*, old Prussian values, such as the "suum cuique" of Frederick II (his religious policies that were relatively free of prejudice),[54] and the salons of Henriette Hertz and Rahel von Varnhagen that were centers and meeting points of Berlin society.[55] The most important thread of traditional continuity in conservative mentality was the "law and order" principle that occupied pride of place. During the Empire, the Prussian state apparatus, pervaded by conservative values and policy guidelines (and itself not free from anti-Semitic prejudices) had on several occasions taken action to suppress anti-Semitic violence and used the police and military to maintain law and order.[56] With the Nazi takeover on 30 January, these traditions (at least in the public image put forth by the DNVP) were automatically given great weight. As guardians and representatives of the State, as its standard-bearers in the upper echelons of the bureaucracy and in parts of the propertied bourgeoisie and, by extension, as representatives of the upper classes *per se*, the conservatives

52. Mommsen, *Parteiprogramme*, 86. Also published in Max Weiß, ed., *Der nationale Wille. Werden und Wirken der Deutschnationalen Volkspartei 1918–1928* (Essen, 1928), 395; and Mosse, "Die deutsche Rechte und die Juden"; Daniel R. Borg, *The Old-Prussian Church and the Weimar Republic. A Study in Political Adjustment, 1917–1921* (Hanover and London, 1984), 195–202.

53. The DNVP never officially sanctioned the *völkisch* anti-Semitism of radical Weimar splinter parties, even though German Jews were virtually excluded from membership after 1924. The campaign for the May 1924 elections was dominated by anti-Semitic slogans, even if renunciation of terror and violence had been officially condemned since the murder of Walter Rathenau in 1922.

54. See *Das Politische Testament Friedrichs des Großen von 1752* (Stuttgart, 1971).

55. Deborah Hertz, *Jewish High Society in Old Regime Berlin* (New Haven, 1988).

56. In Hinterpommern in 1881 (Wehler, *Gesellschaftsgeschichte*, III, 930) and, the most notorious case, in Konitz in West Prussia. See Christoph Nonn, *Eine Stadt sucht einen Mörder. Gericht, Gewalt und Antisemitismus im Kaiserreich* (Göttingen, 2002); Helmut Walser Smith, *Die Geschichte des Schlachters. Mord und Antisemitismus in einer deutschen Kleinstadt* (Göttingen, 2002). On the prejudice of the Prussian administration, see Werner Angress, "Prussia's Army and the Jewish Reserve Officer Controversy before World War I," in James Sheehan, ed., *Imperial Germany* (New York and London, 1976), 93–129.

were under an implicit obligation to oppose actively the violent attacks of SA hordes and anti-Semitic boycotts. Since conservatives considered themselves keepers and trustees of the State, they owed it to their identity and self-image to maintain at least a semblance of legality and the rule of law. One could hardly take pride in a state in which SA thugs controlled the streets, in which random violence reigned, and where vested rights were trampled over with abandon. Would it be worth representing a state or being involved in its administration and government in which such behavior was the norm? The *raison d'être* and sheer self-preservation of conservatives thus forced the obligation upon them to oppose openly anti-Semitic violence and take a public stance against it. If they failed in this, they would forfeit their self-proclaimed role as guardians of the state, especially since the vast majority of German Jews were, above all, Germans, whose families had lived in Germany for generations and who trusted in the restraining influence of the conservative State apparatus to protect them from Nazi violence.[57] The conduct of the German National People's Party in power, as *Regierungspartei*, toward anti-Semitic transgressions and those who sought protection from Nazi violence was, therefore, an important litmus test of the identity of the whole party, leaders and members alike.

The conservatives' dilemma during their uneasy alliance with the Nazis first became manifest in their relationship with national-minded German Jews, many of whom had risked their lives for Germany in the First World War,[58] and found themselves facing an externally-imposed identity crisis after 30 January 1933. In August 1914, the overwhelming majority of German Jews had demonstrated how much they considered themselves part of the German nation. Among a majority of German Jews, "... enthusiastic expressions of loyalty and of obligation to fulfill one's duty as a German" were

---

57. Regarding the assimilation of German Jews, Peter Gay commented on Wilhelminean Germany: "Das Deutsche der jüdischen Kultur jener Jahrzehnte ist nicht als Versuch der Verstellung zu verstehen. Es handelte sich nicht um Selbstverleugnung, sondern um das Gefühl, an einer Kultur Anteil zu haben, die aufrechte Kosmopoliten wie Schiller und Kant oder Zierden des modernen Humanismus wie Goethe hervorgebracht hatte," and "Wenn Deutschlands Juden in diesen Jahrzehnten . . . sich persönlichen Beleidigungen ausgesetzt sahen, so erlebten sie dies alles folglich als Deutsche." See Peter Gay, "Begegnung mit der Moderne—Deutsche Juden in der deutschen Kultur," in Mosse, ed., *Juden im Wilheminischen Deutschland*, 241–313, esp. 243.

58. Moshe Zimmermann, *Die Deutschen Juden 1914–1945* (Munich, 1997), 2; Barkai, *Wehr Dich*, 55–100.

the rule, whereby it was significant that the different political and religious groups of German Jews focused on the Russian Empire as their "natural" enemy.[59] Of the 615,000 German Jews in 1910, over 10,000 volunteered, over 100,000 served in the army and of these, 12,000 were killed in action.[60] These numbers correspond to the relative percentage of the non-Jewish German population[61] serving in the army and killed in action. This is surprising given the fact that German Jews were excluded from the officer corps and (after 1885) were even prevented from becoming reserve officers.[62] Thus, by dint of prejudice and custom, German Jews were excluded from participating in the military establishment and often were forced to serve in positions not commensurate with the level of their training or skill. All the more emphasis, then, must be placed on their patriotic contribution. In the first months of the war, the patriotic spirit of German Jews, their willingness to sacrifice themselves, and the atmosphere of *Burgfrieden* had the desired effect: discriminatory

59. Zimmermann, *Die Deutschen Juden 1914–1945*, 2–3. The initially dominant image of *Burgfrieden* and social harmony—the SPD Reichstag deputy Ludwig Franck, who volunteered for war service and was killed in September 1914, is the best-known example—did not last long. At the very latest, it ended with the 1916 *Judenzählung* by the army that had been ordered by the military authorities. See Jochmann, "Die Ausbreitung des Antisemitismus," 409–510. In 1914, Jewish organizations, such as the *Centralverein* and the *Verband deutscher Juden*, had called upon their members in a joint statement to dedicate all their energy to the fatherland, "over and above regular duty." Even the *Zionistische Vereinigung für Deutschland* expressed the hope that Zionist youth "will with fiery hearts rush to the colors." Berding, *Moderner Antisemitismus*, 165–178; Egmont Zechlin, *Die deutsche Politik und die Juden im Ersten Weltkrieg* (Göttingen, 1969); Friedländer, "Die politischen Veränderungen der Kriegszeit," 27–65.

60. Berding, *Antisemitismus*, 166; Zimmermann, *Die deutschen Juden*, 2; Friedländer, "Die politischen Veränderungen der Kriegszeit," 27–67, esp. 38.

61. Nipperdey, *Arbeitswelt und Bürgergeist*, 412. According to Nipperdey 17.3 percent of German Jews had served in the war (as opposed to 18.7 percent of non-Jews); of those 77 percent were at the front (78 percent); 11–12 percent of those were killed (13–14 percent). The slight deviations are explained by the different age structure of German Jews, urbanization, and the exclusion of Jews from the officer corps.

62. Except for minor exceptions in Bavaria. See Nipperdey, *Arbeitswelt und Bürgergeist*, 401. Of twenty-five thousand one-year volunteers (the *"Einjährig Freiwillige"*) of Jewish origin, who joined the army as potential officer cadets between 1885 and 1914, only twenty-one were able to advance to the rank of lieutenant in the reserves; Wehler, *Gesellschaftsgeschichte*, III, 1065–66.

measures were eased and Jews were promoted to officer ranks.[63] Even dyed-in-the-wool anti-Semites, such as Houston Stewart Chamberlain, had words of praise for the war contribution of German Jews: ". . . they perform their duty as Germans against the enemy in the field of battle or at home."[64] According to a report of the Association for the Defense against anti-Semitism of November 1915, five thousand Jewish German soldiers had already been awarded the Iron Cross and 650 others had been accorded comparable decorations.[65]

Nationale Juden

National-minded German Jews, especially those who had actively fought on the German side, found themselves in a difficult position once the Nazis were in power. Less than fifteen years before, they had fought and died for Germany. Now they were unwanted and ostracized, labeled parasites, enemies of the German people, and a danger to the very country they had served all their lives and whose values and guiding principles had become their own. An open letter published at the end of March 1933 in the *Deutsche Allgemeine Zeitung* under the headline "Professions of a Jewish Frontline Soldier" characterized the inherent plight in which they found themselves in 1933:[66] "For almost four-and-a-half years, I was a soldier at the front, I was fighting in Flanders and France . . . and lost my only brother on the Western Front. When today I hear and read that

---

63. Thirty thousand received decorations for bravery; two thousand became officers (Berding, *Antisemitismus*, 166).

64. Houston S. Chamberlain, *Kriegsaufsätze* (Munich, 1915), 46; also Jochmann, "Die Ausbreitung des Antisemitismus," 409–511, esp. 411. "Germany has ten times as many Jews [as England] and where are they now? As if wiped away from the tremendous cataclysm; no longer recognizable as Jews, for they perform their duty as Germans before the enemy or at home."

65. Jochmann, "Ausbreitung des Antisemitismus," 421; Friedländer, "Veränderungen," 38.

66. BA Berlin-Lichterfelde, "DNVP, Politischer Schriftwechsel," R 8005, no. 19, 56. The letter was dated 21 March 1933. The *Deutsche Allgemeine Zeitung* (*DAZ*) was one of the Reich's most important daily newspapers. Due to its extensive foreign reporting, this national conservative newspaper was cofinanced by the German Foreign Office. Internationally, it was one of Germany's most widely read newspapers. From the summer of 1932, the *DAZ* advocated Hitler's participation in government. See Norbert Frei and Johannes Schmitz, *Journalismus im Dritten Reich*, 3rd ed. (Munich, 1999), 59–63.

Jews as a whole are being condemned as un–German, I consider that the most bitter of injustices. Then I get out my military papers and go over the large number of campaigns and battles in which I have taken part and find the assessments "very good" and "excellent." The good old Iron Cross lies there as well. . . . Must I live from now on as a second-rate citizen in the *Heimat* of my parents and forefathers, for whom I have fought and suffered like the others? Should I be torn from the world of my friends simply because I am of Jewish origin?"[67] This open letter reflected the dilemma of tens of thousands of people and, as the DNVP records show, became a topic of intense debate among conservative German Jews. In these discussions opinions were voiced which, only months later, could either no longer be aired or would be rendered obsolete by the rapid, and seemingly inexorable, consolidation of power by the Nazis.

In this context, Gerhard Lissa, a Jewish businessman from Berlin-Zehlendorf, reported about a meeting of former frontline soldiers, "organized by a number of ex-servicemen's leagues, such as the *Stahlhelm*, the SA, the *Kyffhäuser Bund*, and the *Reichsbund jüdischer Frontsoldaten*."[68] In the course of this meeting, "many shameful things occurred. Jewish [soldiers] crippled and blinded in the war were insulted and abused by young rascals, who had never heard the whistle of a bullet."[69] Lissa's own personal and financial situation appeared equally hopeless. Lissa wrote: "A fortune accumulated by grandfathers through dogged work was completely invested in war bonds and thereby dissipated into thin air, . . . my uncles voluntarily participated in the war of 1870, and . . . both my family and I have for a long time been spiritually assimilated into the Teutonic world." It is thus hardly surprising that when speaking about it, he was seized by "boundless rage over the injustice" by which "every

---

67. The author of the letter, Dr. Paul Rosenthal, ended with an appeal to all ex-comrades: "Do not forget us in these days. Do not forsake us; protect us from humiliating generalizations and stand up for us, so that in the national-minded Germany of today an old frontline soldier may participate in the reconstruction, even if he was born a Jew." BA Berlin-Lichterfelde, "DNVP, Politischer Schriftwechsel," R 8005, no. 19, 56.

68. 27 March 1933 at BA Berlin-Lichterfelde, "DNVP, Politischer Schriftwechsel," R 8005, no. 19, "Lissa an Lindner," 57. In 1921 the *Deutsche Kriegerbund*, founded in 1872, amalgamated with the *Kyffhäuserbund*, founded in 1898, to become the *Deutscher Reichskriegerbund Kyffhäuser*. In 1930, it had about three million members organized into thirty thousand organizations.

69. Ibid.

Jew is thrown into a pot with swindlers, rogues, and traitors to the Fatherland."[70]

National-minded Jews (who included not only the relatively few conservative and most liberal German Jews, but also the majority of the large number of war veterans) were psychologically most affected by the provocations and boycotts, since they shared fundamental political principles, standards of behavior, and values with non-Jewish Germans.[71] All of the physical and financial sacrifices—grandchildren, sons, fathers, and siblings killed in the Great War, the fortunes painstakingly amassed and lost through war and inflation—had now become meaningless and futile. In addition to personal predicaments, impending financial ruin threatened Lissa's very existence, since "recently payments of bills have been refused under the justification that one no longer has to pay Jews because a new dispensation of justice will soon be in place in Germany."[72] The entire world order had been rendered incomprehensible, and help was nowhere in sight. From foreign countries, such as Britain and the USA, Germany's former World War I adversaries, national-minded Jews expected and wanted no help. Lissa's attitude toward foreigners was characterized by apprehension and distrust: "Foreign voices are a nuisance and only create mischief. Here we see the same elements at work that leveled inflammatory propaganda and vilified Germans as barbarians during the war."[73]

How did the German conservative party, the leadership and members of the DNVP, behave toward national-minded Jews? Could these German Jews, who had served in the war and endured sacrifices and privations for Germany, count on the help of the DNVP (which, after all, considered itself the party of all national-minded Germans)? The internal confidential correspondence of the DNVP discloses that there was a range of reactions. First, direct rejection: military service, past sacrifices, even an impeccable national pedigree mattered less when it came to Germans who were Jewish. The party leadership was especially adamant in refusing to accommodate German Jews. A case in point is that of Dr. Vogel.

70. Ibid.

71. See Jakob Wassermann, *Mein Weg als Deutscher und Jude*, 2nd ed. (Munich, 1999), 48 (first published in 1921). See in particular what Wassermann said about himself and the German language.

72. 31 March 1933 at BA Berlin-Lichterfelde, "DNVP, Politischer Schriftwechsel," R 8005, no. 19 "Lissa an Rohr," 52–54.

73. Ibid., 58.

The DNVP Frankfurt am Main district association warmly recommended Vogel's admission in a letter to the party's Berlin head
office, with characteristic wording: "He was Jewish; two years ago
[he] was baptized as a Protestant.[74] According to the testimony of
his parson [he has] been absolutely un-Jewish and always oriented
toward the Right. . . . Vogel has lost his fortune in the Inflation and
is generally considered to be a poor, decent, and upright man." The
rejection of Dr. Vogel's application from Berlin was, however, terse
and pointed. No words were wasted on his character.[75] Even a man
with what were considered at the time to be impeccable national
credentials, the jurist Dr. Erich Gisbert, was deemed worthy of only
a short, very formal acknowledgement when he sought help in a
matter that concerned his very existence. Gisbert, a former member
of the DNVP, a signatory of the Hugenberg-sponsored "People's
Rebellion against the Young Plan," related to Prussian generals
through his mother and, baptized and confirmed in the Protestant
church, had been forced to resign from his post in the Chamber of
Commerce and Industry in Berlin.[76] Now, in order to facilitate his
reinstatement, he requested from the DNVP head office confirmation of his membership and participation in the anti-Young Plan
referendum campaign.[77] He was, however, only pithily and formally
referred to his former DNVP Land and county associations.[78] Notably lacking were any words of sympathy or regret.

The entire political climate of the winter and spring of 1933 was
poisoned by suspicion and mutual recrimination. A characteristic
example is the case of Heinrich and Hans Wassermeyer. The chairman of the DNVP Mittelrhein Land Association, *Justizrat* Heinrich
Wassermeyer,[79] feared that his son, working in Altona near Hamburg, might run into trouble with the Nazis. Wassermeyer therefore

74. 18 April 1933 at BA Berlin-Lichterfelde, "DNVP, Kirchen- und Religionsangelegenheiten," R 8005, no. 48, 47. In the appeals from local organizations, it was consistently emphasized that either the applicants or their parents
had converted to Christianity.

75. 5 May 1933 at BA Berlin-Lichterfelde, "DNVP, Kirchen- und Religionsangelegenheiten," R 8005, no. 48, 46. "We should like to warn against the
admission of Herr Dr. Vogel. The stipulation in our statutes that prohibits the
admission of Jews does not exclusively refer to religion."

76. 3 April 1933 at BA Berlin-Lichterfelde, "DNVP, Kirchen- und Religionsangelegenheiten," R 8005, no. 48, 56–58.

77. Ibid., 54–55.

78. Ibid., 53.

79. *Taschenbuch der Deutschnationalen Volkspartei* (Berlin, 1929), 27.

requested that the DNVP chairman in Altona look after his son Hans.[80] It is telling that the father found it necessary in his request to stress the German National leanings of his son and to point out that he had been a frontline soldier in the war and had later participated in the struggle against the communists.[81] When the son, Dr. Hans Wassermeyer, presented himself at the DNVP Altona district office to apply for admission into the party, the chairman of the Altona DNVP office experienced an unpleasant surprise: "We were astounded to see by his appearance that we were dealing with a Jew; after making inquiries we learned that his wife was also from a well-known Hamburg Jewish family."[82] Now full of mistrust, the chairman of the Altona DNVP requested information from Berlin about père Wassermeyer,[83] "especially whether he is a Jew and as such leader of a party organization." Yet the concerns of the Altona chairman were precipitate. Two days later, the DNVP Mittelrhein Land Association reported that Dr. Heinrich Wassermeyer was "not Jewish."[84] Rather, the Wassermeyer family was "an old established Christian Bonn family. Dr. Hans Wassermeyer's mother is also descended from an established Christian family. The suppositions concerning the Jewish origins of Dr. Wassermeyer are thus entirely erroneous."[85] This case showed clearly that after 30 January every German was subject to all-pervading suspicion. The entire society, even "national" constituencies, including the chairman of a DNVP Land Association, was affected. It subsequently transpired that no confidentiality was accorded to the internal background check on the Wassermeyer family, so that the publication of the fact that the son's wife was Jewish cast aspersions on the entire family.[86]

In analyzing the multitude of reactions to Jewish applications for admission to the DNVP, anti-Semitic attacks, the boycott of Jewish shops on 1 April 1933, violence against Jews, dismissals, general

---

80. 14 March 1933 at BA Berlin-Lichterfelde, "DNVP, Kirchen- und Religionsangelegenheiten," R 8005, no. 48, 36.

81. Ibid.

82. 29 March 1933 at BA Berlin-Lichterfelde, "DNVP, Kirchen- und Religionsangelegenheiten," R 8005, no. 48, 35.

83. Ibid., 35. "We shall not accept Herr Dr. Wassermeyer Jr., particularly since two doctors from the Altona hospital, who are members of our party, strongly came out against him."

84. 31 March 1933 at BA Berlin-Lichterfelde, "DNVP, Kirchen- und Religionsangelegenheiten," R 8005, no. 48, 34.

85. Ibid.

86. Père Wassermeyer lost trust in his party; his son suffered professionally.

discrimination, and discriminatory local legislation, two broad types of responses emerge: (1) isolated protests from individual DNVP members against anti-Semitic measures (often in the form of letters to the party leadership) and even attempts to lend succor, on the one hand; and (2) disapprobation, rejection, resentment, prejudice, and a pronounced anti-Semitic predisposition, on the other.

Protest, Regret, and Efforts to Help

German Nationals, who had kept close company with German Jews for many years, often perceived the sweeping discrimination as extremely unjust. Voices of protest were raised in particular in Frankfurt am Main,[87] where German Jews had been firmly ensconced for generations, prospered, and often acquired a reputation as public benefactors. In Frankfurt, as in most other German cities, the percentage of the Jewish population had been declining slightly since 1900. By 1933, 4.7 percent of the 555, 857 inhabitants were Jewish,[88] giving Frankfurt the highest percentage of Jewish inhabitants of any German city, well ahead of Berlin (3.8 percent) and Breslau (3.2 percent).[89] One noteworthy example of protest against anti-Jewish discrimination was an open letter to Hugenberg about the boycott of 1 April written by the longtime DNVP member Adele Kappus that was forwarded from the DNVP Frankfurt office to Berlin.[90] It would be "imprudent and unworthy of Germany," according to Kappus, "to start treating the century-long established Jewish people as pariahs, people who feel German and who have performed valued services to their Fatherland and Christian compatriots for

87. On the Jewish community in Frankfurt and the extent to which Frankfurt Jews were assimilated, see Leo Löwenthal, *Mitmachen wollte ich nie* (Frankfurt, 1981).

88. Thamer, *Verführung und Gewalt*, 258. In 1905, 7 percent of Frankfurt's population had been Jewish. Peter Pulzer, "Die jüdische Beteiligung," 189.

89. Thamer, *Verführung und Gewalt*, 258.

90. 12 April 1933 at BA Berlin-Lichterfelde, "DNVP, Kirchen- und Religionsangelegenheiten," R 8005, no. 48, "Offener Brief an Herrn Geheimrat Hugenberg," 63–64. It was generally known that Hugenberg's friend Reinhold Quaatz was half-Jewish, and that Hugenberg had Jewish employees in his publishing house, the *Scherlverlag*. On Hugenberg, see Mosse, "Die deutsche Rechte und die Juden," 183–249, who emphasized that "there was no mention of the *Judenproblem*" in any of Hugenberg's speeches (231).

hundreds of years."[91] In Frankfurt "the Christian and Jewish econo-
mies are so interconnected" that one could not damage one part
without injuring the other.[92] For the past thirty-two years, she her-
self had been an employee of a large Jewish-owned antiquarian and
export book dealership that had been in existence for 148 years and
whose proprietors (who, during the First World War, had been sta-
tioned at the front for four years) had treated her over the years
with "probity, generosity, and goodwill."[93] Now the business faced
bankruptcy and she and her colleagues had received their notices.
Kappus concluded her letter in an undertone of ominous foreboding: "If things continue in this vein, many who have once whole-
heartedly welcomed the national revolution will turn their backs
on it in anger. Make no mistake about the mood of the masses, it
is pervaded by disillusionment and bitterness."[94] The response from
Berlin contained merely the grudging admission that "the measures
had been extraordinarily harsh, and had thus triggered legitimate
resentment,"[95] along with stereotypical, apologetic formulas stressing that the DNVP was not responsible for the boycott.[96] Lacking,
perhaps deliberately, were any words of sympathy or regret for the
blatant injustice suffered by so many national-minded Jews. There
are a number of explanations for this extraordinarily tepid response
from the DNVP leadership in Berlin, ranging from genuine indifference and lack of empathy to fear of appearing too "pro-Jewish"
and uncertainty as to which policy line would emerge triumphant.
Kappus's letter highlighted the tension in the DNVP's reaction to

91. BA Berlin-Lichterfelde, "DNVP, Kirchen- und Religionsangelegenheiten," R 8005, no. 48, 64.
92. Ibid., 63. On the effect of the boycott, Adele Kappus remarked: "One
has the impression that with the entire undertaking the arrow strikes back at the
archer."
93. Ibid., 63–64.
94. Ibid., 64. The DNVP Frankfurt county association forwarded Adele
Kappus's letter to the head office in Berlin with the not-very-hopeful query,
"Will these lines have any impact?" (ibid., 62).
95. 26 April 1933 at BA Berlin-Lichterfelde, "DNVP, Kirchen- und Religionsangelegenheiten," R 8005, no. 48, 60.
96. Ibid: "Let me point out that it is neither the DNVP nor the national
government, but the NSDAP, which is responsible for the boycott and, last but
not least, those *Bürger* who flock to the swastika banner *en masse* instead of voting
for the Kampffront Schwarz-Weiß-Rot, not to mention the German People's
Party which, especially in Frankfurt, had been very popular with Jewish voters.
If we take this last fact into account, your former masters, or at least their following, are not without guilt for the current development."

anti-Semitic transgressions: indignant opposition induced by moral or patriotic concerns voiced by DNVP members and local organizations, on the one hand, and tacit or outright support used to further the DNVP head office's large scale political strategy, on the other.

The most urgent and comprehensive charges leveled against the Nazi terror also came from Frankfurt, straight from the office of the local DNVP district association (written on DNVP letterhead) by the Vice-President of Frankfurt's *Oberlandesgericht* (Provincial High Court and Court of Appeal).[97] According to the author of the complaint, Frankfurt was "under the thumb of the NSDAP leadership, repressed more brutally than during the 1918 revolution. Fear and panic have gained a hold over all public and family life,"[98] and Roland Freisler, *Ministerialdirektor* in the Prussian Ministry of Justice in March 1933, had lashed out "in a public harangue against Jews, transmitted over loudspeaker, which might result in a pogrom breaking out any day now."[99] The Vice-President of the *Oberlandesgericht* plainly spelled out the debt of gratitude that Frankfurt, in his opinion, owed its Jewish population: "The majority of local Jews have been residents of Frankfurt am Main or its surroundings for centuries. Among them are the city's greatest public benefactors, people responsible for almost all public charity work. A large number of Jews have served at the front or lost their sons in the war. Frankfurt's magnificent cultural facilities would never have come into being without Jewish donations. The spirit that prevails in these old Jewish families must, for the most part, be considered as genuinely conservative."[100] Unfortunately, he had been unable to prevent terror from making its way even into the *Oberlandesgericht*. The Jewish judges, among whom were "the most competent members of the Law Courts," had been forcibly suspended, and "the terror against Jewish lawyers" was so distressing that they "were virtually driven to suicide."[101] The letter further mentions "the all-pervasive terror

97. 3 April 1933 at BA Berlin-Lichterfelde, "DNVP, Politischer Schriftwechsel," R 8005, no. 19, "Hehdermann [? name partially illegible] an Hergt," 63–64.
98. Ibid., 63.
99. Ibid. Roland Freisler (1893–1945) began his career as a lawyer in Kassel and later became a deputy to the provincial Diet of Hessen-Nassau, which explains his proximity to Frankfurt.
100. Ibid.
101. Ibid., 63 verso. Among the lawyers there were many "whose irreproachable character and flawless management have been known to me for years." There was an atmosphere of "most bitter despair since only very few of them are left with some property," having lost all their savings in the Inflation.

in public life"[102] and the criminal acts committed with impunity by
the SA, which "the police not only tolerate but even countenance
and encourage."[103] Thirty-five Jewish businessmen had been led
with their hands held high "through the busiest streets of the city"
and "children of Jewish families, who had long ceased to belong to
the world of Judaism and had been raised as Christians, have been
chased out of the schools."[104] These goings-on were injurious to the
reputation of the DNVP, and it was high time to put a stop to them:
"Desperation prevails throughout the bourgeoisie of the city to the
point that it will be detrimental to the dignity of our party if it does
not remedy the situation as quickly as possible."[105] The judiciary no
longer dared "to counter the terror" since its members had ceased to
believe in the autonomy of the judicial branch. There was still some
hope that the German National members of the Cabinet would succeed in making sure that the constitutionally guaranteed foundations of the Rechtsstaat "were not encroached upon, at least for the
time being."[106] Yet, one had to concede that "due to the complete
silence of these Cabinet members . . . confidence in their influence
was waning with each passing day."[107]

   This letter of the Vice-President of the Frankfurt Provincial High
Court at least gives vent to indignation over National Socialist violence, rage over crimes perpetrated against Frankfurt's Jews, shame
over the impotence, haplessness, and inactivity of his own party,
and dismay at the erosion of the Rechtsstaat. At the same time, the
author had the foreboding that worse was still to come: "Even our
Frankfurter Post did not risk publishing my exceedingly moderate
article, 'Back to Law and Order,' because the publisher feared that
the SA might smash his printing plant to pieces. I was advised by
friends not to sign my name to this article as otherwise I might be
threatened with protective custody."[108] The Frankfurt judge's letter

---

   102. Ibid.
   103. Ibid., 63–63 verso.
   104. Ibid., 64.
   105. Ibid.
   106. Ibid. Now, the complaint continued, they would have to deal with the
dire consequence "that, with the adoption of the Enabling Act, the constitutional foundations of the Rechtsstaat have been placed at the will and discretion
of the current government."
   107. Ibid.
   108. Ibid., 63 verso-64. "Protective custody" was a euphemism for com-
mittal to a concentration camp. Starting in mid March 1933, even members of
the German elite (and whose position appeared to be more secure than that of

makes two things clear: (1) The number and scale of infringements and violent acts in the winter and spring of 1933 were enormous; and (2) attacks and crimes were so well known, occurring as they did right under everyone's noses, that one had to look away deliberately in order not to see them. DNVP party offices in particular were alerted to many of these transgressions since it was naturally expected that the Nazis' conservative alliance partner still would be in a position to intervene. Even when the determination and readiness to help existed (which was not often in the case of most German Nationals), the actual ability to help was frequently limited. If the German National Vice-President of an *Oberlandesgericht* was curtailed in his capacity to intercede, how much more helpless must others have felt.

The records thus indicate few cases of active help. Not only was it difficult to lend succor—given the climate of fear and intimidation and the corresponding threat to oneself and one's family—but also the will and the readiness to offer assistance was often lacking. Hugenberg, for example, who (according to his American biographer) cannot be accused of being a dyed-in-the-wool anti-Semite,[109] surrounded himself with the aura of a busy Minister, whose vital ministerial activities determined the health and well-being of the German economy. Since he even neglected his duties as chairman of the DNVP to the point that his deputy, Friedrich von Winterfeld, had to do his work, Hugenberg had a plausible excuse for not having the time to tackle other "problems."[110]

---

a high-ranking German National judge?) found themselves threatened by this kind of "protective custody," which often accounted for the fact that many remained silent in the face of Nazi provocation.

109. Leopold, *Alfred Hugenberg*, 22. Leopold writes of Hugenberg's "pragmatic" attitude toward anti-Semitism: "Hugenberg considered anti-Semitism a tool which could be exploited and discarded; he himself measured a man by his loyalty to the nation rather than by the purity of his racial pedigree." (22); "Nationalist Jews played an important role in his press concern and an even more important one in the Ufa. Even in political life, one of the men most intimately associated with Hugenberg, Reinhold Quaatz, was reportedly the cousin of Ludwig Holländer, the chairman of the Central Association of Germans of the Jewish Faith," (185, note 138). See also Mosse, "Die deutsche Rechte und die Juden," 183–249; esp. 231–233.

110. The nearly 68-year-old was plagued by ill-health, and those close to him had orders to make sure that he was not approached with unwelcome petitions and requests. See Weiß and Hoser, eds., *Die Deutschnationalen*, 234–244. For complaints directed to Hugenberg, see BA Koblenz, N 1231, Nachlaß Hugenberg, no. 89: "Ausschreitungen der NSDAP gegen DNVP Mitglieder."

Instead, it was Papen's office in the Vice Chancellory to which most complaints were directed. Especially since Papen had resigned his position as *Reichskommissar* for Prussia to make way for Göring in the first half of April 1933, he was free to take on other responsibilities. Papen lent active support in the case of the historian Ludwig Dehio, Archivist at the State Archives in Berlin-Dahlem who, as a result of the Law on the Restoration of a Professional Civil Service of 7 April, was in danger of losing his post.[111] A faultless national pedigree and a prominent name—Dehio was the son of the famous art historian Georg Dehio—worked to his advantage.[112] Dehio also had the good fortune to have well-connected, conservative friends who interceded on his behalf. One of them, Dr. Wedepohl, wrote a long letter to Papen, in which he praised Dehio's nationalist background.[113] He had met Dehio during the war as an infantry officer; knew that as a boy, Dehio had already been received in the house of Paul de Lagarde (a well known anti-Semite),[114] and that Dehio's father had been "found worthy of the highest honors of the German Reich." In Dehio's case at least, the ring of his family name and the patriotic significance of his father's work prompted Papen to intervene. At Wedepohl's suggestion, Papen turned to Hindenburg's *Staatssekretär* Otto Meissner with the request that Meissner approach Hindenburg, asking him to use his influence on Dehio's behalf.[115] Meissner promptly replied (in an unusually obliging tone) that he had forwarded Dehio's case with Hindenburg's special recommendation to the Prussian Minister of Culture, requesting "favorable reconsideration" of the case. In his correspondence about the matter,

111. Regarding the Law on the Restoration of a Professional Civil Service, see Joseph Walk, *Das Sonderrecht für die Juden im NS-Staat*, 2nd ed. (Heidelberg, 1996), 12, and Friedländer, *Nazi Germany and the Jews*, 27–46.

112. Georg Dehio (1850–1932) was the organizer and chief collaborator in the *Handbuch der deutschen Kunstdenkmäler* (1905–1912), often referred to as "the Dehio." Dehio's other seminal work was *Geschichte der deutschen Kunst* (1919–1925). As Nipperdey remarked, "Emphasis on the national element" constituted the common denominator in Dehio's work (*Arbeitswelt und Bürgergeist*, 645).

113. Pfingsten 1933 at BA Berlin-Lichterfelde, "Stellvertreter des Reichskanzlers, Kanzlei von Papen," R 53, no. 86, 76–80.

114. Ibid., 77–78. Paul de Lagarde (1827–1891), whose original name was Paul Bötticher, became known as a cultural critic and famous Orientalist. See Fritz Stern, *The Politics of Cultural Despair* (Berkeley and Los Angeles, 1972).

115. 19 June 1933 at BA Berlin-Lichterfelde, "Stellvertreter des Reichskanzlers, Kanzlei von Papen," R 53, no. 86, 82.

Meissner emphasized that Hindenburg had awarded Dehio's father the *Adlerschild* in 1930 "because of the patriotic significance of his creative work."[116] Meissner's intervention had some impact: during the Third Reich, Dehio was no longer allowed to publish his work, but at least he was "tolerated" as an archivist in the *Hohenzollernsche Hausarchiv.*

Rejection and Disapprobation

The cases cited above were the exception rather than the rule. Viewed as a whole, most German Nationals were not critics of Nazi attacks or reluctant incriminators or powerless onlookers seized by fury over the attacks they witnessed, or even helpers in the crisis. As has been shown, a wide cross-section of the party rank and file disapproved of the lawlessness of excesses and the brutality of the attacks. Some, like Adele Kappus, were themselves adversely affected by the boycott and objected to the treatment of their Jewish employers; most believed that a dividing line had to be drawn between the old established German Jews and those who had come to Germany since the war. Some complained about the erosion of the Rechtsstaat and realized that a section of Germany's brightest and most educated citizens stood in danger of being victimized, driven out, and possibly destroyed. Yet the mainstream conservative reaction to the multitude of Nazi excesses during the Nazi seizure of power was characterized largely by the resentment and prejudice that had traditionally been a component of the DNVP's anti-Semitic orientation. Conservatives had always considered German Jews the vanguard of an unwelcome modernity, undermining tradition, customs, and the good old ways. In addition to these traditional anti-Jewish motifs, already present in German conservatism during the Empire, two further elements figured prominently at the beginning of the Third Reich. First, conservatives did not want to let themselves be

116. Ibid., 83. The decoration carried the dedication, "To Georg Dehio, the great teacher and historiographer of German art." Papen's office immediately notified Wedepohl on 26 June 1933 (ibid., 85). The heartfelt tone of the letter leads one to expect a positive outcome. On Dehio, see Volker Berghahn, "Ludwig Dehio," in Hans-Ulrich Wehler, ed., *Deutsche Historiker* (Göttingen, 1973), 473–492; Theodor Schieder, "Ludwig Dehio zum Gedächtnis," *Historische Zeitschrift* 201 (1965), 1–12; Thomas Beckers, *Abkehr von Preußen. Ludwig Dehio und die deutsche Geschichtswissenschaft nach 1945* (Aichach, 2001).

outdone on any issue brought to the fore in public life; second, it was becoming increasingly clear that, under the changed conditions that prevailed after 30 January, leading DNVP members and functionaries dared to show their true colors and came out into the open with *völkisch* ideas that they had long harbored. The various shades of anti-Semitism and its degrees of intensity reflect the DNVP's disparate roots: from the moderate liberal-conservative influences of the Free Conservative Party of the Empire which, in some ways, had been closer politically to the National Liberals than to the German Conservative Party, all the way to the extremely anti-Semitic elements of the former Christian Social Party and the Association of German National Shop Assistants. Though the extreme anti-Semitic wing had been pushed out of the party at the Görlitz party congress of 1922, individual instances of *völkisch* orientation lived on, as illustrated below.

Graphic examples of the anti-Semitic orientation of party administrators and bureaucrats can be found in their attitude toward the boycott of 1 April 1933. While the NSDAP was chiefly responsible for its organization, many local and regional DNVP associations participated in the boycott (in contrast to statements of the party head office in Berlin, which, as in its correspondence with Adele Kappus, had often flatly denied any participation of the DNVP). A series of documents clearly indicates that instructions to join in the boycott were distributed from the head office in Berlin. The Posen-Westpreußen Land Association, for example, reported to Berlin on 1 April 1933: "Telephoned instructions to get the *Kampfring* ready for the propaganda campaign urging that 'Germans buy only German goods' have been executed without delay."[117] On 28 March the DNVP head office had already sent out telegrams to twenty-five Land Associations: "Arrange processions as soon as possible with placards saying 'Germans buy only German goods and Germans buy only from Germans' and immediately submit photographs."[118]

117. 1 April 1933 at BA Berlin-Lichterfelde, "DNVP, Kirchen- und Religionsangelegenheiten," R 8005, no. 48, 104. The report continued: "We repeatedly had the placards carried through the entire town and have achieved a satisfactory mobilizing effect, especially since we had been the first to do this."
118. BA Berlin-Lichterfelde, "DNVP, Kirchen- und Religionsangelegenheiten," R 8005, no. 48, 106. The circular telegram was sent to, among others, the DNVP Land Associations of Niederrhein, Westfalen-Ost, Arnsberg, Mittelrhein, Düsseldorf-Ost, Hannover-Süd, Braunschweig, Merseburg, Magdeburg, Dresden, and Leipzig.

Transmission did not always proceed without a hitch. In one instance, the DNVP *Landesgeschäftsführer* of Baden anxiously cabled to Berlin on 1 April: "We never received any propaganda materials against foreign merchandise."[119] The instructions of the head office to the Land Associations were passed on to the *Bezirksgruppen* (district groups) which, in turn, sent their performance reports about organized processions on 1 April back to Berlin.[120] For the most part, the entire DNVP, from the leadership in Berlin (*Bundesvorstand*) down to the *Bezirksgruppen* strenuously endeavored to leave its mark on the boycott of 1 April. When party organizations did exclude themselves from action, their reasons for doing so had little to do with moral scruples or attachment to humanitarian principles. The Gotha *Bezirksgruppe* reported, for example, that it would not allow any placards to be carried through the streets: "The Nazis have already done that for days and if we were to enter the arena now, it would only look like a pale imitation, and would have absolutely no effect."[121] The DNVP leadership brushed off and disregarded appeals by DNVP members upon whom the severity of the boycott weighed heavily, even if the victims were patriotic Jews. On several occasions members took exception to the boycott and concomitant discrimination. A DNVP member from Hattingen on the Ruhr, for example, complained that a local Jewish dentist, "a strongly national-minded man through-and-through," who, due to his nationalist convictions "suffered much at the hands of the Left," had now been deprived of his practice. The same member complained that a Jewish factory owner, "a benefactor such as Hattingen and its surroundings had, as far as I know, never seen before" was now discriminated against just like all the other Jews.[122] The answer from the Berlin head office basically repudiated the justification of these grievances, pointing out that even though not everyone was happy with "the so-called *Judenaktion*," one had to consider "that we are in the midst of a revolution and that things one would not

119. 1 April 1933 at BA Berlin-Lichterfelde, "DNVP, Kirchen- und Religionsangelegenheiten," R 8005, no. 48, 105.

120. See, for example, 1 April 1933 at BA Berlin-Lichterfelde, ibid., "Bericht der Bezirksgruppe Sonneberg in Thüringen," 107.

121. 30 March 1933, ibid., 108. Instead they had "put up the appropriate posters in our exhibition windows, as well as in our display cases."

122. 1 April 1933 at BA Berlin-Lichterfelde, "DNVP, Kirchen- und Religionsangelegenheiten," R 8005, no. 48, 68–69.

countenance in normal times have now become unavoidable."[123] The DNVP head office hereby articulated a policy that spoke to the inherent contradiction in the DNVP's approach toward German Jews: one should consider that the "position one takes on the Jews [is], after all, a fundamental one that cannot depend on whether or not a particular Jew is a decent human being or not."[124] In this particular case, the position of the DNVP head office is unequivocal: "Religious points of view play no role with regard to the position on Judaism; rather, the rejection of Jews issues from political considerations."[125]

Even more anti-Semitic than the party leadership or bureaucracy was the type of DNVP party member whose opposition to Jews was based not solely on considerations of political expediency but on *völkisch* racial convictions. How high the percentage of such dyed-in-the-wool *völkisch* anti-Semites was within the DNVP at the end of the Republic and the beginning of the Third Reich is difficult to gauge. But that this very type of conservative existed is beyond question. A prime example of one such extreme nationalist and *völkisch*-thinking German National was the Württemberg physician Bubenhöfer, a member of the *Vorstand* (executive committee) of the Württemberg DNVP, well acquainted with Vice-Chancellor Papen, and (as he wrote about himself in a letter to Papen) a "man known for his nationalist convictions in the whole Land of Württemberg."[126] A long letter Bubenhöfer wrote to Papen on 11 April 1933, accompanied by a political discourse in which Bubenhöfer expounded upon his political ideas, throws light on the Weltanschauung of conservative *völkisch* anti-Semites.[127] As Bubenhöfer explained, in 1932 he had encouraged the leadership of the Württemberg DNVP to merge their party with the Nazis, mainly in order to reinvigorate the non-Socialist wing of

123. Ibid., 67.

124. Ibid.

125. Ibid. In defense of their own inactivity the letter ended with the words: "Incidentally, now that the boycott is over, further measures will have a firm legal grounding."

126. 11 April 1933 at BA Berlin-Lichterfelde, "Stellvertreter des Reichskanzlers, Kanzlei von Papen," R 53, no. 80, 157 verso. Bubenhöfer was known mainly as the founder of a *"Deutsch-Völkischer Orden"*; see also Werner Braatz, "The Counter-Revolution in 1933 as viewed in two Documents addressed to Vice-Chancellor Papen," *International Review of Social History* 19 (1974), 115–127.

127. Ibid., 158–162.

the NSDAP and thereby, as Bubenhöfer expected, Hitler's position in the party. Bubenhöfer knew himself to be completely in accord with Hitler's policies; there was no significant difference "between his [i.e., Hitler's] resolution of the social question and that of the German Nationals . . ."[128] A strong German National wing within the Nazi Party would reinforce the "Christian conservative" world-view within the NSDAP.[129] An independent DNVP had, in any case, lost its justification. Bubenhöfer waxes enthusiastic about the "dazzlingly drastic measures since 5 March," and sees himself completely in accord "with so many points of the NSDAP."[130] By and large, however, "the revolution [had been] . . . too bloodless,"[131] and too lenient on "elements of an alien race,"[132] which was Bubenhöfer's way of referring to the "intellectual leaders of socialism." These leaders "must be killed on a wide scale. Only when this poison is eliminated will we again be able to get at the soul of the German worker."[133] To Bubenhöfer it seemed that the "boycott against Judaism has been wholly inadequate," since he did not believe "that a revolution achieves its ends without deliberate terror."[134] Germans were far too good-natured to take vigorous action, whereas the terror of the Russian revolution had petrified the whole world: "And, when all is said and done, who, after all, were the fathers of the Russian revolution? Jews. I do not say that we should imitate these Jewish methods, but we must, through correspondingly tough concerted action against Jews in Germany and their supremacy in all fields, imbue their blood relations throughout the world with a holy fear, otherwise they won't be silenced. We must use German Jews as hostages against Jewish financial power. This kind of talk they will

128. Ibid., 158 verso.
129. Ibid., 158.
130. Ibid., 159.
131. Ibid., 159 verso.
132. Ibid., 160.
133. Ibid. It had been a recurring theme of the Right's accusations since the First World War that Jewish leaders had steered the German workers' movement into increasingly radical waters. See Friedländer, "Die politischen Veränderungen der Kriegszeit," 27–67; Werner Angress, "Juden im politischen Leben der Revolutionszeit," in Mosse, ed., *Deutsches Judentum in Krieg und Revolution*, 137–317; Friedländer, *Nazi Germany and the Jews*, 73–113.
134. BA Berlin-Lichterfelde, "Stellvertreter des Reichskanzlers, Kanzlei von Papen," R 53, no. 80, 160.

understand."[135] In this and other points Bubenhöfer's political views were in no way different from those of even radical National Socialists. The principal distinction between National Socialism and the conservative anti-Semitic physician Bubenhöfer lies paradoxically in the fact that Bubenhöfer disapproved of public health care and other social policies.[136] Bubenhöfer's views may not have been particularly exceptional; however, German Nationals of the Bubenhöfer orientation were certainly not typical. Insofar as they did exist, they were found mainly in the *Bildungsbürgertum* and among the East Elbian aristocracy.[137]

The German National Predicament

In the first months after the Nazi seizure of power, German Nationals were concerned that they might be regarded as too *judenfreundlich* ("Jew-friendly") since they feared making the DNVP unpopular with their larger coalition partner. In the eyes of most Nazis, German Nationals had only reluctantly supported boycott measures and had been, all in all, too halfhearted when it came to anti-Semitic measures. This anxiety of being considered "lukewarm" was mirrored in an inquiry by the German National *Altenburger Landes-Zeitung* to the DNVP head office: "One of our readers discussed anti-Semitism with a Nazi, who accused German Nationals of protecting Jews, since 40–50% of the journalists in Hugenberg's *Scherlverlag*

---

135. Ibid. This extreme language underlined Bubenhöfer's affinity to National Socialism, a fact further highlighted by his statements on eugenics (160–162), where he speaks of *"Aufnordung"* (160) and the "forcible sterilization of all racially-inferior elements" (160 verso), as well as of the need for "gradual de-urbanization," since "the large cities . . . ultimately mean the death of a people" (160 verso).

136. Ibid., 160 verso-161. So, for example, when he quoted in obvious affirmation: "It is not that we have lost the war in spite of our social welfare legislation, but because of it." National Socialists would also hardly have spoken of the "futile and immoral equal, direct, and secret franchise" (161).

137. Malinowski, *Vom Kaiser zum Führer*; Heike Ströhle-Bühler, *Studentischer Antisemitismus in der Weimarer Republik* (Frankfurt, 1991); and Helma Brunck, *Die deutschen Burschenschaften in der Weimarer Republik und im Nationalsozialismus* (Munich, 1999). On the anti-Semitism of the Weimar *Bildungsbürgertum* see Mommsen, *The Rise and Fall of Weimar Democracy*, 304–305; and Winkler, *Weimar 1918–1933*, 293–294.

[publishing house] are Jewish."[138] The head office hastened to assure the *Altenburger Landes-Zeitung* that among the approximately 100 journalists there were "now, at most, four who would fit this description."[139] In the German National camp, one was obviously eager to allay the suspicion that Hugenberg employed a significant number of Jewish journalists in his publishing house. On the other hand, the existing anti-Semitism of moderate German Nationals was of a different nature than that of the National Socialists. The Nazis took pride in their conspicuous anti-Semitism, for it indicated the extent to which individual Nazi party members were committed to the movement.[140] The conservatives, while certainly not free of anti-Semitic prejudices themselves, considered each individual case carefully and, if possible, tried to hide behind the provision of existing laws and proceed accordingly. The roundabout and tortuous tactics employed to exclude half-Jews from admittance into the DNVP testified to the fact that even the DNVP leadership felt a certain embarrassment about rejecting them. German National county and district boards, familiar with particular local circumstances and impressed by the impeccable national "credentials" of Jewish (or partly Jewish) applicants, and by their good name and public donations, were, as a rule, more receptive to admitting applicants than the DNVP head office in Berlin. The leadership in Berlin was desperately at pains to show that the party could not be accused of being *judenfreundlich* and was therefore more inclined to be disapproving and reject applications of German Jews. The county

138. 11 April 1933 at BA Berlin-Lichterfelde, "DNVP, Kirchen- und Religionsangelegenheiten," R 8005, no. 48, 52. Altenburg in Thuringia had 42,570 inhabitants in 1925; see *Statistisches Jahrbuch für das Deutsche Reich*, 52 (Berlin 1933), 11.

139. 3 May 1933 at BA Berlin-Lichterfelde, "DNVP, Kirchen- und Religionsangelegenheiten," R 8005, no. 48, 51: "In the meantime, the number may have decreased further. Total elimination, however, can be achieved only gradually."

140. Sebastian Haffner, *Germany: Jekyll & Hyde. 1939—Deutschland von innen betrachtet* (Berlin, 1996). The book was originally written in wartime England in 1939–1940. Haffner emphasized the "fundamental importance of anti-Semitism for the Nazis," which had the function of welding them together "through an iron chain" of jointly committed crimes: "Der Antisemitismus dient wie bestimmte Mut- und Bewährungsproben, die vor der Aufnahme von Kandidaten in die alten Ritterorden oder die modernen Geheimbünde zur Feststellung der Verschwiegenheit und des Gehorsams angewendet wurden, der Auslese und Prüfung. Die Prüfung zur Feststellung der Eignung als Nazi ist jedoch keine Mutprobe, sondern dient dem Nachweis der Skrupellosigkeit" (70).

and district boards, on the other hand, considered each individual case with care. A strictly defined policy *per se* did not exist. The later a case came forward, the greater the chance of refusal. What was still subject to a long debate in the winter of 1933 was likely to be thrown out without much ado in April or May. This rapid spread of anti-Semitic sentiment on the part of the DNVP leadership reflects the speed of Hitler's successful consolidation of power and the DNVP's acknowledgement of that fact. The party leadership obviously felt it had to join the fray or suffer the potentially debilitating political consequences. But there were exceptions even to this rule of thumb. In the winter of 1933, any case that appeared ambiguous was still disputed at length and produced an extensive correspondence, in which contradictory opinions clashed.

One case in particular, that of the practicing physician Dr. Behrend from Pomerania, illustrates how deeply anti-Semitism was rooted in the DNVP and how much the party membership was torn over this issue. In February and March 1933 the Behrend case divided the entire Pomerania Land Association, the party's largest and most influential regional organization since the inception of the DNVP.[141] In mid-February 1933 a prominent member of the DNVP Kolberg *Ortsgruppe* wrote a letter requesting mediation from the Land Association in the provincial capital of Stettin in a matter regarding Dr. Behrend, who was characterized as "the son of a Jewish father and a Christian mother. The father converted to Christianity upon his marriage."[142] At the behest of Kolberg's local DNVP leader, Dr. Behrend and his non-Jewish wife had joined the party. The letter continued: "Behrend did his duty in the war and occupied a position of considerable prominence in Kolberg, . . . frequented the best social circles," and politically "had never stood out before." Even though "his sole inherent defect" consisted in the fact "that he is the son of a Jewish father and thus half Jewish," a number of party members raised serious objections to Behrend's membership in the DNVP.[143] On the other hand, a group of members interceded on Behrend's behalf and insisted that he

141. Traditionally, the DNVP had been most successful in Pomerania. In the elections for the provincial Diet, the party attained the following results: 48.5 percent in 1925, 40.8 percent in 1929 and, even in 1933, 18.4 percent of the vote. See Falter et al., eds., *Wahlen und Abstimmungen*, 104.

142. 14 February 1933 at BA Berlin-Lichterfelde, "DNVP, Kirchen- und Religionsangelegenheiten," R 8005, no. 48, 147.

143. Ibid., 147 verso.

be allowed to remain a member. They even threatened their own withdrawal if Behrend were forced to leave the party. In this difficult situation, the local group hoped for help from the Land Association.[144] Behrend's opponents also turned to the Land Association. A colleague of Behrend, *Oberstabsarzt* Dr. Haenisch, argued that Behrend's membership in the DNVP only caused the party harm, since it would "leave us wide open to Nazi attacks."[145] Dr. Haenisch openly threatened (just as Behrend's defenders had in making the opposite case) to resign from the party should Behrend stay in it. He also made it plain that his opinion about Behrend was shared by many; there were other German Nationals who "strongly disapprove of any affiliation with Judaism from a *völkisch*-racial standpoint and who refuse to collaborate closely with people who are so thoroughly Jewish by virtue of blood [ties]."[146] Former Captain von Hertzberg, a cousin of the Pomeranian DNVP chairman Georg von Zitzewitz,[147] a prominent member of the Kolberg DNVP, and a strict opponent of Behrend's acceptance, claimed in his letter to Zitzewitz that there were "Freemasons and half-Jews who cannot go to the Nazis, because they are on their blacklist. They now seek admission to the DNVP which, in their opinion, is not as *völkisch*-oriented, and because they need some form of reinsurance."[148] Von Hertzberg warned that the DNVP stood in danger of losing a large number of its best members unless indiscriminate admission into the party was curtailed. Then "inferior scum" would gain the upper hand in the party. Therefore, the party must not allow itself "to be burdened with Jews and Jewish riffraff"; it must "be *völkisch* and *judenrein* (free of Jews) or it won't exist at all."[149] Von Hertzberg threatened (like others before him) to leave the party if Behrend were to remain a member.

---

144. Ibid.

145. 21 February 1933 at ibid., 146–146 verso. A number of years prior to 1933, Behrend had remarked to the Kolberg *Stahlhelm* leader that ". . . with my nose and my ancestry no one can expect me to be a German National" (146).

146. Ibid., 146 verso.

147. Georg von Zitzewitz, born in 1892, member of the Prussian Landtag 1932–1933, DNVP Reichstag deputy in 1924 and 1933.

148. 21 February 1933 at BA Berlin-Lichterfelde, "DNVP, Kirchen- und Religionsangelegenheiten," R 8005, no. 48, 142.

149. Ibid. Von Hertzberg wrote about Behrend that he was blacklisted by the Nazis "because he is a half-Jew and also behaved like a Jew," and wanted to use the DNVP "in order to protect himself."

The DNVP Pomerania Land Association, to whom all of these letters were directed, naturally found itself in an awkward dilemma so shortly before the 5 March elections. It did not risk making a ruling since, regardless of how the issue was decided, DNVP members were sure to be offended one way or another. The matter was passed on to Berlin with the recommendation: "The affair is not to be considered as very urgent." Instead, dilatory tactics were to be pursued: "We have advised the Kolberg local association to appeal to the party court, in order to drag this thing out."[150] The final verdict now rested with Berlin, where the matter was not taken lightly. The *geschäftsführende Vorstandsmitglied* (manager of the party's day-to-day affairs), Major Nagel, with whom the decision rested, drafted a carefully worded response to Stettin, which he diligently revised before sending the final letter to the Stettin Land Association on 23 March.[151] In this letter he urgently advised "to refrain from an appeal to the party court," since if "a general decision is made, then the party will certainly be harmed."[152] Nagel clearly outlined the party's predicament: "There may be doubt as to whether the statutes according to which Jews may not become members refer to religion or race." If now, on this highly sensitive question of accepting half-Jews as members, "a fundamental decision is issued to the effect . . . that half-Jews can be admitted, this would cause immense damage in *völkisch*-oriented circles and probably cost us a great many members."[153] This was all the more true "in the extraordinarily charged climate of the present age" and provided "National Socialists with materials against us that could not be more injurious." In the present case, Nagel continued, it would have been best to tell Behrend to withdraw his application for membership.

By the middle of May, the DNVP had lost most of its local strongholds to the more dynamic Nazi party, whose predominance

150. 2 March 1933 at BA Berlin-Lichterfelde, "DNVP, Kirchen- und Religionsangelegenheiten," R 8005, no. 48, 141.
151. Ibid., 140–140 verso. In his draft, Nagel wrote that in the case of a general decision against the acceptance of half-Jews "in all likelihood a great many very valuable members might be lost to us." He omitted this sentence, which might well be interpreted as "pro-Jewish," from the final text of the letter. Even in intraparty correspondence, fear of appearing too favorably disposed toward what now had become the "national enemy" was all-pervasive.
152. 23 March 1933 at BA Berlin-Lichterfelde, "DNVP, Kirchen- und Religionsangelegenheiten," R 8005, no. 48, 136.
153. Ibid.

had grown consistently after 5 March. The renaming of the DNVP as the "German National Front" at the beginning of May had been the symbolic expression of the party's increasing alignment with the Nazis (and the adoption of their methods). By the spring of 1933, conservatives had thus become exceedingly anxious to avoid any political move that might be construed as a provocation to its more powerful coalition partner. In May 1933, the Frankfurt am Main county association, for example, warmly recommended "the admission of a gentleman who was Jewish." This referred to "*Generaldirektor* Professor Dr. Salomon, [who] according to one of our prominent leaders, [has been] baptized for 40 years," and "enjoys quite a good reputation here in Frankfurt," a man one can "absolutely rely upon."[154] Despite this glowing introduction, this request met with an immediate refusal from Berlin.[155] In the case of the apparently less promising application of the lawyer Ledien, who had applied for membership to the DNVP Merseburg Land Association and who is described as a "baptized Jew, but also a World War I combatant" who had always been "involved in patriotic endeavors,"[156] the Berlin Office procrastinated, recommending that "the matter be deferred for several months."[157]

The unpredictable decisions of the central office in Berlin and the uncertainty they produced were connected in part with the tumultuous nature of day-to-day politics, the growing insecurity and waning strength of the German Nationals, and the absence of a consistent policy on the part of the DNVP. Efforts in that direction lacked resoluteness. On 27 March 1933, for example, Major Hans Nagel wrote to the Berlin Land Association: "The DNVP statutes include the passage that Jews are not allowed to join the party. The

---

154. 2 May 1933 at BA Berlin-Lichterfelde, "DNVP, Kirchen- und Religionsangelegenheiten," R 8005, no. 48, 29.

155. 10 May 1933 at ibid., 28. Here the applicant is rejected with reference to the statutes.

156. 12 May 1933 at BA Berlin-Lichterfelde, "DNVP, Kirchen- und Religionsangelegenheiten," R 8005, no. 48, 17.

157. 26 May 1933 at ibid., 16. These stalling tactics are frequently employed. One case in point is that of the Gelsenkirchen physician Dr. Block, who wrote to the DNVP head office on 1 March, asking whether the DNVP would accept Jews. He requested an immediate answer "since Sunday is election day." The negative response followed only on 5 April, that is, a month after the elections. See BA Berlin-Lichterfelde, "DNVP, Kirchen- und Religionsangelegenheiten," R 8005, no. 48, 93–94.

statutes do not contain a precise definition of who is a Jew. In the committees responsible for accepting new members the opinion has, however, gained ground that persons who are born Jewish and then convert to Christianity must not be accepted into the party."[158] In mid May, a good six weeks later, more direct language was employed. The response to a letter from a DNVP member who, on account of his ancestry, had been suspended from his local branch[159] was couched in no uncertain terms: "According to party statutes, Jews cannot be accepted into the German National Front. It is not religion but ethnic origin that is decisive in the characterization of 'Jewish.' If you have been accepted into our party and are a member of the Jewish race, it is only because we were not aware of that fact. Therefore, we cannot consider the expulsion from your local group as unjustified."[160] Was this, in fact, a first step toward the adoption of the racist anti-Semitism of the Nazis?

Conclusion

Only a few months after the demise of Weimar democracy, there was no institution or party left to which German Jews could turn for effective aid. As already mentioned, due to the intervention of the aged *Reichspräsident* Paul von Hindenburg, war veterans, relatives of soldiers killed in action, and those who had lost sons in the war gained a reprieve and were temporarily exempted from discriminatory legislation. But the DNVP, the party that, more than any other, had been the standard-bearer of the conservative German establishment, the embodiment of the values of the Empire, the bureaucracy, and the traditions of the old Prussian *Rechtsstaat*, had failed abysmally when put to the test. In this, it was not alone. Other pillars of the German establishment remained inactive either because they were deeply divided on the issue of anti-Semitism and the nature of Nazi terror, as with the Protestant Church hierarchy,

---

158. 27 March 1933 at BA Berlin-Lichterfelde, "DNVP, Kirchen- und Religionsangelegenheiten," R 8005, no. 48, 125. The large number of applications for membership is explained by the (erroneous) belief that membership in the DNVP would offer protection from Nazi violence.

159. Ibid., 26–27.

160. 14 May 1933 at BA Berlin-Lichterfelde, "DNVP, Kirchen- und Religionsangelegenheiten," R 8005, no. 48, 25.

or they were anti-Semitic themselves, as with sections of the German Foreign Office.[161] The DNVP had always spoken out against random violence and, as late as March 1933, opposed "in principle terrorizing any segment of the population."[162] But this was mere rhetoric. In practical terms, this opposition had amounted to very little. In the final analysis, it was a combination of practical obstacles (such as the sheer fear of confronting the Nazis) and the anti-Semitic convictions of DNVP members and leaders alike that prevented the DNVP from standing up for the rights of fellow German citizens, even if they had fought in the Great War and suffered as a result of German defeat and inflation. The conservatives' anti-Semitism was multifaceted: its cultural aspects were strong in the predominantly Protestant DNVP and its political overtones powerful in a right-wing party that associated Jews with opposing political creeds from left liberalism to socialism and communism. Finally, as Bubenhöfer's example demonstrated, even *völkisch* orientations were extant in a party that counted among its antecedents remainders of the *völkisch* splinter groups of the Empire, even if most of those found a more natural home under the roof of the NSDAP.

On an individual level, there was some protest, empathy, and occasionally also willingness to help. This even included local party organizations. The documents have revealed some cognitive dissonance on the part of many German Nationals, who were often torn between their positive experiences with German Jews based on shared professional or personal bonds and the political expediencies generated by the wave of anti-Semitism that accompanied the Nazi seizure of power. The DNVP's Berlin head office, meanwhile, was dealing with abstract policy, not with neighbors in distress. DNVP policymakers were ready (though, perhaps, with a certain reluctance) to use anti-Semitism to advance their political position, even if this meant abandoning other central tenets, such as upholding the Rechtsstaat, or respecting and defending German Jews for their merits and sacrifices for the fatherland. DNVP policymakers knew they were playing a dangerous game. By not intervening to stop Nazi violence and discrimination, they implicitly sanctioned them; by not standing up to an all-pervasive culture of fear, they allowed

---

161. Scholder, *Die Kirchen und das Dritte Reich*, 364–401; Donald M. McKale, "From Weimar to Nazism: Abteilung III of the German Foreign Office and the Support of Anti-Semitism, 1931–1935," *LBIYB* 32 (1987), 297–308.
162. Mosse, "Die deutsche Rechte und die Juden," note 24.

anti-Semitic attacks to go unpunished. Other casualties were the much-vaunted Prussian bureaucratic tradition, and, in the end, those very principles conservatives took pride in (though no longer embodied), such as decency, the rule of law, and the maintenance of civic order. Through their alliance with the Nazis, they themselves had helped to create an environment that doomed the very world order they professed to uphold.

Chapter VI

Rebellion against the Inevitable

The Tribulations of Spring 1933

At the beginning of April 1933, Major Hans Nagel, the *geschäfts-führendes Vorstandsmitglied* (party manager) of the DNVP in Berlin, received a long registered letter from the DNVP Konstanz district association (on Lake Constance), which reflected the mood among that district's party members.[1] At a function organized by the Konstanz chapter of the conservative Berlin Herrenclub[2] on 18 March, a German National speaker from Berlin had argued that the DNVP Reichstag faction was currently divided into three groups: the first was made up of Hugenberg and his followers, though Hugenberg concentrated almost exclusively on his various ministerial offices; the second and presumably largest included those who "advocated immediate fusion with Hitler and the National Socialists"; and the third had formed around deputy chairman Friedrich von Winterfeld, who wanted to carry the party forward as an independent force "in the spirit of Old Prussia."[3] Given current tensions and

1. Major Hans Nagel, born 1872, retired army major.
2. There were branches of the Herrenclub throughout the Reich. Mostly conservative in orientation, the club sought to bring together not only party members but also "personalities from business, politics, arts and sciences, public administration and the military." For a general characterization, see Fritz Günther von Tschirschky, *Erinnerungen eines Hochverräters* (Stuttgart, 1972), 56–60.
3. 4 April 1933 at BA Berlin-Lichterfelde, "DNVP, Krisen in der Partei," R 8005, no. 11, 6–11. The speech was given by a Dr. Sievers at a closed meeting of the Konstanz branch of the Herrenclub.

contradictions, the speaker maintained, it was but a matter of time
before the DNVP would be wholly absorbed by National Socialism.[4] As the letter writer reported, this speech of a DNVP representative from the capital caused immense consternation among
German Nationals in Konstanz. The Konstanz district association
strongly urged that the DNVP be preserved as a counterweight to
National Socialism, for otherwise the danger of a Nazi dictatorship
would become very real, even though "the highly developed German *Volk* in its intellectual, cultural, ethnic, and finally, political
diversity would never countenance a fascist regime and one-party
dictatorship, no matter how things appeared at the moment. We
are not Italians."[5] The unrest caused in Konstanz by this speech
was heightened "by the surprising resignation of Dr. Oberfohren,"
chairman of the DNVP Reichstag faction and Hugenberg's long-
time confidant.[6]

The unlawful search of the DNVP faction leader's office and
house, followed by his resignation at the end of March and finally
his death on 7 May—the circumstances of which were never fully
clarified—inaugurated the beginning of the last chapter in the party's history. Ernst Oberfohren, born in Mühlheim/Ruhr in 1881
and a *Gymnasium* teacher by profession, joined the DNVP shortly
after its foundation, then served as a member of the National Assembly and became DNVP Reichstag deputy for Schleswig-Holstein in
1920.[7] In the intra-party strife that followed losses in the May 1928
Reichstag election, Oberfohren sided with Hugenberg. As Hugenberg's confidant, he succeeded Kuno Graf von Westarp as Reichstag
faction leader in December 1929. Until Hitler's accession to power,
Oberfohren was known as Hugenberg's intimate advisor and close
comrade-in-arms. Initially, despite reservations, he also seemed to
have supported the alliance with the NSDAP, which he saw as an
opportunity for the DNVP to attain governing power at long last.[8]
The alliance with the NSDAP, however, must have been difficult for
Oberfohren to swallow, since he had been involved in acrimonious

4. Ibid., 8.
5. Ibid., 10.
6. Ibid., 8.
7. Peter Wulf, "Ernst Oberfohren und die DNVP am Ende der Weimarer
Republik," in Erich Hoffmann and Peter Wulf, eds., *Wir bauen das Reich. Aufstieg
und erste Herrschaftsjahre des Nationalsozialismus in Schleswig-Holstein* (Neumünster,
1983), 165–187.
8. Ibid., 179.

disagreements with the NSDAP in Schleswig-Holstein in 1931 and 1932. After the Reichstag elections of May and December 1924, the DNVP had become the strongest party there with 33 percent of the vote, well ahead of even the SPD.[9] After 1928, Oberfohren, much to his chagrin, was a powerless onlooker as the NSDAP rapidly undermined the position of his party. In the July 1932 Reichstag elections, the NSDAP gained 51 percent of the vote in Schleswig-Holstein, while the DNVP was reduced to a mere 6.6 percent.[10]

Oberfohren also had the opportunity to learn firsthand about Nazi machinations, given that the neighboring *Freistaat* Oldenburg had had a National Socialist government since May 1932. Dr. Ernst Evers, DNVP leader for the Lübeck region, which at that time was part of Oldenburg (today comparable approximately to the Eutin district), gave several speeches warning of the violent measures used by the Nazis in Schleswig-Holstein.[11] Since the Lübeck-Eutin district of the Oldenburg territory was surrounded by Schleswig-Holstein, Oberfohren had ample opportunity to become acquainted with the reality of Nazi rule well before 1933. The ruthlessness with which the Nazis exercised their power in Oldenburg in the summer and autumn of 1932 should have served as a clear warning to all German Nationals, since it exposed only too plainly the unlawful nature of National Socialist rule. The vindictiveness of the Nazi government in Oldenburg and Oberfohren's tense relationship with the Schleswig-Holstein *Gauleiter* Hinrich Lohse served to increase his mistrust toward National Socialism and its adherents.[12] It is

9. Jürgen Falter et al., eds., *Wahlen und Abstimmungen in der Weimarer Republik. Materialien zum Wahlverhalten 1919–1933* (Munich, 1986), 70. In the elections to the National Assembly, the SPD had obtained 45.7 percent, as opposed to 7.7 for the DNVP; in May 1924, the DNVP had surpassed the SPD, by 31 to 24.9 percent; in December 1924 the ratio was 33 to 30.3. Ibid., 67–70.

10. Ibid., 71–75. Whereas the NSDAP obtained only 4 percent in Schleswig-Holstein in 1928 (compared with 23 for the DNVP), it attained 27 percent in September 1930 (DNVP 6.1) and 51 percent in July 1932 (DNVP 6.6). That the same voters supported the two parties became apparent in the November 1932 elections, when the NSDAP dropped to 45.7 percent while the DNVP increased its share to 10.3.

11. Lawrence D. Stokes, "Conservative Opposition to Nazism in Eutin, Schleswig-Holstein, 1932–1933," in Francis R. Nicosia and Lawrence D. Stokes, eds., *Germans against Nazism. Essays in Honor of Peter Hoffmann* (New York and Oxford, 1990), 37–57.

12. See Wulf, "Ernst Oberfohren und die DNVP." Hinrich Lohse (1896–1964), who had been *Gauleiter* in Schleswig-Holstein since 1925, became *Oberpräsident* of the province on 29 March 1933; later, from November 1941 to

difficult to discern which factor was more important in Oberfohren's decision to agree initially to his party's alliance with the NSDAP: his loyalty to Hugenberg, to whom he was beholden for his position within the party, or the chance for the DNVP to participate in governing the country. It is certain that very soon after 30 January 1933 Oberfohren realized that it had been a mistake to tie the DNVP to the Nazi party, and by mid February he already started to oppose Hugenberg's course and argued vehemently against a tight alliance with Hitler. On 10 February, Reinhold Quaatz noted in his diary: "Four hour long faction session. Strong sentiment against Hugenberg whipped up by Oberfohren."[13] On 12 February, Oberfohren openly expressed his opposition to Hugenberg's political course in a conversation with Quaatz. This was prompted by Hugenberg's demand that all DNVP deputies commit to a solemn declaration that would compel them to support unreservedly all Cabinet decisions. According to Quaatz, Oberfohren said that "this would be the desired way out for him," that is, the final reason to break with Hugenberg.[14] The declaration was indeed designed to give Hugenberg carte blanche: "I hereby give my word of honor to the leader of the DNVP that, in the case of my election to the Reichstag, I shall unreservedly support those measures of the Cabinet of the government of national consolidation designated by him."[15] With this declaration, Hugenberg obviously wanted to impose party discipline: whoever did not comply would no longer be put on the party's electoral list. On 7 March, Quaatz noted that Oberfohren seemed to be gaining supporters within the party against Hugenberg[16] and on 12 March, Hugenberg, now fully aware of the treacherous behavior of his faction chairman, confided to Quaatz: "Oberfohren will not again be elected faction chair."[17] Despite his strong resistance to Hugenberg's policies, Oberfohren's own views were just as antiparliamentarian and opposed to Weimar democracy as Hugenberg's. At an election rally on 17 February, for example, he declared: "Once

1944, he was Reich Commissar for the Baltic countries and Belarussia (*Reichskommissariat Ostland*). See Hermann Weiß, ed., *Biographisches Lexikon zum Dritten Reich*, 2nd ed. (Frankfurt, 1998), 304–305; Robert S. Wistrich, *Who's Who in Nazi Germany* (London and New York, 1995), 159.

13. Weiß and Hoser, eds., *Die Deutschnationalen*, 233.
14. Ibid., diary entry of 12 February 1933, 234.
15. Ibid., 244, note 50.
16. Ibid., diary entry of 7 March 1933, 229.
17. Ibid., diary entry of 12 March 1933, 241.

we have gained a majority [on 5 March], we will not play the parliamentary game. Then an Enabling Act will be drawn up and the
Reichstag will be sent home for one or two years."[18] Further dis-
agreement broke out during a tumultuous faction meeting on 20
March: "Hugenberg gave a very clumsy report. Oberfohren stirred
up trouble," while in another meeting two days later, which took
place without Hugenberg, Oberfohren got "the faction to come out
in support of him."[19] This seems surprising, given that tension must
have arisen between Oberfohren and the DNVP parliamentary faction just before 22 March, as former chancellor Heinrich Brüning of
the Center Party reported in his memoirs. On the bus trip to the
ceremonial opening of the Reichstag in Potsdam on 21 March,
"Oberfohren of the German National faction did not sit with his
own faction in their bus, but instead sat by himself in one of ours."[20]
During the next faction meeting on 24 March, open conflict erupted
between Hugenberg and Oberfohren, in the course of which
Hugenberg apparently succeeded in getting the faction to side with
him.[21] In the meantime, it had not escaped the National Socialists
that the DNVP faction chairman had become a dangerous opponent, who agitated against them within his party. Oberfohren's disagreements with Hugenberg were well known and, in the tense
atmosphere of March 1933, when Nazi surveillance of their opponents was the order of the day, it was practically to be expected that
Oberfohren's telephone calls would be monitored.[22] The Prussian
police, now led by a National Socialist as acting Interior Minister
(Hermann Göring), were thus informed of Oberfohren's activities
down to the last detail. Before his return to his native Kiel,

18. *Frankfurter Zeitung*, Nr. 133, 18 February 1933, cited in Morsey, "Das 'Ermächtigungsgesetz' vom 24. März 1933," 25, note 1.

19. Quaatz, diary entry of 22 March, in Weiß and Hoser, eds., *Die Deutschna-tionalen*, 243–244. Even though Oberfohren and Quaatz had few common points of reference, Brüning mentions both in the same breath in his memoirs, prais-ing them as independent financial experts: "For men such as Oberfohren and Quaatz, as well as Hilferding and Hertz of the SPD, it was ultimately not so important which parties formed the government. What mattered to them was attaining a guarantee of loyal cooperation and a responsible fiscal policy." Hein-rich Brüning, *Memoiren 1918–1934* (Stuttgart, 1970), 115.

20. Brüning, *Memoiren*, 657. Since special buses had been rented for each party, Oberfohren's action was highly unusual.

21. Wulf, "Ernst Oberfohren und die DNVP," 182.

22. Fritz Tobias, *Der Reichstagsbrand. Legende und Wirklichkeit* (Rastatt, 1962), 174–175.

Oberfohren had a long phone conversation with his Berlin secretary on 26 March to give her instructions about the copying and possible distribution of letters directed against Hugenberg from his opponents inside the party.[23] Göring immediately ordered searches of Oberfohren's Berlin office and Kiel house; these took place on 26 and 27 March.[24] Several of the letters were seized in early April, and the Nazi paper *Braunschweiger Landeszeitung* published excerpts from them with piquant, unflattering details about Hugenberg. Despite the blatant breach of Oberfohren's immunity as a Reichstag deputy, his own party failed to protest the unlawful actions of the police. No doubt intimidated by this ruthless employment of state power, compromised by the letters, which at the very least indicated his disloyalty toward Hugenberg—an indelible blot on one's escutcheon among conservatives who constantly mouthed the ideal of *Nibelungentreue*—and totally deserted by his party, Oberfohren became resigned to his political fate. At the end of March, he relinquished his Reichstag seat and withdrew embittered to Kiel.[25] When press reports about Oberfohren's resignation appeared on 30 and 31 March, there was great surprise among the general public, especially since on 23 March (following the DNVP faction meeting that had gone in Oberfohren's favor) premature reports of his re-election as DNVP faction chair had appeared.[26] Speculation as to the reasons behind Oberfohren's surprising step initially led to a futile guessing game.[27] Since the accounts of the *Braunschweiger Landeszeitung*

23. These were letters from DNVP members critical of Hugenberg, which Oberfohren had collected for further distribution. See Wulf, "Ernst Oberfohren und die DNVP," 182–184.

24. Ibid., 183–184. Hiller von Gaertingen, "DNVP," 596, dates the house searches 29 and 30 March. Broszat, *Der Staat Hitlers*, 121, and Hans-Ullrich Thamer, *Verführung und Gewalt. Deutschland 1933–1945* (Berlin, 1986), 286, also date the office search on 29 March. The surveys by Broszat and Thamer presumably followed Hiller von Gaertingen, whereas Wulf carried out his own archival research in Schleswig-Holstein and may therefore be considered the most reliable source. According to Wulf, the search in Oberfohren's Berlin office already took place on 26 March, that of his Kiel apartment on the morning of 27 March; see Wulf, "Ernst Oberfohren und die DNVP," 183.

25. Wulf, "Ernst Oberfohren und die DNVP," 184.

26. See, for example, "Dr. Oberfohren wieder Vorsitzender der deutschnationalen Reichstagsfraktion," *Pommersche Tagespost*, 23 March at BA Berlin-Lichterfelde, "Pressearchiv Reichslandbund, Organisiertes Bürgertum," R 8034 II, no. 9021, 6.

27. See, for example, "Mandatsniederlegung des deutschnationalen Fraktionsführers Dr. Oberfohren," *Deutsche Zeitung*, 30 March 1933; "Unsere Meinung,"

regarding the letters critical of Hugenberg were reprinted by other National Socialist newspapers (especially in Schleswig-Holstein), Hugenberg was compelled to make a public announcement about the Oberfohren matter at a DNVP faction meeting on 12 April. After all, in letters now made public there was talk to the effect that Hugenberg "was useless as a minister" and that he had to "disappear."[28] Press coverage on the issue was extensive, especially in the Berlin press—the *Berliner Tageblatt*, the *12 Uhr Blatt*, and the *Deutsche Zeitung*—and made the front pages.[29] According to extensive, mutually corroborating newspaper reports, which reproduced Hugenberg's explanation to the DNVP faction, Oberfohren was dissatisfied with the policies Hugenberg had adopted since Hitler came to power and freely gave vent to these feelings during his last faction meeting of 24 March. During the search of Oberfohren's office, anonymous circulars had been unearthed that, according to the sworn testimony of Oberfohren's secretary, had been dictated by Oberfohren himself and prepared by him for distribution. According to Hugenberg, who emphasized that the searches had taken place without his knowledge, Oberfohren's sudden resignation had to be taken as confirmation of his secretary's statement and, in effect, as an admission of guilt. The very fact that the chairman of the parliamentary faction had conspired against him, Hugenberg contended, made it impossible to undertake any legal steps regarding the "doubtlessly illegal" searches.[30] In his post as faction chair, Oberfohren was succeeded by Otto Schmidt-Hannover,[31] former

---

Deutsche Allgemeine Zeitung, 31 March, at BA Berlin-Lichterfelde, "Pressearchiv Reichslandbund," R 8034 II, no. 9021, ibid.

28. Wulf, "Ernst Oberfohren und die DNVP," 184, note 84.

29. These articles are collected in BA Berlin-Lichterfelde, "Pressearchiv Reichslandbund, DNVP Parteitage," R 8034 II, no. 4334, 65–66; and "Pressearchiv Reichslandbund, Organisiertes Bürgertum," R 8034 II, no. 9021, 7–9. On the Oberfohren case, see also Leopold, *Alfred Hugenberg*, 148–150 and Hiller von Gaertingen, "Die Deutschnationale Volkspartei," 596–597. Karl-Dietrich Bracher, *Stufen der Machtergreifung* (Berlin, 1974), 291, merely states that Oberfohren had been "replaced" by Otto Schmidt-Hannover on 11 April 1933 and does not mention that he resigned his mandate.

30. According to identical reports of 12 April in the *12 Uhr Blatt*, the *Deutsche Zeitung*, *Der Tag*, and the *München-Augsburger Abendzeitung*, Oberfohren disputed the charge of writing the circulars himself. See Leopold, *Alfred Hugenberg*, 255, note 64.

31. Otto Schmidt-Hannover (from the electoral district Hannover), born 1888 (there was another Schmidt in the DNVP faction who hailed from Neukölln). According to Schmidt-Hannover's memoirs, *Umdenken oder Anarchie*

World War I officer, member of the DNVP Reichstag faction since 1924, and a close associate of Hugenberg. Hugenberg's tacit admission that personal animosities were more important to him than constitutional principles is indeed revealing. Since his former comrade-in-arms was evidently in the process of betraying him, Hugenberg had a ready-made alibi for his inaction: due process could be dispensed with in the case of betrayal. On the other hand, one might argue that he was simply afraid to challenge Göring, especially since Oberfohren's career had ended anyway.[32]

On Monday 8 May, scarcely a month after these events, the press reported that the former DNVP faction chairman, Dr. Ernst Oberfohren, had shot himself in his Kiel apartment and died.[33] Murder as the cause of death seemed more likely than suicide, given recent history: Oberfohren's known aversion to National Socialism, his hostility toward the Schleswig-Holstein Gauleiter Hinrich Lohse, the continuous campaign against Oberfohren in the Nazi press, and the ever-spreading Nazi despotism and reign of terror that had also claimed numerous casualties in Schleswig-Holstein.[34] To add to all this, the entire Schleswig-Holstein SA held rallies in Kiel at which explicit threats against opponents of the regime were made.[35] In DNVP circles people were equally reluctant to subscribe to the suicide version. Hugenberg, for example, cautioned the party

---

(Göttingen, 1959), 349, Oberfohren suffered a "mental and physical collapse" on 22 March, which seems hardly likely, since Oberfohren participated in the party faction meeting of 24 March. Schmidt-Hannover also argued that Oberfohren blamed Hugenberg for remaining in the government after the Reichstag fire since he believed that Nazis had set the blaze.

32. On 11 April Hitler appointed Göring to the office of deputy Reich Commissar and Minister President of Prussia after Franz von Papen had resigned as Prussian Reich Commissar on 7 April. In his numerous protests to Hitler and Göring about Nazi attacks, Hugenberg had always been concerned solely with DNVP members. He never protested the principle of these attacks, that is, he never defended the abstract idea of the Rechtsstaat, even though it was generally expected that the DNVP would uphold *rechtsstaatliche Grundsätze*.

33. See BA Berlin-Lichterfelde, "Pressearchiv Reichslandbund, Organisiertes Bürgertum," R 8034 II, no. 9021, 30. Oberfohren's body was discovered by the maid, since his wife was away from home at the time. On Oberfohren's death, see also Fritz Tobias, *The Reichstag Fire* (New York, 1964), 104–109.

34. See also Schmidt-Hannover, *Umdenken oder Anarchie*, 350, who argues that suicide would not have been compatible with Oberfohren's religious beliefs.

35. Wulf, "Ernst Oberfohren und die DNVP," 186; Schmidt-Hannover, *Umdenken oder Anarchie*, 350; Hiller von Gaertingen, "DNVP," 606.

executive board during the DNVP's last meeting before its dissolution: "If any report should be circulated in the near future that I was
said to have committed suicide, please be assured that this will not
be the truth."[36]

The theory that Oberfohren was murdered emerged in passing
after the Second World War in memoirs and historical accounts,
whose authors usually made references to a questionable suicide. In
the summer of 1933 the KPD had published a *Braunbuch* about the
Reichstag fire in which the Nazis were accused of being the arsonists.
Included was the so-called "Oberfohren Memorandum" that allegedly identified National Socialists as the perpetrators. According to
the *Braunbuch*, Oberfohren had collected incriminating evidence in
his capacity as the faction chair of one of the two governing parties.
This evidence, summarized in his memorandum, supposedly sealed
his fate, and as an opponent of National Socialism and a bothersome
witness to their actions, according to the *Braunbuch*, he was killed
by the Nazis. Due to its communist authorship, contemporaries dis-
counted the *Braunbuch* allegations, especially since Oberfohren was
then no longer alive to set matters straight. In 1962 Fritz Tobias finally relegated these and other contentions to the realm of legend.[37]
Today the general assumption is that Oberfohren did indeed commit
suicide, a view bolstered by the testimony of Oberfohren's widow,
who categorically ruled out murder.[38] It still remains unclear when

36. Schmidt-Hannover, *Umdenken oder Anarchie*, 354.

37. Fritz Tobias, *Der Reichstagsbrand. Legende und Wirklichkeit* (Rastatt, 1962),
171–192; Wulf, "Ernst Oberfohren und die DNVP," 166. For the English text
of the "Oberfohren Memorandum," see Fritz Tobias, *The Reichstag Fire* (New
York, 1964), 293–312. First hints of the existence of a confidential note that
charged the Nazis with setting fire to the Reichstag appeared (without nam-
ing names) in two articles in the *Manchester Guardian*. Tobias minutely speci-
fies textual contradictions and inconsistencies and shows that the awkward style
of the memorandum cannot be reconciled with Oberfohren's excellent formal
education. ("In fact, the German text of the Memorandum was written by an
uneducated hack and could not possibly have stemmed from the pen of Dr.
Oberfohren, who had studied at the Universities of Berlin, Bonn and Kiel."
Tobias, *Reichstag Fire*, 110).

38. *Der Spiegel*, no. 48 (1959), 49; Hiller von Gaertingen, "DNVP," 606,
note 7. Broszat, *Der Staat Hitlers*, 121, writes of the "mysterious suicide" of
Oberfohren. Tobias refers to the widow's letter: "My husband was not killed
by the Nazis; however, he felt he had become the object of a campaign of persecution and, realizing that the Nazi dictatorship was bound to lead to disaster
for Germany and her people, he committed suicide in black despair." Tobias,
The Reichstag Fire, 109. On 3 May, Oberfohren already had mentioned suicide

exactly Oberfohren turned against Hugenberg, in what political direction he would have steered the DNVP faction, what actions he
might have taken against the DNVP's powerful coalition partner,
and what, in the end, was the direct cause of his death—or—the
reasons for his suicide.

"False Friends": Nazis Turn Their "Revolutionary Fervor" against German Nationals

Oberfohren's death, which the National Socialist press unanimously
interpreted as a suicide, was naturally exploited for propaganda
purposes. Oberfohren, having studied at several universities, epitomized in many ways the traditional *Bildungsbürger* and the values of
the intellectual elite, the *Bildungsbürgertum*. In the Nazi press he was
now portrayed as a relic of a bygone era, whose demise was long
overdue, and his death presented as a symptom of the deep crisis in
which the bourgeoisie was mired. The age of a bourgeois way of
life, including bourgeois behavior, manners, and elitist education—
the main purpose of which was to establish and perpetuate class
barriers—was now, so the argument went, over. The youth of the
new Germany rejected the bourgeoisie, with its outmoded formalities and values, and looked down upon its members as inferior in
character and personality. Triumphantly the Nazi press proclaimed
that the epoch of bourgeois arrogance, superciliousness, formalized
education, ostentatious wealth, and class conceit was now consigned
to the past.[39]

In April and May 1933, the National Socialists turned their attention to the DNVP as the main impediment on the road to complete
power and accordingly fought them at every turn. This battle took
place in full public view. Nazi leaders made no bones about the fact
that the elimination of "*die Reaktion*"—and by that they meant the

---

to a journalist and spoken of the countless threats made against him. In a letter to Hugenberg, published by the German National press service a day after
Oberfohren's death, Oberfohren had spoken of his inner anguish ("I myself have
suffered almost superhuman agonies during the last few weeks . . ." Tobias, ibid.,
108–109).

39. BA Berlin-Lichterfelde, "Pressearchiv des Reichslandbundes, Nationalsozialisten und DNVP," Vol. II, 16 September 1932–13 July 1933," R 8034 II,
no. 9030, 183; "Das Ende des Bürgers. Zum Selbstmord Dr. Oberfohrens," 9
May 1933.

conservative establishment—was their next objective. "Everywhere among the people one speaks of a second revolution that is about to occur," Joseph Goebbels noted in his diary on 18 April: "This means nothing else than that the first revolution has not yet come to a proper conclusion. We will now soon have to deal with the Re-action. The revolution must stop nowhere."[40] Nazi attacks against the conservative *"Reaktion"* took place on multiple fronts, as they simultaneously attempted to replace the German National People's Party as the party that represented German conservative values and traditions, to remove German National officials from political and administrative positions, as well as posts in professional associations, and to intimidate or terrorize members of the DNVP and its affili-ated organizations.

In the fratricidal struggle of nationalist forces, National Social-ists increasingly tread upon the time-honored turf of German Na-tionals and began to preempt national symbols traditionally claimed by conservatives. The goal was to supplant the German Nation-als as the main standard-bearers of traditional national symbols, of nationalism, and of a Prussian past that stood for military might and success. Though the Nazis vehemently attacked bourgeois, con-servative values, they made every effort to co-opt symbols of the German past that had customarily been associated with conserva-tives. In Silesia, a former stronghold of the German Nationals that was now firmly in Nazi hands, the NSDAP employed its politics of symbols to contest the DNVP's claim to be heir to the tradition of the wars of liberation against France in 1813.[41] At the beginning of April 1933, National Socialists celebrated the 120th anniversary of the swearing in of the *Lützower Freikorps* with great pageantry and exploited the occasion by proclaiming that the same martial spirit of revolutionary awakening that had animated Lützow's vol-unteer corps 120 years before now pervaded the National Socialist movement.[42] In 1813, as in 1933, Silesia was proclaimed to be the

40. Joseph Goebbels, *Vom Kaiserhof zur Reichskanzlei. Eine historische Darstel-lung in Tagebuchblättern* (Munich, 1940), 300.

41. In provincial district elections in Lower Silesia, the DNVP gained 26 percent of the vote in 1925, 22 in 1929, and 9 in 1933; the NSDAP obtained a mere 5.2 percent in 1929, but 51.7 in 1933. See Falter, "Wahlen und Abstim-mungen in der Weimarer Republik," 105.

42. BA Berlin-Lichterfelde, "DNVP, Politischer Schriftwechsel 1933," R 8005, no. 19, 43. The *Freikorps* of Adolf Freiherr von Lützow (1782–1834) was a symbol of mass rebellion against Napoleon, though it is debatable whether

birthplace of the German nation. German Nationals, who attended the celebration, must have been struck by the perverse combination of symbols: Luther's chorale "Nun danket alle Gott," the hymn *par excellence* of patriotic Prussians, was followed by the "Horst Wessel Lied," the SA marching song and Nazi hymn. The National Socialist Silesian Gauleiter and *Oberpräsident* of Lower Silesia, Helmuth Brückner, crowned the paradoxical spectacle by ending the ceremony with a warning against "false" friends. The open enemies, he said, had been taken care of; now it was the turn of the false friend, who must be fought with the same ruthlessness.[43] This was an unmistakable reference to the German Nationals. For the Nazis, appropriating national symbols and celebrations was a means to bolster their own legitimacy and was necessarily directed against their own political ally. Brückner's words were no hollow threat.

In the spring, the DNVP Berlin headquarters, other central party offices, and DNVP deputies found themselves swamped with a flood of complaints about Nazi attacks from all corners of the Reich. This testified to the fact that all was not well between the unequal coalition partners. Friedrich von Winterfeld, the deputy party chairman, received alarming reports from Wiesbaden, according to which the NSDAP had instigated local coup attempts in the Prussian province of Hessen-Nassau to remove the incumbent *Landräte* (the heads of county administrations) and take over their administrative offices. The DNVP *Gauverband* Wiesbaden, painfully aware of the impotence of its own party, requested that Winterfeld contact Papen and ask for his assistance.[44] At the same time, a complaint was delivered from neighboring Frankfurt to the effect that the DNVP was passed over as vacant municipal posts were being filled, even though the German Nationals had competent experts, who were

---

mass revolts ever took place. Known as the "Black Band" because of its uniforms, it attracted many students and often operated behind enemy lines. See "120-Jahr Feier der Vereidigung des Lützower Freikorps," *Schlesischer Volksbote*, no. 79, 3 April 1933.

43. BA Berlin-Lichterfelde, "DNVP, Politischer Schriftwechsel 1933," R 8005, no. 19, 43. Helmuth Brückner, born 1896 in Peilau/Silesia, died in a Soviet camp, probably in 1954. Officer in the First World War; later participated in Upper Silesian border skirmishes. NSDAP Reichstag deputy since September 1930, from 25 March 1933 *Oberpräsident* of Lower Silesia; expelled from the party in December 1934 in the wake of events surrounding the Röhm putsch.

44. 8 April 1933 at BA Berlin-Lichterfelde, "DNVP, Politischer Schriftwechsel 1933," R 8005, no. 19, 61–61 verso. "Gauverband Wiesbaden an Dr. v. Winterfeld."

"understandably" missing among the Nazis: "We hardly have the feeling here that we have a brother party next to us, as we are simply being pushed against the wall . . ."[45] The DNVP Hannover East Land Association in Lüneburg reported that German National mayors of rural communities might defect to the NSDAP just to be confirmed in their offices. In several instances this had already happened. And at the higher appellate court (*Oberlandesgericht*) in Celle, a German National judge was about to be replaced with a member of the Nazi party. Unless the situation was quickly remedied, German National officials would soon be ousted from all influential positions.[46] From Magdeburg came the alarming communication that the Nazi *Gauleiter* of Magdeburg-Anhalt, Wilhelm Loeper, had circulated allegations in the local Nazi press that the SPD and DNVP were voting each other onto municipal councils to keep National Socialists out. Loeper threatened that "potential traitors to the idea of the national revolution would be taught otherwise," a warning aimed directly at the German Nationals.[47] From Berlin, a DNVP deputy of the Prussian parliament reported that many teachers and other civil servants, who had traditionally leaned to the political left but suddenly switched allegiance to become newly minted NSDAP members, were now given preference over experienced conservative civil servants in the appointment to new posts. As a result, the conservative, national-minded electorate felt abandoned and hoped that a solid legal basis for the "national awakening" could soon be established.[48] Further complaints arrived from Thuringia, where National Socialists under the direction of *Gauleiter* Fritz Sauckel kept gatherings of the ex-servicemen's organization *Stahlhelm* under close

45. 8 April 1933 at BA Berlin-Lichterfelde, "DNVP, Politischer Schriftwechsel 1933," R 8005, no. 19, 62–62 verso, "Carl Hill an Exzellenz Hergt."

46. 5 April 1933 at BA Berlin-Lichterfelde, "DNVP, Politischer Schriftwechsel 1933," R 8005, no. 19, 65–68.

47. 7 April 1933 at BA Berlin-Lichterfelde, "DNVP, Politischer Schriftwechsel 1933," R 8005, no. 19, 87. "Anruf Fischer Magdeburg." See also the *Magdeburger Tageszeitung* of 9 April. The SPD was outlawed on 22 June 1933. In his appeal to his "party comrades," Loeper wrote: "Since this kind of betrayal of the nation is directed against the national revolution, I ask you to take the necessary revolutionary measures that will teach a lesson to potential traitors of the national revolution." Wilhelm Loeper (1883–1935), a professional officer, forced to resign from the Reichswehr after his participation in the Beer Hall putsch in 1923. He became *Gauleiter* of Magdeburg-Anhalt in 1928.

48. 4 April 1933 at BA Berlin-Lichterfelde, "DNVP, Politischer Schriftwechsel," R 8005, no. 19, 88.

surveillance, allegedly to forestall the admission of Marxists.[49] In a disquieting dispatch from East Prussia it was mentioned that Nazis there were wantonly taking advantage of their unchecked power, not paying heed to the orders from the county and district councilor (*Landrat* and *Regierungspräsident*). DNVP members had thus become defenseless prey[50] and felt virtually outlawed. In the Neumark (DNVP Frankfurt/Oder Land Association), the administrative heads of small communities were practically forced to abandon the DNVP for the NSDAP to keep their posts, and many German Nationals joined the NSDAP purely for fear of being discriminated against. DNVP members there now seemed almost completely barred from holding posts in municipal administrations,[51] while it was all too apparent that local Nazi leaders openly disregarded directives from the party leadership in Berlin that were aimed at maintaining a truce between the NSDAP and DNVP.

From the town of Arendsee in the Altmark, for example, came a plea for assistance from a German National mayor, who, fearing the loss of his position and pension, as well as the instigation of disciplinary proceedings, sought protection from the local NSDAP.[52] From Reichenbach in the Silesian Erzgebirge came the complaint that the NSDAP was trying to place "its inexperienced and uneducated functionaries" into positions everywhere, while "national-minded, patriotic men were being more fiercely opposed than Marxists.[53] Protests that "national-minded, patriotic" citizens, and no longer only Marxists, had now become the prime target of attacks were voiced frequently. The discouraging realization that no help could be expected from the police, who would not even follow up on

49. 4 April 1933 at BA Berlin-Lichterfelde, "DNVP, Politischer Schriftwechsel," R 8005, no. 19, 90–92. Fritz Sauckel, 1894–1946, *Gauleiter* of Thuringia since 1927; Prime Minister and Minister of the Interior of Thuringia since 26 August 1932; appointed *Reichsstatthalter* (Reich Governor) on 5 May 1933. For his role in the deportation and exploitation of millions of forced laborers he was sentenced to death in Nuremberg on 1 October 1946.

50. 7 April 1933 at BA Berlin-Lichterfelde, "DNVP, Politischer Schriftwechsel," R 8005, no. 19, "Landesverband Ostpreußen an Parteizentrale," 94–95 verso (the term used was "*vogelfrei*").

51. 1 April 1933 at BA Berlin-Lichterfelde, "DNVP, Politischer Schriftwechsel," R 8005, no. 19, 101–103.

52. 3 April 1933 at BA Berlin-Lichterfelde, "DNVP, Politischer Schriftwechsel," R 8005, no. 19, 44–45.

53. Ibid., 42.

complaints, became widespread.[54] The DNVP head office, to which most complaints were directed, was hardly in a position to provide help. But even though little could be done to bring the reported assaults under control, they were at least documented, and Hugenberg could raise this matter during Cabinet meetings. SPD and Center Party members, by contrast, had far fewer venues to air grievances or lodge complaints, and virtually no opportunity to publicize the assaults made against them. During the months of the seizure of power, especially in the spring of 1933, many crimes thus remained not only unpunished, but also completely undocumented.

Loss of Influence in Economic and Professional Organizations

Besides an obvious loss of influence in local politics, where the conservative *Bürgertum* had traditionally been well represented, German Nationals were even ousted from their traditional bastions—economic organizations and professional and civil service associations. As early as 4 April, at a meeting in the Reich Chancellery, Hugenberg complained that "recently SA men had arrested leaders and affiliates of Commercial Chambers, who were registered members of the DNVP." Hermann Göring, who as provisional Prussian Interior Minister was ultimately responsible for these incursions, countered that the arrests were made "at the instigation of the responsible public prosecutor" (which was clearly not true) and that, in any case, the composition of the Chambers of Commerce in no way reflected "current political conditions," so that it was "not possible for him to restrain the SA."[55] Göring knew only too well that

54. This is emphasized, for example, in a letter of 7 April addressed to DNVP headquarters: "We enclose herewith a complaint about a National Socialist encroachment. For well known reasons we refrained from forwarding this to police headquarters" (ibid., "Politischer Schriftwechsel," 40). The Prussian police were directly subordinate to Göring and, as such, bound by his directives. Following the takeover of the remaining governments by mid March, the situation there had become similar to that in Prussia. Since the livelihood of the ordinary policeman and his family depended entirely on whether he obeyed the orders of his Nazi superiors, it would be unrealistic to expect noncompliance.

55. BA Berlin-Lichterfelde, "Reichskanzlei, NSDAP," R 43 II, no. 1195, 207–208, "Auszug aus der Niederschrift über die Sitzung des Reichsministeriums" of 4 April 1933; reprinted in Karl-Heinz Minuth, ed., *Akten der Reichskanzlei*, 293–294; see also BA Koblenz, Nachlaß Hugenberg, N 1231, no. 89, "Ausschreitungen der NSDAP gegen DNVP Mitglieder."

practically all such actions had their roots in deliberate provocations by the local SA, and that the majority of the arrests were carried out without warrants. All told, however, Hugenberg's protests did have some success. At a Cabinet meeting on 22 April, Hitler and Göring promised to take the necessary measures to stop interference with business associations and public authorities.[56] With immediate effect, subordinate bureaus of Nazi party organizations were thereupon prohibited from appointing commissioners, who might take over business corporations, banks, or professional organizations and thus disrupt economic and political life.[57]

Nevertheless, complaints and calls for help continued throughout April and May. The Frankfurt chairman of the *Reichsverband Deutscher Dentisten*, Alex Stein, for example, complained in a letter to Hugenberg about National Socialist incursions. In a recent meeting of his organization, a specially dispatched Nazi leader had announced that, just as in parliaments, National Socialists must in the future comprise 51 percent of the executive boards of German dental associations,[58] which required the removal of the current German National chairman. Stein lamented that the way in which "big brother bullies us around" was no longer bearable.[59] Everyone was afraid "to suffer economic harm if they did not side with National Socialism."[60] Stein consequently requested that Hugenberg use his influence inside the government to ensure that "no more violent intrusions in professional associations occur . . ."[61] Another dental association, the *Reichsverband der Zahnärzte*, which was also to be brought in line with Nazi policies, lodged a similar complaint. When the Lübeck dentist Karl Mauss was elected executive chairman of the district chapter of this association, attending Nazi members rejected the outcome with the argument that only

56. See Minuth, ed., *Akten der Reichskanzlei*, 365. It would be wrong to assume that the Nazi leadership wanted to mollify Hugenberg, while lower ranks were carrying out attacks against German Nationals. It was in the interest of Nazi leaders to give the impression that law and order prevailed in Germany in order to pacify public opinion inside the country and abroad. In April and May, they took the danger of foreign intervention very seriously.

57. See also Hiller von Gaertingen, "DNVP," 600.

58. 1 April 1933 at BA Berlin-Lichterfelde, "Akten der Reichskanzlei, NSDAP," R 43 II, no. 1195, 233–235, esp. 234.

59. Ibid., 234.

60. Ibid., 235.

61. Ibid., 235. Hugenberg forwarded a report of this incident together with other complaints to Hitler on 12 April; see BA Berlin-Lichterfelde, "Akten der Reichskanzlei, NSDAP," R 43 II, no. 1195, 211–212.

an NSDAP member could be elected executive chairman. Mauss complained about the absurdity of demanding such a biased party-political connection for a representative of a professional body, especially since there were only a few Nazi party members among his colleagues, and most of them had joined only recently.[62] These cases were representative of a more general phenomenon. DNVP members voiced the concern that "German National chairmen of commercial and business associations, who are not exactly fighters by nature, are letting themselves be removed from office to the detriment of the German National cause."[63] And on 12 April the *Leipziger Neueste Nachrichten* ran an article under the headline, "The Bringing into Line of Civil Service Organizations," reporting that an official announcement had been issued in the Leipzig district declaring that professional associations of industry, commerce, and trade now could be headed only by men who "belong to the NSDAP and the DNVP, under the direction of National Socialists."[64] Civil servants had as much reason for concern as members of the professions. The leaders of the *Deutschnationaler Lehrerbund* (German National Teachers Association), for example, complained to Hindenburg in early May that in the formation of the new all–encompassing German *Erziehungsgemeinschaft* (educational community), teachers were not allowed to belong to any party other than the NSDAP, and that those teachers who refused to join would lose their positions.[65] Enclosed with the complaint was a statement of obligation to the NS Teachers Association, which all teachers had to join.[66] But by now, demands

62. 8 April 1933 at BA Berlin-Lichterfelde, "DNVP, Politischer Schriftwechsel," R 8005, no. 19, 18–19. Complaints were also sent to the *Arbeitsausschuß deutschnationaler Industrieller* regarding rumors "that boards of all non-political business associations would need a 51 percent majority of National Socialists." See "DNVP, Politischer Schriftwechsel," 12 April 1933, 1–3, esp. 2.

63. 12 April 1933 at BA Berlin-Lichterfelde, "DNVP, Politischer Schriftwechsel 1933," 3.

64. BA Berlin-Lichterfelde, "Politischer Schriftwechsel, DNVP," 5. "Gleichschaltung von Beamtenorganisationen."

65. 6 May 1933 at BA Berlin-Lichterfelde, "Akten der Reichskanzlei, DNVP," R 43 I, no. 2655, 235–237, esp. 235.

66. BA Berlin-Lichterfelde, "Akten der Reichskanzlei, DNVP," I, no. 2655, 239, 241; "Aufnahme-Erklärung" of the National Socialist Teachers Association and "Rundschreiben des Kreisleiters des NSLB." Especially noticeable is the threatening tone of the Kreisleiter's letter: "It must be expressly brought to the attention of the associations that their distancing themselves from the NSLB is evidence of their attitude towards the state. Those concerned have to bear the ensuing consequences." Ibid., 241.

of German Nationals for equal treatment had become futile. The very fact that complainants addressed their appeals to Hindenburg and not to Hugenberg—the chairman of the DNVP—was clear evidence of the powerlessness of the party.

Physical Violence and the Threat of Arrest

Fear—and not merely of discrimination—was widespread among conservatives in the spring of 1933. The fear was well grounded, since threats of physical violence had become a daily event. National Socialists, for example, vehemently opposed the formation of German National "factory cells," a kind of workers' committee, in public enterprises. To thwart the formation of such cells within Berlin's great public transportation company, the BVG, National Socialists threatened German National workers that they would "smash to pieces every bone in their bodies."[67] Another complaint charged that Nazis countered the formation of German National factory cells with measures that smacked of terror.[68] In fact, the characterization of Nazi measures as terrorist in nature was not inappropriate, as documented in a twenty-five page letter from Hugenberg to Hitler regarding a multitude of violent SA and SS attacks against members of the DNVP and its affiliated organizations.[69] Among other things, this letter recounted arrests of German National *Kampfring* members by the SA and SS in Munich, arbitrary arrests of DNVP members in their private residences without arrest warrants, and the exclusion of German Nationals from professional associations. Many of the attacks were marked by extraordinary and gratuitous

67. 5 April 1933 at BA Berlin-Lichterfelde, "DNVP, Politischer Schrift-wechsel 1933," R 8005, no. 19, 35–37.

68. 2 April 1933 at BA Berlin-Lichterfelde, "DNVP, Politischer Schrift-wechsel 1933," R 8005, no. 19, 7.

69. 12 April 1933 at BA Berlin-Lichterfelde, "Akten der Reichskanzlei, NSDAP," R 34, II, no. 1195, 211–235. Hugenberg's letter was sent simultaneously to Reich Interior Minister Wilhelm Frick and the provisional Prussian Interior Minister (and since 11 April Minister President) Hermann Göring. The incidents reported by Hugenberg all took place in early April. For more cases of violent attacks on DNVP members see BA Koblenz, Nachlaß Hugenberg, N 1231, no. 89, "Ausschreitungen der NSDAP gegen DNVP Mitglieder."

brutality, such as the assault by twenty-five SA men on an elderly couple in their home in Lippe.[70]

Assaults often grew out of personal animosities. Much pent-up hatred and bitterness had accumulated during the *Kampfzeit*, the "years of struggle," when NSDAP members and organizations were often suppressed and subjected to discrimination. But times had radically changed.[71] Now that the Nazi movement had prevailed against all the odds and triumphed over its adversaries, with its leader elevated to the chancellorship and holding in his hands plenipotentiary powers thanks to the Reichstag Fire Decree and the Enabling Act, the time for revenge had come. With the KPD and SPD largely emasculated, their leaders arrested or driven into emigration, and the Center Party—as the Enabling Act had shown—amenable to cooperation, the principal remaining obstacle that stood between the Nazis and total power was the DNVP and, more broadly, the conservative *Bürgertum*, with its firmly anchored power basis in local politics, the municipalities, and in local and district administrations. To the simple SA man—uneducated, barred from "good" society, and filled with resentment, destructive fury, a paranoid fear of conspiracy, and hatred against "those up there"—the conservative *Bürgertum* had always been suspect. The communist *"Rotfront"* of the *Horst Wessel Lied* was the natural enemy, but the German Nationals and those they represented—a conservative *Bürgertum*[72] that had always looked down with scorn on the ordinary National Socialist—were execrated with the greatest of passion by the average SA trooper. The Nazis successfully tapped into this class resentment: the visceral hatred on the part of those petty bourgeois or already proletarian Germans who feared further social decline that was directed against the established *Bürgertum*, even though that class had also suffered a precipitous economic decline following war, inflation, and depression. Their common nationalist orientation—the bond that seemed to unite Nazis and the conservative *Bürgertum*—paled by comparison to these class-based animosities. Now, in April and May 1933,

70. Ibid., BA Berlin-Lichterfelde, "Akten der Reichskanzlei, NSDAP," 226–227.

71. See the autobiographies of individual Nazis gathered in the Abel Collection at the Hoover Institution on War, Revolution and Peace, Stanford, California (Boxes 1–8); Theodor Abel, *Why Hitler Came into Power* (Cambridge, Mass., 1986); Peter Merkl, *Political Violence under the Swastika: 581 Early Nazis* (Princeton, 1975).

72. In the Horst Wessel Lied they figured as the *"Reaktion."*

members of the NSDAP and other Nazi organizations could finally discharge their pent-up hatred with impunity and complete abandon in the certainty of their newly gained strength and unassailability. The Nazi leadership, for the most part, would have preferred to keep a lid on these animosities until they were even more firmly ensconced in power, but they could not always control spontaneous outbreaks of local hostilities against German Nationals and their organizations. Even though little appeared in the press or even in DNVP party publications, the number of incidents contained in the files was legion. Since the victims of these violent assaults were German Nationals, whose party was still in a governing alliance with the NSDAP, the ruthlessness and brutality with which the perpetrators proceeded is almost beyond belief. According to a report by the DNVP party manager of East-Saxony, for example, four members of the German National *Kampfring* were taken into custody by National Socialists on 22 April and then ". . . put up against the wall and interrogated individually, in the process of which every one of them was flogged with large whips so that all four bear the marks to this day."[73] Beatings with rubber truncheons followed. One of the four was consigned to Hohnstein, a recently opened concentration camp near the *Festung Königstein*, where the beating continued; another suffered a burst eardrum during the abuse, and a third, a severely disabled war veteran, had a nervous shock. The report concluded: "Conditions in the Dresdner Volkshaus, and in Hohnstein . . . and probably in other places as well, are such that they are comparable to what we know of CHEKA rule in Russia."[74] In his rejoinder to these accusations, the Nazi police commissioner of Dresden, SA *Gruppenführer* Georg von Detten, explained, not very plausibly, that the four members of the German National *Kampfring* had been expelled from the SA because of "irregularities," and that some of them had several previous convictions, so that the

---

73. 25 April 1933 at BA Berlin-Lichterfelde, "Akten der Reichskanzlei, NSDAP," R 43, II, no. 1195, 282–285, "Bericht des Landesgeschäftsführers, Landesverband Ost-Sachsen." This report is reprinted in Minuth, ed., *Akten der Reichskanzlei*, 396–398.

74. Ibid., BA Berlin-Lichterfelde, "Reichskanzlei, NSDAP," 285. It was also mentioned that "German National personalities had repeatedly been arrested arbitrarily" and that "in the formations of the NSDAP, which are mostly comprised of younger men, . . . Bolshevik elements set the tone."

"use of force was after all understandable."[75] As to concentration camps, no complaints had been levied so far: "We received on the contrary a large number of thank you letters of former protective detainees, who praised the exemplary treatment they received and especially commended the excellent educational work performed by the guards on duty."[76] Detten's report was passed on to Lammers, *Staatssekretär* in the Reich Chancellery, and to the office of the Reich president.[77] Von Detten knew full well that he could get away with such assertions. He did not have to convince anyone and could rely on automatic acceptance of his Nazi phraseology regarding the "excellent educational work of the guards"—lies that were fed to the public. The assault on the four German National *Kampfring* members turned out to be unusual only in that it caused quite a stir and, through the state secretaries Lammers and Meissner, was brought to Hitler's and Hindenburg's attention.[78]

Even political prominence did not protect against assaults. In a letter to Hindenburg, Prussian Landtag deputy Paul Rüffer, one of the founders and leaders of the German National workers movement, complained that he was violently attacked at a rally in Holstein on 11 May, during the course of which he was knocked down by young Nazis and almost thrown down a flight of stairs. Since 1918 he had spoken at numerous rallies, often surrounded by opponents, but nobody had ever dared to lay a hand upon him. Now, as a sixty-year-old man, he had to undergo the humiliating experience of getting knocked down by "young, immature thugs."[79] The irony that members of his party's own ally had meted out this treatment to him did not escape his attention, though assaults on German Nationals were not infrequent, for he had noticed "that *Unterführer*

75. 18 May 1933 at BA Berlin-Lichterfelde, "Akten der Reichskanzlei, NSDAP," R 43, II, no. 1195, 323. The *Kampfring*, or *Kampfgemeinschaft junger Deutschnationaler*, was reorganized in 1931 out of the *Kampfstaffeln* of the DNVP. See Gisbert J. Gemein, "Die DNVP in Düsseldorf 1918–1933" (Ph.D. diss., Cologne, 1969), 131–133.

76. Ibid., BA Berlin-Lichterfelde, "Akten der Reichskanzlei," 323 verso. Georg von Detten (1887–1934), head of the political office of the SA; Police Commissioner and leader of the Dresden SA, killed during the Röhm putsch.

77. Minuth, ed., *Akten der Reichskanzlei*, 395.

78. Ibid., 395–398. See also von Detten's reports of 8 May 1933 and 18 May 1933 at BA Berlin-Lichterfelde, "Akten der Reichskanzlei, NSDAP," R 43 II, no. 1195, 323–23 verso; 324–324 verso.

79. 12 May 1933 at BA Berlin-Lichterfelde, "Rüffer an Hindenburg," in "Akten der Reichskanzlei, NSDAP," R 43 II, no. 1195, 354–357.

of the NSDAP simply do not follow governmental instructions, but instead made politics off their own bat."[80] He had contacted Hindenburg directly since it was well known that the Interior Ministry did not follow up on complaints regarding violent attacks.[81]

The brutality of Nazi attacks against German Nationals appears to match that used against Communists and Social Democrats prior to April 1933. By April and May 1933, when the Republican parties and their organizations had disappeared from the streets, its leaders arrested, gone into hiding, or emigrated, the SA could train all its aggression on the German Nationals and their political meetings. At the beginning of May 1933, for example, the SA disrupted a DNVP gathering in Berlin that was guarded by German National *Kampfstaffeln*. The police, called in to provide protection against the threateningly gathering SA, greeted the storm troopers with "Heil Hitler" and left the scene.[82] Moments later, two hundred SA men armed with pistols, blackjacks, brass knuckles, and other weapons stormed the assembly. In the course of the ensuing brawl with the unarmed *Kampfstaffel* members, more than twenty German Nationals wound up with severe injuries—the SA even beat up the first-aid attendants and ambulance drivers, who tried to remove the casualties. In addition to knocked out teeth and severe injuries to the head and abdomen, there were also a number of bullet wounds.[83] Even though the German Nationals immediately filed charges against the SA, there were few illusions that these would be acted upon, let alone have serious consequences for the attackers.

Such incidents naturally gave rise to all-pervasive fear and insecurity. There was ample ground for this, given that the slightest

80. Ibid., 356.

81. In order to protect himself in the face of growing Nazi influence, Rüffer wrote a letter to Hitler on the following day, in which he assured the Reich Chancellor—in the most charming tone—of his loyalty. 13 May at BA Berlin-Lichterfelde, "Akten der Reichskanzlei, NSDAP," R 43, II, no. 1195, 351–353.

82. See the detailed description of the incident in the "Mitteilungen der Deutschnationalen Front," 12 May 1933 at BA Berlin-Lichterfelde, "Pressearchiv des Reichslandbundes, Nationalsozialisten und DNVP," R 8034 II, no. 9030, 184.

83. Ibid., 184. This incident reveals much about the tension-ridden alliance between Nazis and German Nationals; it was thoroughly described in an internal DNVP party publication, but barely mentioned in the press. For further instances of attacks on members of the *Kampfstaffeln* see BA Koblenz, Nachlaß Hugenberg, N 1231, no. 89, "Ausschreitungen der NSDAP gegen DNVP Mitglieder," 5.

criticism of Nazi measures or opposition to their actions could result in arrest. The deputy chairman of the DNVP *Ortsgruppe* in the Berlin suburb of Bernau and *Studiendirektor* at the local *Gymnasium*, Wullenweber, for example, was arrested because he allegedly forbade his pupils to collect money for a Hitler portrait. Soon after the arrest, however, it emerged that Wullenweber had merely asked a female colleague not to collect money, in order to avoid the unnecessary expense for parents; instead he would attend to the Hitler portrait himself. When the DNVP party manager Major Nagel went to Bernau to get Wullenweber released, the police informed him that they had instructions to follow NSDAP directives.[84] The fact that a seemingly inconsequential incident about a Hitler portrait, which had obviously been based on a misunderstanding, could lead to the arrest of an "upstanding patriotic man," a DNVP member who had a sound reputation as a local *Gymnasium* teacher, must have made the German Nationals acutely aware of their precarious position in a public life that was increasingly monopolized by the Nazis.

For the German Nationals it would have been difficult, if not impossible, to answer violence with violence. Germany's Rechtsstaat tradition, especially as emblazoned in the legalistic thinking of traditional conservatives, made it difficult to counter violent attacks directly, because countermeasures required legal sanction. For a party that claimed to represent the *Bürgertum* and the conservative upper classes, civic peace, order, and the rule of law were top priorities. Violence could not spontaneously be answered by counterviolence, even if the opportunity presented itself. The National Socialists, on the other hand, were not restrained in their conduct by any scruples. The countless lawless actions of local Nazis, even though rarely sanctioned by any directives from Berlin, and often originating from the vindictiveness and personal ambitions of local Nazi leaders, furthered the cause of the Nazi takeover, since they had the effect of driving German Nationals from political and economic positions of power. On the local and regional level, the months of April and May 1933 thus witnessed a dramatic change in the actual balance of power. A report to Hugenberg from Karlsruhe, the capital of Baden,

---

84. See reports in the *Pommersche Tagespost* of 22 April and in the *Deutsche Zeitung* of 23 April, at BA Berlin-Lichterfelde, "Reichslandbund, Pressearchiv, Nationalsozialisten und DNVP," R 8034 II, no. 9030," 176. When Major Nagel tried to contact the *Staatssekretär* in the Prussian Interior Ministry, Ludwig Grauert, he was threatened with arrest himself.

vividly summarized the reality on the ground: "In Baden it is an almost daily occurrence that mayors and municipal officials—in many
cases German Nationals—are deposed or arrested by local NSDAP
formations. Someone from the ranks of the SA or SS, usually without a mandate, arrives at City Hall with a few armed followers and
without much ado deposes or arrests the mayor. Inquiries with the
district office reveal that no order for such an action was issued. On
our appeal, most of those arrested were then again released, often,
however, only after days."[85] Similar incidents and a comparable
modus operandi were reported from all regions of the Reich. Since
the German Nationals were all too aware of the embarrassing fact
that they had helped conjure up the evil spirits, which they were
now unable to exorcise, some reports are accompanied by (possibly unconscious) excuses for Nazi behavior, such as the comment
that "during times of revolution, some violent transgressions are
unavoidable."[86] To counter the increasing erosion of his power base,
Hugenberg emphasized in a speech to the DNVP Reichstag faction
on 11 April that the German Nationals were "fully-fledged and self-
confident co-combatants" in the national revolution: "We do not
belong to the kind of pathetic *Bürgertum* that cowardly retreats from
the position entrusted to it in difficult and turbulent times." The
German Nationals, he proclaimed, were needed for Germany's future: "All revolutions carry within themselves the danger that they
go overboard and overshoot their mark, that they end in radicalism,
severance from their history, and thus in spiritual and material destruction." The German Nationals, Hugenberg argued, guaranteed
the maintenance of order, the rule of law, and the transformation
of the "revolution of 1933" into a truly "German resurrection."[87]
Yet, Hugenberg refused to recognize that German Nationals had no
power to determine the course of the "revolution of 1933," which

85. 5 April at BA Berlin-Lichterfelde, "Akten der Reichskanzlei, NSDAP,"
R 43 II, no. 1195, 244. It was also mentioned that personal quarrels were settled
with the help of state authorities. "It cannot be reconciled with the concept of a
Rechtsstaat that, as unfortunately often happens, personal feuds or old enmities
are settled with the help of individual groups or even the organs of state, i.e. state
power."
86. Ibid., 244 verso.
87. "Im Kampf für Deutschland," *Der Tag*, 12 April 1933, at BA Berlin-
Lichterfelde, "Pressearchiv Reichslandbund, DNVP Parteitage," R 8034 II, no.
4334, 66.

would ultimately turn against both them and the entire conservative *Bürgertum*.

The Vain Struggle to Survive: German Nationals Imitate Nazi Styles

Due to incessant Nazi attacks and acts of violence against DNVP members; the Nazis' successful appropriation of German traditions; and the erosion of the DNVP's traditional power base in society, local politics, and professional organizations, the identity of the conservative party was shaken to its very foundations. As the March election results had indicated and as subsequent developments from the takeover of the Länder governments to the Enabling Act had made crystal clear to every German National, the Nazi party and its organizations were the single engine driving the national revolution. The DNVP appeared to have become politically superfluous, especially since the NSDAP no longer needed conservative votes to obtain a majority in the Reichstag after the KPD had been banned. The Nazis had surpassed the German Nationals in all areas of political competition, perhaps most significantly in the area of symbolic politics, that is, in the maintenance and respect for national traditions and festivals, which the Nazis stage-managed adroitly and with enormous pomp. The grandiose spectacle in Potsdam, with its emphasis on the symbiosis of former *grandeur* and the new spirit of the "awakening" nation, had shown that the Nazis wanted to cultivate the legacy of the Prussian past, appropriate it, and manipulate it toward their own ends.[88] Ubiquitous posters showing Frederick the Great, Bismarck, Hindenburg, and Hitler next to each other intimated a historical continuity, suggesting that the simple soldier of the World War was the rightful heir to the legacy of the Prussian king, the Iron Chancellor, and the Field Marshal. National Socialist propaganda never tired of evoking the continuity between the "new" Germany and the Prussian past and of stressing the movement's bounden duty to live up to the Prussian heritage. In an age of economic depression, unemployment, and widespread uncertainty, all of which contributed to discrediting traditional *bürgerliche* values,

88. André François-Poncet provides an insightful description of the Potsdam ceremony in *The Fateful Years. Memoirs of a French Ambassador in Berlin 1931–1938* (New York, 1949), 60–65, as does Düsterberg, *Der Stahlhelm und Hitler*, 48–51.

it is quite plausible that—if one turned a blind eye to the criminal behavior of its members—the Nazi movement appeared as a more timely successor to austere Prussian traditions than the self-satisfied and stolid *haute bourgeoisie*, whose world seemed destined to crumble in any case. In the spring of 1933, politically guileless and unsophisticated individuals may well have believed in the possibility of blending Old Prussian traditions with National Socialist ideals. Marginalized by the success of this strategy, German Nationals desperately fought to justify their legitimacy. The only recourse left to the party was to stress its own political indispensability, even though many of its members had begun to doubt it themselves.

The DNVP tried to prove its political value and preserve its identity in three different ways. First, German Nationals strenuously pointed out that the Enabling Act depended on the current composition of the Reich government and argued that without the DNVP as coalition partner, the Enabling Act would cease being valid.[89] This assertion was questionable from a legal standpoint, since the constitutional scholar Carl Schmitt had already pointed out that even with Hugenberg's resignation from the government the law would not automatically lose its validity.[90] In the non–German National press it was thus generally noted that Hugenberg's views were "constitutionally not tenable," since "two constitutional authorities, Carl Schmitt and Koellreutter, point out that in this case the present government would be represented solely by the leader of the National Socialist movement, Adolf Hitler."[91] Putting aside legal interpretations, political reality would soon unmask the absurdity of

---

89. BA Berlin-Lichterfelde, "Reichslandbund Pressearchiv, Organisiertes Bürgertum," R 8034 II, no. 9021, 9; "Wie wir es sehen. Hugenbergs Erklärung," and "Straffe Organisation der DNVP," *Deutsche Zeitung*, 12 April 1933.

90. On 1 April; see Carl Schmitt, "Das Gesetz zur Behebung der Not von Volk und Reich," *Deutsche Juristenzeitung* 38 (1933), 456–458. A collection of legal assessments of the validity of the Act can be found in Morsey, *Ermächtigungsgesetz*, 91–99. Otto Schmidt-Hannover, in his *Umdenken oder Anarchie*, 351–352, emphasized that the Enabling Act conferred "special authority only on the 'present government.'" Even though he must have known better, Schmidt-Hannover argued that Hugenberg could have "invoked a kind of veto right by threat of resignation or actual resignation."

91. BA Berlin-Lichterfelde, "Pressearchiv Reichslandbund, Organisiertes Bürgertum," R 8034 II, no. 9021, 14; *Tägliche Rundschau*, 27 April 1933. Hugenberg's desire to assert the political relevance of the DNVP was thus dashed by the realities of constitutional law which, in this case, the Nazis willingly recognized.

Hugenberg's hopes that the DNVP could remain politically signifi-cant.[92] At this point, the Nazis hardly required legal justifications to substantiate their claim to power. By the beginning of May, after the enormously successful May Day celebrations and the crushing of the trade unions that followed the next day, it became very clear that the Nazis would never allow any legal considerations to force them out of the positions they had so successfully usurped.

As a second, almost instinctive means of underscoring the neces-sity of their participation in government, German National politi-cians stressed the danger of foreign encirclement. In April 1933 they repeatedly called for the domestic unity of national-minded forces in the face of foreign threats. This reference to foreign affairs threw into the forefront the great common denominator of the "national front"—the demand for the revision of the Treaty of Versailles and the regaining of German might—while emphasizing the need for domestic peace, an end to Nazi attacks, and the deceleration of "the revolution":[93] "The tempo of domestic reform should also be lim-ited in consideration of the dangerous foreign situation. Desires to organize and propagandize must be of secondary importance when compared to the great goal of the revision of Versailles, the recovery of the German right to be adequately armed, and the rescue of the bleeding *Ostmark*."[94] Foreign encirclement, conjured up by the "call of radical French and Polish circles for a preventive war" and an "Anglo-French-American united front," made domestic unity of all

92. In a speech on 20 April, Hugenberg tried to quell rumors according to which "the continued presence of German Nationals in the Reich govern-ment was a question of but a few more days or weeks." Hugenberg emphasized the solemn "confirmation of this government by the Reich President" and the "circumstance that the Enabling Act was predicated on the continuance of the present Reich government." See *Der Nationale Wille*, 22 April 1933, no. 17, 213; also Gaertingen, "DNVP," 646.

93. The concept of "revolution" had become commonplace during the spring and summer of 1933 to characterize the radical political and social changes that had taken place. It was a term also used by Nazi opponents. On 1 August 1933, for example, Max Planck wrote to Fritz Haber: "The one thing that gives me some relief in this feeling of wretched forlornness is the thought that we are living in catastrophic times, which every revolution brings in its wake, and that much of what happens we must bear like a natural disaster without worrying whether things might be different." Quoted in Fritz Stern, *Das feine Schweigen* (Munich, 1999), 57.

94. "Straffe Organisation der DNVP," *Deutsche Zeitung*, 12 April 1933," at BA Berlin-Lichterfelde, "Pressearchiv Reichslandbund, Organisiertes Bürger-tum," R 8934 II, no. 9021, 9.

national-minded and patriotic forces imperative.[95] The new DNVP faction chair, Otto Schmidt-Hannover, in particular, never tired of evoking the specter of an "external political threat to Germany," warning that "French-Polish politics . . . are desperately looking for the opportunity to intervene in German domestic developments."[96] This also gave him the chance to call for a further buildup of military armaments, a demand that saw him in full agreement with his coalition partner.

Thirdly, in the hope of sharing in the success of National Socialism, the DNVP frantically attempted to conform to the new Zeitgeist by altering its organizational structure and revitalizing its presentational style. In the course of the March election campaign it had become painfully apparent that the DNVP had little to offer those who were gripped by fervent excitement over the national uprising. In contrast to the Nazi party, the DNVP was far from being any sort of "community of struggle" (the concept of *Kampfgemeinschaft* was frequently evoked), and it could also hardly be described as a "modern activist communal movement," into which German Nationals such as Eduard Stadtler wanted to mold it.[97] Hugenberg's much-vaunted *Führertum* lacked charisma and was unable to inspire the commitment and spirit of sacrifice that was so common among National Socialists.[98] The DNVP now tried to compensate for its lack of dynamism with organizational strengths. At the beginning of April 1933, new German National professional organizations

95. "Straffe Organisation der DNVP," *Deutsche Zeitung*, 12 April 1933, at ibid.

96. BA Berlin-Lichterfelde, "Pressearchiv Reichslandbund, Organisiertes Bürgertum," ibid., 11; "Forderungen der DNVP zur Wehrfrage," *Deutsche Zeitung* 13 April 1933; "Entscheidende Fragen," *Der Tag*, 28 April 1933; "Hugenberg spricht vor seiner Partei," *Tägliche Rundschau*, 29 April 1933.

97. For example, in a speech at the Stettin party congress in September 1931: ". . . the German National Party has definitively changed its organizational face towards the movement character of a modern activist communal movement; it has turned into the pure body of adherents of a self-confident, creative personality that has become a manifestation of political leadership. In a word, the German National Party has become a Hugenberg-movement." In *Unsere Partei*, 1 October 1931, nos. 18/19, 221; and Gaertingen, "DNVP," 625. Eduard Stadtler, born 1886, defected to the NSDAP in May 1933, just weeks before the dissolution of his own party.

98. For the best examples for the prevalence of *"Opferbereitschaft"* (readiness to sacrifice oneself) among Nazi followers, see the 593 biographies in the Abel Collection at the Hoover Institution on War, Revolution and Peace, Stanford, California (Boxes 1–8).

were called into life that were modeled on those of the NSDAP or directly copied from the Nazi originals. This was more than an effort to organize party-dependent professional associations. In the final instance it was nothing less than the endeavor to transform the DNVP from a traditional political party into a movement, one with an all-encompassing worldview in the manner of the Social Democrats or the National Socialists.[99]

On 4 April, the Reich Association of German National Jurists was formed, and four days later the Union of German National Economists; this was followed by the Reich Alliance of German National Physicians and the Association of German National Veterinarians.[100] In addition, the DNVP also instituted the National Socialist leadership principle.[101] A decree passed down by the party leadership on 18 April ordered that, from this point on, current chairmen of DNVP Land Associations and county and local groups would no longer be elected, but appointed by the "leader" of the next higher organizational level. They also could be removed from their post at any time. Closely following the Nazi model, their official designations were changed to "*Landesführer, Kreisführer* und *Ortsgruppenführer.*"[102] The boards of Land Associations, county, and local groups were changed to advisory committees (*Beiräte*): "The *Beiräte* are to give counsel; the Führer will make the decisions."[103] For the DNVP, this was more than just a break with party practice; it was a betrayal of a longstanding Prussian tradition. Even in the heyday of its rule, in the first half of the nineteenth century, the

---

99. In political science literature, a political movement, as opposed to a traditional political party, has the following characteristics: 1) an all-encompassing worldview and an emphasis on values, not just specific interests; 2) an attempt to organize wide-ranging social groups of all types affiliated with and responsible to the party organization; 3) an attempt to capture support outside the party's traditional voter base.

100. Following the above order: *Reichsbund deutschnationaler Juristen*; *Bund deutschnationaler Volkswirte*; *Reichsverband deutschnationaler Ärzte*; *Bund deutschnationaler Tierärzte*. Even non-academics were included, such as an organization for tradesmen, the *Deutschnationaler Bund des gewerblichen Mittelstandes*; see also Hiller von Gaertingen, "DNVP," 598.

101. "Kampfbewegung statt Partei. Der Führergedanke im Aufbau der Deutschnationalen Volkspartei," *Der Tag*, 19 April 1933.

102. BA Berlin-Lichterfelde, "Pressearchiv Reichslandbund, Organisiertes Bürgertum," R 8034 II, no. 9021, 11; "Bekanntmachung über die Eintragung des Führerprinzips in der DNVP," *Der Nationale Wille*, 22 April 1933, no. 17, 222.

103. "Kampfbewegung statt Partei," *Der Tag*, 19 April 1933.

supposedly staunchly authoritarian Prussian bureaucracy had always practiced the "collegiate" principle:[104] it was not the leader of the collegiate body, the *Regierungspräsident*, who made the decision (as was the case in the French prefecture system), but the majority in the college of councilors. The "Führer" principle was contrary to Prussian political traditions and, in fact, deeply un-Prussian.

In some instances, German National adaptation to National Socialist ways went further than organizational changes; it included conversions in language and patterns of thought. On 8 May 1933, for example, the DNVP Reichenbach district association in Silesia[105] sent a "resolution," that is, a programmatic statement, to *Volkskanzler* Hitler that condemned class hatred, along with the mentality of class struggle and "class conceit," while accentuating National Socialist "values," such as "personality" and the "performance principle."[106] The ultimate goal of this missive to Hitler was to underscore the demand for equality with the "brothers-in-arms of the NSDAP," something that had long since ceased to be self-evident, and to emphasize that German Nationals no longer lingered in "reactionary" modes of behavior and thought. The German Nationals from Reichenbach hoped to attain equal treatment by proffering assurance of unquestioning loyalty in their alliance with the NSDAP, whereby their self-denial went so far as to extol values and employ words that were strikingly similar to those propagated by National Socialism.

104. As Thomas Nipperdey has pointed out, the Prussian administration was a *"diskutierende Verwaltung,"* an administration in whose councils, boards, and committees free discussions reigned supreme, at least at the higher levels. See Nipperdey, *Deutsche Geschichte, 1800–1866* (Munich, 1983), 333. Strongholds of collegial debate were the *Regierungen*, the body of councilors in a district, chaired by a *Regierungspräsident*, who was only a *primus inter pares* among higher officials. In Prussia, the principal of collective responsibility and competence prevailed over the French prefect system; this had the advantage that decisions were jointly reached, whereas the prefect system vested the president of an administrative body with the sole responsibility. See Hermann Beck, *The Origins of the Authoritarian Welfare State in Prussia. Conservatives, Bureaucracy and the Social Question, 1815–1870* (Ann Arbor, 1995), 128–129, and "The Social Policies of Prussian Officials: The Bureaucracy in a New Light." *The Journal of Modern History* 64 (1992), 263–298.

105. Reichenbach in the *Regierungsbezirk* Breslau had a population of 16,342 (1925).

106. 8 May 1933 at BA Berlin-Lichterfelde, "Akten der Reichskanzlei, DNVP," R 43 I, no. 2655, 255–255 verso.

Yet, despite all adversities and attempts to adapt to Nazi methods, even in the spring of 1933 the DNVP still had not entirely lost its will to self-assertion and, in some instances, even resistance to its overpowering ally. In mid April, in a loudly advertised reckoning with their own past, German Nationals boasted that they had now streamlined their organization and still remained legitimate bearers of the national idea.[107] Clear lines were also then drawn between the DNVP and its ally: the party had never been simply a big interest group but, from the start, it had been committed to the supreme "ideals of nationalism and the national community." For this reason, the DNVP saw no need to pay any heed to the "callow rascals" of the NSDAP, young thugs who had recently joined the Nazi party and now indulged in an overzealous nationalism. Without the DNVP, "without its struggle, without its parliamentary ventures, everything that today is taken for granted, everything that today a suspicious flag-waving chauvinism, shouting itself hoarse, can freely express, might be completely silenced and forgotten in Germany."[108] As late as early May 1933, the head of the Pomeranian Land Association, Georg von Zitzewitz, sharply distanced himself from National Socialism. At a gathering of Pomeranian county leaders (*Kreisführer*) in Stettin, he asserted that the "Prussian conservative Mensch" was bound "to the God-given order of the state in Lutheran freedom."[109] On these grounds alone, he was obliged to reject "collectivism" and "leveling tendencies"—a clear implicit critique of collectivist streaks in Nazi ideology. Von Zitzewitz claimed that because of their long-standing affiliation with the national movement, German Nationals perceived any violation of equality as a flagrant injustice.[110] But such

---

107. BA Berlin-Lichterfelde, "Pressearchiv Reichslandbund, Organisiertes Bürgertum," R 8034 II, no. 9021, 10a, "Der deutschnationale Weg," *Parlamentarische Beilage*, 13 April 1933. Here it was emphasized that the party had cast off all elements of doubtful loyalty and economic opportunists, who had voted for the Dawes Plan or been sympathetic to Locarno.

108. Ibid., "Der deutschnationale Weg," 10a, sheet 2.

109. BA Berlin-Lichterfelde, "Pressearchiv Reichslandbund, DNVP Parteitage," R 8034 II, no. 4334, 73, "Konservativer Staatsglaube," *Pommersche Tagespost*, 7 May 1933.

110. Ibid. Von Zitzewitz mentioned that the German Nationals had been fighting against Marxism since 1918, whereas National Socialists were relative newcomers in this struggle. The fact that German Nationals were not accepted as equals meant that they were unappreciated in their "national devotion" and in what they had "accomplished in forcefully preparing the ground for the national state."

critical voices were in the minority. At a meeting of the DNVP leadership on 3 May, participants agreed to change their party's name to Deutschnationale Front (DNF or German National Front), which amounted to a further concession to the Nazi movement and a final renunciation of the multiparty state.[111] The grounds provided for this action were that to those who had banded together in the DNVP to "fight against the republican–democratic system . . . the party was never an end in itself, but instead a necessary measure to survive on the battlefield of the parliamentary state."[112] At the same time, DNVP leaders triumphantly proclaimed that "the democratic parliamentary system of Weimar is dead."[113] The more prescient members of the now-renamed DNF must have recognized by this point that the complete demise of the "system" of Weimar was not necessarily advantageous to their fate or to that of their German National Front.

In the first half of May, the Nazi press, sensing the innate weakness of the German Nationals, initiated a major offensive against Hugenberg personally, throwing aspersions on his professional competence as a government minister, coupled with demands that he be replaced by a National Socialist. On 9 May 1933, for example, the National Socialist *Oberbürgermeister* of Hagen in Westphalia sent a telegram to the Reich Government that was widely circulated in the German press, in which he demanded Hugenberg's dismissal from the government, alleging that he no longer enjoyed the support of working Germans.[114] Whether this demand really arose spontaneously from within the Hagen NSDAP, as the *Oberbürgermeister* claimed, or whether it was "ordered" by the Nazi leadership remains open to

111. BA Berlin-Lichterfelde, "Pressearchiv Reichslandbund, DNVP Partei-tage," R 8034 II, no. 4334, 72. "Deutschnationale Front," *Deutsche Zeitung*, 4 May 1933, and "Pressearchiv Reichslandbund, Organisiertes Bürgertum," R 8034 II, no. 9021, 24–26.

112. "Deutschnationale Front," *Deutsche Zeitung*, 4 May 1933.

113. Ibid. The party leadership further emphasized the "camaraderie of 30 January," the "self-evident assertion of full equality," the restitution of a "firm legal order," the "integrity of an incorruptible civil service," and "an economy protected from experiments and wanton interference." These demands, however, fell on deaf ears, since no real power could be marshaled to support them.

114. BA Berlin-Lichterfelde, "Pressearchiv Reichslandbund, Organisiertes Bürgertum," R 8034 II, no. 9021, 30a; "Die Deutschnationale Front gegen den Hagener Oberbürgermeister," *Mitteilungen der Deutschnationalen Front*, 19 May 1933. Hagen in Westphalia had a population of 147,052 in 1933; see *Statistisches Jahrbuch für das Deutsche Reich*, 52 (1933), 7.

interpretation. The Hagen incident attracted nationwide attention and was by no means the only one of its kind. The German National Front answered such attacks by insisting that Hugenberg was indispensable as a *Fachminister* (departmental minister) who enjoyed the full trust of Reich Chancellor Hitler, and by reverting to the usual specter of external threats. Internal discord had to be avoided at all cost, the argument ran, since the current political situation "was of the greatest concern," given that "Germany's situation is deadly serious. At the moment, it tolerates less than ever incitation of the masses."[115] The increasing attacks on the German National "leader" were answered, in the second half of May, with a flood of declarations affirming steadfast solidarity with Hugenberg.[116] As a practical defense measure against Nazi attacks, German Nationals organized assemblies in various parts of the Reich at which participants solemnly pledged "unswerving allegiance to Hugenberg."[117] A characteristic incantation came from the German National county group of Niederbarnim: "Faced with the mighty goal and difficult task of the protection of Germany's borders and German states, all internal conflict must cease."[118]

All these affirmations and testimonials of solidarity, loyalty oaths, and demands for equality were a last stand against an end that was drawing inexorably closer. A speech by Joseph Goebbels on 19 May in Berlin regarding the "current state of the German revolution" illustrates just how hopeless the DNVP's overall position had become by the second half of May.[119] Goebbels barely mentioned the NSDAP's German National coalition partner, but instead maintained that "the National Socialist movement has become the State itself."[120] The inner rationale under which the NSDAP operated

---

115. Ibid.

116. BA Berlin-Lichterfelde, "Pressearchiv Reichslandbund, Organisiertes Bürgertum," R 8034 II, no. 9021, 31–33; *Mitteilungen der Deutschnationalen Front,* 19 May 1933.

117. *Mitteilungen der Deutschnationalen Front,* 32a.

118. Ibid., 32a. Declarations of solidarity with Hugenberg came from the entire Reich, coupled with the demand for "equal treatment of our members politically, professionally and economically."

119. BA Berlin-Lichterfelde, "Akten der Reichskanzlei, NSDAP," R 43 II, no. 1195, 327–333; "Dr. Goebbels über den Stand der deutschen Revolution," *Wolff's Telegraphisches Büro,* 84. Jahrgang, no 1212. Goebbels was named "Minister of Propaganda and Public Enlightenment" on 13 March. He became the fourth Nazi in the Cabinet.

120. Ibid., 327 verso.

heretofore would now be applied to the "entire structure of the State and the people," and this was a development that could naturally be brought to its successful conclusion only by National Socialists.[121] Goebbels continued that there must never be any doubt "that this new State has been hard-won by a minority," which now intended to realize the fruits of its labor. While National Socialists did not want "to exclude anyone from the *Volk* at large," they alone had the right to determine how the State should be "constituted internally and externally."[122] Goebbels aimed his speech solely at his Nazi audience—the German National Front, still the NSDAP's coalition partner, was not mentioned. The omission was a reflection of the party's increasingly ominous situation. But then, by the second half of May, the Nazis had already begun to initiate bans against DNF meetings, and a number of prominent German Nationals had defected to the NSDAP. The demise of the DNF, and the tradition of the German National brand of conservatism it had carried with it, was now well within sight.

121. Ibid., ". . . either the Germany of future generations will operate on the legal basis (*Gesetzlichkeit*) that has characterized the life of this party [i.e., the NSDAP], or Germany will have no future at all."

122. Ibid., 327 verso. The National Socialists will lead the way to the future "as the *avant garde* of the German revolution," and they will "ensure that nothing will ever stop this revolution." Ibid., 328.

Chapter VII

IGNOMINIOUS DEMISE

Defections, Prohibitions, and Final Dissolution

A Change in Climate

An understanding of the contemporary Zeitgeist is necessary to explain the rapid disappearance of old established parties such as the liberal parties, Center, and SPD (whose roots reached back to the *Vormärz*) from the political stage without a last-ditch stand, and the ignominious end of the DNVP, which resembled a melting away more than a last convulsive struggle. Between the end of March and the end of June, during the long spring of 1933, dramatic changes took place not only in the political climate and public mood, but also in the consciousness of a majority of the population. Without proper appreciation of the spirit of the age it is difficult to ascertain how the National Socialists could make such easy game of their coalition partner and why the conservative edifice collapsed like a house of cards. As the Nazis began to eliminate their political opponents, they concurrently strove to undermine traditional political allegiances. Under the impetus of Nazi coercion, traditional political ties started breaking down, and interest groups and associations sought new organizational links by which they could continue to operate under the watchful eye of a state that was increasingly dominated by the Nazis. Interest groups, professional associations, and political parties that had not yet suffered the direct wrath of the NSDAP had to strategize in the face of what seemed to be the inevitable consolidation of Nazi power. When it became clear that they could not oppose the Nazis and continue to survive, many attempted to accommodate themselves to Nazi rule. They either began to join NS-sanctioned organizations or to accept Nazi restrictions on their own. Members of banished organizations frequently turned to the DNVP or to associations close to it, such as the *Stahlhelm*, as the only organizational outlet for their activities (or shelter for personal safety) in the new political climate. The resulting increase of SPD and *Reichsbanner* members in the German National People's Party and its organizations would, on the other hand, soon provide the Nazis with an excuse to turn against their own coalition partner with the charge that they had been infiltrated by leftist elements and thus had to be dissolved.

Three brief examples illustrate the accommodation made to the growing dominance of National Socialist power. The unions were among the first to begin assessing their limited options under Nazi rule. Even before the Enabling Act, the General Association of German Trade Unions (ADGB), under the leadership of Theodor Leipart,[1] publicly distanced itself from the SPD and signaled its willingness for social and economic cooperation "regardless which type of regime controls the state."[2] Quite obviously, countless Nazi attacks, the "arbitrariness of Nazi measures," and the "uncertainty of legal conditions," which had compelled Leipart to send a plea for help to Hindenburg on 10 March, had apparently all had the desired effect.[3] Yet, the accommodation shown by the ADGB proved to be in vain, as is evidenced by another letter of protest to Hindenburg dated 5 April 1933, in which further complaints were made about the "monstrous terror" directed against union functionaries.[4] The Catholic Church, after first recoiling from Nazism, eventually sought ways to protect its institutional and doctrinal autonomy. Another milestone was thus the declaration by Catholic bishops on 28 March that dropped previous prohibitions and warnings against National Socialism and instead urged loyalty toward lawful authorities

1. The *Allgemeiner Deutscher Gewerkschaftsbund*, founded in 1919, was first led by Carl Legien (1861–1920) and then by Theodor Leipart (1867–1947) from 1921 to 1933.

2. Gotthard Jasper, *Die gescheiterte Zähmung, Wege zur Machtergreifung Hitlers 1930–1934* (Frankfurt, 1986), 166; Broszat, *Der Staat Hitlers*, 7th ed. (Munich, 1978), 113; Winkler, *Der Weg in die Katastrophe*, 89–98.

3. "Der Bundesvorstand des ADGB an den Reichspräsidenten," 10 March 1933, in Minuth, ed., *Akten der Reichskanzlei*, 188–189.

4. Ibid., 189, note 4.

and conscientious fulfillment of civic duties.[5] But it was the accommodation of political parties that paved the way for the ultimate domination of National Socialism. The Center and liberal parties' approval of the Enabling Act was one of the first ominous signs of a momentous change in the political climate and cannot be explained solely as a combination of the readiness to cooperate with Hitler and fear of reprisals. It also indicated that party leadership and deputies were incapable of resisting the tide of public feeling, which practically demanded acceptance of the Act.[6] A further unmistakable sign of the times was that countless Social Democrats, Communists, and members of the republican *Reichsbanner* sought refuge after the March elections with nationalist organizations, such as the DNVP *Kampfstaffeln* and the *Stahlhelm*. The DNVP itself also saw an artificial boost in popularity, as many defectors from the leftist camp joined its ranks. For many, the motivation for joining was not so much opportunism as a fear of retribution by the SA and a basic need for security. On 15 April, the union leadership welcomed the government's declaration that the first of May was to become a "legal holiday in honor of national labor,"[7] and four days later the ADGB's national executive committee (*Bundesausschuß*) issued instructions "to take part solemnly in the official celebrations."[8] Thanks to the willing collaboration of the unions, the "Day of National Labor" turned into a monumental propaganda success for the National Socialists, something that even opponents of the regime, such as the French Ambassador André François-Poncet and the author Erich Ebermayer, were grudgingly forced to acknowledge.[9] The news on

5. This declaration was made following Hitler's public announcement confirming the inviolability of Catholic doctrine. See Klaus Scholder, *Die Kirchen und das Dritte Reich*, Vol. I, *Vorgeschichte und Zeit der Illusion 1918–1934* (Frankfurt, 1977), 300–322. On 13 March 1933 the Pope already had praised the anticommunist stance of the new government. Munich Cardinal Richard Faulhaber (1869–1952) reported to the Bavarian bishops after his return from Rome on 20 April: "In Rome, National Socialism and fascism are judged to be the only salvation from communism and Bolshevism. The Holy Father views this from afar, seeing not the concomitant side-effects, but only the larger goal." (Ibid., 307.)

6. See chapter 3 above.

7. Winkler, *Der Weg in die Katastrophe*, 921, describes this as an act of public submission.

8. And this despite continuing SA attacks against union functionaries (Ibid., 922).

9. François-Poncet, *The Fateful Years*, 66–74. Ebermayer, *Denn heute gehört uns Deutschland*, 72–73, conveys the euphoric atmosphere: "Hindenburg and

the following day that union halls and buildings throughout the entire Reich had been occupied by members of Nazi organizations received less attention in light of the success of the 1 May holiday.[10] Even the Social Democrats no longer seemed to take excessive umbrage against the regime for these attacks. Hitler's conciliatory foreign policy speech during the Reichstag session of 17 May,[11] attended by about half of the SPD Reichstag faction and applauded by those present, blurred the favorable impression of staunch protest against Nazi repression that had been created by the SPD's rejection of the Enabling Act. The session was staged in such a way that all deputies rose at the end of the speech (which indeed gave little cause for objection)—including the SPD deputies. This, in turn, created the misleading impression that all of Germany had closed ranks with the regime.[12] The speaker of parliament, Hermann Göring, was thus in a position to close the session with the words: "The world has seen: the German people are united when their destiny is at stake."[13]

The overbearing propaganda, solicitation, and publicity for the Hitler government went so far that even Goebbels came out against "nationalist kitsch," a phenomenon that Ebermayer described in some detail: "All the lowest instincts of taste seem to have been unleashed by the National Socialist movement and its victory. Busts of the Führer made out of lard are the least of it. Toilet paper: "we

---

Hitler drive through a line of tens of thousands of people to the castle. Incomparable storms of jubilation!. . . . Later, workers' delegations from throughout the Reich arrive by airplane at Tempelhof to be greeted by Goebbels. They take their midday meal with Hitler . . . Now it truly seems as if the whole of German labor pays homage to the Führer."

10. Ebermayer commented: ". . . every real success, which gains them a few million more of the formerly undecided, is usually followed by some kind of completely unlawful brutality which, in advance, has been legitimated by the success and is drowned out by its lingering inebriation and euphoria." Ibid., 73.

11. Winkler characterized the speech as the "most measured and conciliatory [Hitler] had ever made." See *Der Weg in die Katastrophe*, 935.

12. See Winkler, *Der Weg in die Katastrophe*, 932–937. There was intense debate within the SPD Reichstag faction over the party's participation in the session of 17 May. Following a threat by Nazi Interior Minister Frick, there was reason to fear for the lives of incarcerated Social Democrats unless the party proved cooperative, which prompted a majority of the faction to favor participation. Even Ebermayer found words of praise for Hitler's Reichstag speech: "Bravo! If one of us had said that or were to say it, he would already be under lock and key." *Denn heute gehört uns Deutschland*, 89.

13. Winkler, *Der Weg in die Katastrophe*, 936.

crack down" is not bad either. And the post card industry!"[14] In petitions to the Reich Chancellery,[15] coffeehouse owners asked permission to name their shops after Hitler, rose growers their roses, and mayors of villages requested name changes into "Hitlershöhe" and the like. As documented in the bimonthly reports of district governors, the *Regierungspräsidenten*, a government-friendly mood, even if it did not turn into ecstatic enthusiasm, generally seemed to catch on in the spring of 1933. On 20 April 1933, for example, the *Regierungspräsident* of Upper and Middle Franconia related reports from county offices, according to which "the take-over is viewed more sympathetically, even among circles not previously well disposed toward the NSDAP, and there are indications, namely in workers' circles, that point to a certain leaning toward the new government."[16]

This drift toward the new regime, even by those who formerly opposed National Socialism, was often based on support for strengthening central power. The centralizing measures taken by the National Socialists, such as the two laws for the *Gleichschaltung* of the Länder of 31 March and 7 April 1933 that more or less put an end to the century-old semi-sovereignty of the individual states, paradoxically were more popular with the declared opponents of National Socialism than with the Nazis' conservative coalition partner.[17]

14. Ebermayer, more amused than outraged, on 18 April 1933 in *Denn heute gehört uns Deutschland*, 65.

15. See Beatrice and Helmut Heiber, eds., *Die Rückseite des Hakenkreuzes. Absonderliches aus den Akten des Dritten Reiches*, 2nd ed. (Munich, 1994), 119–120.

16. Martin Broszat et al., eds., *Bayern in der NS Zeit. Soziale Lage und politisches Verhalten der Bevölkerung im Spiegel vertraulicher Berichte* (Munich and Vienna, 1977), vol. I, 210; reprinted in Josef and Ruth Becker, eds., *Hitlers Machtergreifung*, 2nd ed. (Munich, 1992), 248.

17. The *Vorläufiges Gesetz zur Gleichschaltung der Länder mit dem Reich* (Provisional Law on the Coordination of the Länder with the Reich) of 31 March 1933 regulated the new organization of state parliaments and local representative bodies. Their composition was now made to conform with the election results of 5 March. The *Zweites Gesetz zur Gleichschaltung der Länder mit dem Reich* of 7 April decreed the appointment of Reich Governors. Papen resigned as Reich Commissar for Prussia on 7 April; Hitler reserved the Reich Governorship for Prussia for himself and, on 11 April, appointed Göring as Deputy Reich Governor and Minister President of Prussia. Contemporaries considered these laws an attempt to restructure the relationship between Reich and Länder. On 30 January 1934 the federally oriented constitutional structure was finally annulled by the *Gesetz über den Neuaufbau des Reiches* (Law on the Reorganization of the Reich), though a comprehensive reform of the Reich was never implemented. See Martin Broszat, *Der Staat Hitlers*, 151–162.

Conservatives had traditionally supported the preservation of the power and rights of the individual Länder; overall, they favored the maintenance and perpetuation of regional and particularist powers and decentralization in general, while vociferously opposing administrative uniformity, standardization, and political centralization.[18] The practice of appointing Reich Governors from Berlin was diametrically opposed to their conservative belief in the federal principle and in regional checks and balances, because the new policy abolished the autonomy of the Länder and undermined restraints on centralized power. In the early years of the Weimar Republic, Matthias Erzberger's transfer of tax authority from the individual states to the Reich and the establishment of a uniform Reich tax board "had been vehemently fought by the entire Right."[19] In April 1933, the liberal Reichstag deputy and future president of West Germany, Theodor Heuss, wrote that Hugo Preuß (the left liberal father of the Weimar Constitution) would have been greatly pleased by the *Gleichschaltungsgesetze* (the "co-ordination legislation"), noting that Nazi opponents more readily agreed with Nazi centralizing measures and *Gleichschaltung* policies than "those conservative German publicists who had served as Hitler's intellectual vanguard among the so-called educated elite [and] who now have to admit that this was not exactly what they had envisioned."[20] Following the adoption of the laws, a surprised Thomas Mann noted in his diary that the *Frankfurter Zeitung*, a paper renowned for its liberal views, celebrated "the radical centralization of the Reich as a great historic deed, despite the fact that it manifested little respect for historic tradition and long-standing national idiosyncrasies," musing that "the thousand year old fragmentation of Germans was brought to an end in one fell swoop."[21]

18. See Beck, "The Changing Concerns of Prussian Conservatism, 1830–1914," in Phillip Dwyer, ed., *Modern Prussian History, 1830–1947*, Vol. II (London, 2001), 86–106.

19. Lutz Graf Schwerin von Krosigk, *Memoiren* (Stuttgart, 1977), 94.

20. Theodor Heuss (1884–1963), "Das Schicksal des Reiches," *Die Hilfe*, no. 39, 22 April 1933, 224–227. Heuss, a deputy of the DDP and its successor, the Staatspartei, was an expert on constitutional issues during the Weimar years and President of West Germany from 1949 to 1959. Hugo Preuß (1860–1925) was Professor of Constitutional Law and Minister of the Interior in the Scheidemann Cabinet from February to June 1919. He drew up the first draft of the Weimar Constitution, which gave rise to protest by the Länder because of its centralist orientation and was subsequently revised.

21. Thomas Mann, *Tagebücher 1933–1934*, ed. by Peter de Mendelsohn (Frankfurt, 1977), 45–46.

Possibly the most impressive phenomenon that illustrated the subjective authenticity of the enthusiasm for the Hitler movement was the large number of genuine, non-opportunistic conversions to National Socialism. Alongside an army of many hundreds of thousands of *"Märzgefallenen"*[22]—opportunists who streamed into the party for personal advancement or to safeguard themselves and their families—were thousands, including many from the ranks of former opponents, who became National Socialists out of conviction. Their conversion was at times comparable to a religious experience, one that transformed them into zealous Nazis with a mission. Erich Ebermayer, son of the liberal *Oberreichsanwalt* (the highest prosecutor of the Reich) Ludwig Ebermayer,[23] a well-known author, some of whose books were required reading in upper levels of *Gymnasium* before they were eventually banned in May and June 1933, provides impressive examples—representative, each in its own way—from different spheres of life. First, there was the president of the German Supreme Court, *Reichsgerichtspräsident* Erwin Bumke, a friend of the Ebermayer family, "a man above reproach, anything but a Nazi,"[24] who was ordered to make his inaugural visit to Hitler at the beginning of May: "Bumke was in a bad mood and had absolutely no desire, as a high official of the Prussian school, to offer his hand to this political upstart."[25] Yet, following his return from Berlin,

22. The "casualties of March" who, due to the change in political climate, suddenly discovered that they had been Nazis all along and now rushed to join the party and its organizations. They were also called *Märzveilchen* (March violets) by the "Old Fighters"—those who had joined the NSDAP early on. When the party was closed to newcomers on 1 May, more than 1.6 million new members had joined since 30 January (out of a total of 2.5 million). This was why one's membership number was deemed to reflect one's loyalty to the cause (the lower the number, the earlier one had joined).

23. Ludwig Ebermayer (1858–1933) was *Oberreichsanwalt* from 1921 to 1926.

24. Ebermayer, *Denn heute gehört uns Deutschland*, 76, entry of 9 May 1933. Erich Bumke (1874–1945) had been President of the *Reichsgericht* in Leipzig since 1929. Since 17 December 1932 he was also acting deputy of the *Reichspräsident* in his capacity as president of the Supreme Court (Article 51 of the Weimar Constitution was amended accordingly; before this the Chancellor had been the designated deputy). In 1939, Hitler extended Bumke's term beyond the legal age limit by decree. When American troops entered Leipzig on 20 April 1945, Bumke committed suicide. See Wolfgang Benz and Hermann Graml, eds., *Biographisches Lexikon zur Weimarer Republik* (Munich, 1988), 50.

25. Ebermayer, *Denn heute gehört uns Deutschland*, 76.

Bumke was as if transformed:[26] "He returned as a convert, or at least
almost converted . . . 'One has no sense of the charm, the warmth,
the power of this leadership-personality, unless one has personally
stood in front of him,' he explained to my father. At the end of the
audience Hitler had tightly gripped his hands, looked long and deep
into his eyes, and said with his resonant voice, 'Help me, Bumke.'
With that the soul catcher had made his score perfect."

Erich Ebermayer also felt isolated in his own surroundings,
where an increasing number of close friends professed allegiance to
National Socialism: "Among my young friends, the very best are
committing themselves body and soul to National Socialism . . .
One cannot debate the issue with them because they just believe.
And there are no logical arguments against faith." But Ebermayer
persisted undaunted: "When today . . . I attempted a conversation and ventured—already weak and powerless as one now feels
when confronted with this youth so flushed with victory—to say
that perhaps our entire old culture, the collection of all the intellectual and artistic possessions of the last five hundred years, may
well be drowned in the maelstrom of our age, the triumphant knave
exclaimed with naïve impertinence: 'And so what, my dear man!
That bit of culture is not really so important! Because according to
the Führer, a Thousand Year Reich is now coming into being that
will create its own new culture!'"[27] In the spring of 1933, politics
commanded all spheres of life. Lifelong friendships broke apart because of disagreements about the nature of National Socialism. As
reported by Ebermayer on 28 April: "Short get-together with my
longtime friend H.W. . . . The damned politics wreaks havoc even
here. H. has become a National Socialist! The notorious 'tabloid
critic and Jew hireling,' as he would be called today, has been converted! Not before, but after the *Machtergreifung*. . . . But in H.W.'s
case opportunism does not play a role. He has simply been bowled
over, overawed by the events of the day . . . He positively worships
Hitler. His eyes shine when he speaks of the "Führer."[28] In mid May

26. Ibid., 77. Ebermayer continues: "On that day, without anyone requesting him to do so, Dr. Bumke had the oil painting of the first president of the
Supreme Court, Simson, a Jew who converted to Christianity, removed from
the Great Festival Hall of the Reichsgericht."

27. Ibid., 75–76.

28. Ebermayer, *Denn heute gehört uns Deutschland*, 69. Ebermayer continues
resignedly: "But it is painful. Above all when I consider that there are now millions like him in Germany who have suddenly 'seen the light'. . . . These are
people endowed with sight who have been blinded."

1933, shortly after the official announcement of the prohibition of his books, Ebermayer wrote about a National Socialism ". . . that we have been able to observe for years" and that he thought had been discarded: "If now, in the frenzy of events, it suddenly seems to appear in a different light, it was not insight but temptation and bedazzlement."[29] When remembering H.W., who "had been my good loyal friend through many years of my youth,"[30] Ebermayer commented on the mood in the spring of 1933: "How murderously politics interferes with everything! How it severs ties overnight that had been considered unbreakable! The closer the friendship, the more impossible appears its continuation when it is undermined by an opposing view of the world."[31]

Spring 1933 marked the first high point of the regime's popularity, comparable with the mood after the fall of France in June 1940. In 1933, hopes vested in the regime were geared mainly toward domestic renewal and unity; the road to dictatorship was being paved without apparent awareness that the dictatorship itself would mark the final milestone. In the spring of 1933, the popularity of National Socialism still was based on the restoration of order and the fulfillment of the regime's promise of national unity. This, after all, provided a welcome contrast to the fragmentation and unpopular party infighting of the Weimar Republic. In these early months, even men who were later to gain notoriety as opponents of the regime placed their hopes in National Socialism.[32] One of the most glittering and enigmatic personalities to fall into this category was Otto Dibelius, *Generalsuperintendent* (head of the Protestant church) of Brandenburg since 1925 and, as Klaus Scholder wrote: ". . . with his 45 years the youngest *Generalsuperintendent* of the Prussian Church and without

29. Ebermayer, entry of 15 May 1933, 85.

30. Ibid., 86–87. This was in reaction to the words in one of H.W.'s letters: "It is quite true that politics today takes priority over everything else, because Germany has given us the genius Adolf Hitler. I am ashamed only of one thing—that we were skeptical and lacked faith for too long in this leader and did not recognize his greatness in the full enormity and uniqueness of its power much sooner. Therefore I now feel an even stronger duty for blind and unquestioning allegiance. . . . "

31. Ibid.

32. A prominent example is the man who spearheaded the assassination attempt on Hitler, Claus Graf von Stauffenberg. He had supported Hitler as candidate for President against Hindenburg in 1932. See Peter Hoffmann, *Stauffenberg. A Family History, 1905–1944* (Cambridge, 1995), 69.

doubt the most capable."[33] Though no supporter of the Weimar
Republic and, until March 1933, not unfavorably disposed toward
National Socialism, Dibelius soon distanced himself from the Hitler
regime because he rejected its encroachment upon church affairs.
Removed from his post in June of 1933 and briefly arrested in 1937,
he soon became one of the most prominent figures of the oppositional German Confessional Church during the Third Reich[34] and
one of the very few who dared to protest publicly. Even though Dibelius welcomed the advent of the Hitler government and its electoral success of 5 March, he nevertheless admonished the pastors of
Brandenburg in a confidential circular on 8 March that "the church
must remain the conscience of the state."[35] Even his high-spirited
patriotic sermon in the Potsdam Nikolai Church on 21 March, the
"Day of Potsdam," was not free of critical overtones, though it focused on the theme of domestic unity—with Dibelius making comparisons to the Reichstag opening on 4 August 1914, symbol of the
manifestation of German unity at the beginning of the First World
War. It was thus all the more astonishing when Dibelius, in a radio
broadcast on 4 April, in which he addressed the American population, asked for more sympathetic understanding for the new regime and its methods and clearly downplayed violent Nazi attacks.[36]
In his speech, which highlights the reasons for the popularity of

33. Scholder, in his seminal study *Die Kirchen und das Dritte Reich*, 42.
34. On Dibelius, see Benz and Graml, eds., *Biografisches Lexikon zur Weimarer Republik*, 59–60; Weiß, ed., *Biografisches Lexikon zum Dritten Reich*, 83–84;
Robert S. Wistrich, ed., *Who's Who in Nazi Germany* (London and New York,
1995), 38; Klaus Scholder, "Otto Dibelius," *Zeitschrift für Theologie und Kirche* 78
(1981), 90–104. After the war Dibelius was accused of not speaking out against
the Nazi extermination policy, even though he had known about it from Kurt
Gerstein.
35. See "Rundbrief des Generalsuperintendenten Otto Dibelius," in Becker
and Becker, eds., *Hitlers Machtergreifung*, 129–132, esp. 131. Dibelius criticized
"pastors going around their communities sporting party badges and greeting
their parishioners with Heil Hitler." Ibid., 132. On account of this circular, Dibelius became involved in a dispute with the Brandenburg *Oberpräsident* (provincial governor) and *Gauleiter* of the Kurmark, Wilhelm Kube, who had founded
a church party out of which emerged the "German Christians." See Scholder,
Kirchen, 277–300.
36. Reprinted in Becker and Becker, eds., *Hitlers Machtergreifung*, 207–211.
Dibelius depicted the anti-Semitic boycott of 1 April as a defensive measure. On
the other hand, he was speaking to a foreign audience, trying to elicit understanding for Germany, and was thus disposed to distort reality and paint a rosy
picture.

Nazism, Dibelius drew the picture of a people who, after a long inner struggle, had finally found themselves again, despite the burdensome handicap of the Weimar Republic: "From the inner decay to which we were driven during the past 15 years, we want to return to a Christian and genuinely German way of life. Have confidence that the German people are at the point of finding themselves again." The movement now sweeping Germany meant "a return to the good German traditions."[37] In his radio broadcast, Dibelius evoked the danger of a communist revolution—a fear all too real for many Germans—fed by reports of horrors from Bolshevik Russia, memories of "communist terror" in Munich in 1919, and the 1921 communist revolt in Thuringia. National Socialism appeared as a savior from those dangers: "With rising anxiety we asked ourselves: when will the Bolshevik revolution break loose?. . . . Well, now it has turned out differently than we thought possible. The revolution has been defeated without street fighting or loss of blood. The new government has removed communist agitators and their allies from public life with thoroughgoing and drastic measures."[38] While Dibelius, in his Potsdam sermon of 21 March, made references to the fact that the Germans were "not yet a united people,"[39] he ended his radio speech—only two weeks later—on a very different note: "Today the German Reich is united and strongly joined together as never before in our history. Millions of German hearts are imbued with the impassioned wish that the German name will again stand pure and unblemished before the eyes of the world."[40] This

37. Ibid., 210–211.
38. Ibid., 208. Dibelius presented a vivid picture of the noticeable relief that was then being felt all across Germany. He conceded that there had been "transgressions," but maintained that public life as a whole remained a "picture of order and discipline."
39. Partially reprinted in Becker and Becker, eds., *Hitlers Machtergreifung*, 156–157; Günther van Norden, *Der deutsche Protestantismus im Jahr der nationalsozialistischen Machtergreifung* (Gütersloh, 1979), 52–55.
40. "Rundfunkansprache des Generalsuperintendenten der Kurmark, Otto Dibelius vom 4. April," in Becker and Becker, eds., *Hitlers Machtergreifung*, 207–211, esp. 210. Dibelius's speech made it clear that even in the eyes of critical observers, National Socialism could point to two important successes by the spring of 1933: (1) In contrast to Weimar, the people were not divided into a large number of parties, but seemed united as a nation, in public perception partially because of the centralization of the Reich; (2) "order" had been reestablished and the Communist danger was eliminated. It was also an immense asset for the regime to have men of Dibelius's great moral authority on its side.

desire, as history has sadly demonstrated, would remain unfulfilled. Had Dibelius ventured to say openly what he had seen, heard, and known about National Socialism and its methods between 30 January and early April 1933, he would have realized that his hopes were bound to be dashed.

But like Dibelius, millions reveled in deluding themselves, though they must have known otherwise. Underneath the surface, dictatorship had already become reality. Apart from the multitude of violent attacks and the establishment of concentration camps, in the spring of 1933 the dictatorship was already weaving itself into the fabric of German society in all of its layers and nuances. Hand in hand with a tremendous upsurge in the popularity of National Socialism and—among some sections of the population—a growing feeling of solidarity, of a nascent "organic" national community reminiscent of August 1914,[41] there developed an insidious, all-encompassing repression that also constituted an essential component of the changed climate of the spring of 1933. In April, the German population was informed through its daily press that the "dissemination of unsubstantiated rumors was a punishable offense." If spreading of rumors resulted in severe damage "to the Reich or one of the Länder," it was punishable by a prison term. Punishment fell under the jurisdiction of special courts, which would recognize neither probation nor parole.[42] Though insidious in their potentially totalitarian impact, these measures did not initially affect the majority of Germans, since the dissemination of negative rumors or—in the jargon of the day, "horror propaganda"—was expected to emanate solely from Communists or Social Democrats, so that this regulation could be explained away as "self protection" of the regime. Of greater underlying danger and incalculable in its impact was a decree of 22

---

41. For parallels between the Nazi takeover and August 1914 see Peter Fritzsche, *Germans into Nazis* (Cambridge, Mass., 1998), 148. "For conservatives and Stahlhelmers, for 'Tory' workers and rural protesters, as well as for Hitler's voters, long years of opposition to the Weimar Republic had finally culminated in the victory of January 1933, a moment which overcame the shame of November 1918 and restored the promise of August 1914, when Germans had pulled together for the national cause. In other words, the National Socialists tapped into a more generic 'national socialist' consensus that extended well beyond Hitler's party and his electorate."

42. Otfried Brügge, ed., *Hannover wird nationalsozialistisch. Quellenlesebuch zur Machtübernahme* (Hannover, 1981), 33. Even the careless repetition of rumors, that is, without malicious intent, was to be punished with a three-month jail sentence or a fine, so that even harmless gossip could have serious consequences.

June 1933, initially directed toward the administration of the Prussian Interior Ministry, to combat the so-called *"Miesmachertum"* (a defeatist attitude that manifested itself in veiled criticism) inside the Ministry.[43] According to the ordinance, it had been observed that civil servants and employees in the Ministry "had made comments in their conversations with other persons that were designed to generate dissatisfaction with the measures of the national government and thus sow distrust."[44] Such persons could "accurately be described with the term '*Miesmacher*' . . ."[45] In future such *Miesmachertum* would be considered "a form of Marxist agitation," and *Miesmacher* were thus "viewed as hidden Marxists who were still continuing their Marxist activities."[46] In plain language, this meant that even the most benign critical comment, however justified, by a member of the Prussian administration would be viewed as "Marxist agitation." The decree thus nipped any criticism in the bud in a particularly drastic fashion. Furthermore, "all civil servants, employees and workers" were ordered to "remain on the look-out for such cases in question and to report immediately any person concerned." This again bears Göring's mark, as the formulation is reminiscent of his decree of 17 February 1933 to the Prussian police.[47] Göring further stressed that he would view non-observance of the duty to report offenders as a "declaration of solidarity with such rabble-rousers and agitators."[48] This decree broke with all the traditions of the Prussian administration. Even in the first half of the nineteenth century, when most states in the German Confederation

43. "Bekämpfung des sogenannten Miesmachertums," *Ministerialblatt für die preußische innere Verwaltung*, at Geheimes Staatsarchiv Preußischer Kulturbesitz, Berlin-Dahlem (GStAPK), "Preußisches Staatsministerium," Rep. 90, no. 2326, 222. The decree was addressed to provincial and district governors, presidents of police, county councilors (*Landräte*), and the communities and communal associations and was thus bound to reach every Prussian administrative official.

44. GStAPK, Ibid., 222.

45. The ordinance differed substantially in its tone from the language traditionally used in comparable ordinances, as may be ascertained by the colloquial expression "*Miesmacher*," which was regionally colored and not at all common in southern Germany. See also Broszat, *Der Staat Hitlers*, 145.

46. GStAPK, Ibid., 222.

47. Hsi-Huey Liang, *The Berlin Police Force in the Weimar Republic* (Berkeley and Los Angeles, 1970), 171–172; Bracher, Sauer, Schulz, *Die nationalsozialistische Machtergreifung*, 2nd ed. (Köln and Opladen, 1962), 72–74.

48. "Bekämpfung des sogenannten Miesmachertums," at Geheimes Staatsarchiv Preußischer Kulturbesitz, Berlin-Dahlem, "Preußisches Staatsministerium," Rep. 90, no. 2326, 222.

eagerly adopted Metternich's police state methods, the Prussian civil service remained a "debating administration."[49] With Göring's ordinance against *"Miesmachertum,"* Prussian civil servants, from the lowest employee to the *Oberpräsident,* were fitted with a muzzle and had implanted a pair of scissors in their heads that censored every original idea and critical thought, eliminated constructive criticism, and firmly implanted the virus of the police state in every Prussian district, county, and local authority.

But by the late spring of 1933 this was neither new nor revolutionary, since by then the surveillance state had long become a reality. By the end of April, the French Ambassador in Berlin reported to his Foreign Minister that correspondence and telephone calls of diplomatic missions in Berlin were being monitored. He himself knew from the son of German Foreign Minister Neurath that even officials in the German Foreign Office were subjected to close political control. And a colleague of François-Poncet, upon entering an SA office, had chanced to overhear a recording of a telephone conversation that he himself had conducted that very morning.[50] In addition to the constant and all-too-justified fear of eavesdroppers, the omnipresent "ear against the wall," and denunciation by neighbors and colleagues that from March onwards spread like a plague, in the spring of 1933 there was unprecedented coercion to prove one's nationalist orientation and openly demonstrate one's nationalist sensibilities by taking part in National Socialist celebrations and rites. It soon became obligatory, for example, to raise the swastika flag on days that marked National Socialist festive occasions, such as 20 April and 1 May. Whoever refrained from participating would be reported. This coercion to take part and join in—with concomitant sanctions for offenders—became established policy in the spring of 1933. Erich Ebermayer, for example, reported that a horde of SA men had climbed over the garden fence of his parents' house in Leipzig and, with a battle cry of "the swine haven't hung out the flag, they need to be taught a lesson," demolished the entire garden, simply because his mother had failed to comply with the obligatory

49. Thomas Nipperdey, *Deutsche Geschichte* (Munich, 1983), 333 (see also chapter 6 above).

50. François-Poncet to Paul Boncour, 24 April 1933, in *Documents Diplomatiques Français 1932–1939. Première Série*, vol. III (Paris, 1966), 312–313. (The recording was made on a phonographic record.)

flag raising.[51] And on 14 July 1933 Reich Interior Minister Wilhelm Frick made the "Heil Hitler" salute obligatory for all civil servants; the *Hitlergruß* thus soon served to differentiate between those who sympathized with the Nazis and those who opposed them.[52] Whoever did not want to come under suspicion of adopting a critical stance toward the regime was well advised always to shout loudly "Heil Hitler" as the established public greeting. Whoever wanted to express reservations about the regime could signal his defiance with a simple "Guten Tag."

At the same time, a mental and intellectual censorship set in which Central and Western Europe had not experienced since the Inquisition. At the end of April, there was already talk of black and white lists, of proscribed and acceptable authors.[53] The well-known book burning of 10 May was only the public expression of an already poisoned atmosphere, and the authors who were publicly outlawed on that day by no means included all of those whose works were banned.[54] Aside from the fact that the outlawed author was soon avoided like the plague, even in his own familiar surroundings,[55] the general knowledge about banned books led to reluctant self-censorship. Certain books could no longer be purchased and even if one owned a copy, one scarcely dared to read such books in public, on a park bench, or in the subway. Bookcases in the home were censored accordingly: the works of Thomas and Heinrich Mann, Stefan Zweig, Erich Maria Remarque, and other "undesirable" authors vanished to the back row, covered up by books of authors

51. Ebermayer, *Denn heute gehört uns Deutschland,* 140. The incident occurred on the occasion of Hitler's visit in Leipzig in mid July 1933. It was reported by Ebermayer's mother in a letter to her son, who was not in Leipzig at the time. As Ebermayer noted, his mother was lucky that the incident did not culminate in a home invasion.

52. Cuno Horkenbach, ed., *Das Deutsche Reich von 1918 bis heute,* vol. 4 (Berlin, 1935), 284.

53. Oskar Loerke, *Tagebücher 1903–1939,* ed. by Hermann Kasack, 2nd ed. (Heidelberg and Darmstadt, 1955), 272.

54. Erich Ebermayer's name, for example, was initially not on the long list of prohibited authors whose books were publicly burned, such as Stefan Zweig, Franz Werfel, Fritz von Unruh, Ernst Toller, Erich Maria Remarque, Berthold Brecht, Heinrich Mann, Walter Hasenclever, Theodor Wolff, Arnold Zweig, and many others. Relief was great, but of short duration. Four days later, Ebermayer found out that his novels were likewise prohibited; Ebermayer, *Denn heute gehört uns Deutschland,* 79, 83–84.

55. Ibid., entry of 16 May 1933, 86.

tolerated by the regime. Aside from the encroachment of politics into the private sphere of life, this inevitably led to mistrust and caution even among one's friends and imposed restrictions on social discourse, because people took care to invite into their homes only those whom they could absolutely trust. Even this social development in the micro-sphere of private life—increased distrust that undermined existing private circles—was ultimately grist for the mill of the evolving dictatorship. Its omnipresent menace appeared even more acute and dangerous, because Hindenburg, still the superior authority and last safeguard against Nazi arbitrariness and despotism, became increasingly inactive, so that the door to lawlessness was now opened wide. On 23 July, for example, the American *chargé d'affaires*, George A. Gordon, reported to his Secretary of State that the President evinced no reaction at all when SA units took "aggressive action against various [of his] Junker neighbors" several days earlier, even though the attack "could only be interpreted in the nature of a veritable challenge and of wanting to see how far they could go."[56] Even more audacious, SA guards replaced the *Stahlhelm* guard at Hindenburg's estate in Neudeck, "without asking the President's leave or consent and without . . . his doing anything about it."[57] Since Hindenburg had been the last effective source of appeal and check on Hitler's power, there were now no more restraints to arbitrary actions. Hugenberg and the DNVP, though much was expected of them,[58] were utterly powerless and unable to protect even their own members. The petitions addressed to Papen in the spring of 1933 already provide an unmistakable foretaste of the complete absence of legal protection for the individual in the Third Reich and the powerlessness of third parties to intercede— even the Vice Chancellor of the Reich. The following is one case history among many: in early June 1933 the Westphals, a Cologne

56. 23 June 1933, "The Chargé in Germany (Gordon) to the Acting Secretary of State" *Foreign Relations of the United States. Diplomatic Papers*, Vol. II, 1933 (Washington, 1949), 234. (The *chargé d'affaires* transacts diplomatic business during the temporary absence of an ambassador.) Brüning and Treviranus mentioned this incident to Gordon on the occasion of a dinner on 22 June.

57. Ibid., 235.

58. Georg Bernhard, the former editor of the liberal *Vossische Zeitung*, is a telling example of how the influence of the DNVP was overrated. Even in the late spring of 1933, he was convinced that "in the long run German Nationals are bound to constitute an obstacle for the implementation of Nazism's racial idiocies." In Georg Bernhard, *Die deutsche Tragödie. Selbstmord einer Republik* (Prague, 1933), 25. Chapter 5 above tells a very different story.

couple in their mid sixties, reported a raid by an SS detachment of eleven armed men on their family home. The raid took place at midnight between 24 and 25 April and involved a prolonged, three-hour-long search of the Westphal's home and the SS's theft of money and other valuables. The couple's protests over the confiscation of three savings books were answered by the threat of one SS trooper to "shut your trap or I'll smack you one on your mug." The police and city administration had behaved in exemplary fashion, but were powerless against the SS in their effort to have the valuables restored.[59] The theft insurance company refused payment on the grounds that the SS commando represented legitimate state authority. The couple then pleadingly turned to Papen, as the "one who paved the way for the German revolution," with the request to bring to bear his influence on the *Gauleitung* (Nazi party authorities at the *Gau* level) to have the stolen items returned.[60] All Papen was able to do, however, was to convey his regret through his assistant Carl-Friedrich von Savigny that "mistakes and transgressions are not always avoidable in such turbulent times as today."[61] He was unable to help. By the spring of 1933, every German was conscious of the fact that the civil administration could no longer assert itself against the Nazi party and its organizations. Police, public prosecutors, and county councils felt powerless and remained inactive when confronted with open breaches of the law, well aware that they were in no position to counter injustices.[62] With respect to unwarranted arrests, public prosecutors' offices could merely ascertain that no

59. 6 June 1933 at BA Berlin-Lichterfelde, "Stellvertreter des Reichskanzlers, Kanzlei von Papen," R 53, no. 184, 74–75.

60. Ibid., 75.

61. 19 June 1933 at BA Berlin-Lichterfelde, "Kanzlei von Papen," R 53, no. 184, 76. Von Savigny, well aware that this was only one infraction of many that would remain unatoned, wrote to the Westphals that "an intervention in pending proceedings is . . . on principle inadmissible."

62. The lawlessness of the half year following 30 January 1933 went so far that there were already cases of *Sippenhaft* (in which entire family clans were held liable for the actions of one of their members). Thus, five of Philipp Scheidemann's relatives were interned in a concentration camp after he had published an article in the *New York Times* that was critical of the Nazi regime. Scheidemann managed to obtain the release of his relatives only after a public disavowal of his own article. He was expatriated on 23 August 1933, and his personal property was confiscated. See Becker and Becker, eds., *Hitlers Machtergreifung*, 377; Bracher et al., *Die nationalsozialistische Machtergreifung*, 2nd ed. (Cologne, Opladen, 1962), 301.

grounds existed for an arrest, but they were unable to intervene or make restitution. The professional morale of civil servants and the civil administration suffered accordingly. Failure to act undermined the professional ethos of individual officials and of the civil administration as a whole. As a form of self-defense or to have an alibi for their own inactivity, many officials (as, in fact, the German population as a whole) tended to gloss over infractions and attacks and shrug them off as unavoidable side-effects of the "revolution." It was this climate of nationalist ecstasy and lawlessness, of euphoria and wanton arbitrariness, of hope and tight surveillance, that set the stage for the final act in the history of the DNVP.

Prohibitions, Desertions, and Dissolutions

The first major prohibitions that led to temporary bans of organizations close to the DNVP, such as the *Stahlhelm*, began already at the end of March in the small northern German state of Braunschweig, where National Socialists had participated in government since 1931.[63] In fact, it was Braunschweig's National Socialist Interior Minister (and later *Ministerpräsident*) Dietrich Klagges who had made it possible for Hitler to obtain German citizenship in February 1932, thereby enabling him to stand as a candidate in the presidential elections of March and April 1932.[64] The DVP, DNVP, and SPD had traditionally been strongly represented in Braunschweig, so that acrimonious political conflicts were inevitable.[65] Since 1931 Braunschweig was thus a testing ground for the NSDAP and, in Volker Berghahn's words, "a kind of pocket-book edition of the

63. Braunschweig, with an area of 3,672.05 square kilometers, was only 6.6 times as large as Lake Constance. It had a population of 518,736 (16 June 1933), less than one-eighth of that of Berlin.

64. On Braunschweig politics in the early 1930s, see Ernst-August Roloff, *Bürgertum und Nationalsozialismus 1930–1933. Braunschweigs Weg ins Dritte Reich* (Hannover, 1961). The author is the son of the former DNVP parliamentary faction leader in the Braunschweig Landtag. Dietrich Klagges (1891–1971) had been a Nazi party member since 1925.

65. In the Braunschweig Landtag elections of 7 December 1924, which took place concurrently with the Reichstag elections, the DVP received 17.2 percent of the vote; the DNVP 18.5; and the SPD 37.4 (and 46.2 in the Landtag election of 27 November 1927); Falter, *Wahlen und Abstimmungen*, 92.

'Third Reich'."[66] Following the *Machtergreifung*, the Braunschweig *Stahlhelm* had helped curb the influence of the SPD and was prominent in actions against largely Social Democratic communities and districts. After 5 March, the Braunschweig *Stahlhelm* itself became a target of SA attacks.[67] On 20 March, the Braunschweig *Stahlhelm* leader Ernst Schrader complained to Theodor Duesterberg,[68] one of the two national leaders of the organization, about the Nazi attacks, since Duesterberg's reservations about National Socialism were generally known. To strengthen the position of the Braunschweig *Stahlhelm* and augment its membership, Schrader decided to accept a large influx of new members from now-banned organizations, such as the republican *Reichsbanner*, who were either not welcome in the SA or preferred non-Nazi organizations. For this purpose the Braunschweig *Stahlhelm* decided upon an agreement with a Braunschweig *Reichsbanner* leader that provided for the acceptance of 150 of its members.[69] Thus, on 27 March the Braunschweig *Stahlhelm* office was swamped by a horde of hundreds of applicants that kept growing during the course of the day. The confusion, the jostling of the crowd, and the ongoing, very public recruitment of former Social Democrats and some Communists provided Nazi Interior Minister Klagges with the excuse to intervene under the pretext that a *Stahlhelm* instigated coup was underway. SA auxiliary police and the SS subsequently arrested two thousand *Stahlhelm* members and about 1,200 "Marxists," many of whom were seriously injured in the process.[70] The Braunschweig *Stahlhelm* was immediately disbanded,

66. Volker Berghahn, *Der Stahlhelm. Bund der Frontsoldaten 1918–1945* (Düsseldorf, 1966), 263.

67. Roloff, *Bürgertum und Nationalsozialismus*, 146–151; Bracher, *Stufen der Machtergreifung*, 288–289; Berghahn, *Der Stahlhelm*, 263–266; Theodor Duesterberg, *Der Stahlhelm und Hitler*, 45–46.

68. Theodor Duesterberg (1875–1950) was second *Bundesführer* of the *Stahlhelm*, co-equal with Franz Seldte, who was the first *Bundesführer* (both since 1924).

69. See Berghahn, *Stahlhelm*, 264; Roloff, *Bürgertum*, 148–149. This agreement ran counter to the previous conduct of the *Stahlhelm*, which had fought the *Reichsbanner* and SPD in Braunschweig. In the circumstances, it was thus reasonable to assume that the action was aimed at the Nazis.

70. Roloff, *Bürgertum*, 149: "Ambulances transported the wounded the whole day without a break, the traces of the horrible bloodbath remained visible for a long time thereafter . . . large puddles of blood testified to the fact that the Stahlhelmers suffered the same fate at the same hour in the Volksfreund-Haus as the Social Democrats, who were still being beaten to death there." Duesterberg's

though the head national leader of the organization, Franz Seldte, who had founded the *Stahlhelm* in 1918 and was now Minister of Labor (*Reichsarbeitsminister*) in the Hitler Cabinet, managed to get the ban rescinded on 1 April 1933. As a precondition for lifting the ban, Seldte had promised to initiate disciplinary measures against the Braunschweig *Stahlhelm* leadership. At this point it was in Seldte's as well as in Hitler's interest to downplay, minimize, and resolve the Braunschweig incident as quickly as possible, since it had attracted much unfavorable attention throughout the Reich by highlighting the tension between Nazis and German Nationals. During a Cabinet meeting on 29 March, Hitler thus hastened to confirm that "the situation had been completely cleared up" and that there remained "no trace of ill-will between the Minister of Labor and the National Socialist members of the Reich Cabinet."[71]

While Hitler tried to pacify his Cabinet colleagues over the *Stahlhelm* affair, he was determined to remove *Stahlhelm* leader Theodor Duesterberg, who had been the DNVP presidential candidate in March 1932, and whom Hitler secretly suspected of being behind the Braunschweig incident.[72] It was not without reason that the Nazis considered Duesterberg an obstacle in their efforts to eliminate the *Stahlhelm* as an independent political force.[73] Duesterberg had put *Stahlhelm* troopers on alert between 3–6 March to prevent Nazi rioting and attacks before and after the 5 March elections. On the whole, however, the *Stahlhelm*'s role was ambiguous to say the least, and more help than hindrance to the Nazis, especially since the organization actively participated, often together with the SA, in *Gleichschaltung* measures and in eliminating the opposition,

---

account, *Der Stahlhelm und Hitler*, contains occasional inconsistencies regarding the order of events.

71. Minuth, ed., *Akten der Reichskanzlei*, 270. Contrary to what might reasonably be expected, DNVP chairman Hugenberg rarely participated in Cabinet discussions about these or other decisive political issues. His colleague in the Cabinet, Minister of Finance Lutz Graf Schwerin von Krosigk, noted disapprovingly that Hugenberg evinced no interest in general political questions "even when, as with the Enabling Act and the law to purge the bureaucracy, these were of the utmost significance." Lutz Graf Schwerin von Krosigk, *Es geschah in Deutschland* (Tübingen and Stuttgart, 1951), 174.

72. In his memoirs, *Der Stahlhelm und Hitler*, 46, Duesterberg reported that Hitler accosted him angrily at a diplomatic reception shortly after the events of Braunschweig: "It was you who first gave your leader Schrader the order to stage a putsch. It is therefore your fault." Ibid.

73. Ibid., 46–47; Berghahn, *Der Stahlhelm*, 251.

even if this meant resorting to force. In his public pronouncements Duesterberg supported the National Socialist government,[74] while his personal experiences and implied criticisms had marked him as an enemy of the Nazis. As a candidate in the 1932 presidential elections, he had been mocked and scorned by the Nazi press on account of his Jewish grandfather, and his own veiled criticism[75]—when, for example, he pointed out that among Socialists and Catholics there were also hundreds of thousands of honorable front-line soldiers— indicated that his allegiance could not be relied upon.

Seldte was quick to perceive that Duesterberg had to be forced from his position to ensure the survival of the *Stahlhelm* as an independent organization. After Duesterberg had shown no interest in becoming *Oberpräsident* of the Grenzmark, a position offered to him by Papen and Meissner, and also turned down an extended holiday proposed by Seldte (a yearlong world tour), Seldte knew he had to take action.[76] This would prove difficult, since a majority of the *Stahlhelm*'s twenty-three *Landesverbandsführer* (Land Association leaders), whose consent was needed for a lawful discharge, supported Duesterberg. Thus, at the meeting of the *Stahlhelm*'s national council on 1 April 1933, Seldte was compelled to withdraw the letter in which he had called on Duesterberg to resign, due to pressure from the majority of the other *Stahlhelm* leaders. At this meeting, Duesterberg was even elevated to "Acting *Bundesführer*," since

74. For example, in a speech in Leipzig on 15 March 1933: "We know how much the frontline fighters Göring and Hitler esteem the old comrades from the World War now gathered in the Stahlhelm and how close comrade Seldte is to the men in the cabinet." Cited in Berghahn, *Der Stahlhelm*, 254. As leader of an organization that was officially represented in the government, Duesterberg had to condone its actions, whether he agreed with them or not.

75. Berghahn, *Der Stahlhelm*, 250. Duesterberg's occasional criticism of Nazism was not free of contradictions, since he himself was anti-democratic and had always rejected the Weimar Republic.

76. Duesterberg, *Der Stahlhelm und Hitler*, 52–53. The events that led to Duesterberg's dismissal on 26 April 1933 are described in detail in "Die gewaltsame Amtsenthebung des 2. B.F. Duesterberg," at BA Berlin-Lichterfelde, "Stellvertreter des Reichskanzlers, Kanzlei von Papen," R 53, no. 2, 13–26. This chronologically organized protocol corresponds to the chapter "Das Protokoll über die Führerkrise im Stahlhelm," in Duesterberg, *Der Stahlhelm und Hitler*, 51–63, down to linguistic idiosyncrasies and incorrect dating, except that the chapter in Duesterberg's memoirs is supplemented with his own observations. The protocol was drafted by Major Egon Krieger on 23 May 1933.

Seldte was fully occupied with his ministerial post.[77] In the first half of April it became increasingly clear that Duesterberg's continued presence in his position was detrimental to the organization as a whole but, in a session on 20 April, Seldte's renewed attempt to force Duesterberg's dismissal again failed to gain the support of a majority of *Stahlhelm* leaders. Duesterberg, on the other hand, was prepared to abdicate voluntarily, provided that the continuity and equal standing of the *Stahlhelm* would be guaranteed by this step. Since it was clear to Seldte that Hitler would never agree to any real autonomy of the *Stahlhelm*, and that it would also be impossible to dismiss Duesterberg by dint of a vote, he finally opted for coercion.[78] On 26 April, Seldte's ally, the *Stahlhelm* leader of Greater Berlin, Major Franz von Stephani, stormed Duesterberg's Berlin office, armed and escorted, to present Duesterberg the news of his dismissal. In his memoirs, Duesterberg emphasized that he bowed to force only after von Stephani had given him his word of honor that Hindenburg had also demanded his resignation. This, however, soon turned out to be untrue.[79]

It is striking that in the case of Duesterberg's dismissal, Nazi organizations did not even have to make an appearance to eliminate their rival. By the end of April 1933, the political climate had changed to such an extent that many were eager to remove obstacles from the path of the victorious movement so as to spare themselves. Seldte joined the NSDAP on 26 April and placed the *Stahlhelm* under the

---

77. Duesterberg, *Der Stahlhelm und Hitler*, 53. The "Akten der Kanzlei von Papen," BA Berlin-Lichterfelde, R 53, no. 2, 4–10, contain a confidential commentary on Duesterberg's removal from office with the heading: "Am 24.7.33 an Herrn von Tschirschky zur Einordnung in die geheimen Akten übergeben." Fritz-Günther von Tschirschky was von Papen's assistant. See Fritz-Günther von Tschirschky, *Erinnerungen eines Hochverräters* (Stuttgart, 1972), 95–121. Duesterberg's own account, based on Egon Krieger's chronological breakdown of events, is subjectively colored and condemns Seldte's actions as opportunistic, disloyal, and even dishonest, while Berghahn's examination (*Der Stahlhelm*, 245–263) also sheds light on Seldte's motives, thus making his actions more understandable.

78. See BA Berlin-Lichterfelde, "Stellvertreter des Reichskanzlers, Kanzlei von Papen," R53, no. 2, 20–24; Duesterberg, *Der Stahlhelm und Hitler*, 56–60; Berghahn, *Der Stahlhelm*, 258–261. Berghahn concluded: "Only after the ruins of the German catastrophe does Seldte's behavior appear 'fraudulent.' In the spring of 1933, it was perfectly in line with his principles" (*Der Stahlhelm*, 258–259).

79. Duesterberg, *Der Stahlhelm und Hitler*, 59–60. Duesterberg suspected that Major von Stephani had been deceived by Seldte about Hindenburg's true position. Duesterberg emphasized that on 28 April Hindenburg sent him "a very appreciative letter and a large portrait of himself" (60).

leadership of Hitler, who was also the highest-ranking leader of the SA.[80] This was done in the hope of preserving the *Stahlhelm* as an independent organization for the foreseeable future. At a convention of all *Stahlhelm* leaders on 30 April, the success of Seldte's strategy was confirmed, since only a minority of those attending protested against the *Stahlhelm* now falling under Hitler's authority. With his defection to the Nazi camp, Seldte had correctly assessed the mood of the times.[81]

In the second half of April the first signs of disintegration appeared within the DNVP. On 24 April 1933 the leadership of the Braunschweig DNVP decided, by a vote of 22 to 2, to switch over *en masse* to the NSDAP, which was another manifestation of nationalist euphoria and pro-Nazi ecstasy that epitomized the contemporary Zeitgeist. The German National party chairman in Braunschweig, *Studienrat* Baumann, had already called for "unconditional joyous collaboration with the National Socialist state" in his speech celebrating Hitler's birthday on 20 April.[82] Since all four Landtag deputies of the Battlefront Black-White-Red were among the defectors, the Braunschweig Landtag was the first representative body of a German Land that was comprised solely of National Socialists.[83] The Nazi press made much of the incident and widely circulated the explanation put forth by the Braunschweig German Nationals: "The members of the executive committee of the Braunschweig Land Association do not consider themselves to be changing one party for another, because the party system is dead and we do not wish to see it revived. Germany's fate calls for unified lead-

80. Berghahn, *Der Stahlhelm*, 265–267; Broszat, *Der Staat Hitlers*, 121–122; Hans-Ulrich Thamer, *Verführung und Gewalt. Deutschland 1933–1945* (Berlin, 1986), 288.

81. Berghahn, *Der Stahlhelm*, 262; 266–274. At a meeting with Hitler on 21 June 1933, Seldte relinquished his command over the younger *Stahlhelm* members; only those older than thirty-five remained under his authority. Those from age eighteen to thirty-five were integrated into the SA as *Wehrstahlhelm*.

82. A *Gymnasium* teacher by profession, Baumann maintained that petty criticism and complaining now had to cease, since the nation had to be imbued with one unified will; see Roloff, *Bürgertum*, 158–159. For press reports on the incident see BA Berlin-Lichterfelde, "Pressearchiv Reichslandbund, DNVP und Nationalsozialismus," R 8034 II, no. 9030, 177–180; and "Organisiertes Bürgertum," R 8034 II, no. 9021, 16–20.

83. The KPD and SPD had been eliminated, the Catholic Center was not represented in the Landtag of Protestant Braunschweig, and the DVP had dissolved itself on 26 April; Roloff, *Bürgertum*, 131–161.

ership . . . Rivalry between organizations striving toward the same goals, when the hearts of their members are filled with the same nationalist ardor, is unacceptable to us in light of Germany's grave political situation."[84] The deputy chairman of the Braunschweig DNVP publicly urged Hugenberg to incorporate the entire DNVP into the Nazi party, arguing that Hugenberg's knowledge and expertise could best serve the national government if he merged his party into the "German freedom movement."[85] Hugenberg, resolved to uphold the independence of the DNVP, immediately appointed a new Land Association leader for Braunschweig, so that the party continued to exist even if defections of its members to the NSDAP continued unabated.[86] Even though German Nationals played down the defections as best they could and Hugenberg tenaciously stayed his course to preserve the integrity of the DNVP, this latest incident nevertheless gave rise to fundamental criticism regarding the policies and strategy pursued by the German Nationals. Even voices sympathetic to the party considered Braunschweig to be only the tip of the iceberg. The *Reichsbote*, a paper of "Protestant-nationalist" persuasion, wrote, for example, that the defection of the Braunschweig Land Association was a "symptom of the inner disintegration of the German National leadership . . . who hid behind the enclosure of a departmentalized civil service and a bureaucratic party machine . . ."[87] Hugenberg was accused of having isolated himself from the public by shutting himself away in his ministerial offices, and the German Nationals were blamed for neglecting political propaganda, having made armchair decisions "from a bureaucratic ivory tower."

84. "Landesverband Braunschweig der DNVP zur NSDAP übergetreten," *Völkischer Beobachter*, 25 April 1933.

85. BA Berlin-Lichterfelde, "Pressearchiv Reichslandbund, DNVP und Nationalsoialismus," R 8034 II, no. 9030, 179; "Nicht eine Partei, sondern Deutschland," *Völkischer Beobachter*, 26 April 1933.

86. Roloff, *Bürgertum*, 159; BA Berlin-Lichterfelde, "Pressearchiv Reichslandbund, DNVP und Nationalsozialismus," no. 9030, 180–181, esp. "Hugenbergs sturer Kampf," *Der Jungdeutsche*, 28 April 1933; "Die Braunschweiger Austritte. Erklärung der DNVP," *Berliner Lokal Anzeiger*, 27 April 1933. In its official explanation, the DNVP emphasized that the members of the Braunschweig executive committee who had defected had previously complained about the Nazis and sought protection from the German National party leadership in Berlin. Their defection, therefore, appeared more like a form of political suicide or desperate self-defense than an act of political conviction.

87. BA Berlin-Lichterfelde, "Pressearchiv Reichslandbund, Organisiertes Bürgertum," R 8034 II, no. 9021, 17, "Wie lange noch Hugenberg?" *Der Reichsbote. Tageszeitung für das evangelische Deutschland*, 26 April 1933.

According to the *Reichsbote*, the Braunschweig defection was unlikely to remain an isolated occurrence, since the German Nationals could no longer exempt themselves from the powerful drive toward the unification of people and state.[88] As a result of the Braunschweig DNVP's defection, widely interpreted as an indication of things to come, the press repeatedly raised the question of whether it was not high time for the German Nationals to merge with National Socialism, since the DNVP had clearly lost its legitimacy as an "autonomous national force."[89]

Throughout the spring, the Nazis had already made a concerted effort to discredit and prosecute a number of conservative personalities who had become bothersome and inconvenient. Dr. Günther Gereke (1893–1970), for example, the Reich Commissar for Job Creation, who had also been a member of Schleicher's Cabinet, was arrested on 24 March on a charge of embezzlement and was dismissed from his post on 27 March.[90] The German National *Oberbürgermeister* of Düsseldorf, Robert Lehr (1883–1956), was detained in mid April 1933 on suspicion of corruption, and the conservative chairman of the *Reichslandbund*, Eberhard Graf von Kalckreuth (1881–1941), whose organization had supported Hitler even before 30 January, was accused of speculation in the grain trade and illegal personal enrichment in early May.[91] His post was filled by a National Socialist.

88. According to the *Reichsbote*, Hugenberg's tenure in office was "but a matter of weeks or days."

89. One headline posed the question concerning the DNVP's status as "Party, or Link in the National Movement?" For reports on this issue, also from the semi-independent Center Party and liberal press, see BA Berlin-Lichterfelde, "Pressearchiv Reichslandbund, Organisiertes Bürgertum," R 8034 II, no. 9021, 18–20.

90. Wolfgang Sauer made it clear that he did not consider these charges conclusive: "In March 1933, he [i.e., Gereke] was one of the first to disappear in the maelstrom of National Socialist terror." In Bracher, Sauer, Schulz, *Die nationalsozialistische Machtergreifung*, 660; also Brüning, *Memoiren*, 660. Gereke was charged with having embezzled a million Reichsmark, partly from Hindenburg's reelection campaign fund. See Minuth, ed., *Akten der Reichskanzlei*, 248; and Günther Gereke, *Ich war königlich-preußischer Landrat* (Berlin/East, 1969).

91. Walter Först, *Robert Lehr als Oberbürgermeister. Ein Kapitel deutscher Kommunalpolitik* (Düsseldorf and Vienna, 1962); Broszat, *Der Staat Hitlers*, 232. According to Brüning (*Memoiren*, 654), Lehr, charged with enriching himself with public funds, remained imprisoned for a year and a half. Bracher argues that the charges against Kalckreuth were based on pure fabrication. See Bracher, *Die nationalsozialistische Machtergreifung*, 188.

Given the rapid accumulation of events unfavorable to the DNVP—Oberfohren's public resignation as leader of the parliamentary faction, the vast number of Nazi attacks on the DNVP and its organizations, Duesterberg's removal and the *Stahlhelm's* subjugation to Hitler's authority, and finally the defection of the DNVP's Braunschweig executive committee—it seemed indeed as if the time had come for the German Nationals to heed the freely given (though unsolicited) advice to merge their organizations into the National Socialist movement as long as this was still possible. Hitler apparently arrived at the same conclusion at around the beginning of May when, in an uncharacteristically gracious manner, he proposed that Hugenberg unite the DNVP with the NSDAP, an offer that Hugenberg rejected in an equally friendly, but firm, manner.[92] Hugenberg must have realized that Hitler's genial approach had to be taken with a grain of salt, as it was a mere testing of the political waters and likely to be followed up with further, less genial invitations.

On 3 May, at a session of the DNVP party executive that included German National Reichstag and Landtag deputies in order to give its decisions more weight,[93] participants placed renewed emphasis on parity with the NSDAP, despite a fundamentally altered situation. This continued insistence on equality possibly was meant only as a demonstration of the party's own right to exist.[94] Considering the circumstances, the gesture seemed hollow given that German National defections continued on a local basis in May.[95] In the National Socialist press, the negative coverage of Hugenberg recommenced in the second half of May, combined with renewed calls for his resignation.[96] Declarations of solidarity by German

92. Borchmeyer, *Hugenbergs Ringen*, Part I, 36 and 81. This apologetically formulated tract from Hugenberg's attorney contains materials used in Hugenberg's de-nazification proceedings. See also Hiller von Gaertingen, "DNVP," 603.

93. It was also on 3 May that the decision was made to rename the DNVP the *Deutschnationale Front*, DNF.

94. BA Berlin-Lichterfelde, "Pressearchiv Reichslandbund, Organisiertes Bürgertum," R 8034 II, no. 9021, 24–27.

95. At the beginning of May, for example, the DNVP chairman in the Berlin suburb of Rudow defected to the NSDAP. See BA Berlin-Lichterfelde, "Pressearchiv Reichslandbund, Organisiertes Bürgertum," no. 9021, 28a.

96. BA Berlin-Lichterfelde, "Pressearchiv Reichslandbund, Organisiertes Bürgertum," R 8034 II, 30a.

National organizations that expressed their "trust" in Hugenberg did little to improve his standing, for they smacked too much of having been "made to order."[97] The inherent weakness of their position was brought home to the German Nationals when three of their prominent representatives, Emil Berndt, Axel Freiherr von Freytagh-Loringhoven, and Horst von Restorff, met with Hitler on 30 May to give vent to various concerns and discuss pressing problems of the day.[98]

By then, it had become clear that the Nazis would welcome any opportunity to charge German Nationals or their affiliated organizations with promoting infiltration by socialists or communists, which could then be used as a pretext for further bans. They found such an opportunity at the end of May with the German National paramilitary organizations, the *Kampfstaffeln*, which had become a catch-all vessel for banned leftist paramilitary groups, such as the republican *Reichsbanner*, and accordingly began to swell in numbers. Hitler wanted the *Kampfstaffeln* dissolved and made it plain to the delegation that he would no longer tolerate the existence of the German National defense organization.[99] When Emil Berndt, the spokesman of the delegation, rejected dissolution, the German National deputation was treated to one of Hitler's hysterical tantrums, in the course of which he threatened to "then simply let his SA begin shooting and start a three day bloodbath, until nothing was left."[100] Since the *Kampfstaffeln*, despite growing numbers, which by May 1933 had reached almost 100,000, were hopelessly inferior to the SA, the delegation silently endured Hitler's outburst. Hitler's fit of anger was connected with an incident in Hamburg, where on 29 May the "*Kampfring* of young German Nationals" had been banned on the basis of the Reichstag Fire Decree. As the president of the Hamburg police explained in his letter to *Staatssekretär* for the Interior Hans Pfundtner, the *Kampfring* had accepted former *Reichsbanner* members with "bad reputations" and "on occasion even

---

97. For examples of such "Declarations of Solidarity," see "*Mitteilungen der deutschnationalen Front*," 19 May 1933.

98. The meeting had been arranged well beforehand. Emil Berndt, Reichstag deputy, 1920–1933; Axel Freiherr von Freytagh-Loringhoven, Reichstag deputy, 1924–1933; Horst von Restorff, chairman of the DNVP East Prussian Land Association.

99. Borchmeyer, *Hugenbergs Ringen*, 35.

100. Borchmeyer, *Hugenbergs Ringen*, 35; Schmidt-Hannover, *Umdenken oder Anarchie*, 353; Hiller von Gaertingen, "DNVP," 606.

communists."[101] The strength of the Hamburg *Kampfring* had risen
from fifty members at the end of January to a current membership
of four hundred, with the increase coming mainly "from Marxist
circles." Even though *Reichskampfring* leader Herbert von Bismarck
regularly issued directives to delete from the membership lists all
those who had joined after 30 January 1933 but had formerly been
members of the KPD, the SPD, and the *Reichsbanner* and its affiliated organizations, and who had been active in those organizations
after 1 January 1932, *Kampfringe* all over the Reich saw a significant
influx "from Marxist circles."[102] New prohibitions were thus clearly
in the offing and only a matter of time in coming. In fact, the next
Nazi ban on a *Kampfring* organization would follow on 15 June in
Dortmund.[103]

But already before then, at the very beginning of June, the DNF
was shaken by yet another scandal, when two prominent German
Nationals, Eduard Stadtler and Martin Spahn, left the party to join
the NSDAP.[104] Stadler had become well-known in extreme right-
wing circles after 1918. In 1919 he had promulgated the idea of a "national socialism" that, to him, as he wrote in 1935, encompassed the
reconciliation of Prussian militarism and socialism.[105] Spahn, who

101. 31 May 1933 at BA Berlin-Lichterfelde, "Reichskanzlei, DNVP, April
1931–April 1938," R 43 I, no. 2655, 249. On the reaction of the press, see BA
Berlin-Lichterfelde, "Pressearchiv Reichslandbund, Organisiertes Bürgertum,"
R 8034 II, no. 9021, 35, esp. "Zusammenbruch der Parteien! Das Ende des
politischen Bürgertums," *Generalanzeiger*, 31 May 1933; "Proteste im Hugenberg
Lager," *Rundschau*, 31 May 1933. Hans Pfundtner (1881–1945); as *Staatssekretär*
in the Reich Interior Ministry he participated in the drafting of the Nuremberg
Laws; resigned his post in 1943, and committed suicide on 25 April 1945 in
Berlin.
102. 31 May 1933 at BA Berlin-Lichterfelde, "Reichskanzlei, DNVP, April
1931–April 1938," R 43 I, no. 2655, 249. Brawls between the SA and the *Stahlhelm* had taken place because the SA had mistaken *Stahlhelm* uniforms for those
of the *Kampfringe*. A ban thus became necessary in the "interest of good relations" between the *Stahlhelm* and the SA.
103. Hiller von Gaertingen, "Das Ende der DNVP im Frühjahr 1933," in
Gotthard Jasper, ed., *Von Weimar zu Hitler 1930–1933* (Cologne and Berlin,
1968), 276; *Berliner Lokalanzeiger* of 15 June 1933.
104. For the extensive press coverage, especially in the Nazi press, see BA
Berlin-Lichterfelde, "Pressearchiv Reichslandbund, Organisiertes Bürgertum,"
34–46; and "DNVP und Nationalsozialismus," 186 and 192.
105. Rüdiger Stutz, "Stetigkeit und Wandlungen in der politischen Karriere
eines Rechtsextremisten. Zur Entwicklung Eduard Stadtlers von der Novemberrevolution bis 1933," *Zeitschrift für Geschichtswissenschaft* 34 (1986), 797–806.

had been a prominent Alsacian Center Party politician, switched to the DNVP in 1921 because of his estrangement from the increasingly leftist orientation, as he saw it, of the Center.[106] Spahn's switch helped the DNVP, with its mostly Protestant membership, increase its Catholic electorate by about 6 to 8 percent.[107]

Even before Hitler became Chancellor, Stadtler and Spahn were at the center of the small, but very influential Catholic circle within the DNVP. Despite their apparent closeness to Hugenberg, they were not always on his side.[108] In December 1932, Reinhold Quaatz repeatedly confided to his diary that the "group Stadtler-Spahn-Gisevius" pursued subversive activities against Hugenberg.[109] Weeks after 30 January, Spahn and Stadtler had already given unambiguous signals that they were toying with the idea of switching to the NSDAP. Accordingly, occasional reference is made to the "group of renegades around Stadtler." Threats of defection to the Nazis did not remain without political consequences. As Heinrich Brüning relates in his memoirs, the proposal for revisions to the Enabling Act, which he and Hugenberg allegedly contemplated, had to be relinquished, since twenty-two DNVP Reichstag deputies under Stadtler's leadership had threatened to defect to the NSDAP should

106. Spahn had been a Professor of History in Straßburg since 1901 but left the city in 1918 when the Alsace again became French. In 1902, Spahn married Elisabeth Bracht, sister of Franz Bracht, future Reich Commissar for Prussia and Interior Minister in Schleicher's Cabinet. On Spahn, see Gabriele Clemens, *Martin Spahn und der Rechtskatholizismus in der Weimarer Republik* (Mainz, 1983); for an overview, see Larry E. Jones, "Franz von Papen, the German Center Party, and the Failure of Catholic Conservatism in the Weimar Republic," *Central European History* 38 (2005), 191–217.

107. Clemens, *Martin Spahn*, 173. At the time of his changeover to the DNVP, Spahn was joined by a small group of Catholic noblemen, officers, and high-ranking officials.

108. Reinhold Quaatz, in Weiß and Hoser, eds., *Die Deutschnationalen*, 214. In his entry of 23 November 1932, Quaatz noted: "Hugenberg voices his concern about the Catholic wing: Stadtler, Spahn, Borchmeyer (and Gisevius), who make their own policies. Sua maxima culpa!" With this last comment Quaatz presumably referred to the fact that it was Hugenberg who had brought Spahn into the party. Joseph Borchmeyer acted as Hugenberg's attorney after the war; Hans-Bernd Gisevius also defected to the NSDAP in early June, but later joined the resistance against Hitler.

109. Quaatz, ibid., 218–219. On 16 December 1932 Quaatz mentioned a "move by the group Spahn-Stadtler-Gisevius" against Hugenberg; on 19 December he wrote that the group was carrying out "subversive activities" within the DNVP.

the proposal be acted upon.[110] The defection of Stadtler and Spahn to the NSDAP was thus hardly surprising to political insiders; it was well known that Spahn had considered fusing the DNF with the Nazi party for some time in order to create a more forceful Right.[111] In a 14 May letter to Hugenberg, Spahn recommended the dissolution of the DNF and the incorporation of its members into the NSDAP in return for concessions from Hitler. After Hugenberg rejected this proposal without comment, Spahn's decision to leave the DNF became final.[112] In addition to Spahn and Stadtler, Wilhelm Schmidt, the German National labor leader and chairman of the *Vaterländische Arbeitervereine*, as well as Hans-Bernd Gisevius and Edmund Forschbach, also defected to the NSDAP at the beginning of June.[113]

This matter, embarrassing as it was to the German Nationals, was further aggravated by allegations leveled by Spahn and Stadtler against their former party. Stadtler claimed that the DNF threatened to become a counterrevolutionary force, since it had recently turned into "a gathering point for all those elements dissatisfied with political developments."[114] Spahn and Stadtler even alluded to signs of decay and demoralization within the DNF that seemed to herald imminent collapse. Goebbels's paper *Der Angriff* picked up on this widespread mood: "The German National Front is moving ever closer to that point in time when its undeniable task must be seen as fulfilled and completed."[115] Here, the focus was on a wilting from

---

110. Brüning, *Memoiren 1918–1934*, 652–656. Edmund Forschbach, himself one of those who defected to the NSDAP in June 1933, disputed Brüning's account. See Morsey, *Das Ermächtigungsgesetz*, 178, 180.

111. Clemens, *Martin Spahn*, 202.

112. Ibid., 204.

113. Wilhelm Schmidt, born 1878, chairman of the Fatherland Labor Association, deputy in the Prussian Landtag 1924–1928, and Reichstag 1930–1932; Hans-Bernd Gisevius, born 1904, German National Youth Leader, later member of the *Abwehr* (counterintelligence) and one of the few members of the resistance who survived the war. See his—not always reliable—account, Hans-Bernd Gisevius, *To the Bitter End. The Plot to Kill Hitler* (New York, 1998). Others who left were Edmund Forschbach, who published a short piece on the DNVP's demise, "Die Deutschnationalen. Vom Ende einer Partei," *Politische Meinung* 5 (1960), 12–16, and *Studienassessor* Flume, one of the founders of the *Kampfring junger Deutschnationaler*. See "Raustreten," *Kölnische Zeitung*, 10 June 1933.

114. "Die gegenrevolutionäre DNVP," *Preußischer Pressedienst*, 10 June 1933, at BA Berlin-Lichterfelde, "Pressearchiv Reichslandbund, DNVP und NS," 192a.

115. "Der Weg zu Hitler," *Angriff*, 10 June 1933.

within, an increasing weakness and "bloodlessness," on "the lack of any idealistic power of German National thought," and it was alleged that it was not enough to be national-minded in the face of the "revolutionary resolve of the national uprising."[116] The DNF responded to such attacks by stressing its *raison d'être* as the "champion of conservative, Christian, *völkisch* and social-state concepts" and by condemning the behavior of the Reichstag deputies Spahn, Stadtler, and Schmidt because they had abandoned the DNF without "resigning their mandate, which was a violation of their Christian word of honor and a gross deception of their constituency."[117]

The End

These protests did little to reduce the damage caused. By mid June 1933 it had become clear that another major affair, or perhaps just a minor scandal, would spell doom for the party and usher in its inexorable demise. The end came, as is so often the case, from an unanticipated quarter. Hugenberg, and with him his party, met his downfall where he expected triumph—at the "politically all-decisive London Economic Conference," as the event was hailed in the German National press when it conveyed its best wishes to "our leader Hugenberg" on the eve of the meeting.[118] It would turn out differently: Hugenberg's behavior at the World Economic Conference, which decided little and ended as an abject failure, marked the beginning of the end of both Hugenberg's political career and that of his party.[119]

116. Ibid. Occasionally terms such as "end of the political bourgeoisie" were employed to denote the demise of the bourgeois way of life. See "Das Ende des politischen Bürgertums," *Schlesische Tageszeitung*, 1 June 1933.

117. The DNF adopted the position that Reichstag mandates belonged to the Land Associations and would automatically revert back to them if a deputy crossed the floor to another party. See "Die deutschnationale Reichstagsfraktion zu den Austritten," in "Mitteilungen der DNF," at BA Berlin-Lichterfelde, "Pressearchiv Reichslandbund, Organisiertes Bürgertum," R 8034 II, no. 9021, 49. That the German National spirit seemed unbroken was documented by the foundation of a new paper for younger DNF members, *Der junge Nationalist*, as the conservative daily *Der Tag* reported on 13 June 1933.

118. "In Treue zu Hugenberg," *Westfälische Volkszeitung*, 13 June 1933, at BA Berlin-Lichterfelde "Pressearchiv Reichslandbund, Organisiertes Bürgertum," R 8034 II, no. 9021, 47.

119. In his closing words on behalf of the German delegation, Reichsbank President Schacht spoke of the "failure of an international agreement . . ."

In his function as *Wirtschaftsdiktator*, holding the portfolios for the Ministries of Economics and Agriculture of Prussia and the Reich, Hugenberg hoped to stimulate the domestic market by increasing the purchasing power of farmers, thereby relieving the economic distress in town and country.[120] By the success of these measures he expected that, as "the savior from economic misery," his position in the Cabinet would become unassailable. Through legislation granting debt relief to the agricultural sector and measures favorable to the middle classes, he hoped to be supported by a majority of the population as the person responsible for the country's economic recovery. At this point, influencing the public mood in his favor through palpable economic success appeared the only way to save both his position and his party. In Hugenberg's opinion, fewer restrictions on trade posed a danger to the recovery of the German domestic market. He was therefore determined to avoid concessions on this matter at the London summit at all cost. Foreign Minister von Neurath and Hitler, on the other hand, had different priorities: most notably, to avoid the potentially threatening isolation of Germany.

At the World Economic Summit, held in London between 12 June and 27 July 1933, Hugenberg presented the economic forum with a memorandum on 16 June, in which he offered his own analysis of the Great Depression and proposals for overcoming it. Germany's recovery, he asserted, was in the interest of all nations. To promote German recovery and strengthen Germany's capacity to meet its financial obligations, Hugenberg thought it imperative that Germany be granted possession of colonies, where it could carry out "large projects"; he argued that the "*Volk ohne Raum*" should thereby gain access to regions in which new settlements could be developed.[121]

According to Schacht, the "whole World Economic Conference . . . disbanded without any practical result." See Hjalmar Schacht, *76 Jahre meines Lebens* (Bad Wörishofen, 1953), 395.

120. Anton Ritthaler, "Eine Etappe auf Hitlers Weg zur ungeteilten Macht. Hugenbergs Rücktritt als Reichsminister," *Vierteljahrshefte für Zeitgeschichte* 8 (1960), 193–219; here 196–197; and the "Unterlagen Anton Ritthaler, 1920–1954" ED 307, at the Institut für Zeitgeschichte, Munich.

121. For the English text of the memorandum, see *Documents on German Foreign Policy*, Series C, Vol. I, 562–567; for the German original, see *Akten zur Deutschen Auswärtigen Politik 1918–1945*, Serie C, 1933–1937, Vol. 1, part 2, 557–562. On international reactions, see *Akten zur Deutschen Auswärtigen Politik*, Serie C, Vol. 1, 576–577; 584–586. Hugenberg maintained that the revolution and civil war in Russia lay at the root of the economic crisis. Soviet Foreign

It must have been clear to Hugenberg that he was bound to alienate England and France with this expansive venture, that the Soviet Union would take offense at the demand for new "areas of settlement," and that, regardless of the other states' reactions, his entire memorandum blatantly contradicted the careful tactics Hitler had adopted for the moment, including his 17 May foreign policy speech. Other German conference participants, such as Finance Minister Schwerin von Krosigk, *Reichsbank* President Hjalmar Schacht, and the Foreign Office's Chief Interpreter, Paul Schmidt, were united in their judgment that Hugenberg's untimely and poorly coordinated approach was harmful to himself and made a laughingstock of the entire German delegation.[122] Foreign Minister von Neurath, the leader of the German delegation, thus saw himself obligated to take the undiplomatic step of explaining that Hugenberg's memorandum represented only his personal views and not the official position of the German delegation. Hugenberg had obviously considered the London Economic Conference an opportunity to put forward demands in which he and his Pan-German associates had long been interested, and now seized the chance to prove to his followers that he could advance nationalist claims more decisively than even Hitler.[123] Hugenberg's desperate and almost grotesque attempts to justify his behavior showed all too plainly that he had been perfectly serious about what he wrote.[124] Already on the crossing to England

---

Minister Litvinov, who reacted angrily, was not alone in suspecting that Hugenberg wrote the memorandum at the behest of the Nazis. On 19 June, *Pravda* published an editorial on Hugenberg's memorandum entitled "Don Quixotes of our Age," where it was argued that Hugenberg spelled out what the present German leadership saw as a way out of the present crisis: expansion into the East. See Minuth, ed., *Akten der Reichskanzlei*, 574.

122. Lutz Graf Schwerin von Krosigk, *Es geschah in Deutschland. Menschenbilder unseres Jahrhunderts* (Tübingen and Stuttgart, 1951), 174–178; Schacht, *76 Jahre meines Lebens*, 394–395. Schacht also drew a direct link between Hugenberg's conduct and his resignation ten days later. See also Paul Schmidt, *Statist auf diplomatischer Bühne 1923–1945. Erlebnisse des Chefdolmetschers im Auswärtigen Amt mit den Staatsmännern Europas* (Bonn, 1949), 265–267.

123. When Hugenberg had read the memorandum to the German delegation, Neurath, apparently to observe proprieties, desisted from criticizing him openly. But he advised Hugenberg not to present the memorandum to the Economic Forum and assumed that Hugenberg would follow his instructions. See Schwerin von Krosigk, *Es geschah in Deutschland*, 176.

124. "Denkschrift des Reichswirtschaftsministers über verschiedene Vorgänge auf der Londoner Weltwirtschaftskonferenz," 21 June 1933, in Minuth, ed., *Akten der Reichskanzlei*, 571–575.

from Vlissingen to Harwich he had made it unmistakably clear that he was not prepared to support Neurath's conciliatory course. He was thus the only member of the German delegation who took exception to one passage in Neurath's speech: "The National Socialist government has shown that it is willing to work together with other nations [*Völkern*] in the political arena. It is in this spirit that it approaches the World Economic Conference."[125] Arguing that he had "not come here for a harmonious understanding,"[126] Hugenberg threatened to depart at once unless that sentence was deleted, so that Neurath felt obliged to relent and remove the sentence from his speech.

It was not long before the consequences of Hugenberg's ill-conceived behavior caught up with him. The German Foreign Ministry suppressed the publication of an interview Hugenberg had given in London, and after his return to Germany, he found himself completely isolated in the Cabinet on account of his conduct.[127] In the 23 June 1933 Cabinet meeting, Hugenberg, bursting with righteous indignation, complained to Hitler in front of the assembled Cabinet that Neurath had publicly compromised and disavowed him in London. Hitler and Neurath, who had no interest in further expounding upon an incident that was replete with embarrassment for all involved, did their best to pacify Hugenberg. But when Hugenberg demanded the dismissal of the experienced and respected *Ministerialdirektor* Posse, who coordinated the efforts of the German delegation after the departure of the Ministers, Papen, Neurath, Schwerin von Krosigk, Schacht, Labor Minister Franz Seldte, and eventually Hitler turned against Hugenberg and argued that major changes in the German delegation would be impolitic.[128] During the meeting, "the generally negative opinion of Germany at the Conference" was discussed, as was the upsetting fact that Hugenberg's memorandum had given Germany's adversaries the opportunity for

125. Schmidt, *Statist*, 266.

126. Ibid.

127. Hugenberg had claimed in this interview that the Marxist camp had disseminated false information about the German delegation in the English press. He also insisted that the ideas expressed in his memorandum were in line with those of the Reich government. See Leopold, *Alfred Hugenberg*, 154.

128. *Ministerialdirektor* was the rank just below that of *Staatssekretär*. Posse remained at his post following Hugenberg's resignation and was later promoted to *Staatssekretär* in the Ministry of Economics. See "Ministerbesprechung, anschließend Kabinettsitzung vom 23. Juni," in Minuth, ed., *Akten der Reichskanzlei*, 577–589, esp. 581–582; Krosigk, *Es geschah in Deutschland*, 175–177.

a good many derisive and spiteful comments. Among other things, the "impertinent tone of the Russian note on Hugenberg's memorandum" was also a subject of discussion.[129] Soviet Foreign Secretary Litvinov had fervently rejected the implications of Hugenberg's memorandum and declared that some countries, which had fallen into an "economic morass," saw their last hope "in scatterbrained schemes" and were in danger of becoming the "laughing stock of the entire world."[130] After being thus shown up, isolated, and left with no support in the Reich Cabinet, Hugenberg decided to resign after the meeting, though he initially endeavored to keep his decision secret.[131] The stance of outraged innocence and wounded pride that he adopted during the Cabinet meeting had misfired, and his foreign policy foray and attempt to trump Hitler on the nationalist front not only failed to bring him any kudos, but also served to brand him as a foreign policy embarrassment and troublemaker in the Cabinet.

Meanwhile, on 20 June, after a protracted election campaign in the Free City of Danzig that was supervised by the League of Nations, the NSDAP and the Center Party formed a coalition under the leadership of Hermann Rauschning, a former German National who had switched over to the NSDAP.[132] The German Nationals and the Nazi party had bitterly fought each other during the course of the campaign, with the Nazis training their destructive propaganda on the German Nationals who, for their part, tried to prevent an absolute majority for the NSDAP. In fact, political strife in Danzig was reminiscent of the autumn of 1932 when political antagonism and resentment between the two "national" parties had burst forth with equal vehemence. After the Danzig elections, Hitler felt secure enough to drop any remaining concerns about his coalition partner, and he initiated a decisive move against the German National

129. Minuth, ed., *Akten der Reichskanzlei*, 578.

130. Ibid., 573, note 8; and *Soviet Documents on Foreign Policy*, Vol. III: 1933–1941 (London, New York, 1953), 21–22.

131. The politics of extreme economic self-sufficiency that Hugenberg had advocated in the Cabinet were also rejected by Neurath and initially even by Hitler (who later embraced it) as premature and therefore imprudent. Leopold, *Alfred Hugenberg*, 153. Leopold believes that this was the reason Hitler had offered Neurath the leadership of the delegation.

132. See the Center Party paper *Germania* and the conservative *Der Tag* of 20 June 1933; and Leopold, *Alfred Hugenberg*, 157.

Kampfringe throughout the entire Reich.[133] Ever since the ban on
the Hamburg *Kampfringe* at the end of May, the threat of a general
prohibition had hovered like a Damocles sword over the organization.[134] The majority of *Kampfring* leaders had been summoned to a
national training and indoctrination course (*Reichsschulungskurs*) between 17 and 23 June, so that it was an opportune moment to take
ruthless action against the German National paramilitary organization. On the morning of 21 June, the *Kampfringe* were dissolved and
their assets confiscated on the pretext that investigations had proved
conclusively that communist elements had been accepted into the
organizations.[135] During operations conducted by the police and
SA, a number of DNF offices that had served as coordination points
for the *Kampfstaffeln* were also searched. Letters of protest against
the searches, including that of a DNF Land Association leader, were
to no avail, despite his assurance that the members of his organization were not implicated in any counterrevolutionary endeavors,
but on the contrary, considered it as their noblest purpose to help
build "the new Reich created by the national revolution."[136] At the
same time, youth organizations, such as the *Großdeutsche Bund*—the
Greater German Association, an umbrella organization of the *bün-
disch* youth leagues, led by Vice Admiral Adolf von Trotha—were
banned as well (as a prelude to their incorporation into the Hitler
Youth). In his five-page protest letter to Hindenburg, Trotha, in a
rage fueled by his utter incapacity to fend off the onslaught, rejected

133. One pretext for this was the claim that during searches of SPD offices on
16 June, incriminating evidence against the *Kampfringe* had been found. Hiller
von Gaertingen, "DNVP," 610.

134. The ban had been promulgated on the basis of Article I of the *Reichs-
tagsbrandverordnung*, the Decree on the Protection of the People and the State of
28 February 1933. This article rendered null and void basic rights that had been
guaranteed in the Weimar Constitution, such as Articles 114, 115, 117, 118, 123,
124, and 153, and could be evoked under many conditions.

135. The truth of these assertions is difficult to verify. Even though *Reichs-
kampfringführer* Herbert von Bismarck did everything possible to exclude former
communists and *Reichsbanner* members from the *Kampfringe*, in practice it was
not always possible to prevent German National organizations from becoming a
kind of receptacle for banned leftist organizations, as they represented the only
possibility for legal political activity outside of the NSDAP.

136. 21 June 1933 at BA Berlin-Lichterfelde, "Reichskanzlei, DNVP,
1931–1938," R 43 I, no. 2655, 263–265.

charges that the *Bünde* were reactionary or would "pit themselves against the revolutionary wave of youth."[137]

With a national ban on the *Kampfringe*, Hugenberg's days, as well as those of the German National Front, were numbered. As Theodor Heuss wrote after the prohibition of all parties in July 1933, the dissolution of party-affiliated associations, such as the *Kampfring* of Young German Nationals, had deeply affected the main parties at a psychological, emotional, and spiritual level because their "fighting youth"—the very future and core of political parties—had been wrested from them and, worst of all, nobody had dared to resist.[138] Hugenberg had decided to submit his resignation immediately after the 23 June Cabinet meeting, despite the fact that Hitler and even Neurath, whom Hugenberg had directly attacked, had done their best to downplay Hugenberg's conduct in London, hoping to avoid a Cabinet reshuffle. Initially, Hugenberg informed only a small circle of close personal confidants of his decision and, on 26 June, still refused to make his intention to resign public.[139] Given the ongoing defections of local DNF organizations to the NSDAP, however, as well as the dissolution of more German National associations, it was clear to the party leadership that the DNF could no longer be sustained as an independent organization. The one person who still harbored illusions and wanted to keep the party alive was Hugenberg himself. Since he had paid little attention to the party in recent months and had passed all his authority to deputy chairman Friedrich von Winterfeld, in this final phase of the party's existence the initiative passed more and more to the leading members of the party executive. They finally implemented the dissolution of the DNF against Hugenberg's wishes, but with the agreement of the vast majority of the party executive (now renamed *Führerstab*, or leadership staff). On 26 June, Alexander von Freytagh-Loringhoven was thus instructed by the party executive to ascertain from Nazi Interior Minister Wilhelm Frick the intended plans, if any, for the

137. 23 June 1933 at BA Berlin-Lichterfelde, "Stellvertreter des Reichskanzlers, Kanzlei von Papen," R 53, no. 86, 9–13, esp. 11; see also Minuth, ed., *Akten der Reichskanzlei*, 592–595. Trotha also complained about Nazi attacks and a search of his private quarters.

138. Theodor Heuss, "Ausgang der Parteien," *Die Hilfe 39* (1933), 361–366.

139. See Anton Ritthaler, "Eine Etappe," 193–219; Borchmeyer, *Hugenbergs Ringen*, 82–85; and the "Unterlagen Anton Ritthaler, 1920–1954" ED 307, at the Institut für Zeitgeschichte, Munich.

future existence of the DNF, and eventually to enter into negotiations with Frick on the matter.[140]

Meanwhile, Hugenberg's tender of resignation, in accordance with his instructions, was handed to Hindenburg's adjutant at the President's East Prussian estate in Neudeck, where Hindenburg was in residence.[141] Hugenberg's letter of resignation leveled no accusations or fundamental misgivings about National Socialist methods.[142] It resembled more a letter of complaint about alleged injustices suffered by Hugenberg: the treatment meted out to him at the World Economic Conference, unfulfilled requests with respect to the ministries in his charge, and the forcible dissolution of the German National *Kampfstaffeln*. He mentioned neither the continued validity of the Enabling Act nor the potential political reverberations of his resignation. Possibly in recognition of the political implications that his London memorandum brought in its wake, or of his general political failure, Hugenberg clearly wanted to resign as inconspicuously and uncontroversially as possible. Anton Ritthaler suggested that Hugenberg had elected to take his leave in an agreeable way in order to avoid posing any danger to the continued existence of the party and to ensure that German National officials were not subjected to reprisals.[143] Hugenberg's resignation was accepted without any attempt to make him change his mind.[144] But then, it must have been clear to Hugenberg that he could not expect any encouragement from Hindenburg to extend his stay in office. Hindenburg's

140. Ritthaler, "Eine Etappe," 216–219; Freytagh-Loringhoven had been conferred full authority by his party to negotiate with Frick. When Hugenberg heard about Loringhoven's assignment, he insisted that his intention to resign was not to be mentioned to Frick. Hiller von Gaertingen, "DNVP," 263.

141. According to Leopold, *Alfred Hugenberg*, 161, it was Hugenberg's press spokesman Hans Brosius who traveled to Neudeck; according to Hiller von Gaertingen it was former party chairman Hergt. See also Ritthaler, "Eine Etappe auf Hitlers Weg zur ungeteilten Macht,"193–219, Borchmeyer, *Hugenbergs Ringen*, 82–85; and Gaertingen, "DNVP," 612–616.

142. Reprinted in Ritthaler, "Eine Etappe,"193–219; see also Borchmeyer, *Hugenbergs Ringen*, 82–85; Forschbach, "Die Deutschnationalen: Vom Ende einer Partei," *Politische Meinung* 5 (1960), 12–16; and Leopold, *Alfred Hugenberg*, 151–163.

143. Ritthaler, "Eine Etappe." See also Borchmeyer, *Hugenbergs Ringen*, 82–84.

144. *Documents on British Foreign Policy*, Vol. 5, 387–388; Andreas Dorpalen, *Hindenburg in der Geschichte der Weimarer Republik* (Berlin, Frankfurt, 1966), 444. (This is a slightly updated version of Dorpalen, *Hindenburg and the Weimar Republic*, Princeton, 1964.)

heartfelt emotional appeals to Hugenberg to cooperate with the government during Brüning's chancellorship had been rebuffed too brusquely. Sympathy for the man, whom Hindenburg had only ever experienced as uncooperative, was in any event nonexistent, all the more so as, in the President's eyes, Hugenberg was responsible for divisions within the conservative party and its subsequent inexorable decline.

The central event connected with Hugenberg's resignation was his discussion with Hitler on 27 June. Hitler initially appeared accommodating, though firm on certain points: he asked Hugenberg to reconsider his decision and found words of praise for his ministerial work, but also emphasized that Hugenberg's Undersecretary of State, Hans-Joachim von Rohr, whom Hitler personally disapproved of, would have to be replaced by a National Socialist. The German National Front would have to be disbanded as well, Hitler went on, because its continued existence in conjunction with Hugenberg's resignation might lead to the emergence of a conservative nationalist opposition. Hitler could afford to take an accommodating stance, since he had already been informed by Frick about the Interior Minister's discussion with Freytagh-Loringhoven and thus knew full well that the German Nationals were ready to disband the DNF of their own accord. Hugenberg, on the other hand, did not yet know the result of the talks between Freytagh-Loringhoven and Frick. When Hugenberg continued to insist on his resignation, categorically rejected the dissolution of the DNF, and even suggested to Hitler to take action against "leftist elements" in National Socialist organizations, Hitler abruptly changed tack. He uttered threats to the effect that thousands of German National civil servants would lose their positions, that a battle would flare up all along the line, which would also devour Hugenberg's press and film Empire, and that all would be decided after three days.[145] Despite these threats, Hugenberg continued to insist on his resignation while refusing to sanction the dissolution of the DNF.[146] After his discussion with Hugenberg, Hitler called for Freytagh-Loringhoven and threatened reprisals if the DNF were not dissolved. If, however, the party were to disband voluntarily, he was prepared to be

---

145. Ritthaler, "Eine Etappe," 216–219; Leopold, *Alfred Hugenberg*, 161–162; Hiller von Gaertingen, "DNVP," 612–615.

146. Hugenberg's reaction evidently wrested reluctant respect from Hitler; see Friedrich Hoßbach, *Zwischen Wehrmacht und Hitler 1934–1938* (Wolfenbüttel and Hannover 1949), 35–36.

generous: to release all arrested DNF members and protect them from further arrests, to provide for party employees, and to recognize German Nationals as equal fellow-combatants in the struggle for a nationalist Germany.[147]

Thus, when the DNF's party leadership and executive board reconvened on the afternoon of 27 June, the choice for voluntary dissolution and against Hugenberg's preference to maintain the party as an independent organization had been made. Of the approximately sixty party representatives attending, four voted for Hugenberg and fifty-six for voluntary dissolution. The DNF submitted a "friendship agreement,"[148] in which it affirmed that it would disband in full agreement with the Reich Chancellor, and Hitler put his assurances in writing and made them official that same evening. As would become evident in the following years, this was one of the few sets of promises that Hitler kept with astonishing reliability.[149] Most of the DNF Reichstag deputies were absorbed into the NSDAP faction, and civil servants associated with the German National Front were provided for. This did not mean that the dissolution of the DNF was uncontroversial. In fact, the process of voluntary dissolution, and the concrete steps that led to it, remained a bone of contention in German National circles for years to come.[150]

In the Cabinet session of 30 June that followed Hugenberg's resignation, Hitler welcomed Hugenberg's successors: Kurt Schmitt, an executive director of the Allianz Insurance Company, as Minister of Economics, and the National Socialist Richard Walther

147. German National deputies were to be accepted as guests in the National Socialist Reichstag faction.

148. "Freundschaftsabkommen mit der NSDAP. Deutschnationale Abgeordnete als Hospitanten," *Deutsche Allgemeine Zeitung*, 28 June 1933.

149. See "Reichstelegramm Fricks an den Preußischen Minister des Inneren und die Reichsstatthalter," 27 June 1933 at BA Berlin-Lichterfelde, "Reichskanzlei, DNVP," R 43 I, no. 2655, 273. Frick's telegram contained the order that all DNF members who had been arrested were to be released. Most of the three hundred officials connected with the DNF obtained comparable positions elsewhere.

150. Gottfried Traub complained to Freytag-Loringhoven as late as 1935 that his mandate had been limited to ascertaining the intentions of the Reich government vis-a-vis the DNF and did not include entering into negotiations about conditions that would govern an eventual dissolution. See Ritthaler, "Eine Etappe auf Hitlers Weg zur ungeteilten Macht," 216–217, note 18.

Darré as Minister of Agriculture and Nutrition.[151] He also expressed his regrets about Hugenberg's resignation and his appreciation for Hugenberg's "collaboration and long-time activity for the national cause."[152] In a commentary on Hugenberg's political achievements, the leading Nazi paper, *Völkischer Beobachter,* wrote that Hugenberg deserved much credit as an economic expert and for his struggle against the Young Plan. All in all, however, "Hugenberg never had any 'luck' and had become a tragic personality. Without being personally to blame, the curse of that barren, depleted generation that followed upon Bismarck and that had gambled away the Reich hovered above him."[153] Hugenberg must have expected that a very different appraisal of his merits would sum up his whole life's work when, on 30 January 1933, he steered his party into the fateful alliance with Hitler.

151. Kurt Schmitt (1886–1950), *Generaldirektor* of Allianz Insurance Company since 1921, was appointed Hugenberg's successor as Minister of Economics on 29 June 1933. He was selected in part to silence misgivings from the industrial and commercial sector about possible changes in the economy after Hugenberg's resignation. Schmitt, in turn, was replaced by Hjalmar Schacht on 30 July 1934. Richard Walther Darré (1895–1953) studied agriculture and became an NSDAP Reichstag deputy in the autumn of 1932; he had been leader of the national peasantry (*Reichsbauernführer*) since 4 April 1933 and Hugenberg's successor as Minister of Agriculture and Nutrition since 29 June 1933. He was sentenced to a seven-year term at Nuremberg but was pardoned in 1950.

152. Minuth, ed., *Akten der Reichskanzlei,* 609–610.

153. Quoted in Minuth, ed., *Akten der Reichskanzlei,* 610, note 4.

EPILOGUE

Conservatism, National Socialism, and German History

During the winter and spring of 1933, the Nazis made a strenuous effort to present themselves as in harmony with conservative German and Prussian traditions, or even as the natural result and outgrowth of these traditions. The Nazis made the conservative Prussian past serviceable to their need for political legitimation to an extent hitherto unprecedented. Long before the Second World War, Prussian values became National Socialist values, judged to epitomize the German character, and held up as models to emulate: austerity, thrift, tenacity in the pursuit of one's goals, a preparedness for personal sacrifice, and a willingness to lay down one's life in the service of a higher cause that would win out in the end, even in the face of overwhelming odds. Above all, there was the concept of duty; it was imperative to "fulfill" one's duty to the *Volk* and the Fatherland. Among other things, Nazi propaganda made the Prussian past and the values it imputed to it palpable in the form of grand historic films that enjoyed mass audiences.[1] It was already during the period of the seizure of power that conservatives lost the *Deutungshoheit*, that is, the prerogative to interpret the great

---

1. Such as *Der Choral of Leuthen* (1933), *Fridericus* (1937), and *Der grosse König* (1942).

traditions and historical figures of the past, to the Nazis. From 1933 onwards, the Nazis acted as self-appointed guardians of the national heritage. And they did this with greater aplomb, audacity, and—in many instances—more skill than conservative propagandists during the Weimar Republic before them.

The proposition that Hitler's Third Reich seemed to be the last—and most important—link of a conservative chain of continuity was also accepted at the level of historical scholarship. There were, after all, some apparently real continuities, whereby National Socialism did indeed seem to carry on conservative traditions and beliefs. In a series of thoroughly researched, solid works of scholarship, German historians of the 1930s favorably referred to Prussian conservative theorists and politicians to elucidate the present. This was particularly the case with respect to Prussia's social-conservative tradition. The social conservatism of Josef Maria von Radowitz and Hermann Wagener of the 1840s through 1860s,[2] which had been judged critically by conservative contemporaries, as being too "modern," was resuscitated and held in high esteem during the Third Reich. In their conservative social thought Radowitz and Wagener had advocated the integration of the proletariat into the state: in a "social kingdom" the rural and urban lower classes would help buttress the power of the monarchy, and this in turn would support the poor and needy. Wagener even envisaged the introduction of universal manhood suffrage (long before it was in place in England and France) to strengthen the position of—what were believed to be—the innately patriotic and monarchist tendencies of the working classes and thus also of the monarchy. The integration of the working class, the "Fourth Estate," into the State was also a central concern of the Nazi government,[3] as the Nationalist Socialist Interior Minister Wilhelm Frick demanded in June 1933. Conservative social concepts thus became prototypes held up as examples or, at the very least, as intellectual and political antecedents. That the Prussian conservative

2. Josef Maria von Radowitz (1797–1853), conservative theorist, close friend and advisor of Frederick William IV, and Prussian Foreign Minister (1850); Hermann Wagener (1815–1889), conservative deputy, editor of the *Kreuzzeitung*, and Bismarck's advisor on social issues.

3. Wilhelm Frick, "Der Sinn unserer Zeit," *Nationalsozialistische Monatshefte* 39 (June 1933), 245–246: "The significance of our age lies in overcoming the differences between classes and estates . . . and in the integration of the fourth estate, the German worker, into the state as a citizen with equal rights."

tradition served as an extended prehistory to National Socialist Germany seems to have been accepted as fact by many.

In his examination of Hermann Wagener's influential political journal *Berliner Revue*, for example, the historian Adalbert Hahn remarked that while his study was originally meant as a contribution to the history of the conservative party in the nineteenth century, "it became evident in the course of the investigation that the . . . ideas under consideration here constituted the first emergence of National Socialist concepts in German politics." Hahn expressed the hope that his monograph would help "to promote the understanding of this great German movement of freedom and rejuvenation [i.e. National Socialism]."[4] Here an intellectual and political lineage is clearly established. And Hahn was not alone. In his detailed study on Radowitz, the young historian Walter Früh discovered similar roots. Früh compared the social-conservative concepts of Radowitz with, as he put it, "present day German socialism, the revival of the irrational, organic forces of the *Volksgemeinschaft* . . . the endeavor to realize the restructuring of the whole of the people along *ständisch* lines," which gave rise "to a rekindling of interest in the ideas of German Social Conservatives from the early capitalist age. . . ."[5] Here, too, an intellectual-political ancestry is ascertained. In analyzing the ideas of Hermann Wagener, Adolf Richter—in his 1935 study on Bismarck and the *Arbeiterfrage* during the Prussian constitutional conflict—maintained in the same vein: "If we survey Wagner's ideas as a whole, comparisons to the present day virtually press in upon us."[6] Continuities with social conservatism are also underlined by Walter Frank, a leading Nazi historian and president of the "Reich Institute for the History of the New Germany" in his book about Adolf Stoecker and the Christian Social Movement. According to the author's own testimony, his book "sprang from the experience of the National Socialist movement and its leading personality" and was thus dedicated to Hitler personally.[7] Yet these

---

4. Adalbert Hahn, *Die Berliner Revue. Ein Beitrag zur Geschichte der konservativen Partei zwischen 1855 und 1875* (Berlin, 1934), 4.

5. Walter Früh, *Radowitz als Sozialpolitiker. Seine Gesellschafts- und Wirtschaftsauffassung unter besonderer Berücksichtigung der sozialen Frage* (Diss. Berlin, 1937), 7.

6. Adolf Richter, *Bismarck und die Arbeiterfrage im preußischen Verfassungskonflikt* (Stuttgart, 1935), 34.

7. Walter Frank, *Hofprediger Adolf Stoecker und die christlichsoziale Bewegung*, 2nd ed. (Hamburg, 1934), 9; see also Helmut Heiber, *Walter Frank und sein Reichsinstitut für die Geschichte des neuen Deutschland* (Stuttgart, 1966).

seemingly self-evident and undeniable continuities were deceptive and more or less tenuous. Even in the case of the social-conservative tradition in Prussia they can be only partially verified. The nationalist thrust of National Socialism—namely, to regain the international-minded urban proletariat for the national cause—was absent in both Radowitz and Wagener.

Essentially the National Socialist contention that Nazism and its leading personality represented a natural continuance and culmination point of German history was untrue. It was an extraordinarily successful fabrication, especially since this spurious claim, which initially added greatly to the popularity of the regime, was believed not only by millions of Germans, but also by Nazi Germany's World War II adversaries, to whom it provided an explanation for the otherwise puzzling dynamism, popularity, and success of Nazism. In fact, Allied propaganda during the Second World War was based largely on the assumption that Nazism was a manifestation of things fundamentally German. This was not surprising given that the widespread popularity of the regime and the public jubilation that followed its foreign policy successes and later its military conquests seemed to indicate that an overwhelming majority of Germans closely identified with National Socialism. Yet those Germans whose support for the regime was based on a belief in Nazism's rootedness in German history or in some historically continuous identity were as deceived as outside onlookers, for their beliefs were based on false premises. As argued here, Nazism, though placing itself in the mainstream of German traditions for instrumental reasons was, in many respects, a break with the traditional, conservative way of life. The gigantic spectacle put on at Potsdam on 21 March had been a sham to endow Nazi rule with the mantle of legitimacy. The Nazis abominated the Empire with—what they considered—its stultifying bourgeois culture, its class differences and self-satisfied lackluster bourgeoisie that, so the charge went, had deliberately excluded a sizeable part of the German people from participation in the public life of the nation. As Goebbels had made clear in a rare moment of truth in 1930: "The front that opposes us stretches from Westarp to Thälmann." And he made no bones about his scorn for the more recent Imperial past and its supposed conservative antecedents, despite the Empire's pathbreaking welfare legislation: "The three-class franchise classifying voters along property lines, the social 'pittance' legislation, the 'limited comprehension of the subject,' the 'lord-of-the manor' way of thinking, the industrial capitalistic firebrands—all of these are typical fabrications of conservative reactionaries who, being fully alive to their own incompetence and inability to foster creativity, enviously suppress achievement and progress by others . . ."[8] As was made clear on that occasion, expressions of shared interest with the nationalist bourgeoisie and the heritage of the German past had to be taken with a grain of salt: "There can be absolutely no doubt that a deep ideological chasm yawns between us and them, a fact that needs to be pointed out all the more clearly, the more often we are compelled to form alliances with bourgeois forces in order to attain our tactical goals. They are captives of their own bourgeois mindset."[9] Nazism's "new man" would have a very different way of thinking.

During the spring of 1933, the Nazis concentrated their fire on the conservative establishment or—put differently—the traditional order of things. Whenever traditional state authority clashed with the demands of the rising movement, the conflict ended with the victory of Nazism. Traditional habits and accepted norms were discarded or modified in order to accommodate the new masters, often out of naked fear of Nazi retribution. A Prussian Finance Minister found it difficult to fire a humble office assistant, simply because the person in question had for years been a member of the Nazi party, and a formerly all-powerful *Schulrat* (Schools Inspector) had to fear for his position because of a well-deserved bad grade he once gave to a graduating student, who happened to be a National Socialist. The Nazis attempted to equalize and undermine traditional hierarchies in virtually all spheres of life. The anti-bourgeois thrust of Nazi propaganda, accentuated after mid March 1933 by the insistence that the "national revolution" would now be followed by a "National Socialist revolution," made it clear that "reactionaries"— German conservatives—would hereby be branded as enemies of the revolution itself. Nazis never tired of mocking conservative symbols and values, calling the Kaiser a coward for having left his post, and making it plain that they looked askance at the Second Empire as a whole. The conservative bourgeoisie, they argued, was equally to blame for the catastrophe of 1918, and the main legacy of the bourgeois age was a lasting social rift that had deprived Germany of the loyalty of millions of her best citizens.

---

8. Joseph Goebbels, "Das patriotische Bürgertum," *Nationalsozialistische Monatshefte*, 1. Jahrgang (1930), 221–229; quotations on 225 and 226.
    9. Ibid., 226–227.

National Socialism as an Anti-Bourgeois Movement

To revitalize Germany, in the eyes of National Socialists, it was necessary not only to reorganize the German state, but to replace the *Bürger* with a different kind of human being, a "new man," fit for the struggles of the coming age. Toward that end the "entitlement character" of the bourgeois age had to be abolished, class differences obliterated, and the German worker integrated into the State as a citizen with equal rights. In the spring of 1933, Nazi ideologues attacked the bourgeois way of life at its very core by postulating a "catalogue of virtues," that is, characteristic traits for the new man of National Socialism. Differences between Nazis and conservatives were so sharply emphasized that the chasm between the two camps seemed unbridgeable. In the spring of 1933, the Nazis presented themselves as a protest movement against a *bürgerlich* way of life that was characterized as inherently corrupt and invested with class conceit and social barriers that acted as a ferment of decomposition and *völkisch* discord. Along with that went the denunciation of *bürgerliche* Bildung—the educational refinement and cultivation typical of the university-trained educated bourgeoisie, the *Bildungsbürgertum*, to which Germany owed its reputation in technical expertise, scholarship, and administration. In Germany the *Bildungsbürgertum*, which included not only the professions but also the high civil service, enjoyed greater social prestige than elsewhere in Europe and—before the turmoil and inflation brought about by the First World War—a considerable measure of material security and comfort. Imbued with the certainty of cultural and social superiority, they were initially unlikely prey for the Nazi movement, which they viewed with thinly veiled contempt. In Nazi eyes this educated bourgeoisie epitomized *Bürgerlichkeit* and became a prime object of hate.

A central result of this study is thus the laying bare of the hitherto much neglected but distinctly pronounced anti-bourgeois streak of National Socialism that so prominently came to the fore during the period of the Nazi seizure of power. The anti-bourgeois trait of Nazism was all-pervasive: it was already a prominent theme in Hitler's *Mein Kampf*, became omnipresent in the political struggles of the last phase of the Weimar Republic, and provided a frequent topic in Hitler's wartime monologues.[10] Historians frequently overlooked

10. See Adolf Hitler, *Mein Kampf*, 210th ed. (Munich, 1936), 47, 110, 190, 367, 409, 450, 538, 548, 595, 609, 744; BA Koblenz, ZSg. 103, *Sammlung Lauterbach*,

this anti-bourgeois quality of National Socialism because it seemed puzzling and paradoxical: why would millions who considered themselves "*bürgerlich*" vote for an avowedly anti-bourgeois party? The answer can only be that they, like others, did not take the Nazis at face value and dismissed their anti-bourgeois talk as vapid propaganda. In 1929, Hitler accused bourgeois parties in his *Völkischer Beobachter* of "political unreliability, lukewarm behavior, cowardice, lack of principle, and indolence,"[11] pronouncements that gained widespread notoriety since they were avidly circulated by Nazism's political opponents.[12] Goebbels freely vented his anger in the *Angriff*, arguing that "the eternal bourgeois [is] the mortal enemy of new life," and that negotiations with bourgeois parties could only serve the purpose of "beating the *Bürger* down and trampling him underfoot"; he asserted that National Socialists considered "the *Bürgertum* our mortal enemy," that the "bourgeois ideal [had] to die," and that the *Bürgertum* was unwilling to sacrifice its *Standesdünkel* (social arrogance) on the altar of a true people's community.[13] As early as 1924, Hitler had argued in *Mein Kampf* that, by dint of its shortsighted and egotistical social policies, the *Bürgertum* had radicalized the working classes, that members of the bourgeoisie were imbued with a narrow cast spirit, and that the nationalism of the "indolent and cowardly bourgeois world" lacked strength and conviction.[14] The central and weightiest charge in both Nazi propaganda and *Mein Kampf* concentrated on the bourgeoisie's alleged failure to stand up to Marxism and the revolutionaries of 1918; in short, that the bourgeoisie had "miserably capitulated before the pressure of the street."[15] These charges reappear in various modifications in Hitler's table talk, where he also asserted that *Akademiker* (members of the

---

no. 795: NSDAP und Bürgertum; Henry Picker, ed., *Hitlers Tischgespräche im Führerhauptquartier* (Stuttgart, 1976), 63, 107; Werner Jochmann, ed., *Adolf Hitler. Monologe im Führerhauptquartier. Aufgezeichnet von Heinrich Heim* (Munich, 2000), 51, 123, 143, 156, 160, 220, 228, 250, 328.

  11. "Wer ist Sieger? Das Versagen des Bürgertums im Kampf gegen den Marxismus," *Völkischer Beobachter*, 20 November, 1929 at BA Koblenz, ZSg. 103, *Sammlung Lauterbach*, no. 795: NSDAP und Bürgertum.

  12. "Hitler und das deutsche Bürgertum," *Hannoversche Landeszeitung*, 29 November, 1929 at BA Koblenz, ZSg. 103, *Sammlung Lauterbach*, no. 795: NSDAP und Bürgertum.

  13. See *Der Angriff* of 20 July 1930, 21 August 1930, and 28 March 1931, at BA Koblenz, ZSg. 103, *Sammlung Lauterbach*, no. 795: NSDAP und Bürgertum.

  14. Hitler, *Mein Kampf*, 47–48, 191, 366–367, and 409.

  15. Ibid., 594–595.

Bildungsbürgertum) had no instinct, that the bourgeoisie had no social conscience, but was primarily interested in its own well-being, and that even the national-minded *Bürgertum* was incapable of speaking the language of the people, lacking as they did the necessary spirit of sacrifice and willingness to put the common weal before their own.[16] In short, Hitler made it plain that the *Bürger* could not be used for the political struggle and that he had nothing but contempt for all of them.[17] With his finely honed sensitivities, Thomas Mann, whose *bürgerliche* identity was well developed, was among the few contemporary observers who, from the distance of his exile in Switzerland and France, discerned Nazism's anti-bourgeois quality as one of its principal characteristics. He expressed his indignation by equating the "brown plague" with "bad Bolshevism," by labeling Nazism the "worst kind of Bolshevism," and by considering Nazi leaders "more Bolshevist" than the "simple-minded party members of German Communism."[18]

In contrast to the anti-communism, anti-socialism, and anti-liberalism of the Nazi movement, which have all been sufficiently examined, the pronounced anti-conservatism of National Socialism has not yet been appreciated to its full extent. As has been shown, it virulently came to the fore during the first phase of the *Machtergreifung* during the winter and spring of 1933. In comparison to Italian fascism, National Socialism succeeded in rendering its national-conservative partners powerless within less than half a year. The German conservative elite thus quickly ceased being the Nazis' equal partners. By the late spring of 1933, its members had to be aware of the painful fact that individually, if not as a group, they were dispensable. The fact that the foundation for any alliance based on equality had been destroyed during the first few months after Hitler became Chancellor was not self-evident, given the emphasis the Nazi regime put on custom, order, convention, and traditional values in some of its public pronouncements after Hitler was firmly ensconced in power. In contrast to Italian fascism, the early elimination of its conservative partners enlarged Nazism's room for

---

16. Picker, ed., *Hitlers Tischgespräche*, 107, and 63; Jochmann, ed., *Adolf Hitler. Monologe im Führerhauptquartier*, 65, 143. There is also talk of the *Bürgertum*'s innate cowardice and lack of resolve. See Jochmann, ed., *Adolf Hitler. Monologe im Führerhauptquartier*, 145, 156, 328.

17. Hitler, *Mein Kampf*, 122.

18. Thomas Mann, *Tagebücher 1933–1934* (Frankfurt, 1977), 128, 8, 14 (entries of 6 July, 17 March, 20 March).

maneuver and permitted an early radicalism of the regime.[19] The anti-bourgeois character of Nazism that so prominently came to the fore in the winter and spring of 1933 rendered National Socialism more attractive to the wide masses of the population, including the industrialized working classes to whom it signified that the Third Reich could also become their state. Paradoxically, the spirit of martial vigor, greater social equality, a tight community of all people's comrades, and the elimination of the entitlement character of the bourgeois world, also appealed to vast sections of the bourgeoisie who—after the turmoil of the First World War and its aftermath of all-pervasive political instability, inflation, and finally a Great Depression, with the unprecedented mass unemployment it brought in its wake—seemed to realize that their *bürgerliche Welt* lacked firm foundations.

In propaganda and public presentation the revolutionary Nazi movement continually emphasized differences in worldview and mentality between itself and the tradition-minded German Nationals, so that it was clear from the start that their alliance was based solely on expediency. Given the prominence of the "social revolutionary" element of Nazism, which trained its wrath on the conservative establishment, it would be wrong to maintain that any *Bündnis der Eliten* remained intact during the period of the seizure of power.[20] In the spring of 1933, the Nazis also usurped the place of conservatives as the main guardians of the national heritage and of national traditions. Nazi organizations now laid claim to the inheritance of patriotic Prussia, as illustrated by their celebration of the Wars of Liberation. German Nationals also had reason to fear for their traditional positions of power and influence in local politics and leadership posts in interest groups and associations. The files are replete with complaints by conservative notables who feared for their social and political standing, and increasingly also for their physical safety. Still, the sheer brutality of Nazi attacks on members and supporters of their conservative ally remains astounding. Political prominence offered no protection from attacks. German Nationals were powerless when confronted with this "revolutionary" violence, not only because they found themselves outnumbered by

---

19. See also Wolfgang Schieder, "Faschismus," in Richard von Dülmen, ed., *Fischer Lexikon Geschichte* (Frankfurt, 2003), 199–221.

20. Fritz Fischer, *Bündnis der Eliten. Zur Kontinuität der Machtstrukturen in Deutschland 1871–1945* (Düsseldorf, 1979).

SA thugs, but because they were trapped in their legalistic thinking and thus reluctant to repay violence in kind.

The changing Zeitgeist facilitated and probably accelerated Nazi successes. It worked to the benefit of the speedy *Machtergreifung* in the Länder after 5 March and the thorough implementation of the first phase of the Nazi seizure of power that ended on 14 July 1933. In the spring of 1933, politics had infiltrated all spheres of life, long-time friendships were broken up over political disagreements, and widespread, seemingly genuine enthusiasm held fast large sections of the population that succumbed all too readily to the "temptation" of National Socialism.[21] In fact, this early phase of the Nazi regime saw a first high-point of its popularity. Many who later achieved fame as opponents of the regime initially supported Nazism. After the long futile battles of Weimar, the German people appeared to have found themselves again, since National Socialism seemed to herald a return to cherished German traditions, claimed to have saved the nation from the all-too-real danger of communism, and promised to unify the people in a national community that harked back to the halcyon days of August 1914. But contemporaries often overlooked that all of this went hand in hand with a new kind of perfected re-pression, from concentration camps to *Gesinnungsschnüffelei*—a kind of "mind police" and ideological spying that promoted denuncia-tions, made the dissemination of rumors a punishable offense, and initiated campaigns against *"Miesmacher"*—those who spread a "sour mood."

Pressure to demonstrate one's loyalty in public through obliga-tory flag raising, the utterance of politically motivated greetings (such as a forcefully exclaimed "Heil Hitler"), the self-censorship that went along with the prohibition of books, and the repression of honest personal opinions all worked to destroy traditional German sociability. Traditional social interaction was, in any case, rendered impossible on account of the increasing danger of denunciations. In the eyes of many Germans, the world they knew—their traditional bourgeois universe—ended in 1945. In reality it had ended twelve years earlier—only they failed to realize it at the time.

---

21. Fritz Stern, "National Socialism as Temptation," in Fritz Stern, *Dreams and Delusions. The Drama of German History*, rev. ed. (New Haven, 1999), 147–191.

APPENDIX

Table 1: From Martin Broszat, *Hitler and the Collapse of the Weimar Republic* (Oxford, 1987), 84–85.

	East Prussia	Pomerania
May 1928		
DNVP	312,000 (31.3%)	373,000 (41.6%)
NSDAP	16,000 (1.4%)	13,000 (1.5%)
September 1930		
DNVP	205,000 (19.6%)	242,000 (24.3%)
NSDAP	236,000 (22.5%)	237,000 (24.0%)
July 1932		
DNVP	107,000 (9.5%)	168,000 (15.8%)
NSDAP	536,000 (47.1%)	511,000 (47.9%)

Since the combined number of votes for the SPD and KPD remained roughly the same in both provinces, it can be assumed that the bulk of DNVP voters in East Prussia and Pomerania switched over to the NSDAP. The DNVP also lost 70 percent of its former voters in Schleswig-Holstein and Lower Silesia after 1930, most of whom likewise went over to the NSDAP.

Table 2: From *Statistisches Jahrbuch für*
das Deutsche Reich, **52 (Berlin, 1933), 5.**

Local resident population as of 16 June 1933:	
Prussia:	39,958,073
Hamburg:	1,183,171
Bremen:	366,425
Lübeck:	136,469
Schaumburg-Lippe:	50,469
Hessen:	1,426,830
Baden:	2,429,977
Württemberg:	2,713,150
Saxony:	5,196,386
Bavaria:	7,732,003

Table 3: From *Statistisches Jahrbuch für das Deutsche Reich* **52 (1933), 5.**

The population of these provinces exceeded those of many German states.

Population as of 16 June 1933:	
Brandenburg province (*Gauleiter* Wilhelm Kube)	2,747,520
Schleswig-Holstein (*Gauleiter* Hinrich Lohse)	1,596,811
Silesia (total) (*Gauleiter* Helmut Brückner)	4,716,251
a. Lower Silesia	3,237,241
b. Upper Silesia	1,479,010
Hannover (SA *Gruppenführer* Viktor Lutze)	3,365,610
Filled during the ensuing months:	
East Prussia (*Gauleiter* Erich Koch)	2,356,938
Prussian province of Saxony (SA-*Gruppenführer* Curt von Ulrich)	3,378,948
Pomerania (*Gauleiter* Franz Schwede)	1,942,367

Table 4: From Falter, et al., *Wahlen und Abstimmungen in der Weimarer Republik*, 104.

Following are the comparative results of Landtag elections for the DNVP and NSDAP in the traditional "Old Prussian" provinces east of the river Elbe.

	Pomerania			East Prussia		
	1925	1929	1933	1925	1929	1933
DNVP	48.5%	40.8%	18.4%	45.6%	31.2%	12.7%
NSDAP	—	4.1%	57.9%	—	4.3%	58.2%

	Grenzmark Posen–West Prussia			Brandenburg		
	1925	1929	1933	1925	1929	1933
DNVP	34.7%	33.6%	11.0%	28.6%	29.4%	15.2%
NSDAP	—	4.7%	55.0%	0.4%	5.6%	53.2%

	Lower Silesia		
	1925	1929	1933
DNVP	26.0%	22.0%	9.0%
NSDAP	—	5.2%	51.7%

These provinces had traditionally been the stronghold of Prussian conservatism: the DKP before 1918 and the DNVP thereafter. The majority of DNVP voters switched to the NSDAP after 1930, though it is fair to assume that the old established *Bürgertum* remained faithful to the DNVP.

SELECT BIBLIOGRAPHY

Archival Sources

Bundesarchiv Berlin-Lichterfelde:

Reichslandbund Pressearchiv, R 8034 II (alte Signatur: 61 Re1)
No. 4334: DNVP—Parteitage, Versammlungen der DNVP.
No. 5576: Staats- und Gemeindebeamte, 28. April 1932 bis 17. Dezember 1933.
No. 5613: Nationalsozialismus und Beamte, 29. September 1930 bis 1944.
No. 6147: Parteileben: Konservative Partei, 1905–1908.
No. 6479: NSDAP und Mittelstand.
No. 9021: Organisiertes Bürgertum.
No. 9029: Parteileben Deutschland: Nationalsozialismus und DNVP, vol. I: 1930–1932.
No. 9030: Parteileben Deutschland: Nationalsozialismus und DNVP, vol. II: 16 September 1932 to 13 July 1933.
No. 9251: Nationalsozialistisches Parteileben vom 5 März bis zum 20. August 1933.

Reichslandbund, Generalia, R 8034 I (alte Signatur: 61 Re1)
No. 45: Gleichschaltung und Neuordnung des landwirtschaftlichen Organisationswesens, März 1933 bis Juli 1933.
No. 111: Aufrufe zur politischen Lage, Oktober 1930 bis April 1933.
No. 235: Gleichschaltung des pommerschen Landbundes.

Deutschnationale Volkspartei, R 8005 (alte Signatur: 60 Vo2)
No. 11: Deutschnationale Volkspartei—Krisen in der Partei, 1926 bis 1933.
No. 19: Politischer Schriftwechsel 1933.
No. 44: Kirchen- und Religionsangelegenheiten, Allgemeines, Januar bis Juni 1933.

No. 47: Kirchen- und Religionsangelegenheiten, Katholiken, Februar bis April 1933.

No. 48: Kirchen- und Religionsangelegenheiten, August 1932 bis Juni 1933.

Alldeutscher Verband, R 8048 (alte Signatur: 61 Ve1)

No. 236: Presseausschnitte zu NSDAP, Januar bis Dezember 1933.

No. 238: Störungen von Versammlungen des Alldeutschen Verbandes durch NSDAP, SA, und Polizei.

No. 684: Informationsmaterial über das Kabinett Hitler, Januar 1933 bis Mai 1934.

No. 685: Informationsmaterial über die preußische Regierung, April 1925 bis Oktober 1933.

Deutscher Philologenverband, R 8079 (alte Signatur: 70 Phi1)

No. 8: Auseinandersetzungen mit dem NSLB.

No. 42: Vorstandssitzungen des Deutschen Philologenverbandes, 1931 bis 1934.

No. 46: Rundschreiben des Deutschen Philologenverbandes, Januar bis Dezember 1933.

No. 120: Rundschreiben der Geschäftsstelle des Preußischen Philologenverbandes, Januar 1933 bis Mai 1934.

No. 129: Rundschreiben des Landesverbandes der höheren Beamten Preußens, 1932 bis 1934.

Reichsbund der höheren Beamten, R 8080 (alte Signatur: 70 Re1)

No. 278: NSDAP, Juni 1932 bis April 1933.

No. 287: Nationalsozialistische Beamtenzeitung.

No. 350: Politische Betätigung der Beamten, November 1931 bis Juni 1933.

No. 542: Zeitschrift des Reichsbundes der höheren Beamten.

Reichsverband der höheren Verwaltungsbeamten des Reichs und der Länder, R 8081 (alte Signatur 70 Re1)

No. 9: Rundschreiben des Reichsverbands.

No. 86: Umorganisation der Beamtenverbände.

Reichskanzlei R 43

R 43 I, no. 2655: DNVP: April 1931 bis April 1938.

R 43 II, no. 1195: NSDAP.

Stellvertreter der Reichskanzlei, Kanzlei von Papen, R 53

No. 2: Problematik der Machtübernahme.

No. 23: Rundschreiben, Mai bis Dezember 1933.

No. 71: Allgemeine politische Angelegenheiten.

No. 77: Briefe von Abt Schmitt aus Grüsau/Schlesien.

No. 80: Korrespondenz.

No. 86: Anfragen wegen politischer Verhaftungen.

No. 100: Papen über die nationale Revolution vom 30. Januar.

No. 173: Eingaben und Beschwerden.

No. 184: Die nationale Erhebung.

Nachlaß, Kuno von Westarp 90 We 4.

Bundesarchiv, Außenstelle Berlin
(formerly Berlin Document Center):

Files of "höhere SS Führer" who were members of the *Bildungsbürgertum* and joined the Nazi party during the *Machtergreifungszeit*:

Dr. Hans Fischer, SS-Obersturmbannführer
Dr. Hans Hohl, SS-Obersturmbannführer
Dr. Hans Illgner, SS-Obersturmbannführer
Dr. Paul Löffler, SS-Hauptsturmführer
Dr. Max Ostermaier, SS-Hauptsturmführer
Dr. Fritz Plothe, SS-Hauptsturmführer
Dr. Ernst Roeckl, SS-Hauptsturmführer
Dr. Friedrich Scharf, SS-Standartenführer
Dr. Herbert Scholz, SS-Standartenführer
Dr. Otto Schröder, SS-Hauptsturmführer
Dr. Karl Segler, SS-Hauptsturmführer
Dr. Walter Stahlecker, SS-Standartenführer
Dr. Karl Steinbacher, SS-Obersturmbannführer

Geheimes Staatsarchiv Preußischer Kulturbesitz, Berlin-Dahlem

Preußisches Staatsministerium, Rep. 90, no. 2326.
Akten betreffend das politische Verhalten der Beamten 1933.
Preußisches Staatsministerium, Rep. 90, nos. 2572–2576.
Personalangelegenheiten; Durchführungsverordnungen für Gesetze.
Der Preußische Ministerpräsident, Rep. 90B, no. 184.
Berichte über Morde und sonstige Straftaten innerhalb der SA in Düsseldorf vom 22.2.1933.
Der Preußische Ministerpräsident, Rep. 90B, no. 119.
Bericht über antideutsche Propaganda in den USA, 5 April 1933.
Justizministerium, Rep. 84a, nos. 14501, 14609, 14683, 14689, 14694.
Verfahren gegen das Republikschutzgesetz.
Justizministerium, Rep. 84a, no. 11986.
Strafanzeige gegen den preußischen Innenminister Dr. Severing.
Justizministerium, Rep. 84a, nos. 15112–15194.
Antisemitismus, 1890–1933.
Justizministerium, Rep. 84a, no. 12733.
Mißhandlungen von Reichsbannerführern, jüdischen Ärzten und Rechtsanwälten durch die SA in Berlin, März 1933.
Justizministerium, Rep. 84a, no. 237.
Verbreitung des Gedankengutes der nationalsozialistischen Bewegung in der Beamtenschaft, Erlaßsammlung, 1933–1941.
Ministerium des Innern, Rep. 77.
Abteilung II: Polizeiabteilung, no. 278.
DNVP, 1928–1933.

Bundesarchiv Koblenz:

Liberale Parteien: R 45 II, DVP, nos. 8, 18, 33, 48, 61, and 63.
Liberale Parteien: R 45 III, DDP/Staatspartei, nos. 50, and 61.
Nachlaß Alfred Hugenberg, N 1231, no. 89: Ausschreitung der NSDAP gegen DNVP Mitglieder.
Der Nationale Wille 1933, ZSg. 1–4412.
Sammlung Lauterbach ZSg. 103: no. 795: NSDAP und Bürgertum; no. 828: NSDAP und DNVP; no. 805: NSDAP und Revolution.

Institut für Zeitgeschichte, Munich

Sammlung Anton Ritthaler, 1920–1954 (ED 207).
Nachlaß Herbert Frank (ED 414/4).
Nachlaß Gerhard Masur (ED 216).
Kartei des verbotenen und geheimen Schrifttums, 1933–1944 (ED 186).
Zeugenschrifttum Gereke (ZS 1698).
Zeugenschrifttum Hoegner (ZS 1959).
Zeugenschrifttum Seldte (ZS 1495).
Zeugenschrifttum Duesterberg (ZS 1700).
Zeugenschrifttum von Papen (ZS 354).
Sammlung DNVP Bayern, 1921–1933 (ED 714/1-2).
DNVP Bayern: "Zeitungsausschnitte, Flugblätter" (ED 714/3).
Mackensen von Astfeld, "Ein Preuße im Widerstand: Die obersten Verwaltungsbehörden Pommers vor, während und nach der Machtergreifung" (F 109; Akz. 3884/67).
Korrespondenzen der Regierung Marienwerder mit dem Innenministerium zum "Fall Wilhelm Grieger" (Fa 256).

Hoover Institution on War, Revolution, and Peace, Stanford University

Biographical accounts of early National Socialist followers of the "Abel Collection" at the Hoover Institution (Boxes 1–8). These vary from about 30–40 pages in length to one-page biographies. Originally there were 593 biographies; now there are about 580 biographies left.

Landesarchiv Berlin

Propagandaschriften der NSDAP (F-Rep. 240)
Flugblattsammlung Broschüren der Weimarer Zeit
Plakatsammlung
Der Angriff
Die Hilfe, Halbmonatsschrift
Berliner Illustrierte Zeitung
Berliner Illustrierte Nachtausgabe
Berliner Börsen Zeitung
Berliner Lokalanzeiger

Berliner Tageblatt
Deutsche Allgemeine Zeitung
Frankfurter Zeitung
Germania
Die Hilfe
Neue Preußische und Kreuz-Zeitung
Der Tag
Tägliche Rundschau
Vossische Zeitung

Stadtarchiv Göttingen

Befragungsaktion Ulrich Popplow (Dep. 77)

108 Befragungen von Augenzeugen: Detailed questionnaires of contemporaries, most born between the 1880s and 1910, regarding their own attitudes and behavior and those of others toward National Socialism. Given the astonishing frankness and frequent indiscretions of respondents, this is a valuable source. The interviews were conducted between 1974 and 1978 by Oberstudienrat Ulrich Popplow; some of them are up to forty pages in length.

Stadtarchiv Heidelberg

Sitzungsberichte des Stadtrates 1933 (AA 24b)
Bürgerausschußsitzungen (AA 27)
(suspended between late February and July 1933)
Lokalzeitungen: Heidelberger Tageblatt
Heidelberger Neueste Nachrichten

Stadtarchiv Mannheim

Lokalzeitungen: Neue Mannheimer Zeitung
Hakenkreuzbanner
Ratsprotokoll (Stadtratssitzungen), missing for 1933

Stadtarchiv Saarbrücken

Lokalzeitungen: Saarbrücker Zeitung
Saarbrücker Landeszeitung
Die Volksstimme
Dillinger Tageblatt

Hauptstaatsarchiv Stuttgart

Nachlaß Reinhold Maier (Q 1/8)
Nachlaß Theodor Bäuerle (Q 1/21)

Nachlaß Eugen Bolz (Q 1/25)
Nachlaß Alfred Bofinger (Q 1/31)

Stadtarchiv Stuttgart

Gemeinderatsprotokolle
(no meetings between 23 February and 9 May 1933)
Niederschriften der inneren Abteilung des Gemeinderates
(3 January to 28 March 1933)

Newspapers and the Contemporary Periodical Press

Der Angriff
Die Hilfe, Halbmonatsschrift
Berliner Illustrierte Zeitung
Berliner Illustrierte Nachtausgabe
Berliner Börsen Zeitung
Berliner Lokalanzeiger
Berliner Tageblatt
Breisgauer Zeitung
Der Jungdeutsche
Der Nationale Wille
Der Reichsbote. Tageszeitung für das evangelische Deutschland
Der Tag
Deutsche Allgemeine Zeitung
Deutsche Zeitung
Frankfurter Zeitung
Fränkisches Volksblatt
Freiburger Tagespost
Freiburger Zeitung
Germania
Hakenkreuzbanner
Heidelberger Tageblatt
Heidelberger Neueste Nachrichten
Kölnische Zeitung
Neue Preußische- und Kreuzzeitung
Magdeburger Tageszeitung
München-Augsburger Abendzeitung
Nationale Rundschau
Nationalsozialistische Monatshefte
Neue Mannheimer Zeitung
Ostpreußische Zeitung
Pommersche Tagespost
Rundschau
Saarbrücker Zeitung
Saarbrücker Landeszeitung

Schlesischer Volksbote
Schlesische Tageszeitung
Schwäbische Volkszeitung
Süddeutsche Zeitung
Tägliche Rundschau
Völkischer Beobachter
Volkswacht (Freiburg i. Breisgau)
Vorwärts
Vossische Zeitung
Die Weltbühne
Westdeutscher Beobachter
Westfälische Volkszeitung
Würzburger Generalanzeiger

Published Primary Sources and Secondary Literature

(The following select bibliography lists only those titles cited in the footnotes and those with a direct bearing on the argument.)

Aandahl, Frederick. "The Rise of German Free Conservatism." Ph.D. diss., Princeton, 1955.

Abel, Theodor. *Why Hitler Came into Power*. Cambridge, Mass., 1986.

Adam, Uwe Dietrich. *Judenpolitik im Dritten Reich*. Düsseldorf, 1972.

Akten zur Deutschen Auswärtigen Politik, 1918–1945, Serie C, 1933–1937. *Das Dritte Reich: Die ersten Jahre, 30. Januar bis 14. Oktober 1933*. Vol. I, Parts 1 and 2. Göttingen, 1971.

Allen, William S. *The Nazi Seizure of Power. The Experience of a Single German Town, 1922–1945*. Rev. ed. New York, 1984.

Angress, Werner. "Juden im politischen Leben der Revolutionszeit." In *Deutsches Judentum in Krieg und Revolution 1916–1923*. Ed.Werner Mosse. Tübingen, 1971: 137–317.

———. "Prussia's Army and the Jewish Reserve Officer Controversy before World War I." In *Imperial Germany*. Ed. James Sheehan. New York and London, 1976: 93–129.

Bahne, Siegfried. *Die KPD und das Ende von Weimar*. Frankfurt, 1976.

Bajohr, Frank. *Parvenüs und Profiteure. Korruption in der NS-Zeit*. Frankfurt, 2001.

Baranowski, Shelley. "Continuity and Contingency: Agrarian Elites, Conservative Institutions and East Elbia in Modern German History." *Social History* 12 (1987): 285–308.

Barclay, David E. *Rudolf Wissell als Sozialpolitiker 1890–1933*. Berlin, 1978.

Barkai, Avraham. *"Wehr Dich!" Der Centralverein deutscher Staatsbürger jüdischen Glaubens, 1893–1938*. Munich, 2002.

Baum, Walter. "Die 'Reichsreform' im Dritten Reich." *Vierteljahreshefte für Zeitgeschichte* No. 3 (1955): 36–56.

Beck, Hermann. "The Social Policies of Prussian Officials: The Bureaucracy in a New Light." *Journal of Modern History* 64 (1992): 263–298.

―――. "Conservatives and the Social Question in Nineteenth-Century Prussia." In *Between Reform, Reaction, and Resistance: Studies in the History of German Conservatism from 1789 to 1945*. Eds. Larry E. Jones and James Retallack. London and Providence, 1993: 61–95.

―――. *The Origins of the Authoritarian Welfare State in Prussia. Conservatives, Bureaucracy and the Social Question, 1815–1870*. Ann Arbor, 1995.

―――. "The Changing Concerns of Prussian Conservatism, 1830–1914." In *Modern Prussian History 1830–1947*. Vol. II. Ed. Philip G. Dwyer. London, 2001: 86–106.

Becker, Josef. "Prälat Kaas und das Problem einer Regierungsbeteiligung der NSDAP 1930–1932." *Historische Zeitschrift* 196 (1963): 74–111.

Becker, Josef, and Ruth Becker, eds. *Hitlers Machtergreifung. Dokumente vom Machtantritt Hitlers 30. Januar 1933 bis zur Besiegelung des Einparteienstaates 14. Juli 1933*. 2nd ed. Munich, 1992.

Beckers, Thomas. *Abkehr von Preußen. Ludwig Dehio und die deutsche Geschichtswissenschaft nach 1945*. Aichach, 2001.

Behnen, Michael. *Das Politische Wochenblatt, 1851–1861. Nationalkonservative Publizistik gegen Ständestaat und Polizeistaat*. Göttingen, 1971.

Behrens, Reinhard. "Die Deutschnationalen in Hamburg 1918–1933." Diss., Hamburg, 1973.

Bennathan, Esra. "Die demographische und wirtschaftliche Struktur der Juden." In *Entscheidungsjahr 1932. Zur Judenfrage in der Endphase der Weimarer Republik*. 2nd ed. Ed. Werner Mosse. Tübingen, 1966: 87–135.

Benz, Wolfgang, ed. *Legenden, Lügen, Vorurteile*. 2nd ed. Munich, 1992.

Benz, Wolfgang, and Hermann Graml. *Biographisches Lexikon zur Weimarer Republik*. Munich, 1988.

Berding, Helmut. *Moderner Antisemitismus in Deutschland*. Frankfurt, 1988.

Berghahn, Volker. *Der Stahlhelm. Bund der Frontsoldaten 1918–1945*. Düsseldorf, 1966.

―――. "Ludwig Dehio." In *Deutsche Historiker*. Vol. IV. Ed. Hans-Ulrich Wehler. Göttingen, 1972: 97–116.

Bessel, Richard. "The Potempa Murder." *Central European History* 10 (1977): 241–254.

―――. *Political Violence and the Rise of Nazism: The Storm Troopers in Eastern Germany 1925–1934*. New Haven and London, 1984.

―――. "The Great War in German Memory: The Soldiers of the First World War, Demobilization, and Weimar Political Culture." *German History* 6:1 (1988): 20–34.

―――. *Germany after the First World War*. Oxford, 1993.

Besson, Waldemar. *Württemberg und die deutsche Staatskrise 1928–1933. Eine Studie zur Auflösung der Weimarer Republik*. Stuttgart, 1959.

Blechschmidt, Herbert. "Die Deutschnationale Volkspartei 1918–1920." Diss., Berlin/East, 1970.

Booms, Hans. *Die Deutsch-Konservative Partei. Preußischer Charakter, Reichsauffassung, Nationalbegriff*. Düsseldorf, 1954.

Borchmeyer, Joseph, ed. *Hugenbergs Ringen in deutschen Schicksalsstunden*. 2 vols. Detmold, 1951.

Borg, Daniel R. *The Old-Prussian Church and the Weimar Republic. A Study in Political Adjustment, 1917–1927*. Hanover and London, 1984.

Bracher, Karl-Dietrich, Wolfgang Sauer, and Gerhard Schulz. *Die nationalsozialistische Machtergreifung. Studien zur Errichtung des totalitärien Herrschaftssystems in Deutschland 1933–34.* 2nd ed. Cologne and Opladen, 1962.

————. *Die Auflösung der Weimarer Republik. Eine Studie zum Problem des Machtverfalls in der Demokratie.* 4th ed. Villingen, 1964.

————. "Parteienstaat, Präsidialsystem, Notstand." In *Von Weimar zu Hitler 1930–1933.* Ed. Gotthard Jasper. Köln and Berlin, 1968: 58–72.

————. *Die deutsche Diktatur. Entstehung, Struktur, Folgen des Nationalsozialismus.* 7th ed. Berlin, 1997. The first edition was published in 1969; the English translation in 1970.

————. *Die Stufen der Machtergreifung.* Frankfurt, 1974.

Brackes, Uwe, et al. *Reichstagsbrand—Aufklärung einer historischen Legende.* Munich, 1986.

Brecht, Arnold. *Prelude to Silence: The End of the German Republic.* New York, 1944.

Brenner, Hildegard. *Ende einer bürgerlichen Kunst-Institution: Die politische Formierung der Preußischen Akademie der Künste ab 1933.* Stuttgart, 1972.

Broszat, Martin. *Der Staat Hitlers.* 7th ed. Munich, 1978. English translation: Broszat, Martin. *The Hitler State. The Foundation and Development of the Internal Structure of the Third Reich.* London and New York, 1981.

————. "Nationalsozialistische Konzentrationslager 1933–1945." In *Anatomie des SS-Staates.* Vol. II, 5th ed. Eds. Martin Broszat, Hans-Adolf Jacobsen and Helmut Krausnick. Munich, 1989.

————. *Die Machtergreifung. Der Aufstieg der NSDAP und die Zerstörung der Weimarer Republik.* 5th ed. Munich, 1994. English translation of 1984 original: *Hitler and the Collapse of the Weimar Republic.* Oxford, 1987.

Broszat, Martin, Ulrich Dübber, Walter Hofer, Horst Möller, Heinrich Oberreuter, Jürgen Schmädecke, and Wolfgang Treue. *Deutschlands Weg in die Diktatur: Internationale Konferenz zur Nationalsozialistischen Machtübernahme. Referate und Diskussionen.* Berlin, 1983.

Broszat, Martin, Elke Fröhlich, and Falk Wiesemann, eds. *Bayern in der NS-Zeit. Soziale Lage und politisches Verhalten der Bevölkerung.* 5 vols. Munich and Vienna, 1977–1983.

Brügge, Otfried, et al., eds. *Hannover wird nationalsozialistisch. Ein Quellenlesebuch zur Machtübernahme.* Hannover, 1981.

Brüning, Heinrich. *Memoiren 1918–1934.* Stuttgart, 1970.

Bullock, Alan. *Hitler. A Study in Tyranny.* Rev. ed. New York, 1964.

Burleigh, Michael. *The Third Reich. A New History.* New York, 2000.

Burleigh, Michael, and Wolfgang Wippermann. *The Racial State: Germany 1933–1945.* Cambridge, 1991.

Bussche, Raimund von dem. *Konservatismus in der Weimarer Republik. Die Politisierung des Unpolitischen.* Heidelberg, 1998.

Caplan, Jane. "Strategien und Politik in der Ausbildung der Beamten im Dritten Reich." In *Erziehung und Schulung im Dritten Reich. Teil 2: Hochschule, Erwachsenenbildung.* Ed. Manfred Heinemann. Stuttgart, 1980: 246–260.

————. "Civil Service Support for National Socialism: An Evaluation." In *Der Führerstaat: Mythos und Realität.* Eds. G. Hirschfeld and L. Kettenacker. Stuttgart, 1981: 167–193.

————. *Government without Administration: State and Civil Service in Weimar and Nazi Germany.* Oxford, 1988.

Chanady, Attila. "The Disintegration of the German National People's Party, 1924–1930." *Journal of Modern History* 39 (1967): 65–91.

Chickering, Roger. *We Men who feel most German.* Stanford, 1982.

Clemens, Detlev. *Herr Hitler in Germany. Wahrnehmung und Deutungen des Nationalsozialismus in Großbritannien 1920 bis 1939.* Göttingen, 1996.

Clemens, Gabriele. *Martin Spahn und der Rechtskatholizismus in der Weimarer Republik.* Mainz, 1983.

Conze, Werner. "Die Krise des Parteienstaates in Deutschland 1929/30." *Historische Zeitschrift* 178 (1954): 47–83. Reprinted in *Von Weimar zu Hitler 1930–1933.* Ed. Gotthard Jasper. Cologne and Berlin, 1968: 27–58.

————. "Brünings Politik unter dem Druck der großen Krise." *Historische Zeitschrift* 199 (1964): 529–550.

Conze, Werner, and Hermann Raupach. *Die Staats- und Wirtschaftskrise des Deutschen Reiches, 1929–1933.* Stuttgart, 1967.

Craig, Gordon. *The Politics of the Prussian Army, 1640–1945.* Oxford, 1964.

Craig, Gordon. *Germany 1866–1945.* Oxford, 1978.

Dahrendorf, Ralf. *Gesellschaft und Demokratie in Deutschland.* Munich, 1968.

Dibelius, Otto. *Ein Christ ist immer im Dienst.* Stuttgart, 1963.

Die Deutschnationalen und die Zerstörung der Weimarer Republik. Aus dem Tagebuch von Reinhold Quaatz 1928–1933. Eds. Hermann Weiß and Paul Hoser. Munich, 1989.

Diels, Rudolf. *Lucifer ante Portas. Zwischen Severing und Heydrich.* Stuttgart, 1950.

Dipper, Christoph. "Der deutsche Widerstand und die Juden." *Geschichte und Gesellschaft* 9 (1983): 349–380.

Documents Diplomatiques Français 1932–1939. Première Série. Vol. II: 15 November 1932 to 17 March 1933. Paris, 1966.

Documents Diplomatiques Français 1932–1939. Première Série. Vol. III: 17 March 1933 to 15 July 1933. Paris, 1967.

Documents on British Foreign Policy 1919–1939, 2nd Series. Vol. IV: 1932–1933. London, 1950.

Documents on British Foreign Policy 1919–1939. 2nd Series. Vol. V. London, 1956.

Documents on German Foreign Policy, 1918–1945. Series C. Vol. I: 30 January to 14 October 1933. London and Washington, 1957.

Dorpalen, Andreas. *Hindenburg and the Politics of the Weimar Republic.* Princeton, 1964. German translation: *Hindenburg in der Geschichte der Weimarer Republik.* Frankfurt and Berlin, 1966.

Dörr, Manfred. "Die Deutschnationale Volkspartei 1925–1928." Diss.Phil., Marburg, 1964.

Duesterberg, Theodor. *Der Stahlhelm und Hitler.* Wolfenbüttel and Hannover, 1949.

Düffler, Jost. "Die Machtergreifung und die Rolle der alten Eliten im Dritten Reich." In *Die nationalsozialistische Machtergreifung.* Ed. Wolfgang Michalka. Paderborn, 1983: 182–194.

————. *Nazi Germany 1933–1945. Faith and Annihilation.* Translated from the German by Dean S. McMurry. London and New York, 1996.

Ebermayer, Erich. *Denn heute gehört uns Deutschland . . . Persönliches und politisches Tagebuch. Von der Machtergreifung bis zum 31. Dezember 1935.* Hamburg and Vienna, 1959.

Eley, Geoff. *From Unification to Nazism. Reinterpreting the German Past.* London and Boston, 1986.

———. *Reshaping the German Right. Radical Nationalism and Political Change after Bismarck.* 2nd ed. Ann Arbor, 1991.

———. "Konservative und radikale Nationalisten in Deutschland: Die Schaffung faschistischer Potentiale 1912–1928." In Geoff Eley, *Wilhelminismus, Nationalismus, Faschismus. Zur historischen Kontinuität in Deutschland.* Münster, 1996: 209–248.

Ender, Wolfram. *Konservative und rechtsliberale Deuter des Nationalsozialismus 1930–1945: Eine historisch-politische Kritik.* In Europäische Hochschulschriften: European University Studies. Reihe III: Geschichte und ihre Hilfswissenschaften. Serie III: History and Allied Studies. Vol. 208. Frankfurt am Main, 1984.

Engelhardt, Ulrich. *"Bildungsbürgertum:" Begriffs- und Dogmengeschichte eines Etiketts.* Stuttgart, 1986.

Erger, Johannes. *Der Kapp-Lüttwitz Putsch.* Düsseldorf, 1967.

Eschenburg, Theodor. *Letzten Endes meine ich doch. Erinnerungen, 1933–1999.* Berlin: Siedler, 2000.

Eulenberg, Franz. "Die sozialen Wirkungen der Währungsverhältnisse." *Jahrbücher für Nationalökonomie und Statistik.* Stuttgart, 1924: 748–794.

Evans, Richard J. *The Coming of the Third Reich.* New York, 2004.

Eyck, Erich. *Geschichte der Weimarer Republik.* 2 vols. 4th ed. Erlenbach-Zürich and Stuttgart, 1972. First published in 1956.

Fallada, Hans. *Bauern, Bonzen, und Bomben.* Berlin, 1931.

Falter, Jürgen, Thomas Lindenberger, and Siegfried Schumann. *Wahlen und Abstimmungen in der Weimarer Republik. Materialien zum Wahlverhalten, 1919–1933.* Munich, 1986.

Fattmann, Rainer. *Bildungsbürger in der Defensive: Die akademische Beamtenschaft und der 'Reichsbund der höheren Beamten' in der Weimarer Republik.* Göttingen, 2001.

Faust, Anselm. "Professoren für die NSDAP: Zum politischen Verhalten der Hochschullehrer 1932/33." In *Erziehung und Schulung im Dritten Reich. Teil 2: Hochschule, Erwachsenenbildung.* Ed. Manfred Heinemann. Stuttgart, 1980: 31–49.

Fest, Joachim. *Hitler. Eine Biographie.* Berlin and Frankfurt, 1973.

Feuchtwanger, Edgar J. *From Weimar to Hitler. Germany 1918–1933*, 2nd ed. New York, 1995.

Fischer, Conan J. *Stormtroopers: A Social, Economic and Ideological Analysis, 1929–1935.* London and Boston, 1983.

Flechtheim, Ossip K. *Die KPD in der Weimarer Republik.* Frankfurt, 1969.

Foreign Relations of the United States. Diplomatic Papers 1933. Vol. 2. Washington, 1949.

Forschbach, Edmund. "Die Deutschnationalen. Vom Ende einer Partei." *Politische Meinung* 5 (1960): 12–16.

Först, Walter. *Robert Lehr als Oberbürgermeister. Ein Kapitel deutscher Kommunalpolitik.* Düsseldorf and Vienna, 1962.

François-Ponçet, André. *The Fateful Years. Memoirs of a French Ambassador in Berlin 1931–1938.* New York, 1949.

Frank, Walter. *Hofprediger Adolf Stoecker und die christlichsoziale Bewegung.* 2nd ed. Hamburg, 1935.

Frankel, Richard E. *Bismarck's Shadow. The Cult of Leadership and the Transformation of the German Right, 1898–1945.* Oxford and New York, 2005.

Frei, Norbert. *Der Führerstaat. Nationalsozialistische Herrschaft 1933 bis 1945.* 6th enlarged ed. Munich, 2001. English translation: *National Socialist Rule in Germany: The Führer State 1933–1945.* Translated by Simon B. Steyne. Oxford, 1993.

———. "Wie modern war der Nationalsozialismus?" *Geschichte und Gesellschaft* 19 (1993): 367–387.

Frei, Norbert, and Johannes Schmitz. *Journalismus im Dritten Reich.* 3rd ed. Munich, 1999.

Frick, Wilhelm. "Der Sinn unserer Zeit." *Nationalsozialistische Monatshefte* 39 (June 1933).

Friedenthal, Elisabeth. "Volksbegehren und Volksentscheid über den Youngplan und die deutschnationale Sezession." Diss.phil., Tübingen, 1957.

Friedländer, Saul. "Die politischen Veränderungen der Kriegszeit und ihre Auswirkungen auf die Judenfrage." In *Deutsches Judentum in Krieg und Revolution 1916–1923.* Ed. Werner Mosse. Tübingen, 1971: 27–65.

———. *Nazi Germany and the Jews.* Vol. I. *The Years of Persecution, 1933–1939.* New York, 1997.

Fritz, Werner. "Martin Luther, Friedrich II und Adolf Hitler—der Tag von Potsdam in neuem Licht." In *Preußen und der Nationalsozialismus.* Ed. Volkshochschule Albert Einstein. Potsdamer Gespräche. Tagungsreferate, 5.-7. November 1992.

Fritzsche, Peter. *Rehearsals for Fascism: Populism and Political Mobilization in Weimar Germany.* New York and Oxford, 1990.

———. "Breakdown or Breakthrough? Conservatives and the November Revolution." In *Between Reform, Reaction and Resistance. Studies in the History of German Conservatism from 1789 to 1945.* Eds. Larry E. Jones and James N. Retallack. Providence and Oxford, 1993: 299–329.

———. *Germans into Nazis.* Cambridge, Mass., 1998.

Führer, Karl. "Der Deutsche Reichskriegerbund Kyffhäuser 1930–1934: Politik, Ideologie und Funktion eines 'unpolitischen' Verbandes." *Militärgeschichtliche Mitteilungen* 36 (1984): 57–76.

Gay, Peter. "Begegnung mit der Moderne—Deutsche Juden in der deutschen Kultur." In Werner E. Mosse, *Juden im Wilhelminischen Deutschland, 1890–1914.* 2nd ed. Tübingen, 1998: 241–313.

Gemein, Gisbert J. "Die DNVP in Düsseldorf, 1918–1933." Diss.phil., Cologne, 1968.

Gerlach, Helmut. *Von Rechts nach Links.* Zürich, 1937.

Geyer, Michael. "Etudes in Political History: Reichswehr, NSDAP, and the Seizure of Power." In *The Nazi Machtergreifung.* Ed. Peter D. Stachura. London, 1983: 101–123.

Giles, Geoffrey. "Die Idee der politischen Universitat: Hochschulreform nach der Machtergreifung." In *Erziehung und Schulung im Dritten Reich. Teil 2: Hochschule, Erwachsenenbildung.* Ed. Manfred Heinemann. Stuttgart, 1980: 50–76.

———. "National Socialism and the Educated Elite in the Weimar Republic." In *The Nazi Machtergreifung.* Ed. Peter D. Stachura. London, 1983: 49–67.

———. *Students and National Socialism in Germany.* Princeton, 1985.

Gisevius, Hans-Bernd. *To the Bitter End. The Plot to Kill Hitler.* New York, 1998.

Goebbels, Joseph. *Vom Kaiserhof zur Reichskanzlei. Eine historische Darstellung in Tagebuchblättern. Vom 1. Januar 1932 bis zum 1. Mai 1933.* Munich, 1940.

Golecki, Anton, ed. *Akten der Reichskanzlei. Das Kabinett von Schleicher, 3. Dezember 1932 bis 30. Januar 1933.* Boppard, 1986.

Göring, Hermann. *Reden und Aufsätze.* Ed. Erich Gritzbach, 8th ed. Munich, 1943.

Gradmann, Christoph, and Oliver von Mengersen. *Das Ende der Weimarer Republik und die nationalsozialistische Machtergreifung.* Heidelberg, 1994.

Grathwol, Robert. *Stresemann and the DNVP: Reconciliation or Revenge in German Foreign Policy, 1924–1928.* Lawrence, Kansas, 1980.

Grill, Johnpeter Horst. "Local and Regional Studies on National Socialism: A Review." *Journal of Contemporary History* 21 (1986): 253–294.

Grund, Henning. " 'Preußenschlag' und Staatsgerichtshof im Jahre 1932." Diss. jur., Göttingen, 1976.

Grüttner, Michael. *Studenten im Dritten Reich.* Paderborn, 1995.

Guratzsch, Dankwart. *Macht durch Organisation. Die Grundlegung des Hugenbergschen Presseimperiums.* Düsseldorf, 1973.

Haffner, Otto. "Geschichte und Entwicklung der Freiburger Tagespresse." *Zeitschrift für Geschichtsforschung von Freiburg 34–35.* Freiburg, 1919–1920.

Haffner, Sebastian. *Germany: Jekyll and Hyde: 1939—Deutschland von innen betrachtet.* Berlin, 1996.

———. *Geschichte eines Deutschen. Die Erinnerungen 1914–1933.* 2nd ed. Munich, 2002.

Hagenlücke, Heinz. *Deutsche Vaterlandspartei. Die nationale Rechte am Ende des Kaiserreiches.* Düsseldorf, 1997.

Hale, Oron. *The Captive Press in the Third Reich.* Princeton, 1964.

Hamburger, Franz. "Lehrer zwischen Kaiser und Führer: Der deutsche Philologenverband in der Weimarer Republik. Eine Untersuchung zur Sozialgeschichte der Lehrerorganisationen." Diss.phil., Heidelberg, 1974.

Hamel, Iris. *Völkischer Verband und nationale Gewerkschaft. Der Deutschnationale Handlungsgehilfenverband 1893–1933.* Frankfurt, 1967.

Hamilton, Richard F. *Who Voted for Hitler?* Princeton, 1982.

Hartwig, Edgar. "Konservative Partei." In *Lexikon zur Parteiengeschichte.* Vol. III. Eds. Dieter Fricke, et al. Leipzig, 1983–1986: 283–309.

Hauser, Oswald, ed. *Politische Parteien in Deutschland und Frankreich, 1918–1939.* Wiesbaden, 1969.

Hayes, Peter. " 'A Question Mark with Epaulettes'? Kurt von Schleicher and Weimar Politics." *Journal of Modern History* 52 (March 1980): 35–65.

Heberle, Rudolf. *Landbevölkerung und Nationalsozialismus. Eine soziologische Untersuchung der politischen Willensbildung in Schleswig-Holstein 1918–1932.* Stuttgart, 1963.

Hehl, Ulrich von. "Die Kontroverse um den Reichstagsbrand." *Vierteljahreshefte für Zeitgeschichte* 36 (1988): 259–280.

Heiber, Helmut. *Walter Frank und sein Reichsinstitut für die Geschichte des neuen Deutschland.* Stuttgart, 1966.

Heiber, Helmut, and Beatrice, eds. *Die Rückseite des Hakenkreuzes. Absonderliches aus den Akten des Dritten Reiches.* 2nd ed. Munich, 1994.

Henning, Hansjoachim. *Das Westdeutsche Bürgertum in der Epoche der Hochindustrialisierung 1860–1914. Soziales Verhalten und Soziale Struktur. Teil I: Das Bildungsbürgertum in den Preussischen Westprovinzen.* Wiesbaden, 1972.

Hentschel, Volker. *Weimars letzte Monate. Hitler und der Untergang der Republik.* 2nd ed. Düsseldorf, 1979.

Herbert, Ulrich. *Best. Biographische Studien über Radikalismus, Weltanschauung und Vernunft 1903–1989.* 2nd ed. Bonn, 1996.

Herbst, Ludolf. *Das nationalsozialistische Deutschland, 1933–1945. Die Entfesselung der Gewalt: Rassismus und Krieg.* Frankfurt, 1996.

Hering, Rainer. *Konstruierte Nation. Der Alldeutsche Verband 1890 bis 1939.* Hamburg, 2003.

Hertz, Deborah. *Jewish High Society in Old Regime Berlin.* New Haven, 1988.

Hertzman, Lewis. *DNVP: Right-wing Opposition in the Weimar Republic, 1918–1924.* Lincoln, NE, 1963.

Hildebrand, Klaus. *Das Dritte Reich.* 3rd ed. Munich, 1987. English translation: *The Third Reich.* Translated from the German by P.S. Falla. London and Boston, 1984.

Hill, Leonidas E. "The National-Conservatives and Opposition to the Third Reich before the Second World War." In *Germans Against Nazism: Nonconformity, Opposition and Resistance in the Third Reich. Essays in Honour of Peter Hoffmann.* Eds. Francis R. Nicosia and Lawrence D. Stokes. New York and Oxford, 1990: 221–251.

Hiller von Gaertingen, Friedrich Freiherr. "Die Deutschnationale Volkspartei." In *Das Ende der Parteien 1933.* Eds. Erich Matthias and Rudolf Morsey. Düsseldorf, 1960: 543–652.

———. "Das Ende der DNVP im Frühjahr 1933." In *Von Weimar zu Hitler 1930–1933.* Ed. Gotthard Jasper. Cologne and Berlin, 1968: 246–278.

———. "Monarchismus in der deutschen Republik." In *Die Weimarer Republik: Belagerte Civitas.* Ed. Michael Stürmer. Königstein, 1980: 254–271.

Hitler, Adolf. *Mein Kampf.* 210th ed. Munich, 1936.

Hoffmann, Erich, and Peter Wulf, eds. *Wir bauen das Reich. Aufstieg und erste Herrschaftsjahre des Nationalsozialismus in Schleswig-Holstein.* Neumünster, 1983.

Hoffmann, Gerhard, Werner Bergmann, and Helmut Walser Smith, eds. *Exclusionary Violence.* Ann Arbor, 2002.

Hoffmann, Peter. *Stauffenberg. A Family History, 1905–1944.* Cambridge, 1995.

Holzbach, Heidrun. *Das "System Hugenberg." Die Organisation bürgerlicher Sammlungspolitik vor dem Aufstieg der NSDAP, 1918–1928.* Stuttgart, 1981.

Horkenbach, Cuno, ed. *Das Deutsche Reich von 1918 bis heute.* Vol. IV. Berlin, 1935.

Hörster-Philipps, Ulrike. *Konservative Politik in der Endphase der Weimarer Republik: Die Regierung Franz von Papen.* Cologne, 1982.

Hoßbach, Friedrich. *Zwischen Wehrmacht und Hitler 1934–1938.* Wolfenbüttel and Hannover, 1949.

Hübinger, Gangolf. "Politische Werte und Gesellschaftsbilder des Bildungsbürgertums." *Neue Politische Literatur* 2 (1987): 189–210.

Jackisch, Barry. "Not a Large, but a Strong Right: The Pan-German League, Radical Nationalism, and Rightist Party Politics in Weimar Germany, 1918–1933." Ph.D. Diss. Buffalo, 2000.

James, Harold. *Deutschland in der Weltwirtschaftskrise, 1924–1936*. Stuttgart, 1988.

——. "Economic Reasons for the Collapse of the Weimar Republic." In *Weimar: Why did German Democracy Fail?* Ed. Ian Kershaw. New York, 1990: 30–58.

Jamin, Mathilde. *Zwischen den Klassen: Zur Sozialstruktur der SA-Führerschaft*. Wuppertal, 1984.

Jarausch, Konrad H. "The Crisis of German Professions 1918–1933." *Journal of Contemporary History* 20 (1985): 379–398.

——. "The Perils of Professionalism: Lawyers, Teachers, and Engineers in Nazi Germany." *German Studies Review* 9 (1986): 107–137.

——. "Die Not der geistigen Arbeiter: Akademiker in der Berufskrise, 1918–1933." In *Die Weimarer Republik als Wohlfahrtsstaat: zum Verhältnis von Wirtschafts- und Sozialpolitik in der Industriegesellschaft*. Ed. Werner Abelshauser. Stuttgart, 1987: 280–299.

Jasper, Gotthard. *Die gescheiterte Zähmung: Wege zur Machtergreifung Hitlers 1930–1934*. Frankfurt, 1986.

——, ed. *Von Weimar zu Hitler 1930–1933*. Cologne and Berlin, 1968.

Jesse, Eckhard. "Hermann Rauschning: Der fragwürdige Kronzeuge." In *Die braune Elite* II. Eds. Ronald Smelser, Enrico Syring, and Rainer Zitelmann. Darmstadt, 1993: 193–206.

Jochmann, Werner. *Nationalsozialismus und Revolution. Ursprung und Geschichte der NSDAP in Hamburg, 1922–1933*. Frankfurt, 1963.

——. "Die Ausbreitung des Antisemitismus." In *Deutsches Judentum in Krieg und Revolution, 1916–1923*. Ed. Werner Mosse. Tübingen, 1971: 409–510.

——. "Strukturen und Funktion des deutschen. Antisemitismus." In *Juden im Wilhelminischen Deutschland 1890–1914*, 2nd ed. Ed. Werner Mosse. Tübingen, 1998.

——, ed. *Adolf Hitler. Monologe im Führerhauptquartier. Aufgezeichnet von Heinrich Heim*. Munich, 2000.

Jonas, Erasmus. *Die Volkskonservativen, 1928–1933*. Düsseldorf, 1965.

Jones, Larry E. "Between the Fronts: The German National Union of Commercial Employees from 1928 to 1933." *Journal of Modern History* 48 (1976): 462–482.

——. "Crisis and Realignment. Agrarian Splinter Parties in the Late Weimar Republic, 1928–1933." In *Peasants and Lords in Modern German History*. Ed. Robert G. Moeller. Boston, 1986: 198–232.

——. " 'The Greatest Stupidity of my Life:' Alfred Hugenberg and the Formation of the Hitler Cabinet, January 1933." *Journal of Contemporary History* 27 (1992): 63–87.

——. "Nazis, Conservatives, and the Establishment of the Third Reich, 1932–34." *Tel Aviver Jahrbuch für Deutsche Geschichte: Nationalsozialismus aus heutiger Perspektive* (1994): 41–64.

——. "Franz von Papen, the German Center Party, and the Failure of Catholic Conservatism in the Weimar Republic." *Central European History* 38 (2005): 191–217.

Jones, Larry E., and James N. Retallack, eds. *Between Reform, Reaction and Resistance. Studies in the History of German Conservatism from 1789 to 1945*. Providence & Oxford, 1993.

Jung, Otmar. "Plebiszitärer Durchbruch 1929? Zur Bedeutung von Volksbegehren und Volksentscheid gegen den Young Plan für die NSDAP." *Geschichte und Gesellschaft* 15 (1989): 489–510.

Kater, Michael H. "Zum gegenseitigen Verhältnis von SA und SS in der Sozialgeschichte des Nationalsozialismus von 1925 bis 1939." *Vierteljahresschrift für Sozial- und Wirtschaftsgeschichte* 62 (1975): 339–379.

————. "Die nationalsozialistische Machtergreifung an den deutschen Hochschulen. Zum politischen Verhalten akademischer Lehrer bis 1939." In *Die Freiheit des Anderen. Festschrift fur Martin Hirsch*. Eds. Hans Jochen Vogel, Helmut Simon, and Adalbert Podlech. Baden-Baden, 1981: 49–75.

————. *Doctors under Hitler*. Chapel Hill, 1989.

————. *The Nazi Party*. Cambridge, Mass., 1984.

Kaufmann, Walter H. *Monarchism in the Weimar Republic*. New York, 1953.

Keil, Wilhelm. *Erlebnisse eines Sozialdemokraten*. 2 vols. Stuttgart, 1949.

Kershaw, Ian. *Hitler, 1889–1936: Hubris*. New York, 1999.

————. *The Nazi Dictatorship: Problems and Perspectives of Interpretation*. 4th ed. London, 2000.

————, ed. *Weimar: Why did German Democracy Fail?* New York, 1990.

Klemperer, Klemens von. *Germany's New Conservatism. Its History and Dilemma in the Twentieth Century*. Princeton, 1957.

Kocka, Jürgen. "Bürgertum und Bürgerlichkeit als Probleme der deutschen Geschichte vom späten 18. zum frühen 20. Jahrhundert." In *Bürger und Bürgerlichkeit im Neunzehnten Jahrhundert*. Ed. Jürgen Kocka. Göttingen, 1987: 21–63.

Kolb, Eberhard. *Die Weimarer Republik*. 6th ed. Munich, 2002.

Krabbe, Wolfgang. "Die Bismarckjugend der Deutschnationalen Volkspartei." *German Studies Review* 17:1 (February 1994): 9–32.

Kruck, Alfred. *Geschichte des Alldeutschen Verbandes, 1890–1939*. Wiesbaden, 1954.

Lambach, Walter. "Monarchismus." *Politische Wochenschrift* 4, no. 24 (June 14, 1928).

Leopold, John A. *Alfred Hugenberg. The Radical Nationalist Campaign against the Weimar Republic*. New Haven and London, 1977.

Levy, Richard S. *The Downfall of the Anti-Semitic Political Parties in Imperial Germany*. New Haven and London, 1975.

Liang, Hsi-Huey. *The Berlin Police Force in the Weimar Republic*. Berkeley and Los Angeles, 1970.

Liebe, Werner. *Die Deutschnationale Volkspartei, 1918–1924*. Düsseldorf, 1956.

Link, Werner. *Die amerikanische Stabilisierungspolitik in Deutschland, 1921–1932*. Düsseldorf, 1970.

Loerke, Oskar. *Tagebücher 1903–1939*. 2nd ed. Ed. Hermann Kasack. Heidelberg and Darmstadt, 1955.

Longerich, Peter. *Die braunen Bataillone. Geschichte der SA*. Munich, 1989.

Löwenthal, Leo. *Mitmachen wollte ich nie*. Frankfurt, 1981.

Machtan, Lothar. *Der Kaisersohn bei Hitler*. Hamburg, 2006.

Malinowski, Stephan. *Vom König zum Führer. Deutscher Adel und Nationalsozialismus*. Frankfurt, 2004.

Mann, Thomas. *Tagebücher 1933–1934*. Ed. Peter de Mendelsohn. Frankfurt, 1977.

Martel, Gordon, ed. *Modern Germany Reconsidered, 1870–1945.* London and New York, 1992.

Mason, Timothy. *Social Policy in the Third Reich.* Oxford and New York, 1993.

Matthias, Erich. "Die Sozialdemokratische Partei Deutschlands." In *Das Ende der Parteien 1933.* Eds. Erich Matthias and Rudolf Morsey. Düsseldorf, 1960: 101–278.

Matthias, Erich, and Rudolf Morsey, eds. *Das Ende der Parteien 1933.* Düsseldorf, 1960.

McClelland, Charles E. *The German Experience of Professionalization: Modern learned professions and their organizations from the early nineteenth century to the Hitler era.* Cambridge, 1991.

McKale, Donald M. "From Weimar to Nazism: Abteilung III of the German Foreign Office and the Support of Anti-Semitism, 1931–1935." *Leo Baeck Institute Yearbook* 32 (1987): 297–308.

Meissner, Otto. *Staatssekretär unter Ebert-Hindenburg-Hitler. Der Schicksalsweg des Deutschen Volkes 1918–1945.* Hamburg, 1950.

Mergel, Thomas. "Das Scheitern des deutschen Tory-Konservatismus. Die Umformung der DNVP zu einer rechtsradikalen Partei 1928–1932." *Historische Zeitschrift* 276 (2003): 323–368.

Merkl, Peter. *Political Violence under the Swastika. 581 early Nazis.* Princeton, 1975.

Meyer, Michael, ed. *German-Jewish History in Modern Times. Renewal and Destruction, 1918–1945.* Vol. IV. New York, 1998.

Michalka, Wolfgang, ed. *Die nationalsozialistische Machtergreifung.* Paderborn, 1984.

Michalka, Wolfgang, and Gottfried Niedhart, eds. *Deutsche Geschichte 1918–1933. Dokumente zur Innen- und Außenpolitik.* Frankfurt, 1992.

Minuth, Karl-Heinz, ed. *Akten der Reichskanzlei. Die Regierung Hitler.* Vol. I. Parts I and II, 1933–1934. Boppard, 1983.

———, ed. *Akten der Reichskanzlei. Das Kabinett von Papen, 1. Juni bis 3. Dezember 1932.* 2 vols. Boppard, 1989.

Mohler, Armin. *Die konservative Revolution in Deutschland, 1918–1932.* 2 vols. 3rd ed. Darmstadt, 1990.

Möller, Horst. "Die nationalsozialistische Machtergreifung: Konterrevolution oder Revolution?" *Vierteljahreshefte für Zeitgeschichte* 31 (1983): 25–51.

Mommsen, Hans. *Beamtentum im Dritten Reich.* Stuttgart, 1966.

———. "Nachwort." In David Schoenbaum, *Die braune Revolution.* Munich, 1980: 352–368.

———. "Die Auflösung des Bürgertums seit dem späten 19. Jahrhundert." In *Bürger und Bürgerlichkeit im Neunzehnten Jahrhundert.* Ed. Jürgen Kocka. Göttingen, 1987: 288–315.

———. "Zur Verschränkung traditioneller und faschistischer Führungsgruppen in Deutschland beim Übergang von der Bewegungs- zur Systemphase." In *Faschismus als soziale Bewegung.* Ed. Wolfgang Schieder. Göttingen, 1983: 157–181.

———. "The Reichstag Fire and its Political Consequences." In *Aspects of the Third Reich.* Ed. H.W. Koch. New York, 1985.

———. *From Weimar to Auschwitz.* Princeton, 1991.

————. "National Socialism: Continuity and Change." In Hans Mommsen, *From Weimar to Auschwitz*. Princeton, 1991: 141–163.

————. "Noch einmal: Nationalsozialismus und Modernisierung." *Geschichte und Gesellschaft* 21 (1995): 391–402.

————. *The Rise and Fall of Weimar Democracy*. Translated by Elborg Forster and Larry E. Jones. Chapel Hill and London, 1996.

————, ed. *The Third Reich between Vision and Reality. New Perspectives on German History, 1918–1945*. Oxford and New York, 2001.

Mommsen, Wilhelm, und Günther Franz, eds. *Die deutschen Parteiprogramme 1918–1930*. Leipzig and Berlin 1931.

Morsey, Rudolf. *Zur Entstehung, Authentizität und Kritik von Brünings "Memorien 1918–1934."* Opladen, 1975.

————. *Das 'Ermächtigungsgesetz' vom 24. März 1933. Quellen zur Geschichte und Interpretation des 'Gesetzes zur Behebung der Not von Volk und Reich.'* Düsseldorf, 1992.

Mosse, George L. "Die deutsche Rechte und die Juden." In *Entscheidungsjahr 1932. Zur Judenfrage in der Endphase der Weimarer Republik*. 2nd rev.ed. Ed. Werner E. Mosse. Tübingen, 1966: 183–249.

Mosse, Werner, ed. *Entscheidungsjahr 1932. Zur Judenfrage in der Endphase der Weimarer Republik*. 2nd rev. ed. Tübingen, 1966.

————, ed. *Deutsches Judentum in Krieg und Revolution 1916–1923*. Tübingen, 1971.

————, ed. *Juden im Wilhelminischen Deutschland 1890–1914*. 2nd ed. Tübingen, 1998.

Müller-Jabusch, Maximilian. *Handbuch des öffentlichen Lebens*. 5th ed. Leipzig, 1929.

Neue Deutsche Biographie. Ed. Die Historische Kommission bei der Bayerischen Akademie der Wissenschaften. Berlin, 1953–2006.

Neumann, Siegmund. *Die Parteien der Weimarer Republik*. 5th ed. Ed. Karl-Dietrich Bracher. Stuttgart, 1986.

Nicosia, Francis R., and Lawrence D. Stokes, eds. *Germans against Nazism. Essays in Honor of Peter Hoffmann*. New York and Oxford, 1990.

Niedhart, Gottfried. "Zwischen negativem Deutschlandbild und Primat des Friedens: Großbritannien und der Beginn der nationalsozialistischen Herrschaft in Deutschland." In *Die nationalsozialistische Machtergreifung*. Ed. Wolfgang Michalka. Paderborn and Munich, 1984: 274–287.

Niewyk, Donald L. *The Jews in Weimar Germany*. Baton Rouge and London, 1980.

Nipperdey, Thomas. *Die Organisation der deutschen Parteien vor 1918*. Düsseldorf, 1961.

————. "Antisemitismus: Entstehung, Funktion und Geschichte eines Begriffs." In Thomas Nipperdey, *Gesellschaft, Kultur, Theorie*. Göttingen, 1976: 113–133 and 425–432.

————. *Deutsche Geschichte, 1800–1866*. Munich, 1983.

————. *Nachdenken über die deutsche Geschichte*. Munich, 1986.

————. *Deutsche Geschichte 1866–1918. Arbeitswelt und Bürgergeist*. Munich, 1990.

————. *Machtstaat vor Demokratie. Deutsche Geschichte 1866–1918*. Munich, 1992.

Noakes, Jeremy. "Nazism and Revolution." In *Revolutionary Theory and Political Reality*. Ed. Noel O'Sullivan. Brighton, 1983: 73–100.

————. "German Conservatives and the Third Reich: An Ambiguous Relationship." In *Fascists and Conservatives: The Radical Right and the Establishment in Twentieth-Century Europe.* Ed. Martin Blinkhorn. London, 1990: 71–97.

————. "Nazism and High Society." In *Confronting the Nazi Past: New Debates on Modern German History.* Ed. Michael Burleigh. London, 1996: 51–65.

Noakes, Jeremy, and Geoff Pridham. *Nazism, 1919–1945. A Documentary Reader.* Vol. I. Exeter, 1996.

Nolte, Ernst. "Europäische Revolutionen des 20. Jahrhunderts: Die nationalsozialistische Machtergreifung im historischen Zusammenhang." In *Die nationalsozialistische Machtergreifung.* Ed. Wolfgang Michalka. Paderborn, 1984: 395–410.

————. "Konservatismus und Nationalsozialismus."*Zeitschrift für Politik* 1:11 (January 1964): 5–20.

Nonn, Christoph. *Eine Stadt sucht einen Mörder. Gericht, Gewalt und Antisemitismus im Kaiserreich.* Göttingen, 2002.

Norden, Günther van. *Der deutsche Protestantismus im Jahr der nationalsozialistischen Machtergreifung.* Gütersloh, 1979.

Ossietzky, Carl von. *Rechenschaft. Publizistik aus den Jahren 1913–1933.* Frankfurt, 1972.

O'Sullivan, Noel, ed. *Revolutionary Theory and Political Reality.* Brighton, 1983.

Papen, Franz von. *Der Wahrheit eine Gasse.* Munich, 1952.

Payne, Stanley. *Fascism: Comparison and Definition.* Madison, 1980.

————. *A History of Fascism, 1914–1945.* Madison, 1995.

Petzina, Dieter, Werner Abelshauser, and Anselm Faust. *Sozialgeschichtiches Arbeitsbuch: Materialien zur Statistik des Deutschen Reiches, 1914–1945.* Munich, 1978.

Picker, Henry, ed. *Hitlers Tischgespräche im Führerhauptquartier.* Stuttgart, 1976.

Das Politische Testament Friedrichs des Großen von 1752. Stuttgart, 1971.

Prinz, Michael, and Rainer Zitelmann, eds. *Nationalsozialismus und Modernisierung.* Darmstadt, 1991.

Puhle, Hans-Jürgen. *Agrarische Interessenpolitik und preußischer Konservatismus im wilhelminischen Reich, 1893–1914.* Hannover, 1966.

————. "Conservatism in Modern German History." *Journal of Contemporary History* 13 (1978): 689–720.

Pulzer, Peter. *The Rise of Political Anti-Semitism in Germany and Austria.* Rev. ed. Cambridge, Mass., 1988.

————. "Die jüdische Beteiligung an der Politik." In *Juden im Wilhelminischen Deutschland 1890–1914.* 2nd ed. Ed. Werner Mosse. Tübingen, 1998.

————. *Jews and the German State. The Political History of a Minority, 1848–1933.* Oxford, 1992.

Retallack, James. *Notables of the Right. The Conservative Party and Political Mobilization in Germany, 1876–1918.* London & Boston, 1988.

Rheins, Carl J. "The Verband Nationaldeutscher Juden, 1921–1933." *Leo Baeck Institute Yearbook,* 25 (1980): 243–268.

Ritter, Gerhard. *Carl Goerdeler und die deutsche Widerstandsbewegung.* Munich, 1964.

Ritthaler, Anton. "Eine Etappe auf Hitlers Weg zur ungeteilten Macht. Hugenbergs Rücktritt als Reichsminister." *Vierteljahreshefte für Zeitgeschichte* 8 (1960): 193–219.

Roloff, Ernst-August. *Bürgertum und Nationalsozialismus 1930–1933. Braunschweigs Weg ins Dritte Reich.* Hannover, 1961.

Rosenberg, Arthur. *Geschichte der Weimarer Republik*, ed. by Kurt Kersten. Hamburg, 1991.

Ruge, Wolfgang. "Deutschnationale Volkspartei 1918–1933." In *Lexikon zur Parteiengeschichte.* Eds. Dieter Fricke, et al. Leipzig, 1983–1986: 476–528.

Runge, Wolfgang. *Politik und Beamtentum im Parteienstaat. Die Demokratisierung der politischen Beamten in Preußen zwischen 1918 und 1932.* Stuttgart, 1965.

Salomon, Felix. *Die neuen Parteiprogramme mit den letzten der alten Parteien zusammengestellt.* 2nd ed. Leipzig and Berlin, 1919.

Saunders, Thomas. "Nazism and Social Revolution." In *Modern Germany Reconsidered, 1870–1945.* Ed. Gordon Martel. London and New York, 1992: 159–178.

Schacht, Hjalmar. *76 Jahre meines Lebens.* Bad Wörishofen, 1953.

Scheck, Raffael. *Alfred von Tirpitz and German Right-Wing Politics, 1914–1930.* Atlantic Highlands, NJ, 1998.

———. *Mothers of the Nation. Right-Wing Women in Weimar Germany.* Oxford and New York, 2004.

Sheehan, James, ed. *Imperial Germany.* New York, London, 1976.

Schieder, Theodor. "Ludwig Dehio zum Gedächtnis." *Historische Zeitschrift* 201 (1965): 1–12.

Schieder, Wolfgang. "Der Faschismus als Vorbild in der Krise der Weimarer Republik." *Historische Zeitschrift* 262 (1996): 73–125.

———. "Fatal Attraction: The German Right and Italian Fascism." In *The Third Reich between Vision and Reality. New Perspectives on German History 1918–1945.* Ed. Hans Mommsen. Oxford and New York, 2001: 39–59.

———, ed. *Faschismus als soziale Bewegung.* Göttingen, 1983.

Schlange-Schöningen, Hans von. *Am Tage danach.* Hamburg, 1946.

Schleunes, Karl A. *The Twisted Road to Auschwitz.* Chicago and London, 1970.

Schmädecke, Jürgen, Alexander Bahar, and Wilfried Kugel. "Der Reichstagsbrand in neuem Licht." *Historische Zeitschrift* 269 (1999): 603–651.

Schmidt, Paul. *Statist auf diplomatischer Bühne 1923–1945. Erlebnisse des Chefdolmetschers im Auswärtigen Amt mit den Staatsmännern Europas.* Bonn, 1949.

Schmidt-Hannover, Otto. *Umdenken oder Anarchie. Männer-Schicksale-Lehren.* Göttingen, 1959.

Schmitt, Carl. "Das Gesetz zur Behebung der Not von Volk und Reich." *Deutsche Juristenzeitung* 38 (1933): 455–458.

Schmitt, Walther. "Unser Wille zum deutschen Sozialismus." *Nationalsozialistische Monatshefte* 35 (February 1933): 82–86.

Schoenbaum, David. *Hitler's Social Revolution: Class and Status in Nazi Germany, 1933–1939.* 2nd ed. New York and London, 1980. German edition: *Die braune Revolution.* Munich, 1980.

Scholder, Klaus. *Die Kirchen und das Dritte Reich. Vorgeschichte und Zeit der Illusionen 1918–1934.* Vol. I. Frankfurt, Berlin, and Vienna, 1977.

———. "Otto Dibelius." *Zeitschrift für Theologie und Kirche* 78 (1981): 90–104.

———, ed. *Die Mittwochs-Gesellschaft. Protokolle des geistigen Deutschland.* Berlin, 1982.

Schulz, Gerhard. *Von Brüning zu Hitler. Zwischen Demokratie und Diktatur.* Vol. III. Berlin, New York, 1992.

Schulze, Hagen. *Weimar: Deutschland, 1917–1933.* 4th ed. Berlin, 1994.

———, ed. *Anpassung oder Widerstand? Aus den Akten des Parteivorstandes der Deutschen Sozialdemokratie 1932–1933.* Bonn and Bad Godesberg, 1975.

Schüddekopf, Ernst-Otto. *Linke Leute von Rechts. Die nationalrevolutionären Minderheiten in der Weimarer Republik.* Stuttgart, 1960.

Schüren, Ulrich. *Der Volksentscheid zur Fürstenenteignung 1926.* Düsseldorf, 1978.

Schwarz, Angela. *Die Reise ins Dritte Reich. Britische Augenzeugen im nationalsozialistischen Deutschland, 1933–1939.* Göttingen, 1993.

Schwarz, Erika. "Rivalität und Bündnis in den Beziehungen der DNVP zur NSDAP: Sommer 1929 bis 1933." Diss., Berlin/East, 1977.

Schwerin von Krosigk, Lutz Graf. *Es geschah in Deutschland. Menschenbilder unseres Jahrhunderts.* Tübingen and Stuttgart, 1951.

———. *Memoiren.* Stuttgart, 1977.

Smelser, Ronald, Enrico Syring, Rainer Zitelmann, eds. *Die braune Elite.* Vol. II. Darmstadt, 1993.

Smith, Helmut Walser. *Die Geschichte des Schlachters. Mord und Antisemitismus in einer deutschen Kleinstadt.* Göttingen, 2002.

Solchany, Jean. "Vom Antimodernismus zum Antitotalitarismus: Konservative Interpretationen des Nationalsozialismus in Deutschland 1945–1949." *Vierteljahreshefte für Zeitgeschichte* 44 (1996): 373–394.

Sontheimer, Kurt. *Antidemokratisches Denken in der Weimarer Republik.* Munich, 1978.

Soviet Documents on Foreign Policy. Vol. III: 1933–1941. Ed. Jane Degras. London, 1953. Reprint New York, 1978.

Staat und NSDAP, 1930–1932. Quellen zur Ära Brüning. Eds. Ilse Maurer and Udo Wengst. Bonn, 1977.

Stasiewski, Bernhard, ed. *Akten deutscher Bischöfe über die Lage der Kirche 1933–1945.* Vol. I. Mainz, 1968.

Statistisches Amt Freiburg, ed. "Die wichtigsten Ergebnisse der Volks-, Berufs- und Betriebszählung vom 16. Juni 1933 in Freiburg/Breisgau." *Beiträge zur Statistik der Stadt Freiburg,* No. 7. Freiburg, 1937.

Statistisches Reichsamt, ed. *Statistisches Jahrbuch für das Deutsche Reich,* 52. Berlin, 1933.

Stehkämper, Hugo, ed. *Der Nachlaß des Reichskanzlers Wilhelm Marx.* Part I. Cologne, 1968.

Stern, Fritz. *The Politics of Cultural Despair.* Berkeley and Los Angeles, 1972.

———. *Gold and Iron: Bismarck, Bleichröder, and the Building of the German Empire.* New York, 1977.

———. *Verspielte Größe. Essays zur deutschen Geschichte des 20. Jahrhunderts.* 2nd ed. Munich, 1998.

———. *Dreams and Delusions. The Drama of German History.* Rev. ed. New Haven and London, 1999.

———. *Das feine Schweigen. Historische Essays.* Munich, 1999.

Stokes, Lawrence D. "Conservative Opposition to Nazism in Eutin, Schleswig-Holstein, 1932–33." In *Germans against Nazism. Essays in Honor of Peter Hoffmann.* Eds. Francis R. Nicosia and Lawrence D. Stokes. New York and Oxford, 1990: 37–57.

Stoltenberg, Gerhard. *Die politischen Strömungen im Schleswig-Holsteinischen Landvolk 1918–1933.* Düsseldorf, 1962.

Striesow, Jan. *Die Deutschnationale Volkspartei und die Völkisch-Radikalen, 1918–1922*. 2 vols. Frankfurt, 1981.

Stromberg, Roland N. "Redemption by War: The Intellectuals and 1914." *Midwest Quarterly* 20 (1979): 211–227.

Stupperich, Amrei. *Volksgemeinschaft oder Arbeitersolidarität. Studien zur Arbeitnehmerpolitik in der Deutschnationalen Volkspartei, 1918–1933*. Göttingen, 1982.

Stürmer, Michael. *Koalition und Opposition in der Weimarer Republik*. Düsseldorf, 1967.

———. "Die konservative Rechte in der Weimarer Republik." In *Politische Parteien in Deutschland und Frankreich, 1918–1939*. Ed. Oswald Hauser. Wiesbaden, 1969: 38–51.

Stutz, Rüdiger. *Die politische Entwicklung Eduard Stadtlers von 1918 bis 1933*. Jena, 1985.

———. "Stetigkeit und Wandlungen in der politischen Karriere eines Rechtsextremisten. Zur Entwicklung Eduard Stadtlers von der Novemberrevolution bis 1933." *Zeitschrift für Geschichtswissenschaft* 34 (1986): 797–806.

Taschenbuch der Deutschnationalen Volkspartei. Published by the Deutschnationale Schriftenvertriebsstelle. Berlin, 1929.

Thamer, Hans-Ulrich. *Verführung und Gewalt. Deutschland 1933–1945*. Berlin, 1986.

Thiele, Peter. "NSDAP und allgemeine innere Staatsverwaltung. Untersuchungen zum Verhältnis von Partei und Staat in Dritten Reich." Diss., Munich, 1967.

Thimme, Annelise. *Flucht in den Mythos. Die Deutschnationale Volkspartei und die Niederlage von 1918*. Göttingen, 1969.

Timpke, Henning, ed. *Dokumente zur Gleichschaltung des Landes Hamburg 1933*. Frankfurt, 1964. Reprint 1983.

Tobias, Fritz. *Der Reichstagsbrand. Legende und Wirklichkeit*. Rastatt, 1962. English translation: *The Reichstag Fire*. New York, 1964.

Treviranus, Gottfried Reinhold. *Das Ende von Weimar: Heinrich Brüning und seine Zeit*. Düsseldorf, 1968.

Trippe, Christian F. *Konservative Verfassungspolitik, 1918–1923. Die DNVP als Opposition in Reich und Ländern*. Düsseldorf, 1995.

Tschirschky, Fritz-Günther von. *Erinnerungen eines Hochverräters*. Stuttgart, 1972.

Turner, Henry Ashby Jr. "Machteliten und Machtübertragung: Die Rolle von Industrie und Agrariern in der deutschen Staatskrise 1930–1933." In *Die deutsche Staatskrise 1930–1933: Handlungsspielräume und Alternativen*. Schriften des Historischen Kollegs, Kolloquien 26. Ed. Heinrich August Winkler. Munich, 1992: 205–214.

———. *Hitler's Thirty Days to Power. January 1933*. Harlow, 1996. German translation: *Hitler's Weg zur Macht. Der Januar 1933*. Munich, 1996.

Ulbricht, Justus H. "Die Bücher des Heimlichen Deutschland: Zur Geschichte Völkischer Verlage in der Weimarer Republik." *Revue d'Allemagne* 22:1 (1990): 401–413.

Ullmann, Hans-Peter. *Interessenverbände in Deutschland*. Frankfurt, 1988.

Ursachen und Folgen. Vom deutschen Zusammenbruch 1918 bis zur staatlichen Neuordnung Deutschlands in der Gegenwart. Eine Urkunden- und Dokumentensammlung zur Zeitgeschichte. Vol. IX. *Die Zertrümmerung des Parteienstaates und die Grundlegung der Diktatur*. Eds. Herbert Michaelis and Ernst Schraepler. Berlin, 1964.

Die Verfassung des Deutschen Reichs vom 11.8.1919. Ed. Hermann Mosler. Reclam ed. Stuttgart, 1972.

Vogelsang, Thilo. *Reichswehr, Staat und NSDAP. Beiträge zur Deutschen Geschichte 1930–1932.* Stuttgart, 1962.

Vogt, Martin, ed. *Akten der Reichskanzlei. Das Kabinett Müller II.* 2 vols. Boppard, 1970–1971.

Voigt, Gerd. *Otto Hoetzsch, 1876–1946. Wissenschaft und Politik im Leben eines deutschen Historikers.* Berlin/East, 1978.

Volk, Ludwig, ed. *Akten Kardinal Michael Faulhabers 1917–1945.* Vol. I, 1917–1934. Mainz, 1975.

Walk, Joseph. *Das Sonderrecht für die Juden im NS-Staat.* 2nd ed. Paderborn and Munich, 1996.

Walker, Denis Paul. "Alfred Hugenberg and the Deutschnationale Volkspartei 1918 to 1930." Diss.phil., Cambridge, 1976.

Walter, Dirk. *Antisemitische Kriminalität und Gewalt. Judenfeindschaft in der Weimarer Republik.* Bonn, 1999.

Wassermann, Jakob. *Mein Weg als Deutscher und Jude.* 2nd ed. Munich, 1999.

Wehler, Hans-Ulrich. *Deutsche Gesellschaftsgeschichte, 1849–1914.* Vol. III. Munich, 1995.

———. *Deutsche Gesellschaftsgeschichte, 1914–1949.* Vol. IV. Munich, 2003.

Weiß, Hermann, ed. *Biographisches Lexikon zum Dritten Reich.* 2nd ed. Frankfurt, 1998.

Weiß, Hermann, and Paul Hoser, eds. *Die Deutschnationalen und die Zerstörung der Weimarer Republik. Aus dem Tagebuch von Reinhold Quaatz 1928–1933.* Munich, 1989.

Weiss, John. *The Fascist Tradition. Radical Right-Wing Extremism in Modern Europe.* New York, 1967.

Weiß, Max, ed. *Der nationale Wille. Werden und Wirken der Deutschnationalen Volkspartei 1918–1928.* Essen, 1928.

Welch, David. "Manufacturing a Consensus: Nazi Propaganda and the Building of a 'National Community.'" *Contemporary European History* 2:1 (1993): 1–15.

Wendt, Bernd-Jürgen. *Deutschland 1933–1945. Das Dritte Reich.* Hannover, 1995.

Wernecke, Klaus, und Peter Heller. *Der vergessene Führer Alfred Hugenberg. Pressemacht und Nationalsozialismus.* Hamburg, 1982.

Wertheimer, Jack. "'The Unwanted Element'—East European Jews in Imperial Germany." *Leo Baeck Institute Yearbook* 26 (1981): 23–46.

Williamson, John G. *Karl Helfferich, 1872–1924. Economist, Financier, Politician.* Princeton, 1971.

Winkler, Heinrich August. *Mittelstand, Demokratie, und Nationalsozialismus.* Cologne, 1972.

———. *Der Schein der Normalität. Arbeiter und Arbeiterbewegung in der Weimarer Republik 1924 bis 1930.* Berlin, 1987.

———. *Der Weg in die Katastrophe. Arbeiter und Arbeiterbewegung in der Weimarer Republik 1930–1933.* 2nd ed. Bonn, 1990.

———. *Weimar, 1918–1933. Die Geschichte der ersten deutschen Demokratie.* Munich, 1993.

Wippermann, Wolfgang. *Europäischer Faschismus im Vergleich, 1922–1982.* Frankfurt, 1983.

———. *Faschismustheorien. Zum Stand der gegenwärtigen Forschung.* 5th rev. ed. Darmstadt, 1989.

Wistrich, Robert S. *Who's Who in Nazi Germany.* London and New York, 1995.

Witt, Peter-Christian. "Eine Denkschrift Otto Hoetzschs vom 5. November 1918." *Vierteljahreshefte für Zeitgeschichte* 21 (1973): 337–357.

Wright, Jonathan, R.C. *'Above Parties:' The Political Attitudes of the German Protestant Church Leadership, 1918–1933.* Oxford, 1974.

Wulf, Peter. "Ernst Oberfohren und die DNVP am Ende der Weimarer Republik." In *Wir bauen das Reich. Aufstieg und erste Herrschaftsjahre des Nationalsozialismus in Schleswig-Holstein.* Eds. Erich Hoffmann and Peter Wulf. Neumünster, 1983: 165–187.

Zechlin, Egmont. *Die deutsche Politik und die Juden im Ersten Weltkrieg.* Göttingen, 1969.

Ziegler, Dieter, ed. *Großbürger und Unternehmer.* Göttingen, 2000.

Ziegler, Leopold. "Edgar Jung: Denkmal und Verdächtnis." *Berliner Hefte für geistiges Leben* No. 4 (1949): 1–12.

Zimmermann, Moshe. *Die Deutschen Juden 1914–1945.* Munich, 1997.

Zollitsch, Wolfgang. "Adel und adelige Machteliten in der Endphase der Weimarer Republik: Standespolitik und agrarische Interessen." In *Die deutsche Staatskrise.* Ed. Heinrich August Winkler. Munich, 1992: 239–256.

———. "Die Erosion des traditionellen Konservatismus. Ländlicher Adel in Preußen zwischen Kaiserreich und Weimarer Republik." In *Parteien im Wandel vom Kaiserreich zur Weimarer Republik.* Eds. Dieter Dowe, Jürgen Kocka, and Heinrich August Winkler. Munich, 1999: 161–182.

INDEX